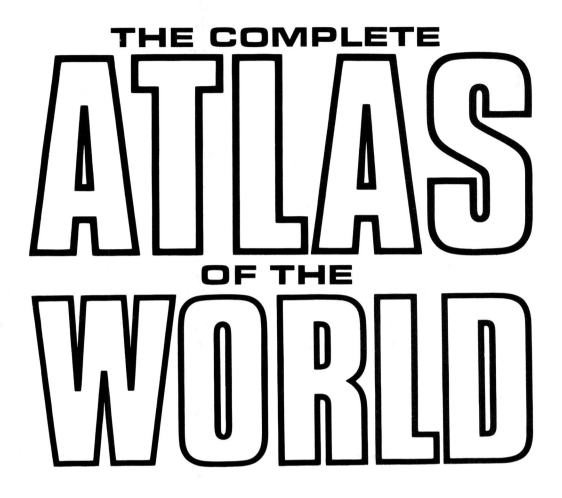

THE COMPLETE ATLAS OF THE WORLD

Written by **Keith Lye**

Colour Library Books

ABOUT THIS ATLAS

Maps are a way of showing, in diagrammatic form, what we know about the Earth. Their use goes back several thousand years. From the days of ancient Greeks, maps were used as a way of summarizing information about the world.

Flat maps of a round world

Because most maps depict the Earth as if it were flat instead of curved, no map can be completely accurate. Hence cartographers have devised different map projections – mathematical ways of projecting the Earth's curvature on to a flat surface – to overcome the inaccuracies inherent in this process. Each projection preserves accurately some of the Earth's features, such as, for example, the shape of the land, its area, or the distances between places. Only a globe can preserve all of them accurately at the same time. But even the largest globes are far less detailed than most maps, and less convenient to carry around.

How to use this atlas

This atlas is divided into two sections. The first section consists of world maps, and provides an overall view of features such as habitats, population, environmental issues, and the Earth's natural resources, on a global scale. The second section looks at the world regionally, and examines closely these same features, as well as providing more detailed information about each country within the region, for example its major imports and exports, or its main religions.

Throughout the atlas, two types of map are used to explain different aspects of the area shown. The first type is called a *topographic* map, and this shows the basic physical features: the height of the land, political boundaries, cities and towns. The second type of map is called a *thematic* map. This presents a particular aspect of the area. Thematic maps include environmental issues, population, and industry. The same themes are examined in each region, so that information between regions can be compared. The world thematic maps give an overview of the extent to which natural and human factors are interrelated around the world.

In this atlas, capital cities are represented by black squares, and cities and towns by black circles. Climate data is provided in the regional section of the atlas and, for this, three places are selected in order to show the variance of temperature and rainfall possible. Flags are also provided for every independent country of the world. At the back of the atlas, there is a glossary to explain terms used, and a gazetteer, which lists where you can find places or features, such as rivers and mountains, in the atlas.

REGIONS OF THE WORLD

Canada & Greenland Canada
United States of America United States of America
Mexico, Central America & The Caribbean Antigua and Barbuda, Bahamas, Barbados, Belize, Costa Rica, Cuba, Dominica, Dominican Republic, El Salvador, Grenada, Guatemala, Haiti, Honduras, Jamaica, Mexico, Nicaragua, Panama, St. Kitts-Nevis, St. Lucia, St. Vincent and the Grenadines, Trinidad and Tobago
South America Argentina, Bolivia, Brazil, Chile, Colombia, Ecuador, Guyana, Paraguay, Peru, Surinam, Uruguay, Venezuela
Nordic Countries Denmark, Finland, Iceland, Norway, Sweden
British Isles Ireland, United Kingdom
France Andorra, France, Monaco
Spain & Portugal Portugal, Spain
Italy & Greece Cyprus, Greece, Italy, Malta, San Marino, Vatican City
Central Europe & The Low Countries Austria, Belgium, Germany, Liechtenstein, Luxembourg, Netherlands, Switzerland
Eastern Europe Albania, Bosnia and Hercegovina, Bulgaria, Croatia, Czech Republic, Hungary, Macedonia, Poland, Romania, Slovakia, Slovenia, Yugoslavia
Russia & Its Neighbours Armenia, Azerbaijan, Belorussia, Estonia, Georgia, Kazakhstan, Kirghizia, Latvia, Lithuania, Moldavia, Mongolia, Russia, Tajikistan, Turkmenistan, Ukraine, Uzbekistan

Middle East Afghanistan, Bahrain, Iran, Iraq, Israel, Jordan, Kuwait, Lebanon, Oman, Qatar, Saudi Arabia, Syria, Turkey, United Arab Emirates, Yemen
Northern Africa Algeria, Chad, Djibouti, Egypt, Eritrea, Ethiopia, Libya, Mali, Mauritania, Morocco, Niger, Somalia, Sudan, Tunisia
Central Africa Benin, Burkina, Burundi, Cameroon, Cape Verde, Central African Republic, Congo, Equatorial Guinea, Gabon, Gambia, Ghana, Guinea, Guinea-Bissau, Ivory Coast, Kenya, Liberia, Nigeria, Rwanda, São Tomé and Príncipe, Senegal, Seychelles, Sierra Leone, Tanzania, Togo, Uganda, Zaire
Southern Africa Angola, Botswana, Comoros, Lesotho, Madagascar, Malawi, Mauritius, Mozambique, Namibia, South Africa, Swaziland, Zambia, Zimbabwe
Indian Subcontinent Bangladesh, Bhutan, India, Maldives, Nepal, Pakistan, Sri Lanka
China & Taiwan China, Taiwan
Southeast Asia Brunei, Burma, Cambodia, Indonesia, Laos, Malaysia, Philippines, Singapore, Thailand, Vietnam
Japan & Korea Japan, North Korea, South Korea
Australia & Its Neighbours Australia, Papua New Guinea
New Zealand & Its Neighbours Fiji, Kiribati, Marshall Islands, Nauru, New Zealand, Solomon Islands, Tonga, Tuvalu, Vanuatu, Western Samoa
Antarctica

CLB 4340
This 1994 edition published for
Colour Library Books Ltd
Godalming Business Centre
Woolsack Way
Godalming
Surrey GU7 1XW

Copyright ©Andromeda Oxford Limited 1994
Planned and produced by:
Andromeda Oxford Limited
11-15 The Vineyard, Abingdon
Oxfordshire, OX14 3PX
ISBN 1-85833-233-8

Printed in the G.C.C.

Flags produced by Lovell Johns, Oxford, U.K. and authenticated by The Flag Research Center, Winchester, Mass. 01890, U.S.A.

CONTENTS

THE WORLD

PHYSICAL

Land covers about 148,300,000 sq. km (57,259,000 sq. mi) of the Earth's surface. The land can be divided broadly into physical regions, whose character is shaped by the topography (surface features) and the climate.

The changing land

Land features such as mountains are constantly changing. While earthquakes and volcanic eruptions cause sudden and catastrophic change, other forces, such as weathering, are slow.

Worn fragments of rock are removed by the forces of erosion. These include running water, particularly in wet regions; glaciers (moving bodies of ice) in cold regions; winds, especially in deserts; and sea waves along coasts. Much of the worn rock is dumped on to sea or lake beds, where it piles up and under pressure over many years forms new rock layers. This is part of the rock cycle, which has continued throughout Earth's history.

The changing map

Other forces operate inside the Earth. Movements in the partly molten mantle affect parts of the overlying lithosphere, the planet's hard outer shell. As these huge blocks, or tectonic plates, move, they cause volcanic eruptions, earthquakes and mountain-building.

Around 180 million years ago, all the world's land areas were joined together in one supercontinent, which geologists call Pangaea. Since then, currents in the mantle have broken up Pangaea and moved the various continents to their present positions. These slow but unceasing movements continue today.

Along the ocean ridges on the deep sea floor, plates are moving apart. New rock is formed from molten material from the mantle.

POLITICAL

While natural forces constantly change physical maps, human factors, such as wars, change political maps. For example, the world map in 1946 was substantially different from that of 1939, when World War II began. Another mainly peaceful upheaval occurred in the 1950s and 1960s when many European colonies in Africa and Asia achieved their independence. Many of the independent nations adopted new names for cities and some physical features.

New nations

The latest upheaval occurred in the early 1990s, when the collapse of many communist governments changed the political map of Europe and Asia. For example, when the former Soviet Union was dissolved in 1991, 15 separate nations were born. The former Yugoslavia also split up into five new nations.

Sovereignty

By 1993, the world contained 188 independent nations. Despite boundary disputes between some neighbouring countries, each nation has a defined territory, which is recognized internationally, and a government that is responsible for making and implementing laws. The independent nations are often called sovereign states, because, unlike dependencies or states and provinces within nations, they recognize no authority higher than their own.

Sovereignty has nothing to do with size. The world's five smallest sovereign states have a combined area of about 110 sq. km (42 sq. mi) and a population of about 72,000. Yet they are sovereign states, unlike Texas, a state within the United States, which covers 692,407 sq. km (267,339 sq. mi) and has 17 million people.

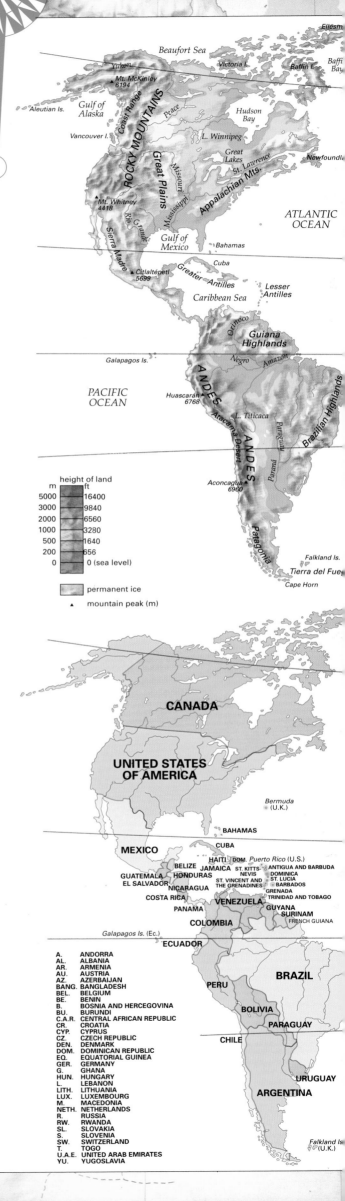

height of land

m	ft
5000	16400
3000	9840
2000	6560
1000	3280
500	1640
200	656
0	0 (sea level)

permanent ice

▲ mountain peak (m)

A. ANDORRA
AL. ALBANIA
AR. ARMENIA
AU. AUSTRIA
AZ. AZERBAIJAN
BANG. BANGLADESH
BEL. BELGIUM
BE. BENIN
B. BOSNIA AND HERCEGOVINA
BU. BURUNDI
C.A.R. CENTRAL AFRICAN REPUBLIC
CR. CROATIA
CYP. CYPRUS
CZ. CZECH REPUBLIC
DEN. DENMARK
DOM. DOMINICAN REPUBLIC
EQ. EQUATORIAL GUINEA
GER. GERMANY
G. GHANA
HUN. HUNGARY
L. LEBANON
LITH. LITHUANIA
LUX. LUXEMBOURG
M. MACEDONIA
NETH. NETHERLANDS
R. RUSSIA
RW. RWANDA
SL. SLOVAKIA
S. SLOVENIA
SW. SWITZERLAND
T. TOGO
U.A.E. UNITED ARAB EMIRATES
YU. YUGOSLAVIA

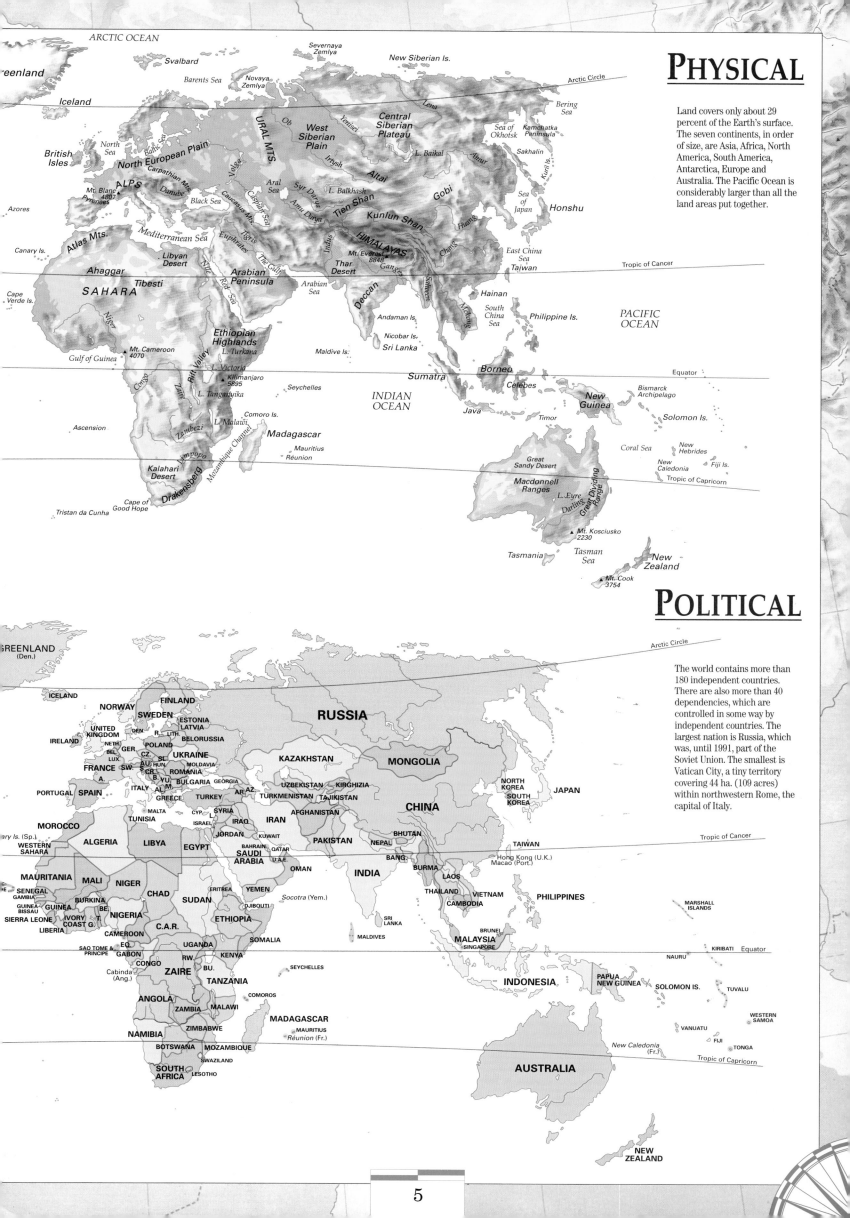

PHYSICAL

Land covers only about 29 percent of the Earth's surface. The seven continents, in order of size, are Asia, Africa, North America, South America, Antarctica, Europe and Australia. The Pacific Ocean is considerably larger than all the land areas put together.

POLITICAL

The world contains more than 180 independent countries. There are also more than 40 dependencies, which are controlled in some way by independent countries. The largest nation is Russia, which was, until 1991, part of the Soviet Union. The smallest is Vatican City, a tiny territory covering 44 ha. (109 acres) within northwestern Rome, the capital of Italy.

THE WORLD

CLIMATE

Hot tropical climates are hot and wet all year.	**tropical**
Tropical monsoon climates have wet and dry seasons.	
Tropical steppe has a short, unreliable rainy season.	
Summers are wet and warm; winters wet and mild.	**subtropical**
Mild and wet winters; summers warm and mostly dry.	
Desert areas with little rain and no cold season.	
It rains all year with no great temperature variation.	**temperate**
These climates have warm summers and cold winters.	
It rains all year with no great temperature variation.	
Subarctic winters are very cold; summers are short.	**cold**
Arctic or icecap climates are freezing all year round.	

The world's climatic zones are affected by latitude, prevailing winds, the terrain, especially high mountain ranges that lie in the path of winds, distance from the sea, and ocean currents.

Surface currents have a marked effect on the climates of coastal regions. Onshore winds passing over cold currents are chilled. Winds passing over warm currents are warmed.

HABITATS

The world can be divided into landscape zones that broadly follow lines of latitude. They include areas around the Equator, the rainforests and savanna (tropical grasslands); deserts and semideserts; the middle latitudes, including the northern coniferous forests; and the cold zones in the high latitudes. Mountains form the fifth zone, but these are not a function of latitude.

Rainforests and savanna

Rainforests flourish in places where it is hot and wet throughout the year. They occur in South America, Central Africa, Southeast Asia and on some Pacific islands. Savanna occurs in tropical regions with a marked dry season.

Arid regions

Deserts are places with an average annual rainfall of less than 25 cm (10 in). Deserts cover about one-seventh of the Earth's land surface.

Middle latitudes

Between the tropics and the polar regions lie the middle latitudes. This zone, with its temperate climates, contains the huge coniferous forests of North America and Eurasia. Dry regions in the middle latitudes include the steppes of Eurasia and the prairies of North America.

Cold zones

Cold zones include the ice sheets of Antarctica and Greenland and treeless tundra regions, where plants grow during the short summer. Plants also grow on high mountain slopes below the permanent snowline. Vegetation zones ranging from tropical to polar occur on the flanks of high mountains near the Equator. This zoning results from the fact that temperatures fall by 0.5°C (1°F) for every 100 m (330 ft) of altitude.

CLIMATE

While weather is the day-to-day, or hour-to-hour, condition of the air, climate is long-term pattern of weather of a place.

Latitude and climate

The Earth's atmosphere is always on the move. The reason for the movement of air is the Sun, whose heat is most concentrated in tropical zones and least effective at the poles. This difference in heating causes a continuous exchange of air and heat between hot tropical and cold polar regions. The prevailing winds—the trade winds, the westerlies and the polar easterlies—are responsible for the heat exchange.

Terrain and climate

While latitude is a major factor affecting climate, several other factors complicate the pattern of world climates. First, winds are affected by the terrain. Warm, moist winds blowing up a mountain range on a coast are chilled. Because their capacity to retain water vapour is reduced by cooling, the water vapour is turned into tiny droplets, which form rain clouds. It rains on the side of the mountain where the clouds rise. Beyond the mountain peaks, the winds become warmer as they descend, picking up moisture and creating a dry region, called a rain shadow.

The influence of the sea

The sea often has a moderating influence on the climate, and moist winds from the ocean usually bring plenty of rain. These moderating effects are felt less and less the farther one travels inland.

Warm ocean currents, such as the Gulf Stream and its extension, the North Atlantic Drift, have a warming effect on northwestern Europe. By contrast, in the same latitude, eastern Canada is chilled by the cold Labrador Current.

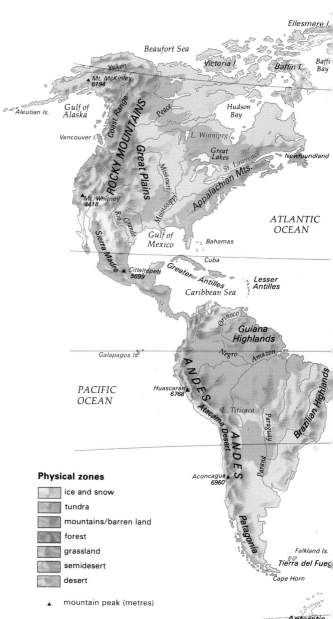

Physical zones

- ice and snow
- tundra
- mountains/barren land
- forest
- grassland
- semidesert
- desert

▲ mountain peak (metres)

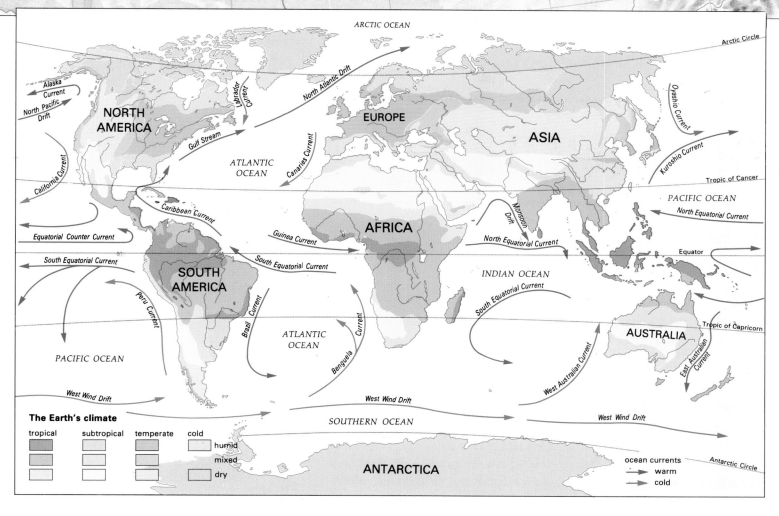

ARCTIC OCEAN

NORTH
AMERICA

EUROPE

ASIA

AFRICA

SOUTH
AMERICA

AUSTRALIA

ANTARCTICA

ATLANTIC
OCEAN

PACIFIC
OCEAN

PACIFIC OCEAN

INDIAN OCEAN

ATLANTIC
OCEAN

SOUTHERN OCEAN

Arctic Circle
Tropic of Cancer
Equator
Tropic of Capricorn
Antarctic Circle

Alaska Current
North Pacific Drift
California Current
Equatorial Counter Current
South Equatorial Current
Peru Current
West Wind Drift
Labrador Current
North Atlantic Drift
Gulf Stream
Canaries Current
Caribbean Current
Guinea Current
South Equatorial Current
Brazil Current
Benguela Current
West Wind Drift
Monsoon Drift
North Equatorial Current
South Equatorial Current
West Australian Current
West Wind Drift
Oyashio Current
Kuroshio Current
North Equatorial Current
East Australian Current

The Earth's climate

tropical | subtropical | temperate | cold
humid
mixed
dry

ocean currents
→ warm
→ cold

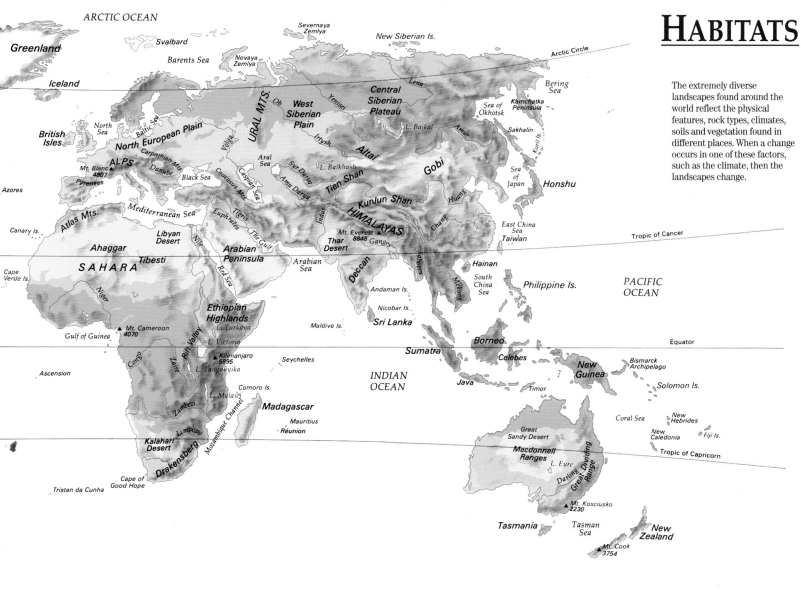

ARCTIC OCEAN

Greenland
Iceland
Svalbard
Barents Sea
Novaya Zemlya
Novaya Zemlya
Severnaya Zemlya
New Siberian Is.
Arctic Circle
Bering Sea
Kamchatka Peninsula
Sea of Okhotsk
Sakhalin
Kuril Is.

British Isles
North Sea
Baltic Sea
North European Plain
Carpathian Mts.
ALPS
Mt. Blanc 4807
Pyrenees
Danube
Black Sea
Caucasus Mts.
URAL MTS.
Ob
West Siberian Plain
Yenisei
Irtysh
Central Siberian Plateau
Lena
L. Baikal
Amur
Altai
Gobi
Kunlun Shan
Tien Shan
Amu Darya
Syr Darya
L. Balkhash
Aral Sea
Caspian Sea
Volga
Sea of Japan
Honshu
Huang
Chang
East China Sea
Taiwan

Azores
Atlas Mts.
Mediterranean Sea
Canary Is.
Libyan Desert
Ahaggar
Tibesti
SAHARA
Cape Verde Is.
Niger
Arabian Peninsula
Red Sea
Nile
The Gulf
Tigris
Euphrates
Indus
Thar Desert
Mt. Everest 8848
Ganges
HIMALAYAS
Arabian Sea
Deccan
Andaman Is.
Nicobar Is.
Maldive Is.
Sri Lanka
Hainan
South China Sea
Philippine Is.
PACIFIC OCEAN
Tropic of Cancer

Ethiopian Highlands
Mt. Cameroon 4070
Gulf of Guinea
L. Turkana
Rift Valley
L. Victoria
Kilimanjaro 5895
L. Tanganyika
Comoro Is.
Seychelles
INDIAN OCEAN
Borneo
Sumatra
Celebes
New Guinea
Java
Timor
Bismarck Archipelago
Solomon Is.
Equator

Ascension
Congo
Zaire
L. Malawi
Zambezi
Madagascar
Mauritius
Réunion
Mozambique Channel
Limpopo
Kalahari Desert
Drakensberg
Cape of Good Hope
Tristan da Cunha
Coral Sea
Great Sandy Desert
Macdonnell Ranges
L. Eyre
Darling
Great Dividing Range
Mt. Kosciusko 2230
New Hebrides
New Caledonia
Fiji Is.
Tropic of Capricorn

Tasmania
Tasman Sea
New Zealand
Mt. Cook 3754

HABITATS

The extremely diverse landscapes found around the world reflect the physical features, rock types, climates, soils and vegetation found in different places. When a change occurs in one of these factors, such as the climate, then the landscapes change.

Weddell Sea
Queen Maud Land
Coats Land
Antarctica
Enderby Land
Wilkes Land
Antarctic Circle

THE WORLD

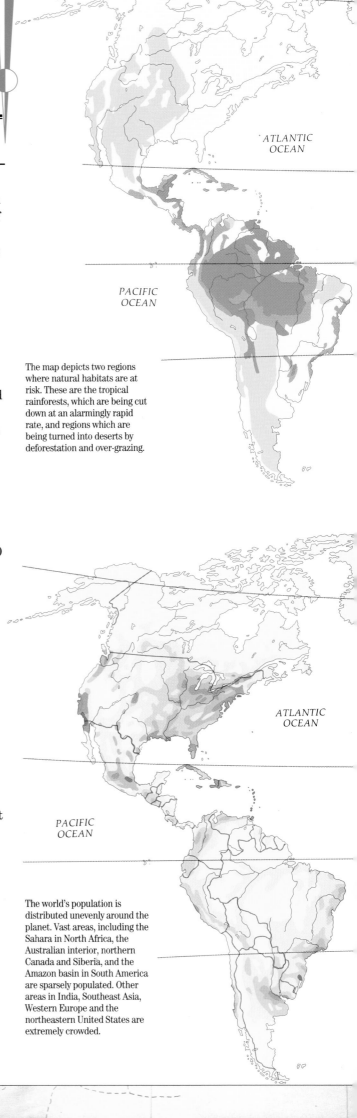

The map depicts two regions where natural habitats are at risk. These are the tropical rainforests, which are being cut down at an alarmingly rapid rate, and regions which are being turned into deserts by deforestation and over-grazing.

The world's population is distributed unevenly around the planet. Vast areas, including the Sahara in North Africa, the Australian interior, northern Canada and Siberia, and the Amazon basin in South America are sparsely populated. Other areas in India, Southeast Asia, Western Europe and the northeastern United States are extremely crowded.

ENVIRONMENTAL ISSUES

The natural habitats around the world are always changing, mainly because world climates vary over periods of hundreds of years. But, in addition to the natural evolution of landscapes, the natural world is now being modified by mounting human activity.

Deforestation

The temperate middle latitudes were once largely covered by deciduous forests of ash, beech, elm, oak, and maple. However, much of the original deciduous forests have been cut down to provide fuel, timber and farmland.

Perhaps the most serious environmental issue in the world today is the destruction of the rainforests in South America, Central Africa and Southeast Asia. These forests contain more than half of the world's species of plants and animals, many of which are rapidly becoming extinct. Rainforest destruction causes climatic change and contributes to global warming.

Desertification

Soil erosion occurs when deforestation, overgrazing and poor farming lays the land bare to the weather. In arid regions, soil erosion can turn fertile land into barren desert. The desertification of semiarid grasslands, such as the Sahel region south of the Sahara, is another major environmental issue.

Other problems

In each of the regional sections in this Atlas there is a map showing local environmental problems. Many of them arise from pollution. Major issues include smog caused by industrial smoke or car exhaust fumes, acid rain, the pollution of rivers and lakes by industrial wastes or untreated sewage, discharges of nuclear radiation, and the extravagant use of water.

POPULATION

In 1992, the world's population totalled about 5,500 million. With an annual population growth rate of 1.7 percent in the early 1990s, the world's population will reach almost 6,500 million by the end of the 20th century and, experts predict, the world population could then double in only 41 years.

The population explosion

Around 10,000 years ago, when people began to grow crops and live in permanent settlements, the world was thinly populated. From around 5 million in 8000 B.C., the population increased steadily to reach 500 million in A.D. 1650. The population then doubled in only 200 years, reaching 1,000 million in 1850. The acceleration of population growth continued. By the mid-1920s, world population had reached nearly 2,000 million, and it passed the 4,000 million mark in the 1970s.

The increases in the last 200 years occurred first in nations which were industrializing. But the rates of population growth in the developed industrial world have recently declined. Today, the highest growth rates are in the developing world.

Where people live

In the early 1990s, about half of the world's people lived on only 5 percent of the world's land area, while about half of the world's land areas contained only about 5 percent of the world's population. The population explosion in areas attractive to settlement and the consequent expansion of city populations have all contributed to pollution, while urban living has created many of the environmental problems that exist today.

Population pressure also affects rural areas, where the increasing demand for food has led to the destruction of natural habitats.

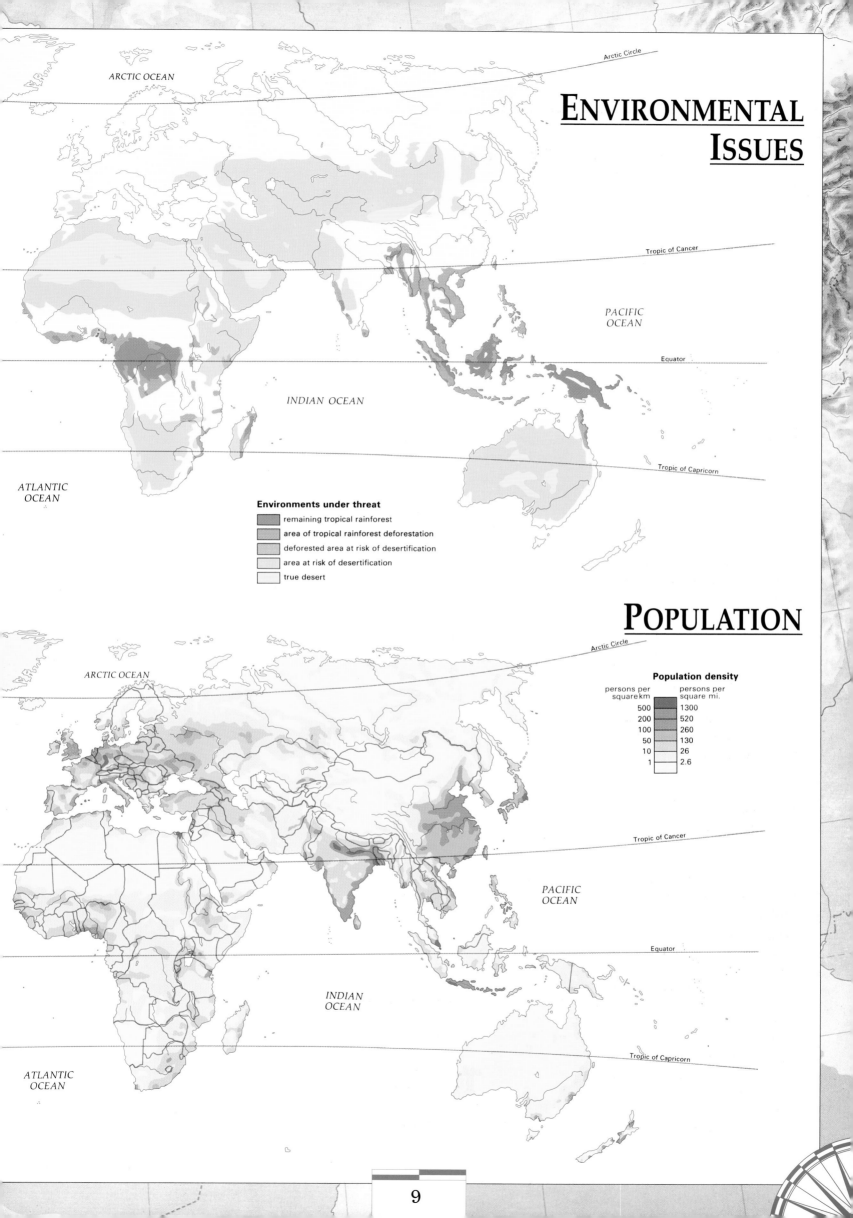

ENVIRONMENTAL ISSUES

ARCTIC OCEAN

Tropic of Cancer

PACIFIC OCEAN

Equator

INDIAN OCEAN

Tropic of Capricorn

ATLANTIC OCEAN

Environments under threat
- remaining tropical rainforest
- area of tropical rainforest deforestation
- deforested area at risk of desertification
- area at risk of desertification
- true desert

POPULATION

ARCTIC OCEAN

Arctic Circle

Population density

persons per square km	persons per square mi.
500	1300
200	520
100	260
50	130
10	26
1	2.6

Tropic of Cancer

PACIFIC OCEAN

Equator

INDIAN OCEAN

Tropic of Capricorn

ATLANTIC OCEAN

THE WORLD

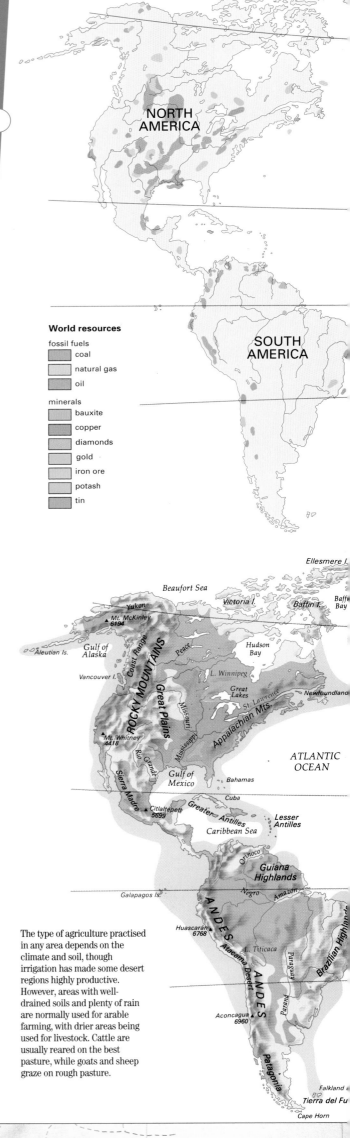

RESOURCES

The world's leading resources include those that provide fuel, together with metals and nonmetallic minerals used in industry.

Energy resources

Coal, oil and natural gas are called fossil fuels because they were formed from once-living organisms. Coal was the main fuel during the British Industrial Revolution in the 19th century. Today, however, oil and natural gas provide about three-fifths of the world's energy.

Fossil fuels are nonrenewable resources and some experts estimate that, at present drilling rates, the world's oil reserves will run out by 2035. Nuclear power remains controversial, and so it seems likely that such renewable energy resources as water and solar power will be increasingly used in the future. Also important is the fact that the use of water and solar power, unlike that of fossil fuels, does not cause pollution.

Mineral reserves

Most minerals are extracted from ores, which are compounds of valuable minerals with other elements. Iron, which is used to make steel, is the most widely used metal. Other major metallic minerals include aluminium, which is obtained from the ore bauxite, copper, lead, tin and zinc. Uranium is also a metal. It has become important because of its use as a nuclear fuel. Nonmetallic minerals include building materials, diamonds, phosphates, and sulphur.

Metals are also nonrenewable resources and some are becoming scarce. As a result, recycling is becoming increasingly common: about half of the iron and one-third of the aluminium now used by industry comes from scrap.

AGRICULTURE

Agriculture is the world's leading industry. Not only does it provide food, but it also produces materials used for the clothing and other industries. Forestry and fishing also are related industries, concerned with producing materials for industry and food.

The development of agriculture

The deliberate planting and harvesting of crops began around 10,000 years ago and, soon afterwards, farming communities began to displace the traditional hunting and gathering economies. Other early developments were the domestication of animals and irrigation. From the 18th century, farming became increasingly mechanized and scientific. Today, agriculture employs only a small proportion of people in the prosperous developed countries. For example, the United States leads the world in agricultural production, yet agriculture employs only about three percent of its workforce. By contrast, a high proportion of people in most developing countries work on the land. Much of the agriculture is carried out at subsistence level – that is, farmers produce enough for their families, with comparatively little left over for sale.

Modern transportation methods, especially the use of refrigeration, has made it possible to move perishable goods around the world. Agriculture is big business.

Forestry and fishing

Forests cover about 30 percent of the Earth's land area. Forestry is the commercial exploitation and management of forests. Wood is a major raw material in industry.

The fishing industry is particularly important in countries, such as Japan, where protein-rich foods are in short supply.

World resources

fossil fuels
- coal
- natural gas
- oil

minerals
- bauxite
- copper
- diamonds
- gold
- iron ore
- potash
- tin

The type of agriculture practised in any area depends on the climate and soil, though irrigation has made some desert regions highly productive. However, areas with well-drained soils and plenty of rain are normally used for arable farming, with drier areas being used for livestock. Cattle are usually reared on the best pasture, while goats and sheep graze on rough pasture.

RESOURCES

The map shows that fossil fuels, particularly oil and gas, are concentrated in the northern hemisphere. North America is especially rich in energy reserves. On the other hand, reserves of metals and other minerals are spread far more evenly around the world.

EUROPE

ASIA

AFRICA

AUSTRALIA

Arctic Circle

Tropic of Cancer

Equator

Tropic of Capricorn

AGRICULTURE

ARCTIC OCEAN

Greenland

Svalbard

Severnaya Zemlya

New Siberian Is.

Iceland

Barents Sea

Novaya Zemlya

Lena

Bering Sea

Kamchatka Peninsula

Central Siberian Plateau

Sea of Okhotsk

Arctic Circle

British Isles

North Sea

Baltic Sea

Ob

West Siberian Plain

Yenisei

L. Baikal

Sakhalin

Kuril Is.

North European Plain

URAL MTS.

Irtysh

Altai

Amur

Greenland

Azores

ALPS
Mt. Blanc 4807
Pyrenees

Carpathian Mts.

Danube

Volga

Aral Sea

Syr Darya

L. Balkhash

Gobi

Sea of Japan

Honshu

Caucasus Mts.

Caspian Sea

Amu Darya

Tien Shan

Kunlun Shan

Huang

Black Sea

Atlas Mts.

Mediterranean Sea

Tigris

Euphrates

The Gulf

Indus

HIMALAYAS

Chang

East China Sea

Taiwan

Tropic of Cancer

Libyan Desert

Nile

Arabian Peninsula

Mt. Everest 8848

Thar Desert

Ganges

Salween

Hainan

Canary Is.

Ahaggar

Tibesti

Red Sea

Arabian Sea

Deccan

Mekong

South China Sea

Philippine Is.

PACIFIC OCEAN

Cape Verde Is.

SAHARA

Niger

Andaman Is.

Nicobar Is.

Sri Lanka

Borneo

Equator

Ethiopian Highlands

Mt. Cameroon 4070

L. Turkana

Maldive Is.

Sumatra

Celebes

New Guinea

Bismarck Archipelago

Gulf of Guinea

L. Victoria

Rift Valley

Kilimanjaro 5895

Seychelles

INDIAN OCEAN

Java

Timor

Solomon Is.

Ascension

Congo

Zaïre

L. Tanganyika

Comoro Is.

Coral Sea

New Hebrides

New Caledonia

Fiji Is.

Zambezi

L. Malawi

Madagascar

Mauritius

Réunion

Mozambique Channel

Great Sandy Desert

Kalahari Desert

Limpopo

Macdonnell Ranges

L. Eyre

Darling

Tropic of Capricorn

Drakensberg

Great Dividing Range

Cape of Good Hope

Mt. Kosciusko 2230

Tristan da Cunha

Tasmania

Tasman Sea

New Zealand

Mt. Cook 3754

Agricultural zones

- arable
- fruit, vegetables and tree crops
- pasture
- rough grazing
- woods and forest
- nonagricultural land

- major fishing grounds
- ▲ mountain peak (metres)

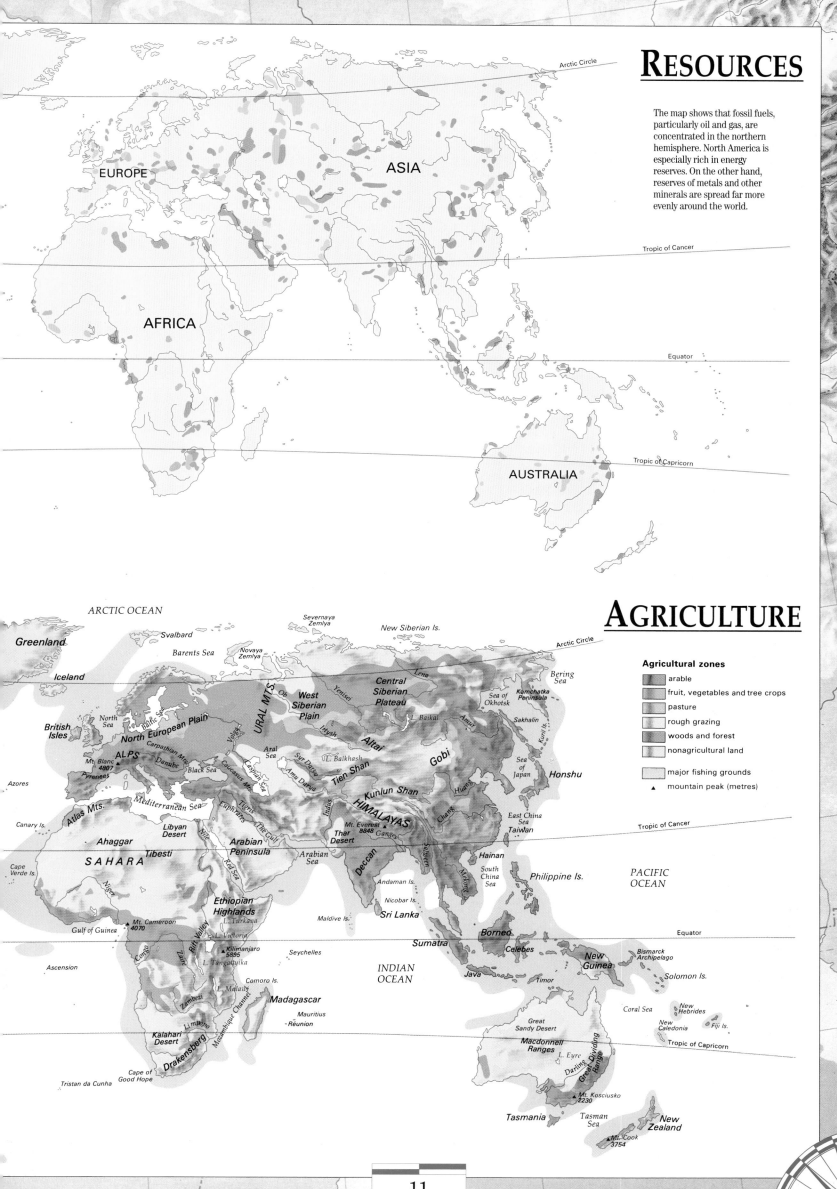

The World

Soils

Soil is one of the Earth's vital resources. Most living things on land could not exist without it. Soil is a complex mixture of worn fragments of rock, humus (the decayed remains of plants and animals), water, air and living organisms. All the living organisms, together with the roots of plants, contribute to breaking down the soil into smaller and smaller pieces.

Soil formation

The character of soil is affected by the parent rock on which it forms. For example, soils that form on shale, a soft rock, usually have a finer texture than those that form on sandstone, which is composed largely of hard grains of quartz.

Soils are usually thin on sloping land, because soil particles tend to move downhill. But they may reach depths of several metres in hollows. In waterlogged areas, dead plants may accumulate to form peat.

Soil types

The most common soil classifications are based on climate. In wet equatorial regions, the heavy rain leaches (dissolves) minerals from the top layers, leaving a red or yellow soil, latosol, which is rich in bauxite.

Brown forest soils are not heavily leached. Their colour comes from the large amount of humus in the top layers. Hot desert soils are often red and sandy, because they are low in humus. Dark-coloured chernozems are soils rich in humus, formed from the remains of the plants that grew on temperate grasslands. By contrast, podzols, the greyish soils of the northern coniferous forest zones, are low in humus. They contain a thin acid layer, overlying a heavily leached layer. Tundra soils are often waterlogged and often remain frozen just below the surface. The frozen subsoil is called permafrost.

Plants

The vegetation in any area is governed by three main factors. First, there are the climate and the geographical conditions that exist today. Second, plants have been affected by past climates, such as ice ages. Third, the world's changing geography, caused by plate movements shifting the continents around, has greatly influenced the course of evolution in various areas.

Botanists have divided the world into six floristic kingdoms, where the major plant families have distinct characteristics in common. The kingdoms are divided into regions.

Holarctic kingdom

The Holarctic (or 'whole northern') includes the cold temperate and subtropical lands of the northern hemisphere. One reason for the similarity between the plants in this kingdom is that the land masses were joined together in recent geological times.

Tropical kingdoms

The Paleotropical ('ancient tropical') kingdom includes most of Africa south of the Sahara and tropical southern Asia. The Neotropical ('new tropical') kingdom in Central and tropical South America has distinctive vegetation, which evolved differently from that of Africa after South America began to move away from Africa from about 140 million years ago. South America was also isolated from North America until about 2.5 million years ago.

The southern kingdoms

The southern kingdoms include the Cape (or South African) kingdom, where the climate is much like that of the Mediterranean kingdom, with its many native species. Finally, there is the Holantarctic kingdom, the southern equivalent of the Holarctic, which includes southern South America and New Zealand.

World soils

- tundra soils
- podzols
- brown earths
- grey forest/steppe soils
- chernozems
- chestnut and brown soils
- red and grey desert soils
- red and brown soils
- red-yellow podzolic soils
- red and yellow soils (latosols)
- dark grey and black tropical soils
- mountain soils

Plants

Plants are found everywhere on Earth, with the greatest number of species in hot and wet tropical regions. The map shows the six main floristic kingdoms, which are further subdivided into regions. These kingdoms and regions reflect both the climate of the areas and the factors that governed the evolution of plant communities over millions of years.

SOILS

The most important factor influencing the development of soils is the climate. Hence, the world distribution of soil types is closely related to the map of climatic zones. Soil types are also influenced by the underlying rocks, terrain, drainage, and vegetation types.

Arctic Circle

Tropic of Cancer

Equator

Tropic of Capricorn

ARCTIC OCEAN

Arctic Circle

CIRCUMBOREAL

CIRCUMBOREAL

ROCKY MOUNTAIN

NORTH AMERICAN ATLANTIC

MADREAN

MACARONESIAN

MEDITERRANEAN

IRANO-TURANIAN

HAWAIIAN

SAHARO-ARABIAN

EASTERN ASIATIC

Tropic of Cancer

CARIBBEAN

ATLANTIC OCEAN

INDIAN

INDOCHINESE

PACIFIC OCEAN

SUDANO-ZAMBEZIAN

GUIANA HIGHLANDS

PACIFIC OCEAN

AMAZONIAN

GUINEO-CONGOLIAN

Equator

MALESIAN

POLYNESIAN

INDIAN OCEAN

NORTHEAST AUSTRALIAN

FIJIAN

POLYNESIAN

ANDEAN

BRAZILIAN

ST HELENA AND ASCENSION

MADAGASCAN

CENTRAL AUSTRALIAN

NEOCALEDONIAN

Tropic of Capricorn

KAROO-NAMIB

UZAMBARA-ZULULAND

SOUTHWEST AUSTRALIAN

FERNANDEZIAN

ATLANTIC OCEAN

CAPE

CHILE-PATAGONIAN

NEOZEYLANDIC

SOUTH SUBANTARCTIC ISLANDS

Floristic Kingdoms

- Holarctic
- Paleotropical
- Neotropical
- Cape
- Australian
- Holantarctic

— Region boundary

Antarctic Circle

THE WORLD

NATURAL VEGETATION

Wilderness areas around the world are amazingly diverse. However, they can be divided into a few general types, which are characterized by the dominant plant communities, such as grassland, tundra, coniferous or broadleaf (deciduous) forest. These broad regions are called biomes.

Living communities

The 14 basic biomes are defined as plant and animal communities that would flourish in those areas if they were left undisturbed. But the wilderness is constantly changing, because some biomes are short-lived. Lakes, for example, are silted by inflowing rivers. Eventually, the hollow containing the lake fills up and a marsh is formed. Finally the lake becomes dry land. Many dry, flat areas in the western United States were once lakes.

Over longer periods, the erosion of mountains and the movements of continents also change landscapes and climates. Plants and animals respond to these changes. Some adapt to the new environment, some migrate and some become extinct.

Biodiversity

There may be as many as 30 million plant and animal species on our planet, even though 98 percent of all the species that have existed are now extinct. Plant and animal species are the basic units of the rich biodiversity on our planet. But human interference is now threatening millions of species, especially in the tropical forests where biodiversity is at its greatest. Experts predict that one-quarter of all the world's plant and animal species face extinction in the next 25 to 50 years, mainly as a result of human destruction of biomes. The future well-being of the Earth may depend on preserving biodiversity.

ANCIENT VEGETATION

Several ice ages have occurred during the Earth's history. Geologists have found evidence of major periods of cooling around 2,300 million years ago, 600 million years ago, around 450 million years ago, and again around 300 million years ago. The most recent ice age was two million years ago.

The Pleistocene Ice Age

The recent, or Pleistocene, Ice Age was not a long period of cold. There were periods of intense cooling, called glacials, when the ice advanced, and periods called interglacials when the climate was warmer than it is today. The ice sheets then melted and retreated. The Pleistocene Ice Age was last at its height between 15,000 and 20,000 years ago. At that time, ice covered about 30 percent of the Earth's land surface. Ice spread over much of the northern hemisphere. Ice sheets reached southern England, the Netherlands and southern Germany. In North America, the ice reached a line roughly joining Seattle in the west to New York City in the east.

Ice ages and vegetation

The effects of the last Ice Age altered all the Earth's climatic and vegetation zones. In the middle latitudes, there developed great areas of tundra, while the tropics became much drier. Huge deserts were formed. However, from about 10,000 years ago, the climate has become generally warmer and plants recolonized the barren tundra zones. Since then, there have been other minor fluctuations, such as the 'Little Ice Age' in Europe between the 15th and 18th centuries.

These natural fluctuations give us some idea of what may happen if global warming, caused by human activity, is allowed to continue.

Biomes
- tropical humid forest
- subtropical and temperate rainforest
- coniferous forest
- tropical dry forest
- temperate broadleaf forest
- evergreen sclerophyll forest and scrubland
- warm desert and semidesert
- cold winter desert and semidesert
- arctic desert and tundra
- tropical grassland and savanna
- temperate grassland
- mountain and highland system
- island system
- lake system

ANCIENT VEGETATION

The map shows the world's vegetation about 18,000 years ago, when the last Ice Age was at its peak. The positions of coastlines were different from those of today, because so much water was frozen in the ice sheets, lowering the sea level. This influenced human development. Dry land bridges were created, enabling early people to migrate from one area to another.

NATURAL VEGETATION

The map shows the 14 main biomes defined by Professor Miklos Udvardy as part of UNESCO's Man and the Biosphere Programme. These range from tropical humid forest to arctic desert and tundra, with special biomes associated with mountains, lakes, and islands.

ARCTIC OCEAN

Greenland
Svalbard
Iceland
Barents Sea
British Isles
North Sea
Baltic Sea
North European Plain
ALPS
Pyrenees
Danube
Black Sea
Atlas Mts.
Mediterranean Sea
Libyan Desert
SAHARA
Nile
Niger
Gulf of Guinea
Congo
Zaire
Rift Valley
L. Victoria
L. Tanganyika
Zambezi
Limpopo
Mozambique Channel
Kalahari Desert
Drakensberg
Cape of Good Hope
Madagascar

URAL MTS.
Ob
West Siberian Plain
Yenisey
Irtysh
Central Siberian Plateau
Lena
Altai
Aral Sea
Volga
Caspian Sea
Syr Darya
Amu Darya
L. Balkhash
Tien Shan
Gobi
Kunlun Shan
HIMALAYAS
Tigris
Euphrates
The Gulf
Arabian Peninsula
Red Sea
Arabian Sea
Thar Desert
Deccan
Ganges
Indus
Salween
Chang
Huang
Mekong
Ethiopian Highlands
Sri Lanka

Bering Sea
Sea of Okhotsk
Amur
Sea of Japan
Honshu
East China Sea
Taiwan
South China Sea
Philippine Is.
PACIFIC OCEAN
Borneo
Sumatra
INDIAN OCEAN
New Guinea
Coral Sea
Macdonnell Ranges
Darling
Great Dividing Range
Tasmania
Tasman Sea
New Zealand

Arctic Circle
Tropic of Cancer
Equator
Tropic of Capricorn

ARCTIC OCEAN
NORTH AMERICA
EUROPE
ASIA
PACIFIC OCEAN
ATLANTIC OCEAN
AFRICA
SOUTH AMERICA
INDIAN OCEAN
PACIFIC OCEAN
AUSTRALIA
ATLANTIC OCEAN
SOUTHERN OCEAN
ANTARCTICA

Arctic Circle
Tropic of Cancer
Equator
Tropic of Capricorn
Antarctic Circle

Vegetation zones 18 000 years ago
- tundra
- forest
- grassland
- semidesert
- desert
- lake

ice thickness
m / ft
9840
6560
3280
0

sea ice in summer
ancient coastline

CANADA & GREENLAND

Northern North America includes Canada, the world's second largest country, and Greenland, the world's largest island. The Arctic islands of Canada are a cold tundra region that contain many glaciers. Two of these islands – Baffin Island and Ellesmere Island – have among the largest islands in the world. About six-sevenths of Greenland is buried under a thick ice sheet, the world's second largest body of ice after the ice sheet of Antarctica.

Canada's most prominent features include the western mountains, the interior plains, the Canadian Shield, the St. Lawrence lowlands and, in the southeast, an extension of the Appalachian region. Canada also shares with the United States the world's largest expanse of fresh water—the Great Lakes.

Because of the climate, about 80 percent of Canadians live within 300 kilometres (about 200 mi) of their southern border. Canada is one of the world's leading mineral exporters and manufacturing nations. Its farming and fishing industries are highly efficient.

Canada has a diverse population. The ancestors of its earliest inhabitants, the Native Americans, entered Canada about 30,000 years ago. They were followed by the Inuits, who also live in Greenland. These two peoples now make up a small minority of the population. Nearly two-thirds of the people today are English- and French-speaking descendants of European settlers, though Canada also has communities from other parts of Europe, notably Germans, Italians and Ukrainians, and from Asia.

Canada and Greenland make up about half of North America. Northern Canada and most of Greenland lie north of the Arctic Circle, and the northern tip of Greenland is about 710 kilometres (440 mi) from the North Pole. Canada's greatest east-west distance is nearly 5,410 kilometres (3,420 mi). This vast distance is reflected by its six time zones. When it is 08.00 in Halifax, it is 03.00 in Vancouver, British Columbia.

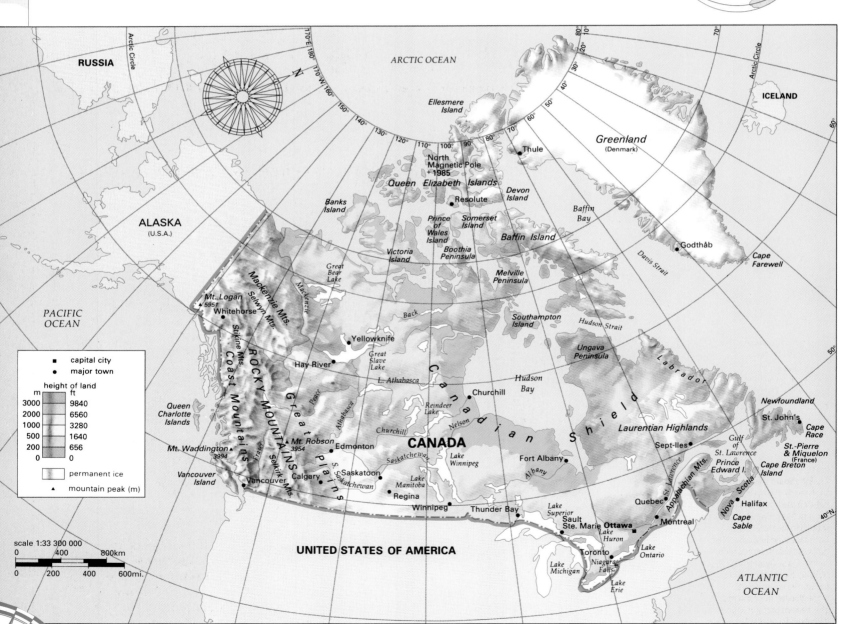

THE POLITICAL AND CULTURAL WORLD

Canada has a federal system of government, but it faces several problems arising from its ethnic diversity. One problem is reconciling the aspirations of the French-speaking people, who form the majority in Quebec, with the different traditions of the English-speaking Canadians. Another problem is how to integrate Native American and Inuit peoples into the modern state.

Greenland is a self-governing province of Denmark, though it is 50 times bigger than that country. To assert its independence, Greenland left the European Community in 1985, though it continued its relationship with Denmark.

COUNTRIES IN THE REGION

Canada

RELIGION

ROMAN CATHOLIC	46.5%
PROTESTANT	41.0%
EASTERN ORTHODOX	1.5%
JEWISH	1.2%
MUSLIM	0.4%
HINDU	0.3%
SIKH	0.3%
NONRELIGIOUS	7.4%
OTHERS	1.4%

ETHNIC COMPOSITION

BRITISH	34.4%
FRENCH	25.7%
GERMAN	3.6%
ITALIAN	2.8%
UKRAINIAN	1.7%
AMERINDIAN AND INUIT	1.5%
CHINESE	1.4%
DUTCH	1.4%
MULTIPLE ORIGIN AND/OR OTHERS	27.5%

FORM OF GOVERNMENT

Federal multiparty parliamentary monarchy with two legislative houses

ECONOMIC INDICATORS: 1990

GDP (US$ billions)	570.15
GNP per capita (US$)	20,470
Annual rate of growth of GDP, 1980-1990	3.4%
Manufacturing as % of GDP	15.0%
Central government spending as % of GNP	23.0%
Merchandise exports (US$ billions)	133.5
Merchandise imports (US$ billions)	126.5
% of GNP donated as development aid	0.44%

WELFARE INDICATORS

Infant mortality rate (per 1,000 live births)	
1965	24
1990	7
Daily food supply available (calories per capita, 1989)	3,482
Population per physician (1984)	510
Teacher-pupil ratio (primary school, 1989)	1 : 16

- ■ capital city
- ● provincial capital

Constitutional changes
In the early 1990s, Canadians debated the future of their country. Many French Canadians wanted to create a French Canadian state in Quebec. One proposed change would set up Nunavut, a self-governing territory for the Inuit to occupy the eastern part of the Northwest Territories. The western part would be a homeland for Native Americans.

Area 9,215,430 sq. km
(3,558,096 sq. mi.)
Population 26,521,000
Capital Ottawa
Chief languages English, French
Currency 1 Canadian dollar (Can $) = 100 cents

Canada

HABITATS

Canada is a cold land, with massive mountain ranges capped by snowy peaks, forests, huge lakes, swift rivers and waterfalls. The Canadian Shield, a bleak region of ancient rock around Hudson Bay, forms the geological core of the country.

LAND

Area   12,151,739 sq. km (4,691,791 sq. mi.)
Highest point   Mount Logan, 5,951 m (19,525 ft)
Lowest point   sea level
Major features   Rocky Mountains, Canadian Shield, Arctic islands, Greenland, world's largest island

WATER

Longest river   Mackenzie, 4,240 km (2,635 mi.)
Largest basin   Mackenzie, 1,764,000 sq. km (681,000 sq. mi.)
Highest average flow   Saint Lawrence, 13,030 cu. m/sec (460,000 cu ft/sec)
Largest lake   Superior, 83,270 sq. km (32,150 sq. mi.), world's largest freshwater lake

NOTABLE THREATENED ENDEMIC SPECIES

Mammals   Vancouver Island marmot (*Marmota vancouverensis*)
Other animals   Lake lamprey (*Lampetra macrostoma*), Copper redhorse fish (*Moxostoma hubbsi*), Periodical cicaca (*Magicicauda septendecim*)
Plants   *Armeria maritima* subsp. *interior*; *Cypripedium candidum* (small white lady's slipper); *Isotria medeoloides* (small whorled fogonia); *Limnanthes macounii*; *Pedicularis furbishiae* (Furbish's lousewort); *Phyllitis japonica* subsp. *americana*; *Plantago cordata*; *Salix planifolia* subsp. *tyrrellii*; *Salix silicicola*; *Senecio newcombei*

CLIMATE

The Arctic has frozen seas and ice caps, with temperatures near freezing point, and tundra regions with brief, chilly summers. Most of Canada has a subarctic climate, with coniferous forests. Only in the south are there climatic regions warm enough for farming.

TEMPERATURE AND PRECIPITATION

| | Temperature °C (°F) | | Altitude m (ft) |
	January	July	
Resolute	−32 (−26)	4 (39)	64 (200)
Vancouver	2 (36)	17 (63)	14 (45)
Winnipeg	−20 (−4)	20 (68)	240 (787)
Montreal	−9 (16)	22 (72)	30 (98)
Halifax	−4 (25)	18 (64)	30 (98)

| | Precipitation mm (in) | | |
	January	July	Year
Resolute	3 (0.1)	21 (0.8)	131 (5.1)
Vancouver	218 (8.5)	31 (1.2)	1,068 (42.0)
Winnipeg	23 (0.9)	79 (3.1)	535 (21.0)
Montreal	83 (3.3)	89 (3.5)	999 (39.3)
Halifax	137 (5.4)	96 (3.8)	1,381 (54.4)

World's highest recorded snowfall in 24 hours, 1,180 mm (46 in), Lake Lakelse, British Columbia

NATURAL HAZARDS

Cold and snowstorms, drought, gales, avalanches, rockfalls and landslides

ENVIRONMENTAL ISSUES

Southeastern Canada suffers from acid rain, part of which results from air pollution originating in the northeastern and midwestern United States. Soil erosion, logging, mining, oil drilling, and water pollution are other hazards.

POPULATION AND WEALTH

Population (millions)	26.6
Population increase (annual population growth rate, % 1960–90)	1.3
Energy use (gigajoules/person)	291
Real purchasing power (US$/person)	17,680

ENVIRONMENTAL INDICATORS

CO_2 emissions (million tonnes carbon/annum)	120
Municipal waste (kg/person/annum)	630
Nuclear waste (cumulative tonnes heavy metal)	11,000
Artificial fertilizer use (kg/ha./annum)	48
Cars (per 1,000 population)	432
Access to safe drinking water (% population)	100

MAJOR ENVIRONMENTAL PROBLEMS AND SOURCES

Air pollution: urban high; acid rain prevalent; high greenhouse gas emissions
River/lake pollution: medium; *sources*: agricultural, sewage, acid deposition
Land pollution: local; *sources*: industrial, urban/household
Waste disposal problems: domestic; industrial; nuclear
Major events: Mississauga (1979), chlorine gas leak during transportation; Saint Basile le Grand (1988), toxic cloud from waste dump fire

HABITATS

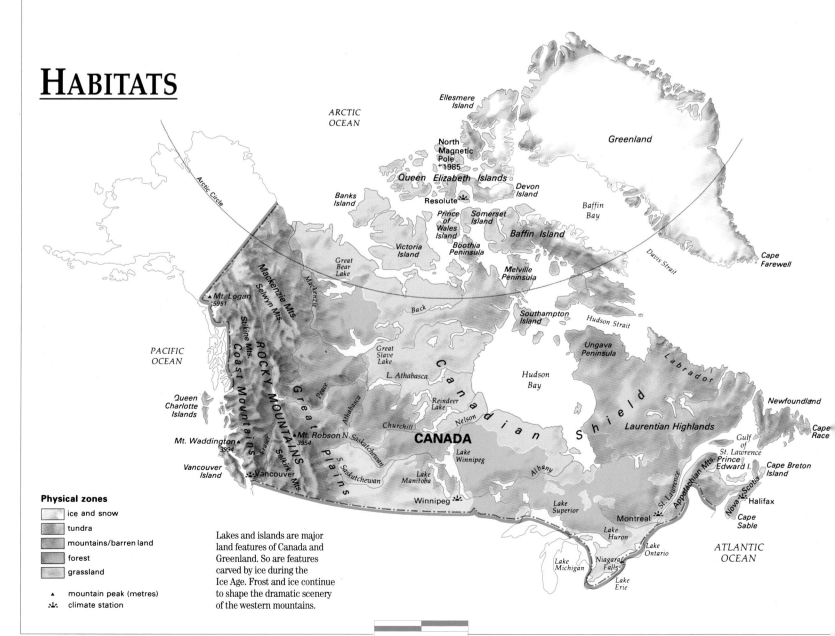

Physical zones
- ice and snow
- tundra
- mountains/barren land
- forest
- grassland

▲ mountain peak (metres)
climate station

Lakes and islands are major land features of Canada and Greenland. So are features carved by ice during the Ice Age. Frost and ice continue to shape the dramatic scenery of the western mountains.

POPULATION

Although Canada's population has doubled since 1945, Canada has one of the world's lowest average population densities. This is the result of a high birth rate and immigration. Most Canadians live near the southern border with the United States.

POPULATION

Total population of region (millions)	26.6
Population density (persons per sq. km)	2.9
Population change (average annual percent 1960–1990)	
Urban	+1.7
Rural	+0.4

URBAN POPULATION

As percentage of total population	
1960	68.9
1990	75.6
Percentage in cities of more than 1 million	29.7

TEN LARGEST CITIES

	Population
Toronto	3,427,000
Montreal	2,921,000
Vancouver	1,381,000
Ottawa †	819,000
Edmonton	785,000
Calgary	671,000
Winnipeg	623,000
Quebec	603,000
Hamilton	557,000
St. Catharines-Niagara	343,000

† denotes capital city

INDUSTRY

Canada is rich in minerals and is a major exporter of raw materials. Manufacturing industries belong to two main groups: those that process raw materials, and those concerned with making products, such as food and vehicles, for home sales.

INDUSTRIAL OUTPUT (US $ billion)

Total	Mining	Manufacturing	Average annual change since 1960
171.3	19.7	94.3	+3.5%

MAJOR PRODUCTS (figures in brackets are percentages of world production)

Energy and minerals	Output	Change since 1960
Coal (mill tonnes)	70.6 (1.5%)	+713%
Oil (mill barrels)	615.7 (2.8%)	+327%
Natural gas (billion cu. metres)	90.8 (4.9%)	+625%
Iron Ore (mill tonnes)	40.8 (7.2%)	+13.5%
Copper (mill tonnes)	0.8 (8.8%)	-8.5%
Lead (mill tonnes)	0.4 (11.5%)	+29%
Zinc (mill tonnes)	1.5 (20.9%)	+14%
Nickel (mill tonnes)	0.2 (24.6%)	-18%
Uranium (1,000 tonnes: U content)	12.4 (33.7%)	No data

Manufactures		
Aluminium (mill tonnes)	1.6 (7.2%)	+72%
Steel (mill tonnes)	15.1 (2.1%)	+286%
Woodpulp (mill tonnes)	21.0 (16.5%)	+16%
Newsprint (mill tonnes)	10.0 (31.5%)	+15%
Sulphuric acid (mill tonnes)	3.8 (1.4%)	+45%
Cars (mill)	2.0 (4.3%)	+509%

AGRICULTURE

Only 8 percent of the land in Canada is used for farming. The best farmland is in the St. Lawrence lowlands and around the Great Lakes. The other main region is the wheat-growing prairie belt. This is the northern part of the Great Plains.

LAND (million hectares)

Total	Agricultural	Arable	Forest/woodland
956 (100%)	78 (8%)	46 (5%)	354 (37%)

FARMERS

472,000 employed in agriculture (4% of workforce)
97 hectares of arable land per person employed in agriculture

MAJOR CROPS

	Area mill ha.	Yield 100kg/ha.	Production mill tonnes	Change since 1963
Wheat	13.5	19.3 (83)	26.0 (5)	+69%
Barley	5.0	27.9 (120)	14.0 (8)	+262%
Rapeseed	2.7	14.4 (101)	3.8 (17)	+1,284%
Oats	1.3	23.7 (129)	3.0 (7)	−51%
Maize	1.0	70.2 (193)	7.0 (2)	+554%
Linseed	0.6	12.3 (216)	0.7 (29)	+42%

MAJOR LIVESTOCK

	Number mill	Production mill tonnes	Change since 1963
Cattle	11.7 (1)	—	+4%
Pigs	10.5 (1)	—	+101%
Milk	—	8.0 (2)	−4%
Fish catch	—	1.6 (2)	—

Numbers in brackets are percentages of world total

POPULATION

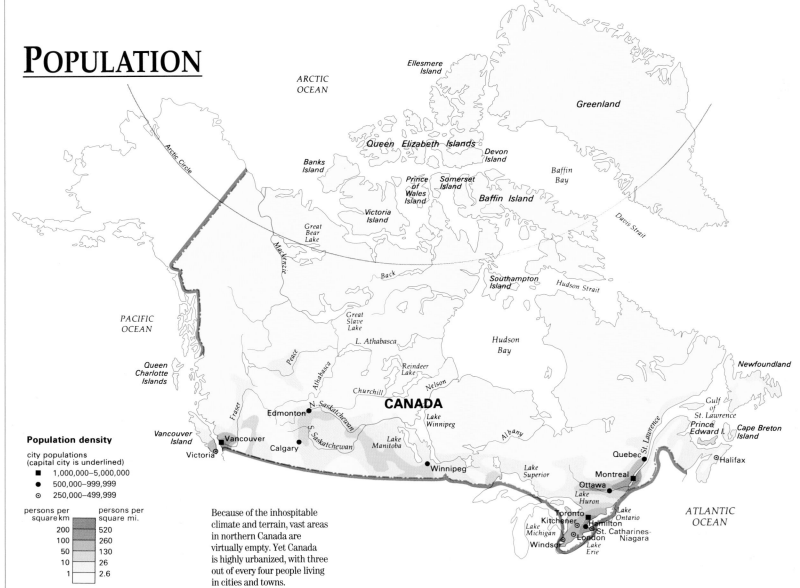

Population density

city populations
(capital city is underlined)

- ■ 1,000,000–5,000,000
- ● 500,000–999,999
- ◉ 250,000–499,999

persons per square km	persons per square mi.
200	520
100	260
50	130
10	26
1	2.6

Because of the inhospitable climate and terrain, vast areas in northern Canada are virtually empty. Yet Canada is highly urbanized, with three out of every four people living in cities and towns.

INDUSTRY

ARCTIC
OCEAN

Ellesmere Island

Greenland

Queen Elizabeth Islands

Devon Island

Banks Island

Baffin Bay

Prince of Wales Island

Somerset Island

Baffin Island

Victoria Island

Davis Strait

PACIFIC
OCEAN

Great Bear Lake

Mackenzie

Back

Southampton Island

Hudson Strait

● Yellowknife

Great Slave Lake

Hudson Bay

○ Churchill

Newfoundland

L. Athabasca

Reindeer Lake

■ St. John's

Peace

● Prince Rupert

Queen Charlotte Islands

Athabasca

Churchill

Nelson

Port Cartier

Gulf of St. Lawrence

■ Port aux Basques

Fraser

Edmonton ◆

N. Saskatchewan

CANADA

Lake Winnipeg

Albany

St. Lawrence

● Sydney

Cape Breton Island

Vancouver Island

Vancouver ◆

Calgary ●

S. Saskatchewan

Lake Manitoba

Quebec ◆

■ Halifax

Regina ●

Winnipeg ◆

Montreal ◆

Thunder Bay ●

Lake Superior

Sudbury ■

Lake Huron

Ottawa ◆

**ATLANTIC
OCEAN**

Toronto ◆

Lake Ontario

Lake Michigan

Windsor ●

Lake Erie

Resources and industry

- ◆ industrial centre
- ○ major port
- ● other town
- —— major road
- —— major railway

mineral resources and fossil fuels
- ● iron and other ferroalloy metal ores
- ● other metal ores
- ■ nonmetallic minerals

- coal
- copper
- iron ore
- lignite (brown coal)
- natural gas
- nickel
- oil

Canada's economy has been based on its rich natural resources, which have brought it export earnings and provided the basis for industrial growth.

AGRICULTURE

ARCTIC
OCEAN

Ellesmere Island

Greenland

North Magnetic Pole +1985

Queen Elizabeth Islands

Devon Island

Banks Island

Baffin Bay

Prince of Wales Island

Somerset Island

Baffin Island

Victoria Island

Boothia Peninsula

Davis Strait

Cape Farewell

PACIFIC
OCEAN

▲ Mt. Logan 5951

Mackenzie Mts.

Selwyn Mts.

Great Bear Lake

Mackenzie

Melville Peninsula

Back

Stikine Mts.

Southampton Island

Hudson Strait

Great Slave Lake

Ungava Peninsula

Labrador

Coast Mountains

ROCKY MOUNTAINS

Great Plains

L. Athabasca

Peace

Hudson Bay

Canadian Shield

Queen Charlotte Islands

Reindeer Lake

Newfoundland

▲ Mt. Robson 3954

Athabasca

Churchill

Laurentian Highlands

Cape Race

Mt. Waddington ▲ 3994

N. Saskatchewan

CANADA

Nelson

Vancouver Island

Selkirk Mts.

S. Saskatchewan

Lake Winnipeg

Albany

St. Lawrence

Gulf of St. Lawrence

Prince Edward I.

Cape Breton Island

Lake Manitoba

Appalachian Mts.

Nova Scotia

Lake Superior

Cape Sable

Lake Huron

**ATLANTIC
OCEAN**

Lake Michigan

Niagara Falls

Lake Ontario

Lake Erie

Agricultural zones

- arable
- arable and grazing
- fruit and vegetables
- rough grazing
- woods and forest
- nonagricultural land

▲ mountain peak (metres)

Canadian agriculture has been limited by physical conditions, namely the cold, harsh climate of the north and the difficult terrain in the western mountains.

United States of America

The United States, the world's fourth largest country, is a land of towering mountain ranges and extensive plains. Prominent land features include the Grand Canyon, great rivers that lead into the interior, deserts, explosive volcanoes in the Cascade Range and wetlands in the southeast. The climate ranges from the icy shores of the Arctic Ocean to the intense heat of the dry Death Valley, in California.

The first inhabitants of the United States, the Native Americans, came from Eurasia around 30,000 years ago across a land bridge over what is now the Bering Strait. They were followed around 6,000 years ago by the ancestors of the Inuit. Since the early 16th century, Europeans and, later, people from almost every part of the world, have made their homes in the United States, the richest country in the world.

The bulk of the United States, comprising 48 of the 50 states, lies between Canada to the north and Mexico to the south. The 49th state, Alaska, is in the northwestern corner of North America. The 50th state, Hawaii, is an island chain situated in the North Pacific Ocean.

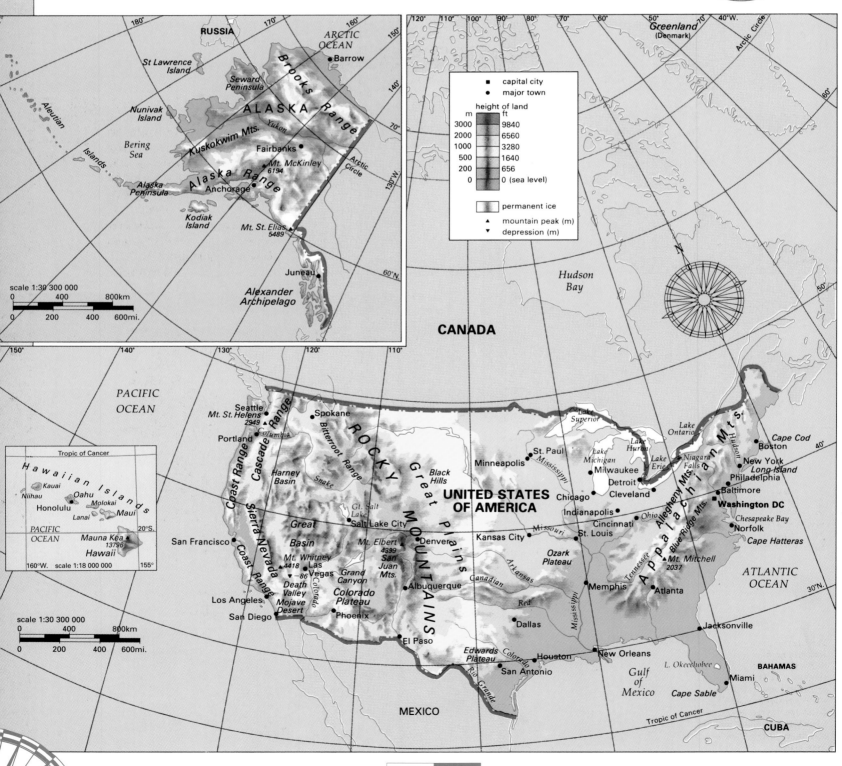

THE POLITICAL AND CULTURAL WORLD

The United States was born during the War of Independence (1775–1783), when the people of the 13 British colonies in the east overthrew British rule. The country expanded westward in the 19th century. Alaska was purchased from Russia in 1867, while Hawaii was annexed in 1898. Both territories became states in 1959.

The United States is a federal republic, whose government has three branches. The executive branch is headed by the president, who is also head of state. The legislative branch includes Congress, which consists of the Senate and House of Representatives. The judicial branch is headed by the Supreme Court.

COUNTRIES IN THE REGION

United States of America

Territories outside the region American Samoa, Guam, Johnston Atoll, Midway Islands, Northern Marianas, Puerto Rico, US Trust Territory of the Pacific Islands (Micronesia, Palau), US Virgin Islands, Wake Island (U.S.A.)

The U.S.A. is composed of 50 states, including Alaska and Hawaii

LANGUAGE

Official language English
Percentage of population by first language
English (79%), Spanish (4%), German (3%), Italian (2%), French (1.3%), Polish (1.2%)
Over 90% of the population can speak English

IMMIGRATION

Percentage of foreign born 6.2
Total immigrants (1987) 601,516
Countries sending most immigrants (1987) Mexico (72,351), Philippines (50,060), China and Taiwan (37,772), Korea (50,060), Cuba (28,916), India (27,803); refugee arrivals 70,000

RELIGION

Protestant (55%), Roman Catholic (29%), nonreligious and atheist (6.8%), Jewish (3.2%), Eastern Orthodox (2.3%), Muslim (1.9%), Hindu (0.2%)

MEMBERSHIP OF INTERNATIONAL ORGANIZATIONS

Colombo Plan, North Atlantic Treaty Organization (NATO), Organization of American States (OAS), Organization for Economic Cooperation and Development (OECD)

STYLE OF GOVERNMENT

Multiparty federal republic with two-chamber assembly

ECONOMIC INDICATORS: 1990

GDP (US$ billions)	5,392
GNP per capita (US$)	21,790
Annual rate of growth of GDP, 1980–1990	3.4%
Manufacturing as % of GDP	17.0%
Central government spending as % of GNP	24.0%
Merchandise exports (US$ billions)	495.3
% of GNP donated as development aid	0.21%

WELFARE INDICATORS

Infant mortality rate (per 1,000 live births)	
1965	25
1990	9
Daily food supply available (calories per capita, 1989)	3,671
Population per physician (1984)	470
Teacher-pupil ratio (primary school, 1989)	1 : 21

Area 9,371,786 sq.km (3,618,467) sq. mi.
Population (1990) 249,224,000
Armed forces army 760,000; navy 591,000; air force 572,000; marines 195,000
Ethnic composition European 84.3%, African 12.4%
Currency 1 United States dollar (US$) = 100 cents
Life expectancy at birth male 73.0 yr; female 80.0 yr

United States of America

- ■ capital city
- ● state capital

CONN. CONNECTICUT
D.C. DISTRICT OF COLUMBIA
DEL. DELAWARE
MD. MARYLAND
MASS. MASSACHUSETTS
MISS. MISSISSIPPI
N.J. NEW JERSEY
R.I. RHODE ISLAND
W. VA. WEST VIRGINIA

The national flag of the United States is popularly called the Stars and Stripes. The 13 alternating red and white stripes represent the original 13 colonies which declared themselves states in 1776. The 50 white stars on a blue background represent the 50 states of today.

HABITATS

The United States is a region of contrasts. In the east, the Appalachian Mountains overlook the eastern Atlantic plains. This range was formed more than 225 million years ago, and has been worn down by erosion. West of the Appalachians lie the interior plains, drained by the Mississippi River and its tributaries.

The land rises to the west to form the higher Great Plains, which are bordered by the Rocky Mountains. Formed within the last 65 million years, the Rockies are higher and more rugged than the Appalachians. West of the Rockies lies a region of basins and ranges formed by upward and downward movements of blocks of land along huge faults (cracks) in the Earth's crust. In the far west lie the Pacific ranges and lowlands. The country's highest mountain is in Alaska.

LAND

Area 9,371,786 sq. km (3,618,467 sq. mi.)
Highest point Mount McKinley, 6,194 m (20,323 ft)
Lowest point Death Valley, −86 m (−282 ft)
Major features Rocky Mountains, Great Plains and central lowlands, Appalachian Mountains

WATER

Longest river Mississippi–Missouri, 6,020 km (3,740 mi.)
Largest basin Mississippi–Missouri, 3,222,000 sq. km (1,224,000 sq. mi.)
Highest average flow Mississippi, 17,500 cu. m/sec (620,000 cu ft/sec)
Largest lake Superior, 83,270 sq km (32,150 sq. mi.)

NOTABLE THREATENED ENDEMIC SPECIES

Mammals Black-footed ferret (Mustela nigripes), Grey bat (Myotis grisescens), Stephens' kangaroo rat (Dipodomys stephensi), Red wolf (Canis rufus), Hawaiian monk seal (Monachus schauinslandi)
Birds California condor (Gymnogyps californianus), nene (Branta sandvicensis), kamao (Myadestes myadestinus), Oahu creeper (Paroreomyza maculata), Hawaiian crow (Corvus hawaiiensis)
Plants Agave arizonica; Asimina rugelii; Cladrastis lutea (American yellowwood); Conradina verticillata (Cumberland rosemary); Fritillaria liliacea (white fritillary); Hudsonia montana (mountain golden heather); Malacothamnus clementinus (San Clemente Island bush-mallow); Pediocactus knowltonii (Knowlton cactus); Prunus gravesii (Graves's beach plum); Rhapidophyllum hystrix (needle palm)
Others San Joaquin leopard lizard (Gambelia silus), Pallid sturgeon (Scaphirhynchus albus), Devil's Hole pupfish (Cyprinodon diabolis), Acorn pearly mussel (Epioblasma haysiana), Little agate shells (Achatinella spp.), No-eyed big-eyed wolf spider (Adelocosa anops), San Francisco forktail damselfly (Ischnura gemina)

HABITATS

Physical zones

- ice and snow
- tundra
- mountains/barren land
- forest
- grassland
- semidesert
- desert

▲ mountain peak (metres)
▼ depression (metres)
☀ climate station

The habitats of the United States range from ice and tundra in Alaska in the far northwest, to forested mountains, flat prairies, hot deserts, and subtropical swamps in the southeast. The Cascade Range contains active volcanoes, such as Mount St. Helens which erupted in 1980. This range, together with the volcanoes in southern Alaska, form part of a huge zone known as the 'Pacific ring of fire'.

ARCTIC OCEAN

Barrow
St. Lawrence Island
Seward Peninsula
Brooks Range
Nunivak Island
ALASKA
Bering Sea
Kuskokwim Mts.
Yukon
Aleutian Is.
Alaska Range
Mt. McKinley 6194
Arctic Circle
Alaska Peninsula
Kodiak Island
Mt. St. Elias 5489

Alexander Archipelago

PACIFIC OCEAN

Mt. St. Helens 2949
Portland
Columbia
Coast Range
Cascade Range
Bitterroot Range
Harney Basin
Snake
Sierra Nevada
San Francisco
Great Basin
Gt. Salt Lake
Coast Range
Mt. Whitney 4418
−86
Death Valley
Mojave Desert
Grand Canyon
Colorado
Sonoran Desert
Colorado Plateau
San Juan Mts.
Mt. Elbert 4399
ROCKY MOUNTAINS
Black Hills
Great Plains
Lake Superior
Mississippi
Missouri
Lake Michigan
Lake Huron
Chicago
Lake Erie
Lake Ontario
Niagara Falls
Hudson
Ohio
Arkansas
UNITED STATES OF AMERICA
Ozark Plateau
Allegheny Mts.
Appalachian Mts.
Blue Ridge Mts.
Mt. Mitchell 2037
Cape Cod
Long Island
Chesapeake Bay
Cape Hatteras
ATLANTIC OCEAN
Canadian
Red
Mississippi
Edwards Plateau
Colorado
Rio Grande
New Orleans
Gulf of Mexico
L. Okeechobee
Cape Sable

CLIMATE

The northeastern and midwestern states have hot summers and cold, snowy winters, while the subtropical southeast has mild winters. The southeast coasts are sometimes hit by hurricanes, while tornadoes occur in the states north of the Gulf of Mexico.

The Pacific coast as far south as San Francisco has a rainy climate, but winters are mild with temperatures mostly above freezing. This area and the southeastern states both receive over 1,000 mm (40 in) of rain every year. The mountains are cooler and wetter than the dry prairies to the east and desert basins, such as Death Valley, in the southwest. California has a Mediterranean climate. The northwest is cooler and wetter. Alaska has polar and subarctic climates, while the tropical climate of Hawaii is moderated by cool trade winds.

TEMPERATURE AND PRECIPITATION

| | Temperature °C (°F) | | Altitude |
	January	July	m (ft)
Barrow	−27 (−17)	4 (39)	7 (13)
Portland	19 (66)	20 (68)	17 (56)
San Francisco	10 (50)	15 (59)	16 (52)
New Orleans	12 (54)	28 (82)	2 (6)
Chicago	−4 (25)	23 (73)	251 (823)

| | Precipitation mm (in) | | |
	January	July	Year
Barrow	5 (0.2)	23 (0.9)	110 (4.3)
Portland	155 (6.1)	13 (0.5)	944 (37.2)
San Francisco	119 (4.7)	0 (0)	475 (18.7)
New Orleans	117 (4.6)	168 (6.5)	1,369 (53.9)
Chicago	51 (2.0)	84 (3.3)	843 (33.2)

NATURAL HAZARDS

Hurricanes and tornadoes in south, earthquakes and volcanic eruptions in west, drought and blizzards in Midwest

CLIMATE

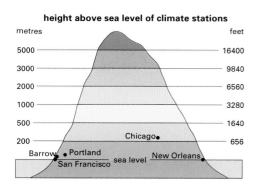

height above sea level of climate stations

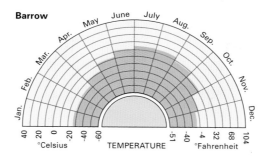
Barrow

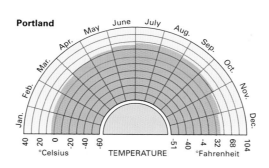
Portland

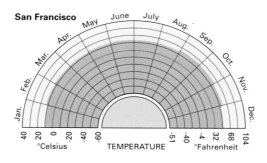
San Francisco

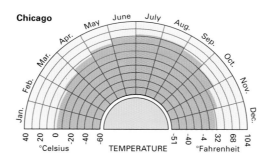
Chicago

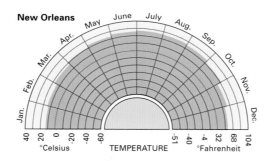
New Orleans

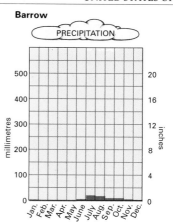
Barrow

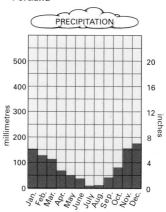
Portland

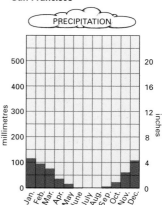
San Francisco

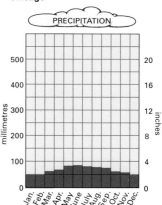
Chicago

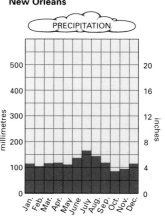
New Orleans

ENVIRONMENTAL ISSUES

Deforestation, large-scale farming, rapid population growth and the development of industrial cities have all contributed to massive environmental changes in the United States in the last 200 years.

One problem was identified in the 1930s, when farming in the dry prairies turned parts of the Midwest into a 'dust bowl'. New farming methods slowed down desertification and some damaged areas were reclaimed, but soil erosion continues to be a problem. Other problems, related to urban growth and rising standards of living, include air pollution, caused by power stations, factories and car emissions, and water pollution, caused by industrial and domestic waste disposal. In the 1960s, people became increasingly aware of the problems. Policies to protect the environment are now vigorously pursued.

POPULATION AND WEALTH

Population (millions)	249.6
Population increase (annual population growth rate, % 1960–90)	1.1
Energy use (gigajoules/person)	280
Real purchasing power (US$/person)	19,850

ENVIRONMENTAL INDICATORS

CO$_2$ emissions (million tonnes carbon/annum)	1,000
Municipal waste (kg/person/annum)	762
Nuclear waste (cumulative tonnes heavy metal)	17,606
Artificial fertilizer use (kg/ha./annum)	93
Cars (per 1,000 population)	550
Access to safe drinking water (% population)	n/a

MAJOR ENVIRONMENTAL PROBLEMS AND SOURCES

Air pollution: locally high, in particular urban; acid rain prevalent; high greenhouse gas emissions
River/lake pollution: medium/high; *sources*: industrial, agricultural, sewage, acid deposition
Marine/coastal pollution: local; *sources*: industrial, agricultural, sewage, oil
Land pollution: locally high; *sources*: industrial, urban/ household, nuclear
Land degradation: *types*: desertification, soil erosion, salinization; *causes*: agriculture, industry
Waste disposal problems: domestic; industrial; nuclear
Resource problems: land use competition
Major events: Love Canal (1978) and Times Beach (1986), evacuated due to chemical pollution; Three Mile Island (1979), nuclear power station accident; *Exxon Valdez* (1989), major oil spill from tanker in sea off Alaska; Dunsmuir (1991), pesticide spill during transportation

ENVIRONMENTAL ISSUES

Key environmental issues

- ● major town or city
- ◖ heavily polluted town or city
- ◗ major pollution event
- ☢ nuclear test site
- ☢ former nuclear test site
- ⌒ heavily polluted river
- —— main oil pipeline
- ⬭ area of groundwater depletion
- ▦ area affected by permafrost

acidity of rain (pH units)
- 4.2 (most acidic)
- 4.4 (least acidic)

areas at risk of desertification
- very high
- high
- moderate
- ▢ true desert

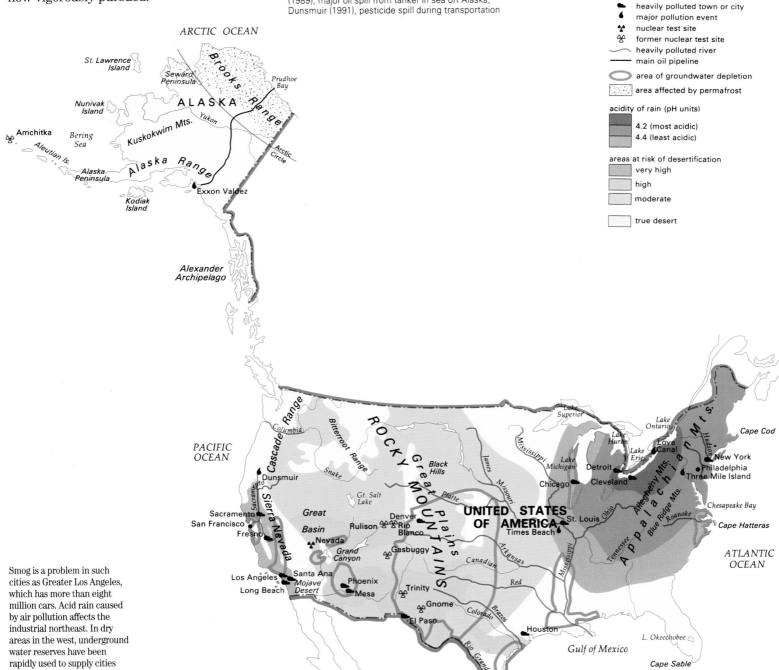

Smog is a problem in such cities as Greater Los Angeles, which has more than eight million cars. Acid rain caused by air pollution affects the industrial northeast. In dry areas in the west, underground water reserves have been rapidly used to supply cities and farmers who irrigate their land. Water shortages are becoming increasingly common.

POPULATION

Between 1890 and 1940, the population of the United States more than doubled from 63 million to 131 million. By 1990, the population had almost doubled again, reaching 249.6 million. This population explosion was caused partly by natural growth, and partly by massive immigration of people from most parts of the world.

The 20th century also saw another change from a mainly rural society to an urban one. In 1900, more than 40 percent of the people lived on farms. By 1991, the percentage had fallen to 1.9. Another trend has been the growth of huge city suburbs, occupied by middle-class people who moved out of the decaying city centres, which were often occupied by poorer ethnic minorities. Some inner cities are being restored, and young people, especially, are moving in.

POPULATION

Total population of region (millions)	249.6
Population density (persons per sq. km)	27.0
Population change (average annual percent 1960–1990)	
Urban	+1.3
Rural	+0.6

URBAN POPULATION

As percentage of total population	
1960	70.0
1990	74.0
Percentage in cities of more than 1 million	49.5

TEN LARGEST CITIES

	Population
New York	18,120,000
Los Angeles	13,770,000
Chicago	8,180,000
San Francisco	6,042,000
Philadelphia	5,963,000
Detroit	4,620,000
Dallas	3,766,000
Boston	3,736,000
Washington DC †	3,734,000
Houston	3,642,000

† denotes capital city

POPULATION

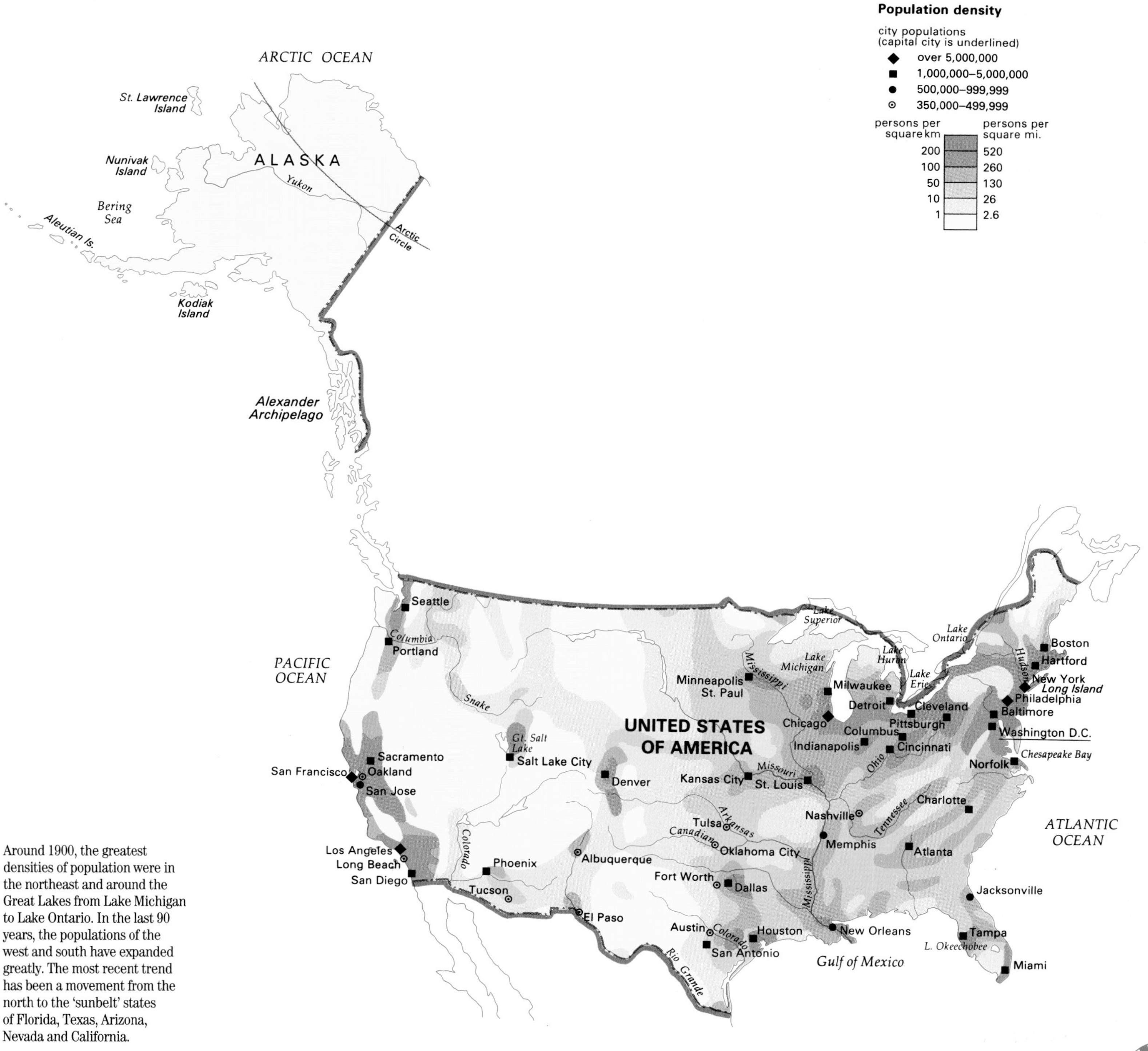
Population density
city populations
(capital city is underlined)
over 5,000,000
1,000,000–5,000,000
500,000–999,999
350,000–499,999
persons per square km
persons per square mi.
200 100 50 10 1
520 260 130 26 2.6
ARCTIC OCEAN
St. Lawrence Island
Nunivak Island
Bering Sea
Aleutian Is.
ALASKA
Yukon
Arctic Circle
Kodiak Island
Alexander Archipelago
PACIFIC OCEAN
UNITED STATES OF AMERICA
ATLANTIC OCEAN
Gulf of Mexico
Seattle
Portland
Columbia
Snake
Sacramento
San Francisco
Oakland
San Jose
Los Angeles
Long Beach
San Diego
Colorado
Phoenix
Tucson
Gt. Salt Lake
Salt Lake City
Denver
Albuquerque
El Paso
Rio Grande
Minneapolis St. Paul
Mississippi
Lake Superior
Lake Michigan
Lake Huron
Lake Erie
Lake Ontario
Milwaukee
Chicago
Detroit
Cleveland
Pittsburgh
Columbus
Indianapolis
Cincinnati
Ohio
Kansas City
St. Louis
Missouri
Nashville
Tennessee
Memphis
Arkansas
Tulsa
Canadian
Oklahoma City
Fort Worth
Dallas
Austin
Colorado
Houston
San Antonio
New Orleans
Atlanta
Charlotte
Norfolk
Chesapeake Bay
Washington D.C.
Baltimore
Philadelphia
New York
Long Island
Hudson
Hartford
Boston
Jacksonville
Tampa
L. Okeechobee
Miami

Around 1900, the greatest densities of population were in the northeast and around the Great Lakes from Lake Michigan to Lake Ontario. In the last 90 years, the populations of the west and south have expanded greatly. The most recent trend has been a movement from the north to the 'sunbelt' states of Florida, Texas, Arizona, Nevada and California.

INDUSTRY

The United States is the world's leading industrial nation. It has huge energy resources, including coal, oil and natural gas. Its mineral resources include most of the materials needed by modern industry. The United States also has rich human resources: a skilled and mobile workforce.

In the early 20th century, the country developed heavy industries, such as iron and steel plants. They supplied the materials for car and machinery manufacturers. In the last 40 years, the emphasis has shifted to light and service industries.

Despite increasing competition from Japan and other Pacific nations, the United States remains a leader in high technology, including microelectronics industries. With its highly developed economy, the United States is also the world's leading trading nation.

INDUSTRIAL OUTPUT (US $ billion)

Total	Mining	Manufacturing	Average annual change since 1960
1,249.5	86.4	1,032.9	+2.1%

INDUSTRIAL WORKERS (millions)
(figures in brackets are percentages of total labour force)

Total	Mining	Manufacturing	Construction
32.96	0.85 (0.7%)	23.1 (19%)	8.0 (6.6%)

MAJOR PRODUCTS (figures in brackets are percentages of total world production)

Energy and minerals	Output	Change since 1960
Coal (mill tonnes)	897.6 (19.2%)	+127%
Oil (mill barrels)	3173.9 (14%)	+24%
Natural gas (billion cu. metres)	488.5 (25.4%)	+36%
Copper (mill tonnes)	1.86 (13.7%)	+28%
Lead (mill tonnes)	1.05 (10.3%)	+72%

Manufactures		
Commercial jet aircraft	2251 (84.5%)*	No data
Domestic/catering ovens, incl. microwaves (mill)	20.5 (21.7%)	No data
Cement (mill tonnes)	67.4 (7%)	+20%
Steel (mill tonnes)	90.1 (12%)	-1%
Cars (mill)	8.0 (25%)	+20%
Televisions (mill)	13.6 (16%)	+133%
Synthetic rubber (mill tonnes)	2.05 (23%)	-19%
Nitrogenous fertilizers (mill tonnes)	9.5 (13%)	+4%
Semiconductors (US $ billion)	22.3 (40%)	N/A

N/A means production had not begun in 1960

* Applies only to noncommunist world in 1989

INDUSTRY

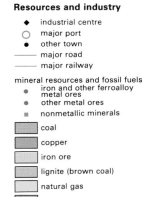

Resources and industry

- ◆ industrial centre
- ○ major port
- ● other town
- — major road
- — major railway

mineral resources and fossil fuels
- ● iron and other ferroalloy metal ores
- ● other metal ores
- ■ nonmetallic minerals

- coal
- copper
- iron ore
- lignite (brown coal)
- natural gas
- oil

Natural resources occur in most parts of the country. For example, major oil-producing states include Texas, Alaska in the north, and Louisiana. California in the west is a major manufacturing state, with high-technology industries in 'Silicon Valley', near San Jose. New York, Illinois, Texas, Michigan, Pennsylvania, and New Jersey are other leading manufacturing states.

ARCTIC OCEAN

St. Lawrence Island
Prudhoe Bay
Nunivak Island
ALASKA
Bering Sea
Yukon
Fairbanks
Aleutian Is.
Anchorage
Arctic Circle
Valdez
Seward
Kodiak Island
Skagway
Alexander Archipelago

PACIFIC OCEAN

Seattle
Columbia
Portland
Butte
Fargo
Duluth
Lake Superior
Minneapolis
Lake Michigan
Lake Huron
Lake Ontario
Portland
Boston
Lake Erie
Buffalo
Milwaukee
Chicago
Detroit
Cleveland
New York
Long Island
Philadelphia
Snake
Pittsburgh
Baltimore
Washington D.C.
Gt. Salt Lake
Salt Lake City
UNITED STATES OF AMERICA
Indianapolis
Missouri
St. Louis
Ohio
Chesapeake Bay
San Francisco
San Jose
Denver
Norfolk
Kansas City
Charlotte
Las Vegas
Colorado
Arkansas
Mississippi
Tennessee
Wilmington
Canadian
Oklahoma City
Atlanta
Charleston
ATLANTIC OCEAN
Los Angeles
Red
San Diego
El Paso
Dallas
Mobile
Jacksonville
Colorado
Houston
New Orleans
Tampa
Rio Grande
San Antonio
Galveston
Gulf of Mexico
L. Okeechobee
Miami

AGRICULTURE

Although farming accounts for only about two percent of the country's gross national product (the value of all goods and services produced), the United States is the world's leading agricultural producer. It not only supplies all its own needs, but it is also the world's leading exporter of agricultural products. For example, it dominates the world's grain markets, especially in wheat.

Farming is highly mechanized, with most farmers using scientific breeding, fertilizers and pest control techniques. Yields are generally high. The great variety of land and climatic types means that the country produces a wide range of products. The United States is a world leader in beef, raised largely on western ranches, citrus fruits, maize and soya beans. It is also a major producer of cotton, dairy and poultry products, pork, tobacco, and vegetables.

LAND (million hectares)

Total	Agricultural	Arable	Forest/woodland
917 (100%)	431 (47%)	188 (20%)	265 (29%)

FARMERS

3.1 million people employed in agriculture (3% of workforce)
61 hectares of arable land per person employed in agriculture

MAJOR CROPS

	Area mill ha.	Yield 100kg/ha.	Production mill tonnes	Change since 1963
Maize	24.0	75.0 (206)	179.6 (39)	+88%
Soya beans	23.1	22.7 (125)	52.3 (52)	+168%
Wheat	22.6	25.3 (109)	57.4 (11)	+74%
Sorghum	4.3	43.8 (297)	18.8 (30)	+35%
Barley	4.1	28.3 (122)	11.5 (6)	+33%
Cotton lint	4.1	7.9 (144)	3.2 (19)	−1%
Vegetables	—	—	28.0 (7)	+46%
Fruit	—	—	25.7 (8)	+50%

MAJOR LIVESTOCK

	Number mill	Production mill tonnes	Change since 1963
Cattle	102.0 (8)	—	−2%
Pigs	51.2 (6)	—	−11%
Milk	—	64.7 (14)	+13%
Fish catch	—	5.7 (6)	—

FOOD SECURITY (cereal exports minus imports)

mill tonnes	% domestic production	% world trade
+74.2	24	34

Numbers in brackets are percentages of world total

AGRICULTURE

Agricultural zones

- arable
- fruit and vegetables
- grazing
- forest with arable and pasture
- nonagricultural land

▲ mountain peak (metres)
▼ depression (metres)

The most extensive arable farming regions are in the interior plains. The main crops are cereals, especially maize and wheat. To the west, the plains are drier and they are used for grazing on ranches. Fruit and vegetable-growing regions are in the southwest, the southeast (especially Florida) and small areas in the northeast.

MEXICO, CENTRAL AMERICA & THE CARIBBEAN

Mexico and Central America together form a land bridge that extends to the northwest tip of South America. The region also includes 13 independent island nations in the Caribbean, two US territories and a number of European dependencies. Rugged scenery, active volcanoes, and subtropical and tropical climates are the main characteristics of the region.

The first inhabitants of the region were the Native Americans, who founded such cultures as the Mayan and Aztec empires. Spain conquered the region in the 16th century and Spanish culture dominates to this day. Other elements in this complex cultural mix are African Americans, other Europeans, and even some Asians, who were introduced as labourers.

The islands of the Greater Antilles (Cuba, Jamaica, Hispaniola and Puerto Rico) formed a single landmass about 100 million years ago. Mexico and Central America became joined to South America between 5 and 2 million years ago. The region was broken up by earth movements and erosion.

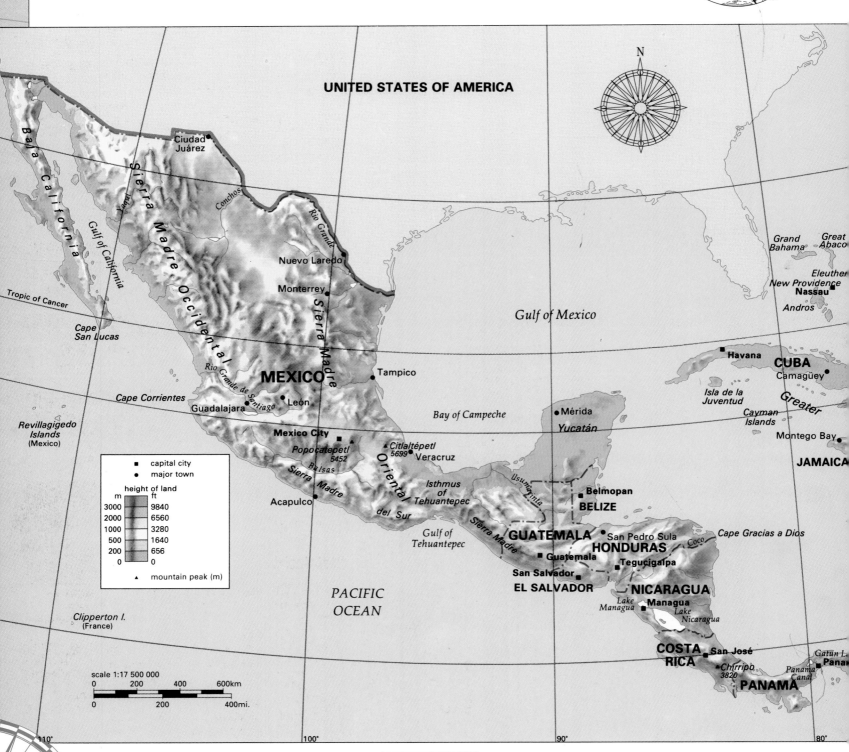

UNITED STATES OF AMERICA

N

Ciudad Juárez

Yaqui
Sierra Madre Occidental
Conchos
Rio Grande
Nuevo Laredo
Monterrey

Tropic of Cancer

Cape San Lucas

Gulf of California

Baja California

Rio Grande de Santiago
Cape Corrientes
Guadalajara
León
MEXICO
Sierra Madre

Tampico

Gulf of Mexico

Grand Bahama
Great Abaco

Eleuther
New Providence
Nassau
Andros

Havana
CUBA
Camagüey

Isla de la Juventud

Cayman Islands

Greater

Montego Bay

JAMAICA

Revillagigedo Islands
(Mexico)

Mexico City
Popocatepetl 5452
Balsas
Citlaltépetl 5699
Veracruz

Bay of Campeche

Mérida
Yucatán

Acapulco
Sierra Madre del Sur
Oriental

Isthmus of Tehuantepec

Usumacinta

Belmopan
BELIZE

Gulf of Tehuantepec

Sierra Madre

GUATEMALA
San Pedro Sula
HONDURAS

Coco

Cape Gracias a Dios

Guatemala
San Salvador
EL SALVADOR
Tegucigalpa

NICARAGUA
Lake Managua
Managua
Lake Nicaragua

PACIFIC OCEAN

COSTA RICA
San José
Chirripó 3820
PANAMA

Gatún L.
Panama Canal
Panam

Clipperton I.
(France)

key
- ■ capital city
- ● major town

height of land

m	ft
3000	9840
2000	6560
1000	3280
500	1640
200	656
0	0

▲ mountain peak (m)

scale 1:17 500 000

0   200   400   600km

0   200   400mi.

110°   100°   90°   80°

THE POLITICAL AND CULTURAL WORLD

Although geographically part of North America, most of the region belongs, culturally, to Latin America. Spanish is the chief language and Roman Catholicism the main religion, though some Native and African Americans combine the Christian faith with some of their own traditional spiritual beliefs.

In the past, the region has suffered much instability. Civilian governments have been overthrown by military groups, while brutal dictatorships and civil war have hampered the region's progress. Cuba is the only communist regime. Its policies were unaffected by the changes in its former ally, the Soviet Union.

COUNTRIES IN THE REGION

Antigua and Barbuda, Bahamas, Barbados, Belize, Costa Rica, Cuba, Dominica, Dominican Republic, El Salvador, Grenada, Guatemala, Haiti, Honduras, Jamaica, Mexico, Nicaragua, Panama, St. Kitts-Nevis, St. Lucia, St. Vincent and the Grenadines, Trinidad and Tobago

Dependencies of other states Anguilla, Bermuda, British Virgin Islands, Cayman Islands (U.K.); Aruba, Netherlands Antilles (Netherlands); Guadeloupe, Martinique (France); Puerto Rico, US Virgin Islands (U.S.A.)

LANGUAGE

Countries with one official language
(English) Antigua and Barbuda, Bahamas, Barbados, Belize, Dominica, Grenada, Jamaica, St. Kitts-Nevis, St. Lucia, St. Vincent and the Grenadines, Trinidad and Tobago; (Spanish) Costa Rica, Cuba, Dominican Republic, El Salvador, Guatemala, Honduras, Mexico, Nicaragua, Panama
Countries with two official languages (Creole, French) Haiti

Other languages spoken in the region include Carib, Nahua and other indigenous languages; creoles and French patois; Hindi (Trinidad and Tobago)

RELIGION

Countries with one major religion
(P) Antigua and Barbuda; (RC) Costa Rica, Cuba, Dominica, Dominican Republic, El Salvador, Honduras, Mexico, Nicaragua
Countries with more than one major religion
(P, RC) Bahamas, Barbados, Belize, Grenada, Jamaica, St. Kitts-Nevis, St. Lucia, St. Vincent and the Grenadines; (P, RC, V) Haiti; (H, M, P, RC) Trinidad and Tobago

Key: H-Hindu, M-Muslim, P-Protestant, RC-Roman Catholic, V-Voodoo

STYLES OF GOVERNMENT

Republics Costa Rica, Cuba, Dominica, Dominican Republic, El Salvador, Guatemala, Haiti, Honduras, Mexico, Nicaragua, Panama, Trinidad and Tobago
Monarchies All other countries of the region
Multiparty states All countries except Cuba, Haiti
One-party states Cuba, Haiti
Military influence Guatemala, Haiti, Honduras

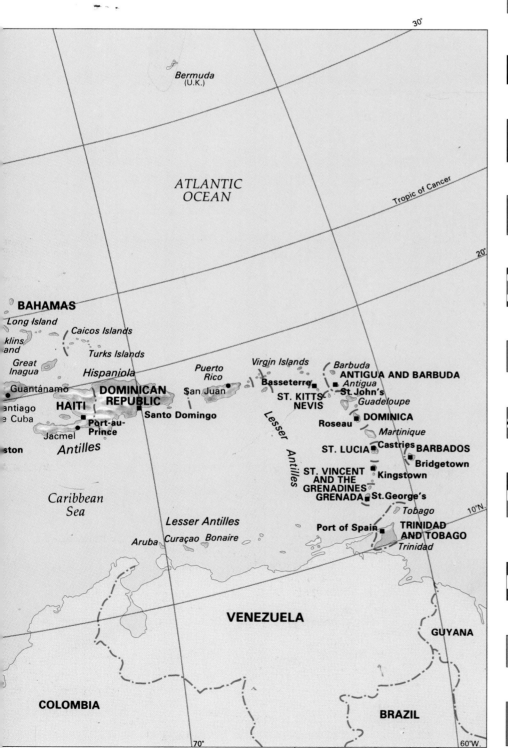

Antigua and Barbuda
Area
442 sq. km
(171 sq. mi.)

Area
27,400 sq. km
(10,579 sq. mi.)
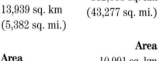
Haiti

Bahamas
Area
13,939 sq. km
(5,382 sq. mi.)

Area
112,088 sq. km
(43,277 sq. mi.)
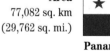
Honduras

Barbados
Area
439 sq. km
(166 sq. mi.)

Area
10,991 sq. km
(4,244 sq. mi.)

Jamaica

Belize
Area
22,965 sq. km
(8,867 sq. mi.)

Area
1,958,201 sq. km
(756,066 sq. mi.)

Mexico

Costa Rica
Area
51,100 sq. km
(19,730 sq. mi.)

Area
120,349 sq. km
(46,467 sq. mi.)
Nicaragua

Cuba
Area
110,861 sq. km
(42,804 sq. mi.)

Area
77,082 sq. km
(29,762 sq. mi.)
Panama

Dominica
Area
750 sq. km
(290 sq. mi.)

Area
269 sq. km
(104 sq. mi.)

St. Kitts-Nevis

Dominican Republic
Area
48,443 sq. km
(18,704 sq. mi.)

Area
617 sq. km
(238 sq. mi.)

St. Lucia

El Salvador
Area
21,041 sq. km
(8,124 sq. mi.)

Area
389 sq. km
(150 sq. mi.)

St. Vincent and the Grenadines

Grenada
Area
345 sq. km
(133 sq. mi.)

Area
5,128 sq. km
(1,980 sq. mi.)

Trinidad and Tobago

Guatemala
Area
108,889 sq. km
(42,042 sq. mi.)

HABITATS

The mainland contains a chain of volcanic highlands that form part of the Pacific 'ring of fire'. Volcanic eruptions and earthquakes are common. Tropical rainforest and heavy rains occur in the northeast and islands, while the northwest is desert or semidesert.

LAND

Area 2,735,515 sq. km (1,056,183 sq. mi.)
Highest point Citlaltépetl, 5,699 m (18,700 ft)
Lowest point Lake Enriquillo, Dominican Republic, −44 m (−144 ft)
Major features volcanic mountain chain and Mexican plateau on isthmus, island chain of the West Indies

WATER

Longest river Conchos–Grande, 2,100 km (1,300 mi.)
Largest basin Grande (part), 445,000 sq. km (172,000 sq. mi.)
Highest average flow Colorado, 104 cu. m/sec (3,700 cu ft/sec), at head of Gulf of California
Largest lake Nicaragua, 8,029 sq. km (3,100 sq. mi.)

NOTABLE THREATENED ENDEMIC SPECIES

Mammals Haitian solenodon (*Solenodon paradoxus*), Central American squirrel monkey (*Saimiri oerstedi*), Volcano rabbit (*Romerolagus diazi*), Jamaican hutia (*Geocapromys brownii*), Gulf of California porpoise (*Phocoena sinus*)
Birds St. Vincent amazon (*Amazona guildingii*), Highland guan (*Penelopina nigra*), Resplendent quetzal (*Pharomachrus mocinno*), Ocellated turkey (*Agriocharis ocellata*), cahow (*Procellaria cahow*)
Plants *Ariocarpus agavoides*; *Auerodendron glaucescens*; *Carpodiptera mirabilis*; *Eupatorium chalceorithales*; *Freziera forerorum*; *Guzmania condensata*; *Ipomoea villifera*; *Lincania retifolia*; *Lycaste suaveolens*; *Streblacanthus parviflorus*
Others Kemp's ridley turtle (*Lepidochelys kempii*), Jamaican ground iguana (*Cyclura collei*), Golden toad (*Bufo periglenes*)

CLIMATE

The climates of Mexico and Central America vary from humid coastlands through cool, temperate plateaus, to cold mountain areas. Northern Mexico has deserts, but the rainfall increases in the south. The tropical Caribbean islands are warm throughout the year.

TEMPERATURE AND PRECIPITATION

	Temperature °C (°F) January	July	Altitude m (ft)
Guayamas	18 (64)	31 (88)	6 (19)
Zacatecas	10 (50)	14 (57)	2,612 (8,567)
Mexico City	12 (54)	18 (64)	2,309 (7,574)
Havana	22 (72)	28 (82)	24 (79)
Bluefields	25 (77)	26 (79)	12 (39)
Seawell	25 (77)	27 (81)	56 (184)

	Precipitation mm (in) January	July	Year
Guayamas	5 (0.2)	43 (1.7)	252 (9.9)
Zacatecas	7 (0.3)	69 (2.7)	313 (12.3)
Mexico City	13 (0.5)	170 (6.7)	726 (28.6)
Havana	71 (2.8)	125 (4.9)	1,167 (45.9)
Bluefields	264 (10.4)	746 (29.4)	4,370 (172.0)
Seawell	68 (2.7)	141 (5.6)	1,273 (59.1)

World's greatest recorded rainfall in 5 minutes, 305 mm (12 in) at Portobello, northern Panama

NATURAL HAZARDS

Earthquakes, landslides, volcanic eruptions, hurricanes

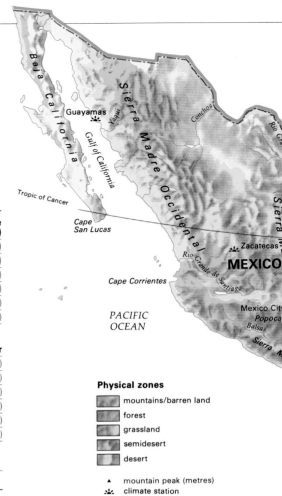

Physical zones

- mountains/barren land
- forest
- grassland
- semidesert
- desert

▲ mountain peak (metres)
⁂ climate station

THE POLITICAL WORLD

The region contains 21 independent nations and 12 dependencies. They include some of the world's oldest European colonies. Spanish settlement began on Hispaniola as early as 1493. Other, later colonizers included the British, Dutch and French. Generally, the passage from colonialism to independence has been peaceful.

■ capital city

HABITATS

Northern Mexico is arid. In central Mexico, two ranges enclose a central, well-watered plateau. Central America has high central ranges, bordered in the east by broad coastal plains.

Gulf of Mexico

Great Abaco

Grand Bahama

Eleuthera

Andros **BAHAMAS**

Long Island

ATLANTIC OCEAN

Caicos Islands

Havana *Acklins Island*

CUBA *Great Inagua* *Turks Islands*

Hispaniola *Puerto Rico* *Virgin Islands* *Barbuda* **ANTIGUA AND BARBUDA**

Isla de la Juventud **DOMINICAN REPUBLIC** *Antigua*

Bay of Campeche

Yucatán

Cayman Islands **HAITI** **ST. KITTS NEVIS** *Guadeloupe*

Citlaltépetl 5699

Bluefields *G r e a t e r A n t i l l e s* **DOMINICA**

JAMAICA *Martinique*

Isthmus of Tehuantepec *L e s s e r A n t i l l e s* **ST. LUCIA** **BARBADOS**

ST. VINCENT AND THE GRENADINES Seawell

Gulf of Tehuantepec **BELIZE**

GUATEMALA *Caribbean Sea* **GRENADA** *Tobago*

Cape Gracias a Dios *Lesser Antilles* **TRINIDAD AND TOBAGO**

HONDURAS *Coco* *Aruba* *Curaçao* *Bonaire* *Trinidad*

Sierra Madre

EL SALVADOR **NICARAGUA**

Lake Managua

Lake Nicaragua

COSTA RICA

Chirripó 3820 *Gatun Lake*

Panama Canal

PANAMA

CLIMATE

height above sea level of climate stations

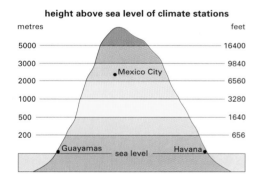

metres	feet
5000	16400
3000	9840
2000 Mexico City	6560
1000	3280
500	1640
200	656
Guayamas sea level Havana	

Guayamas

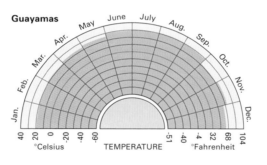

°Celsius   TEMPERATURE   °Fahrenheit

Mexico City

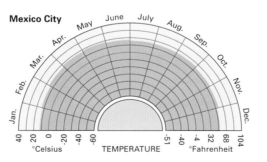

°Celsius   TEMPERATURE   °Fahrenheit

Havana

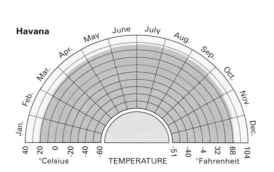

°Celsius   TEMPERATURE   °Fahrenheit

Guayamas

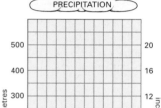

PRECIPITATION

millimetres   inches

Mexico City

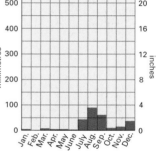

PRECIPITATION

millimetres   inches

Havana

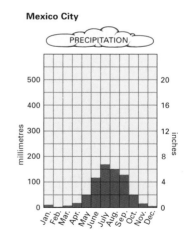

PRECIPITATION

millimetres   inches

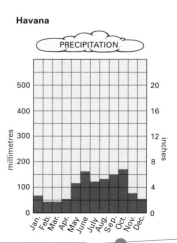

Virgin Islands (U.K.)

Virgin Islands (U.S.A.)

DOMINICAN REPUBLIC

Barbuda **ANTIGUA AND BARBUDA**

St John's *Antigua*

Basseterre **ST KITTS NEVIS**

Puerto Rico (U.S.A.) *Guadeloupe (France)*

Santo Domingo Roseau **DOMINICA**

Martinique (France)

Lesser Antilles **ST LUCIA** Castries **BARBADOS**

ST VINCENT AND THE GRENADINES Bridgetown

Kingstown

GRENADA St George's

Lesser Antilles *Tobago*

Cuba *Netherlands Antilles (Neth.)* **TRINIDAD AND TOBAGO**

Port of Spain *Trinidad*

Bonaire

Curaçao

ENVIRONMENTAL ISSUES

Two key concerns are widespread soil degradation and deforestation in the mountains of mainland Central America and some of the high islands.

Deforestation has in turn caused flooding and the silting of rivers. Other problems include severe air pollution in urban areas, the heavy impact of tourism on coastlines and coral reefs, oil contamination in the Caribbean Sea, and disturbance to the ecology of the seas through overfishing. The main causes are rapid population growth, and the poverty of the people, which put excess pressure on resources.

At present rates of loss, only 5 percent of the region's original rainforest will remain by the year 2010. Where forests have been cleared, erosion and desertification are serious problems.

Rapidly growing urban populations put enormous pressure on the environment, both locally and farther afield. Mexico City alone has over 18 million inhabitants. As rural migrants flock to the cities, more and more food is demanded from already overused farmland, while pollution problems are becoming worse.

POPULATION AND WEALTH

	Highest	Middle	Lowest
Population (millions)	88.6 (Mexico)	5.1 (Honduras)	0.3 (Barbados)
Population increase (annual population growth rate, % 1960–90)	3.3 (Honduras)	2.5 (Panama)	0.3 (Barbados)
Energy use (gigajoules/person)	169 (Trinidad & T)	17 (Panama)	1 (Haiti)
Real purchasing power (US$/person)	6,020 (Barbados)	3,790 (Panama)	970 (Haiti)

ENVIRONMENTAL INDICATORS

	Highest	Middle	Lowest
CO$_2$ emissions (million tonnes carbon/annum)	78 (Mexico)	3.3 (Panama)	0.25 (Barbados)
Deforestation ('000s ha./annum 1980s)	615 (Mexico)	2.3 (Honduras)	0.1 (Cuba)
Artificial fertilizer use (kg/ha./annum)	181 (Costa Rica)	68 (Guatemala)	3 (Haiti)
Cars (per 1,000 population)	203 (Trinidad & T)	43 (Panama)	5 (Haiti)
Access to safe drinking water (% population)	100 (Barbados)	71 (Mexico)	39 (El Salvador)

MAJOR ENVIRONMENTAL PROBLEMS AND SOURCES

Air pollution: urban high
Land degradation: *types*: soil erosion, deforestation; *causes*: agriculture, population pressure
Resource problems: inadequate drinking water and sanitation; coastal flooding
Population problems: population explosion; inadequate health facilities; tourism
Major event: Ixtoc 1 (1979), oil rig fire and leak; Guadalajara (1992), series of gas explosions

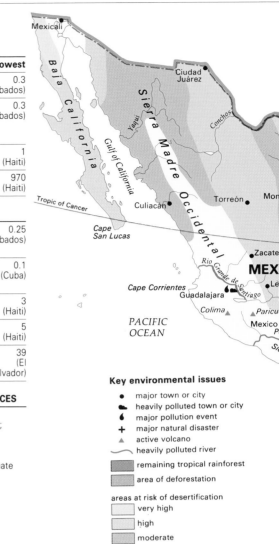

Key environmental issues

- • major town or city
- ⟣ heavily polluted town or city
- ⬧ major pollution event
- + major natural disaster
- ▲ active volcano
- ∼ heavily polluted river
- ▨ remaining tropical rainforest
- ▨ area of deforestation

areas at risk of desertification
- ▫ very high
- ▫ high
- ▨ moderate

POPULATION

Central America and the Caribbean islands were home to people of a wide range of cultures who lived there for at least 12,000 years before Europeans discovered what they called the 'New World' in the late 15th century. After this, waves of Europeans invaded the lands, with dreadful results for the native people. The Spanish seized control of Mexico and the Central American neck of land, and their language, religion and customs prevail there today.

The scattered islands of the Caribbean were colonized by a number of European nations, but the main culture is African, deriving from the millions of slaves shipped there to work in the sugar plantations. People from Asia and Europe also were taken as labourers, making for a great cultural mix.

Until recently, the population was mainly rural, but the decline in traditional farming (and the plantation system) has been the cause of massive movement to the cities. The growth of cities has been rapid and unplanned, leaving millions of people without homes or jobs.

POPULATION

Total population of region (millions)	152.8
Population density (persons per sq. km)	61.1
Population change (average annual percent 1960–1990) Urban Rural	+4.1 +0.9

URBAN POPULATION

As percentage of total population 1960 1990	50.1 71.3
Percentage in cities of more than 1 million	25.9

TEN LARGEST CITIES

	Country	Population
Mexico City †	Mexico	18,748,000
Guadalajara	Mexico	2,587,000
Monterrey	Mexico	2,335,000
Havana †	Cuba	2,059,000
Guatemala †	Guatemala	2,000,000
San Juan †	Puerto Rico	1,816,000
Santo Domingo †	Dominican Republic	1,313,000
Puebla	Mexico	1,218,000
Port-au-Prince †	Haiti	1,144,000
San Salvador †	El Salvador	973,000

† denotes capital city

Population density

city populations
(capital city is underlined)
- ◆ over 5,000,000
- ■ 1,000,000–5,000,000
- ● 500,000–999,999
- ⊙ 250,000–499,999
- × capital city less than 250,000

persons per square km	persons per square mi.
200	520
100	260
50	130
10	26
1	2.6

ENVIRONMENTAL ISSUES

Earthquakes, such as the one which struck Mexico City in 1985, volcanic eruptions and hurricanes on the islands and mainland coasts are natural hazards in the region.

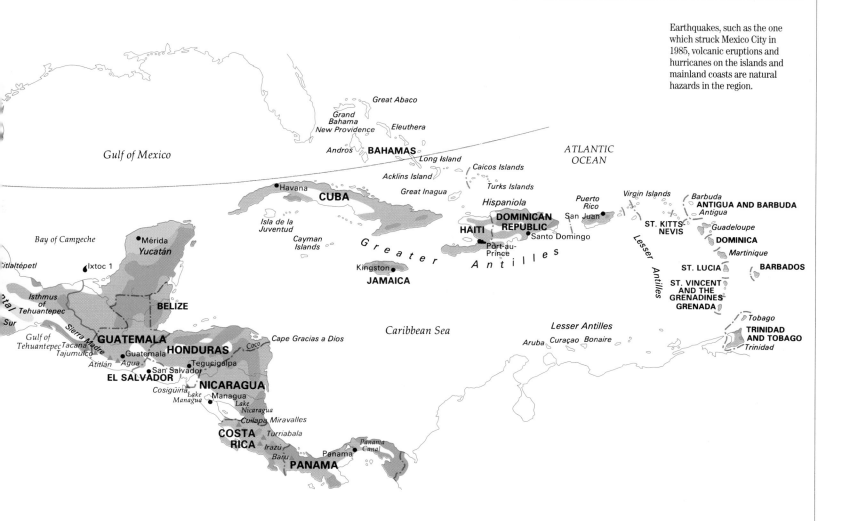

POPULATION

The population of the region used to be mainly rural. But recently enormous numbers of people have moved into the cities. Many new arrivals are poor and have no jobs.

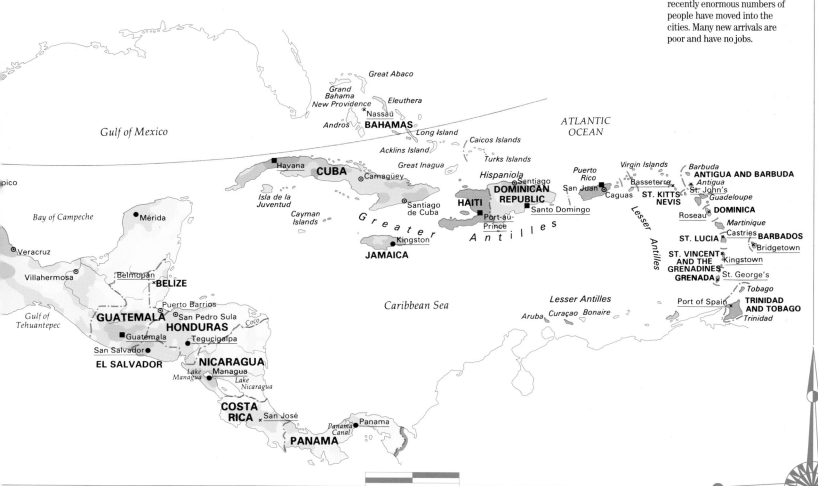

INDUSTRY

The region consists of developing countries which have plenty of resources but lack the money and skilled workers to create truly industrialized economies. Mexico has resources of silver, gold, copper, and oil, and exports crude oil in large quantities. Nicaragua, Guatemala, and Honduras have fewer mineral resources, though Cuba has large nickel reserves and also deposits of limestone, chromium, copper, and iron.

Trinidad and Tobago export oil and process chemicals, fertilizers, and machinery. Like many other countries in the Caribbean, a major industry is tourism. On islands where tourism has not developed widely, agriculture is the main industry. Belize and El Salvador, on the mainland, have small-scale industries which produce goods for the local market. Costa Rica's industries are growing, with products which include cement, clothes, cosmetics, fertilizers, foods, textiles, and medicines. Panama, in the far south, has untapped copper reserves, and small local industries, but the Panama Canal provides income for the country.

INDUSTRIAL OUTPUT (US $ billion)

Total	Mining	Manufacturing	Average annual change since 1960
101.3	9.9	82.2	+5.3%

INDUSTRIAL WORKERS (millions)
(figures in brackets are percentages of total labour force)

Total	Mining	Manufacturing	Construction
9.4	0.7 (1.4%)	6.06 (12.0%)	2.62 (5.2%)

MAJOR PRODUCTS (figures in brackets are percentages of world production)

Energy and minerals	Output	Change since 1960
Oil (mill barrels)	1097.2 (4.8%)	+444%
Bauxite (mill tonnes)	7.5 (7.7%)	-56.3%
Antimony (1,000 tonnes)	3.7 (5.2%)	-18.9%
Silver (1,000 tonnes)	2.4 (12.4%)	+200%
Sulphur (mill tonnes)	2.1 (14.3%)	+33%
Fluorspar (1,000 tonnes)	756 (16.7%)	No data

Manufactures		
Residual fuel oil (mill tonnes)	39.7 (5.4%)	No data
Cement (mill tonnes)	33.7 (3.1%)	+992%
Steel (mill tonnes)	7.6 (1.1%)	+406%
Fertilizer distributors (1,000)	176 (45.8%)	N/A
Rubber footwear (mill pairs)	38.8 (4.3%)	N/A
Soft drinks (mill hectolitres)	56.1 (9.8%)	N/A

N/A means production had not begun in 1960

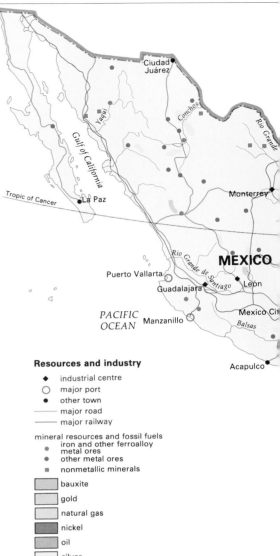

Resources and industry

- ◆ industrial centre
- ○ major port
- ● other town
- — major road
- — major railway

mineral resources and fossil fuels
- ● iron and other ferroalloy metal ores
- ● other metal ores
- ■ nonmetallic minerals

	bauxite
	gold
	natural gas
	nickel
	oil
	silver

AGRICULTURE

Agriculture plays an important part in the region's economy. Root crops were grown in the region 6,000 years ago. Large-scale commercial farming of crops on plantations and of livestock on huge ranches was introduced by the Europeans. There is production of cash crops such as sugar, bananas, and coffee, while the cattle raised on ranches provide meat for consumers in the United States.

Fishing in the Caribbean islands has seen a growth in demand since tourism became a major industry. The moist, warm climate of the region allows a range of tropical crops to be cultivated. Rough pastures in drier areas support cattle ranching. Some groups of people still carry out traditional subsistence farming. Using hand tools, they cultivate maize, beans, and squash as their staple crops, and also rear pigs and poultry as livestock. Subsistence farmers may also grow sorghum, another cereal, potatoes or other root crops, and tropical fruits. In some parts of Cuba, Mexico and Panama, where there is high rainfall or irrigation, rice is the staple grain.

LAND (million hectares)

Total	Agricultural	Arable	Forest/woodland
265 (100%)	132 (50%)	33 (13%)	67 (25%)

FARMERS

16.8 million employed in agriculture (33% of workforce)
2 hectares of arable land per person employed in agriculture

MAJOR CROPS

	Area mill ha.	Yield 100kg/ha.	Production mill tonnes	Change since 1963
Maize	8.8	16.7 (46)	14.6 (3)	+59%
Sugar cane	2.5	600.6 (101)	149.9 (16)	+41%
Dry beans	2.4	5.8 (102)	1.4 (10)	+33%
Sorghum	2.3	29.2 (198)	6.8 (11)	+547%
Bananas	—	—	8.2 (12)	+47%

MAJOR LIVESTOCK

	Number mill	Production mill tonnes	Change since 1963
Cattle	52.5 (4)	—	+45%
Pigs	26.1 (1)	—	+70%
Sheep/goats	20.6 (1)	—	+12%
Milk	—	11.0 (2)	+166%
Fish catch	—	2.0 (2)	—

FOOD SECURITY (cereal exports minus imports)

mill tonnes	% domestic production	% world trade
-8.9	30	4

Numbers in brackets are percentages of world total

Agricultural zones

	arable
	fruit and vegetables
	rough grazing
	woods and forest
	nonagricultural land

- ▲ mountain peak (metres)

INDUSTRY

Mexico is a major oil producer, and the world's leading silver producer. It also has many other valuable deposits. Several island nations have bauxite deposits.

AGRICULTURE

The region produces many tropical crops, including bananas, cotton, maize, and sugar cane, and coffee in highland regions. Livestock are reared in dry areas.

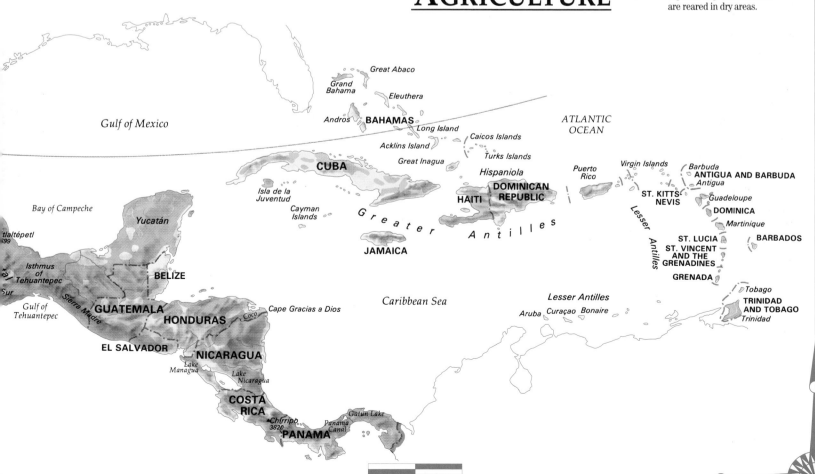

SOUTH AMERICA

South America, the fourth largest continent, contains the Andes Mountains, the world's longest unbroken range, and the mighty River Amazon, which discharges one-fifth of the world's flow of fresh water into the sea.

Extending from the equatorial lands in the north to Cape Horn, which is just 800 km (500 mi) from Antarctica, the continent has a wide range of climates and habitats.

Native Americans migrating from North America reached the southern tip of South America about 8,000 years ago. One group, the Incas, founded a major civilization in the Andes, but it was crushed by Spanish soldiers in the 1530s. The predominant culture in South America today is Latin American. Roman Catholicism is the main religion and Spanish and Portuguese are the chief languages.

South America was once joined to Africa, forming part of the supercontinent of Gondwanaland. When the two continents began to move apart about 150 million years ago, the South Atlantic Ocean opened up between them. Plate movements are still going on, further widening the Atlantic.

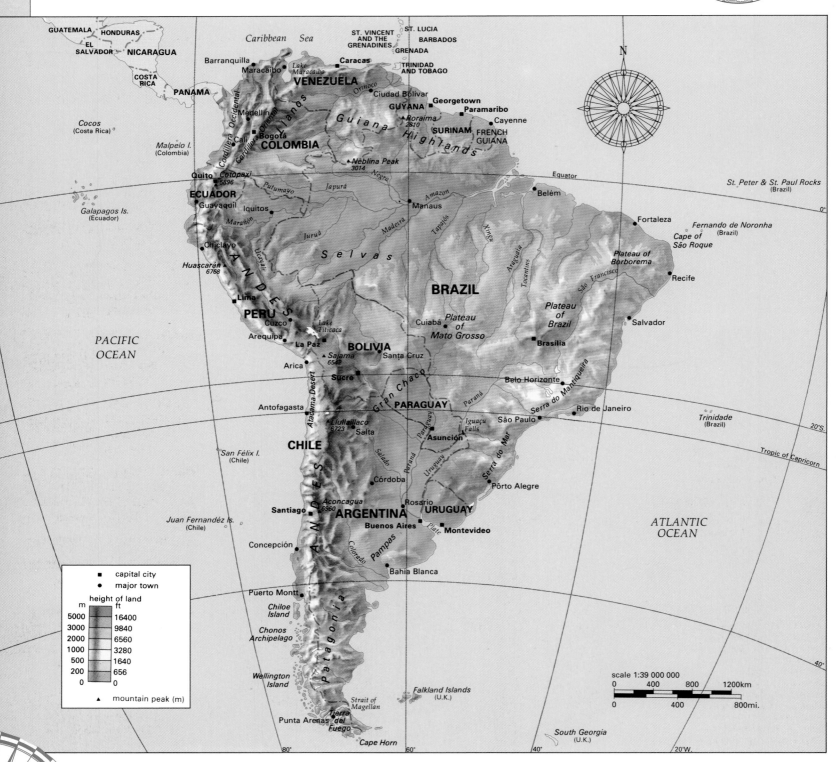

THE POLITICAL AND CULTURAL WORLD

Latin American culture is a complex blend of Native American, European and African influences. The carnivals held in Rio de Janeiro combine Christian and African traditions, while many Native American Roman Catholics combine Christian dogma with some of their old beliefs.

Deep divisions exist between rural people, who are often Native Americans, and urban societies which are often dominated by people of European or of mixed European and Native American descent. In Peru, for example, such differences have led to civil war. Political instability and the suppression of human rights remain features of South American life.

■ capital city

COUNTRIES IN THE REGION
Argentina, Bolivia, Brazil, Chile, Colombia, Ecuador, Guyana, Paraguay, Peru, Surinam, Uruguay, Venezuela

Island territories Easter Island, Juan Fernandez (Chile); Galapagos (Ecuador); Tierra del Fuego (Argentina/Chile)
Dependencies of other states Falkland Islands, South Georgia, South Sandwich Islands (U.K.); French Guiana (France)

LANGUAGE
Countries with one official language (Dutch) Surinam; (English) Guyana; (Portuguese) Brazil; (Spanish) Argentina, Chile, Colombia, Ecuador, Paraguay, Uruguay, Venezuela
Countries with two official languages (Quechua, Spanish) Peru
Country with three official languages (Aymara, Quechua, Spanish) Bolivia

Other languages spoken in the region include Arawak, Carib, Jivaro, Lengua, Mapuche, Sranang, Tongo, Toba and numerous other indigenous languages

RELIGION
Countries with one major religion (RC) Argentina, Bolivia, Brazil, Chile, Colombia, Ecuador, Paraguay, Peru, Venezuela
Countries with more than one major religion (A, N, P, RC) Uruguay; (H, I, M, P, RC) Guyana, Surinam

Key: A-atheist; H-Hindu, I-indigenous religions; M-Muslim, N-nonreligious, P-Protestant, RC-Roman Catholic

STYLES OF GOVERNMENT
Republics All countries of the region
Federal states Argentina, Brazil, Venezuela
Multiparty states All countries of the region except Paraguay
One-party state Paraguay
Military influence Chile, Paraguay

ECONOMIC INDICATORS: 1990

	Brazil	Colombia	Bolivia
GDP (US$ billions)	414.06	41.12	4.48
GNP per capita (US$)	2,680	1,260	630
Annual rate of growth of GDP, 1980–1990	2.7%	3.7%	−0.1%
Manufacturing as % of GDP	26%	21%	13%
Central government spending as % of GNP	36%	15%	19%
Merchandise exports (US$ billions)	31.4	7.1	0.92
Merchandise imports (US$ billions)	20.4	5.6	0.72
% of GNP received as development aid	0.0%	0.2%	10.9%
Total external debt as % of GNP	25.1%	44.5%	100.9%

WELFARE INDICATORS

Infant mortality rate (per 1,000 live births)
1965	104	86	106
1990	57	37	92

Daily food supply available (calories per capita, 1989)
	2,751	2,179	1,916

Population per physician (1984) 1,080 2,598 1,530
Teacher-pupil ratio (primary school, 1989) 1 : 23 1 : 30 1 : 25

Area 1,098,581 sq. km (424,164 sq. mi.)
Population 7,314,000
Bolivia

Area 8,456,508 sq. km (3,265,076 sq. mi.)
Population 150,368,000
Brazil

Area 1,141,748 sq. km (440,831 sq. mi.)
Population 32,978,000
Colombia

Area 269,178 sq. km (103,930 sq. mi.)
Population 10,587,000
Ecuador

Area 215,083 sq. km (83,044 sq. mi.)
Population 796,000
Guyana

Area 406,752 sq. km (157,048 sq. mi.)
Population 4,277,000
Paraguay

Area 163,820 sq. km (63,251 sq. mi.)
Population 422,000
Surinam

Area 912,050 sq. km (352,144 sq. mi.)
Population 19,735,000
Venezuela

Area 1,285,216 sq. km (496,225 sq. mi.)
Population 22,332,000
Peru

Area 756,626 sq. km (292,135 sq. mi.)
Population 13,173,000
Chile

Area 2,780,092 sq. km (1,073,399 sq. mi.)
Population 32,322,000
Argentina

Area 175,016 sq. km (67,574 sq. mi.)
Population 3,094,000
Uruguay

Like many former European colonies, the countries of South America have made slow progress towards democracy and have seen much political upheaval in recent times. There have been periods of military rule in most countries in the region, with resulting human rights abuses. The governments of both Chile and Paraguay are still under the army's influence.

HABITATS

South America covers almost one-seventh of the world's land surface and contains a wide range of habitats. It stretches from north of the Equator almost to Antarctica. The great River Amazon dominates much of the north of the region.

Tropical grasslands, called llanos, are found in the north; rainforests, called selvas, cover large areas around the Equator; temperate grasslands, or pampas, are in the south; hot deserts border the coasts of Peru and Chile; and arid grasslands cover the cold Patagonian region in the south. The western edge of the continent is divided from the east by the great mountain range of the Andes. Extensive mountain habitats, including snowy peaks and high, wind-swept plateaus, or altiplanos, are found in the Andes.

LAND

Area 17,084,526 sq. km (6,874,600 sq. mi.)
Highest point Aconcagua, 6,960 m (22, 836 ft)
Lowest point Salinas Grande, Argentina, −40 m (−131 ft)
Major features Andes, world's longest mountain chain, Guiana Highlands and Plateau of Brazil, Amazon basin

WATER

Longest river Amazon, 6,570 km (4,080 mi.)
Largest basin Amazon, 6,150,000 sq. km (2,375,000 sq. mi.)
Highest average flow Amazon, 180,000 cu. m/sec (6,350,000 cu. ft/sec)
Largest lake Titicaca, 8,340 sq. km (3,220 sq. mi.)
Amazon has world's largest drainage basin and greatest flow
Angel Falls, Venezuela, 979 m (3,212 ft) are world's highest, Iguaçu Falls, Brazil–Argentina, one of the widest, 4 km (2.5 mi.)

NOTABLE THREATENED ENDEMIC SPECIES

Mammals Golden lion tamarin (*Leontopithecus rosalia*), Emperor tamarin (*Saguinus imperator*), Woolly spider monkey (*Brachyteles arachnoides*), Maned wolf (*Chrysocyon brachyurus*), Giant otter (*Pteronura brasiliensis*), Mountain tapir (*Tapirus pinchaque*), Marsh deer (*Blastocerus dichotomus*)
Birds Junin grebe (*Podiceps taczanowskii*), White-winged guan (*Penelope albipennis*), Little blue macaw (*Cyanopsitta spixii*), Esmereldas woodstar (*Acestrura berlepschi*)
Plants Aechmea dichlamydea; Amaryllis traubii; Dalbergia nigra; Dicliptera dodsonii; Glomeropitcairnia erectiflora; Legrandia concinna; Mimosa lanuginosa (snow mimosa); Mutisia retrorsa; Persea theobromifolia (Rio Palenue mahogany); Spergularia congestifolia
Others South American river turtle (*Podocnemis expansa*), Black caiman (*Melanosuchus niger*), Ginger pearlfish (*Cynolebias marmoratus*), Galapagos land snails (*Bulimulus*)

HABITATS

The Andes mountains dominate western South America. The world's largest rainforest covers much of the Amazon basin, while tropical grasslands dominate large parts of the countries in the east. The coast of Peru, in the west, is desert.

Physical zones

- mountains/barren land
- forest
- grassland
- semidesert
- desert

▲ mountain peak (metres)
☀ climate station

CLIMATE

The climates of South America vary greatly. The northern regions straddle the Equator and are hot and rainy. The south has warm temperate to cool climates. Patagonia is arid, but other areas have ample rain. The Andes range contains zones with different climates, depending on the altitude.

Rainfall on the eastern slopes facing the Amazon basin may reach 5,000 mm (200 in) a year. The interior basins and gorges have one-tenth of that rainfall. The western coasts of Peru and northern Chile, though often blanketed in low cloud, have almost no rainfall at all. West of the Andes are some of the world's driest deserts. Central Chile has a Mediterranean climate, with hot, dry summers and warm, moist winters, but the south is rainy with cool summers.

TEMPERATURE AND PRECIPITATION

| | Temperature °C (°F) | | Altitude |
	January	July	m (ft)
Maracaibo	19 (66)	21 (69)	6 (19)
Manaus	27 (80)	28 (82)	44 (144)
La Paz	12 (53)	9 (48)	3,658 (12,000)
Buenos Aires	23 (73)	10 (50)	27 (88)
Ushuaia	9 (48)	2 (36)	6 (20)

| | Precipitation mm (in) | | |
	January	July	Year
Maracaibo	23 (0.9)	109 (4.2)	387 (15.2)
Manaus	249 (9.8)	58 (2.3)	2,102 (82.7)
La Paz	114 (4.4)	10 (0.4)	555 (21.9)
Buenos Aires	79 (3.1)	56 (2.2)	1,027 (40.4)
Ushuaia	58 (2.3)	47 (1.9)	574 (22.6)

Atacama Desert has recorded no rain in 400 years

NATURAL HAZARDS

Volcanic eruptions, earthquakes, landslides and mudslides

CLIMATE

height above sea level of climate stations

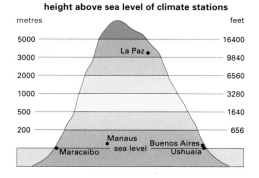

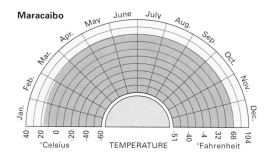
Maracaibo

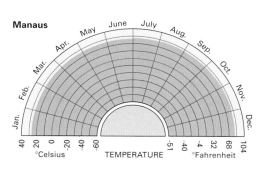
Manaus

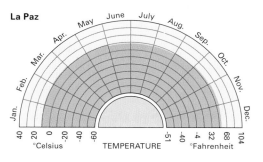
La Paz

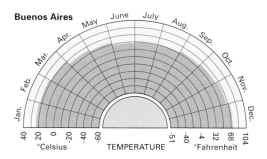
Buenos Aires

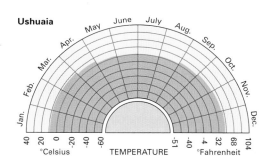
Ushuaia

Maracaibo
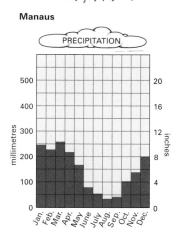

Manaus
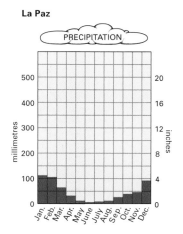

La Paz
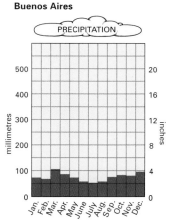

Buenos Aires
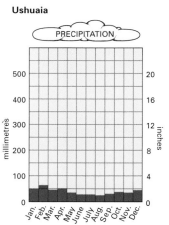

Ushuaia

ENVIRONMENTAL ISSUES

The cutting down of the world's largest rainforest in the Amazon basin, together with the disappearance of the world's richest plant and animal life, has become a symbol of human misuse of the planet. In Colombia, for example, half the forest has been destroyed in the last 50 years. Deforestation also threatens the Native Americans who live there. Nearly 100 groups have been wiped out in the last 90 years.

Soil erosion is severe in many areas, especially the Andes, while heavy industrial and urban pollution and poor conditions of sanitation exist in and around the biggest cities. Economic development and improvements to living conditions have been made a high priority, but the impact on the environment has been great.

POPULATION AND WEALTH

	Highest	Middle	Lowest
Population (millions)	150.4 (Brazil)	13.2 (Chile)	0.4 (Surinam)
Population increase (annual population growth rate, % 1960–90)	3.3 (Venezuela)	2.5 (Colombia)	0.7 (Uruguay)
Energy use (gigajoules/person)	88 (Venezuela)	22 (Brazil)	8 (Paraguay)
Real purchasing power (US$/person)	5,790 (Uruguay)	3,810 (Colombia)	1,480 (Bolivia)

ENVIRONMENTAL INDICATORS

	Highest	Middle	Lowest
CO_2 emissions (million tonnes carbon/annum)	610 (Brazil)	69 (Colombia)	0.3 (Guyana)
Deforestation ('000s ha./annum 1980s)	9,050 (Brazil)	270 (Peru)	3 (Surinam)
Artificial fertilizer use (kg/ha./annum)	162 (Surinam)	43 (Uruguay)	3 (Bolivia)
Cars (per 1,000 population)	126 (Argentina)	33 (Guyana)	2 (Ecuador)
Access to safe drinking water (% population)	96 (Brazil)	61 (Peru)	35 (Paraguay)

MAJOR ENVIRONMENTAL PROBLEMS AND SOURCES

Air pollution: locally high, in particular urban; high greenhouse gas emissions
River pollution: medium; *sources*: agricultural, sewage
Land degradation: *types*: soil erosion, deforestation, habitat destruction; *causes*: agriculture, industry, population pressure
Resource problems: fuelwood shortage; inadequate drinking water and sanitation; land use competition
Population problems: population explosion; urban overcrowding; inadequate health facilities
Major events: Cubatão, Brazil (1984), accident in natural gas/oil refining facility

ENVIRONMENTAL ISSUES

Besides deforestation, South America also suffers soil erosion in upland areas, desertification, urban and industrial pollution, and land degradation caused by mining and the building of dams.

Key environmental issues

- • major town or city
- heavily polluted town or city
- major pollution event
- heavily polluted river
- remaining tropical rainforest
- area of deforestation

areas at risk of desertification
- very high
- high
- moderate
- true desert

POPULATION

South America's population increased by four times between 1930 and 1985. The population explosion is still continuing at about 2 percent a year, making South America's population one of the fastest growing in the world.

In the last 50 years, city populations have also increased rapidly as people have moved away from the countryside. Many cities have elegant districts for the rich elite, and vast shanty towns where the poor live.

For vast numbers of urban dwellers, life is hard. Incomes and standards of living declined throughout the 1980s. The majority now live in overcrowded housing with poor access to services such as water, sanitation, and power. In Venezuela, new city dwellers have built on illegally invaded land.

POPULATION

Total population of region (millions)	296.6
Population density (persons per sq. km)	17.0
Population change (average annual percent 1960–1990)	
Urban	+4.1
Rural	+0.6

URBAN POPULATION

As percentage of total population	
1960	43.2
1990	76.1
Percentage in cities of more than 1 million	12.1

TEN LARGEST CITIES

	Country	Population
São Paulo	Brazil	16,832,000
Rio de Janeiro	Brazil	11,141,000
Buenos Aires †	Argentina	11,126,000
Lima †	Peru	6,234,000
Santiago †	Chile	4,858,000
Bogotá †	Colombia	4,185,000
Belo Horizonte	Brazil	3,446,000
Caracas †	Venezuela	3,247,000
Salvador	Brazil	2,362,000
Fortaleza	Brazil	2,169,000

† denotes capital city

POPULATION

The distribution of South America's population is very uneven. Large areas of forest, mountain and desert are thinly populated, while some coastal areas are overcrowded.

Population density

city populations
(capital city is underlined)

- ◆ over 5,000,000
- ■ 1,000,000–5,000,000
- ● 500,000–999,999
- × capital city less than 500,000

persons per square km	persons per square mi.
200	520
100	260
50	130
10	26
1	2.6

INDUSTRY

Apart from Guyana, the least developed country in the continent, economists classify South American countries as 'middle-income developing nations'. But Argentina and Brazil both have massive industries and are likely to become high-income economies in the 21st century. Argentina's factories process food, especially meat, refine oil, produce chemicals, and make electrical equipment and vehicles. Brazil also produces vehicles, as well as aircraft, cement, chemicals, machinery, textiles, foods, and pharmaceuticals. In most other countries, industry is dominated by mining. Chile is the world's leading copper producer. Other minerals include gold and nitrates. Many minerals are exported as raw materials, where local industries cannot use them.

INDUSTRIAL OUTPUT (US $ billion)

Total	Mining	Manufacturing	Average annual change since 1960
231.5	22.9	181.7	+6.4%

INDUSTRIAL WORKERS (millions)
(figures in brackets are percentages of total labour force)

Total	Mining	Manufacturing	Construction
23.8	0.56 (0.54%)	16.7 (16.3%)	6.6 (6.4%)

MAJOR PRODUCTS (figures in brackets are percentages of world production)

Energy and minerals	Output	Change since 1960
Oil (mill barrels)	2674.0 (11.9%)	+109.6%
Iron Ore (mill tonnes)	119.1 (21.1%)	+91.8%
Bauxite (mill tonnes)	12.9 (13.2%)	+15%
Copper (mill tonnes)	1.8 (21.2%)	+89%
Tin (1,000 tonnes)	59.1 (29.4%)	+72%
Silver (1,000 tonnes)	2.5 (12.9%)	+54%

Manufactures		
Tanning extracts (1,000 tonnes)	57.1 (55.3%)	No data
Coffee extracts (1,000 tonnes)	64.5 (11.6%)	No data
Rubber footwear (mill pairs)	124.7 (13.9%)	No data
Ladies' blouses and underwear (mill)	891.9 (27.9%)	No data
Cement (mill tonnes)	51.6 (4.7%)	+406%
Steel (mill tonnes)	33.9 (4.6%)	+930%
Locks and keys (mill)	271.7 (69.1%)	No data
Electrical fuses (mill)	88.8 (12.7%)	No data

INDUSTRY

South America's many rich resources include bauxite in Surinam, copper in Chile, tin in Bolivia, and oil in Venezuela. Argentina was the first country in the region to set up large manufacturing industries.

Resources and industry

◆ industrial centre
○ major port
● other town
—— major road
—— major railway

mineral resources and fossil fuels
● iron and other ferroalloy metal ores
● other metal ores
■ nonmetallic minerals

bauxite
coal
copper
gold
iron ore
oil
silver
tin

AGRICULTURE

Agriculture employs about a quarter of the workforce and the region produces a wide range of farm products. Argentina's pampas is one of the world's major cereal growing zones. The largest cereal crop is that of maize, the only cereal native to the region. It is the staple crop, and contains up to 15 percent protein. Tropical crops, such as bananas and sugar cane, grow in the north, though in some areas farmers find it more profitable to grow plants for the illegal drug trade. Brazil and Colombia are two of the principal producers of coffee beans. Cattle rearing is the major activity in Brazil and Argentina, while llamas are raised in the high altitudes of the Peruvian Andes. Fishing and forestry are other major industries.

LAND (million hectares)

Total	Agricultural	Arable	Forest/woodland
1,753 (100%)	617 (35%)	116 (7%)	900 (51%)

FARMERS

24.2 million employed in agriculture (24% of workforce)
5 hectares of arable land per person employed in agriculture

MAJOR CROPS

	Area mill ha.	Yield 100kg/ha.	Production mill tonnes	Change since 1963
Maize	19.7	21.2 (58)	41.6 (9)	+133%
Soya beans	13.6	18.9 (99)	25.6 (26)	+6,178%
Wheat	9.6	18.6 (80)	17.9 (3)	+78%
Paddy rice	7.4	21.5 (65)	15.9 (3)	+98%
Sugar cane	5.4	627.7 (105)	337.5 (35)	+197%
Coffee	4.7	6.7 (120)	3.2 (51)	+26%
Bananas	—	—	15.2 (23)	+38%

MAJOR LIVESTOCK

	Number mill	Production mill tonnes	Change since 1963
Cattle	257.8 (20)	—	+73%
Sheep/goats	129.9 (8)	—	−12%
Pigs	53.9 (6)	—	+37%
Milk	—	29.3 (6)	+93%
Fish catch	—	12.0 (13)	—

FOOD SECURITY (cereal exports minus imports)

mill tonnes	% domestic production	% world trade
+4.2	5	2

Numbers in brackets are percentages of world total

AGRICULTURE

Only about one-third of South America is used for agriculture, including simple subsistence farming and high-technology plantations. Large areas are used for grazing.

Caribbean Sea
VENEZUELA
Lake Maracaibo
Orinoco
Llanos
Cordillera Occidental
Cordillera Oriental
Magdalena
GUYANA
Roraima 2810
Guiana Highlands
SURINAM
FRENCH GUIANA
COLOMBIA
Neblina Peak 3014
Cotopaxi 5896
Negro
Equator
ECUADOR
Putumayo
Japurá
Amazon
Cape of São Roque
Marañón
Jurúa
Madeira
Tapajós
Xingu
Plateau of Borborema
Huascarán 6768
Selvas
Araguaia
Tocantins
São Francisco
ANDES
Ucayali
Tapajós
PERU
BRAZIL
Lake Titicaca
Plateau of Mato Grosso
Plateau of Brazil
BOLIVIA
Sajama 6542
PACIFIC OCEAN
Gran Chaco
Paraná
Serra do Mantiqueira
Atacama Desert
PARAGUAY
Paraná
Tropic of Capricorn
Llullaillaco 6723
Iguaçu Falls
Paraguay
Serra do Mar
CHILE
Salado
Paraná
Uruguay
ATLANTIC OCEAN
Aconcagua 6960
Colorado
ARGENTINA
Pampas
URUGUAY
Plate
Chiloe Island
Chonos Archipelago
Patagonia
Wellington Island
Falkland Islands
Strait of Magellan
Tierra del Fuego
Cape Horn

Agricultural zones
- arable
- fruit, vegetables and tree crops
- pasture
- rough grazing
- woods and forest
- nonagricultural land

▲ mountain peak (metres)

NORDIC COUNTRIES

The Nordic countries include Norway and Sweden, Denmark, Finland and Iceland. Glacial erosion has shaped the land, sculpting rugged mountain scenery, deep fjords and many ice-scoured basins which now contain lakes.

Iceland has icecaps and volcanoes. Because it straddles the Atlantic ridge, new crustal rock is being formed in Iceland as the plates on either side of the ridge slowly move apart.

Except for Finnish and Sami (Lapp), the Nordic peoples speak closely related languages. Their historic Viking traditions have given them a distinctive personality and sense of adventure.

Natural resources, including North Sea oil and hydroelectric power supplies in Norway, iron ore in Sweden, fisheries and forests, underpin the economies of the Nordic countries. Farming is important in the south.

The Nordic countries occupy the northwestern corner of Eurasia. They include various islands. The Faeroe Islands and Greenland are Danish, the Jan Mayen Islands, Bear Island and Svalbard are Norwegian, and the Åland islands in the Baltic are Finnish.

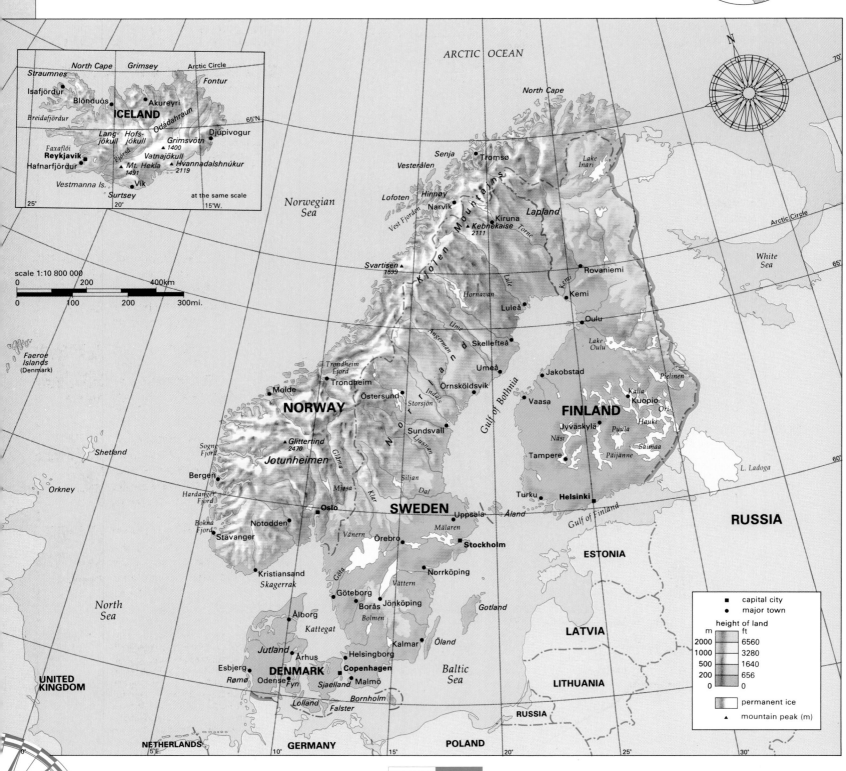

■	capital city			
•	major town			
height of land				
m			ft	
2000			6560	
1000			3280	
500			1640	
200			656	
0			0	
	permanent ice			
▲	mountain peak (m)			

scale 1:10 800 000

THE POLITICAL AND CULTURAL WORLD

The modern Nordic states began to evolve in the early 19th century. Norway became an independent country in 1905, when it broke away from its union with Sweden. In 1944 Iceland broke away from Denmark, which had ceded Schleswig and Holstein to Germany in 1864. Finland declared its independence from Russia in 1917/1918, though it lost land to the Soviet Union in 1944.

Because of their cultural affinity, the Nordic countries collaborate through the Nordic Council of Ministers. Established in 1971, it provides funds for joint institutions. The related Nordic Council is an advisory body.

ECONOMIC INDICATORS: 1990

	Denmark	Norway	Sweden
GDP (US$ billions)	130.96	105.83	228.11
GNP per capita (US$)	22,080	23,120	23,660
Annual rate of growth of GDP, 1980–1990	2.4%	2.9%	2.2%
Manufacturing as % of GDP	20%	15%	24%
Central government spending as % of GNP	41%	46%	42%
Merchandise exports (US$ billions)	35.0	33.8	57.5
Merchandise imports (US$ billions)	31.6	27.2	54.7
% of GNP donated as development aid	0.93%	1.17%	0.90%

WELFARE INDICATORS

Infant mortality rate (per 1,000 live births)			
1965	19	17	13
1990	15	8	6
Daily food supply available (calories per capita, 1989)	3,628	3,326	2,960
Population per physician (1984)	400	450	390
Teacher-pupil ratio (primary school, 1989)	1 : 12	1 : 16	1 : 16

ICELAND
- Reykjavik

NORWAY

SWEDEN

FINLAND

- Oslo

- Stockholm

Helsinki

Åland

Gotland

Öland

DENMARK - Copenhagen

Bornholm

■ capital city

Area 103,000 sq. km (397,68 sq. mi.)
Population 235,000
Currency 1 Icelandic krona (IsK) = 100 aurar
Iceland

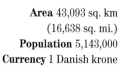

Area 323,878 sq. km (125,050 sq. mi.)
Population 4,212,000
Currency 1 Norwegian krone (NKr) = 100 øre   **Norway**

Area 449,964 sq. km (173,732 sq. mi.)
Population 8,444,000
Currency 1 Swedish krona (SKr) = 100 öre   **Sweden**

Area 338,145 sq. km (130,559 sq. mi.)
Population 4,975,000
Currency 1 markka (Fmk) = 100 pennia   **Finland**

Area 43,093 sq. km (16,638 sq. mi.)
Population 5,143,000
Currency 1 Danish krone (DKr) = 100 øre   **Denmark**

Denmark, Norway and Sweden are constitutional monarchies, whose governments are led by elected prime ministers and cabinets. The monarchs have little real power. Finland and Iceland are democratic republics. Finland's president is the country's chief executive. Iceland's president has little real power.

HABITATS

The glaciated mountain core of Norway and Sweden lies between the indented west coast and the hilly Norrland region. There is tundra in Lapland. Fertile lowland plains are situated in southern Finland, Sweden and Denmark. Iceland is mostly barren.

LAND

Area 1,255,017 sq. km (484,437 sq. mi.)
Highest point Glittertind, 2,470 m (8,104 ft)
Lowest point sea level
Major features islands, fjords, mountains and high plateau in west, lakelands east and west of Gulf of Bothnia, lowlands in south

WATER

Longest river Göta–Klar, 720 km (477 mi.)
Largest basin Kemi, 51,000 sq. km (20,000 sq. mi.)
Highest average flow Kemi, 534 cu. m/sec (19,000 cu. ft/sec)
Largest lake Vänern, 5,390 sq. km (2,080 sq. mi.)

NOTABLE THREATENED NON-ENDEMIC SPECIES

Mammals Grey wolf (Canis lupus), wolverine (Gulo gulo), Polar bear (Ursus maritimus), Harbour porpoise (Phocoena phocoena), Northern bottlenose whale (Hyperoodon ampullatus), Fin whale (Balaenoptera physalus), Blue whale (Balaenoptera musculus), Bowhead whale (Balaena mysticetus), Humpback whale (Megaptera novangliae), narwhal (Monodon monoceros)
Birds Lesser white-fronted goose (Anser erythropus), Red kite (Milvus migrans), White-tailed sea eagle (Haliaeetus albicilla), corncrake (Crex crex)
Plants Braya linearis; Cephalanthera rubra; Gentianella uliginosa; Liparis loeselii; Najas flexilis; Oxytropis deflexa subsp. norvegica; Papaver lapponicum; Platanthera obtusata subsp. oligantha; Polemonium boreale; Potamogeton rutilus
Others Hermit beetle (Osmoderma eremita), Tree snail (Balea perversa), Large blue butterfly (Maculinea arion), Noble crayfish (Astacus astacus)

CLIMATE

The climate of the coasts of Iceland and western Norway is moderated by the North Atlantic Drift. Inland, Iceland has icecaps, while northern Sweden and Finland have subarctic climates. Southern Sweden has mild winters, and Norway the greatest rainfall.

TEMPERATURE AND PRECIPITATION

	Temperature °C (°F)		Altitude
	January	July	m (ft)
Bergen	1 (33)	15 (59)	44 (144)
Oslo	−5 (23)	17 (63)	94 (308)
Stockholm	−3 (27)	18 (64)	44 (144)
Helsinki	−6 (21)	17 (63)	46 (150)
Reykjavik	0 (32)	11 (52)	18 (59)

	Precipitation mm (in)		
	January	July	Year
Bergen	142 (5.6)	143 (5.7)	1,958 (77.1)
Oslo	49 (1.9)	82 (3.2)	740 (29.1)
Stockholm	51 (2.0)	86 (3.3)	555 (21.9)
Helsinki	56 (2.2)	68 (2.7)	641 (25.2)
Reykjavik	90 (3.5)	50 (1.9)	805 (31.7)

NATURAL HAZARDS

Cold, glacier surges, volcanic eruptions in Iceland

ENVIRONMENTAL ISSUES

The main environmental issues in the Nordic countries are pollution of the Baltic Sea and acid rain. Clouds containing acid raindrops drift over from Germany, Poland and the former Soviet Union. Acid rain has poisoned many lakes, rivers and forests.

ENVIRONMENTAL INDICATORS

	Highest	Middle	Lowest
CO_2 emissions (million tonnes carbon/annum)	15 (Denmark)	8.7 (Norway)	0.4 (Iceland)
Municipal waste (kg/person/annum)	474 (Norway)	408 (Finland)	317 (Sweden)
Nuclear waste (cumulative tonnes heavy metal)	1,900 (Sweden)	400 (Finland)	0 (Norway)
Artificial fertilizer use (kg/ha./annum)	2,917 (Iceland)	234 (Denmark)	136 (Sweden)
Cars (per 1,000 population)	406 (Sweden)	377 (Iceland)	311 (Denmark)
Access to safe drinking water (% population)	100 (Sweden)	100 (Iceland)	97 (Finland)

MAJOR ENVIRONMENTAL PROBLEMS AND SOURCES

Air pollution: acid rain prevalent
River/lake pollution: high; *sources:* acid deposition
Marine/coastal pollution: medium; *sources:* industrial, agricultural
Land pollution: local; *sources:* industrial; acid deposition
Major events: Aker river, Oslo (1980), acid leak from factory; Ålesund (1992), oil spill from tanker *Arisan*

HABITATS

Physical zones
- ice and snow
- mountains/barren land
- forest
- grassland
- ▲ mountain peak (metres)
- ⁂ climate station

During the last Ice Age, which ended only about 10,000 years ago, ice sheets advanced and retreated over the region. They left their mark in the many glacial features found in the highlands and lowlands.

ENVIRONMENTAL ISSUES

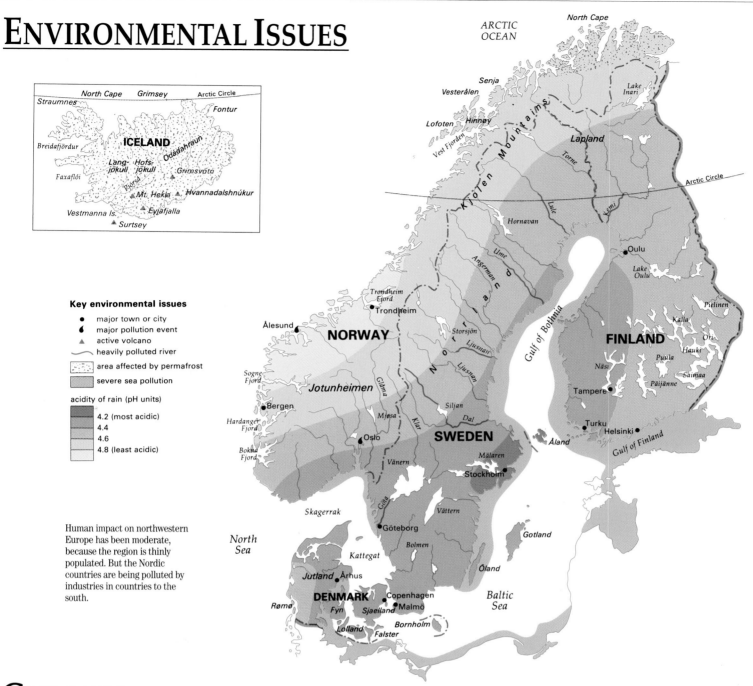

Key environmental issues

- ● major town or city
- ♦ major pollution event
- ▲ active volcano
- ～ heavily polluted river
- ▒ area affected by permafrost
- ▒ severe sea pollution

acidity of rain (pH units)
- 4.2 (most acidic)
- 4.4
- 4.6
- 4.8 (least acidic)

Human impact on northwestern Europe has been moderate, because the region is thinly populated. But the Nordic countries are being polluted by industries in countries to the south.

CLIMATE

height above sea level of climate stations

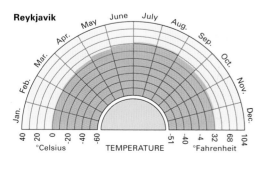

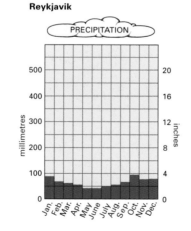

Reykjavik

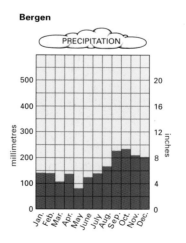

Bergen

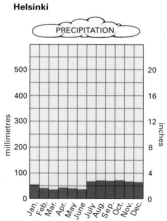

Helsinki

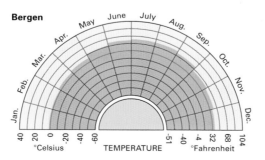

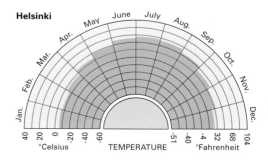

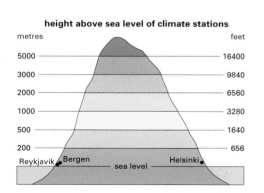

POPULATION

The rugged, mostly forested terrain, combined with the hostile climate, has restricted the population of most Nordic countries to coastal areas except in the far south. Only in Denmark is the population spread evenly, based on a network of farming villages.

POPULATION

Total population of region (millions)	22.9
Population density (persons per sq. km)	20.8
Population change (average annual percent 1960–1990)	
Urban	+0.9
Rural	−1.6

URBAN POPULATION

As percentage of total population	
1960	72.3
1990	82.6
Percentage in cities of more than 1 million	12.1

TEN LARGEST CITIES

	Country	Population
Stockholm †	Sweden	1,471,000
Copenhagen †	Denmark	1,339,000
Helsinki †	Finland	994,000
Oslo †	Norway	726,000
Göteborg	Sweden	720,000
Malmö	Sweden	466,000
Turku	Finland	265,000
Tampere	Finland	261,000
Århus	Denmark	258,000
Bergen	Norway	211,000

† denotes capital city

INDUSTRY

The region's natural resources include offshore oil and gas fields belonging to Denmark and Norway, together with metal ores in Norway and Sweden. Sweden has some of the world's richest iron ore deposits in Lapland. The region's leading industry is papermaking.

INDUSTRIAL OUTPUT (US $ billion)

Total	Mining	Manufacturing	Average annual change since 1960
172.1	23.3	95.7	+3.2%

INDUSTRIAL WORKERS (millions)
(figures in brackets are percentages of total labour force)

Total	Mining	Manufacturing	Construction
3.6	0.36 (2.9%)	2.4 (19.8%)	0.82 (6.7%)

MAJOR PRODUCTS (figures in brackets are percentages of world production)

Energy and minerals	Output	Change since 1960
Oil (mill barrels)	589 (2.6%)	N/A
Natural gas (billion cu. metres)	32 (1.7%)	N/A
Iron Ore (mill tonnes)	22.5 (3.9%)	-13.5%
Copper (mill tonnes)	0.3 (3.7%)	No data
Zinc (mill tonnes)	0.4 (6.2%)	No data

Manufactures		
Woodpulp (mill tonnes)	18.9 (15%)	+1%
Newsprint (mill tonnes)	4.4 (13.8%)	+36%
Steel (mill tonnes)	7.4 (1.1%)	+86.8%
Ships (mill gross tonnes)	0.5 (4.5%)	-59.4%
Cars (mill)	0.5 (1.1%)	+397%
Telecommunications equipment (US $ billion)	7.5 (8.1%)	No data

N/A means production had not begun in 1960

AGRICULTURE

Most of the productive arable land is in Denmark and southern Sweden. Mixed farming is important, especially dairy farming, though livestock is farmed extensively in the south. To the north, farming is combined with the related industries of forestry and fishing.

LAND (million hectares)

Total	Agricultural	Arable	Forest/woodland
117 (117%)	12 (10%)	9 (8%)	60 (52%)

MAJOR CROPS

	Area mill ha.	Yield 100kg/ha.	Production mill tonnes	Change since 1963
Barley	2.2	36.1 (155)	8.1 (4)	+46%
Wheat	0.9	47.5 (204)	4.4 (1)	+129%
Oats	0.9	31.2 (169)	2.8 (7)	−5%
Rapeseed	0.5	18.9 (132)	0.9 (4)	+360%

MAJOR LIVESTOCK

	Number mill	Production mill tonnes	Change since 1963
Pigs	13.4 (2)	—	+25%
Cattle	6.5 (1)	—	−29%
Milk	—	13.4 (3)	−8%
Fish catch	—	6.0 (6)	

Numbers in brackets are percentages of world total

POPULATION

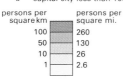

Population density

city populations
(capital city is underlined)

- ■ 1,000,000–5,000,000
- ● 500,000–999,999
- ◉ 250,000–499,999
- ○ 100,000–249,000
- × capital city less than 100,000

persons per square km	persons per square mi.
100	260
50	130
10	26
1	2.6

Most people live in cities and towns which are well-planned, attractive places in which to live. With green parks, woodlands, and often lakes and waterways, they have the appearance of garden cities.

The exploitation of its forests and mineral resources has enabled the Nordic countries to become a major trading region. The region accounts for more than 4.5 percent of world exports.

INDUSTRY

ICELAND

Grimsey · Arctic Circle
Siglufjördur
Hólmavik · Husavik
Akureyri
Breidafjördur · Stykkishólmur · Seydisfjördur
Olafsvik · Djúpivogur
Faxaflói · Þjórsá
Reykjavik
Keflavik · Hafnarfjördur
Vestmanna Is.
Surtsey

Resources and industry
- ◆ industrial centre
- ○ major port
- ● other town
- —— major road
- —— major railway

mineral resources and fossil fuels
- ◆ iron and other ferroalloy metal ores
- ● other metal ores
- ■ nonmetallic minerals

- coal
- copper
- iron ore
- nickel

Map labels (Industry)
Kirkenes
Lake Inari
Senja
Vesterålen
Lofoten
Hinnøy
Narvik
Kiruna
Gällivare
Torne
Arctic Circle
Luleå
Torniö · Kemi
Hornavan
Ume
Ångerman
Trondheim Fjord
Trondheim
Umeå
Kokkola
Pielinen
Ålesund
Kalla
Storsjön
Vaasa
FINLAND
Ori
NORWAY
Pori
Puula
Hauki
Sogne Fjord
Näsi
Bergen
Klar
Dal
Siljan
Tampere
Päijänne
Saimaa
Hardanger Fjord
Mjøsa
Haugesund
Bokna Fjord
Gävle
Turku
Helsinki
Stavanger
SWEDEN
Oslo
Åland
Vänern
Mälaren
Gulf of Finland
Kristiansand
Stockholm
Skagerrak
Norrköping
Trollhättan
Vättern
Göteborg
Gotland
Skagen
Bolmen
North Sea
Kattegat
Öland
Jutland
Århus
Helsingborg
Baltic Sea
Esbjerg
DENMARK
Copenhagen
Rømø
Fyn
Sjælland
Malmö
Lolland
Bornholm
Falster

Gulf of Bothnia
Lake Oulu

AGRICULTURE

ICELAND
North Cape · Grimsey · Arctic Circle
Straumnes · Fontur
Breidafjördur
Odádahraun
Lang-jökull
Hofs-jökull
Grimsvöth 1400
Faxaflói
Vatnajökull
Hvannadalshnúkur 2119
Mt. Hekla 1491
Þjórsá
Vestmanna Is. · Surtsey

Agricultural zones
- arable
- fruit and vegetables
- rough grazing
- woods and forest with some arable
- woods and forest with some grazing
- nonagricultural land

▲ mountain peak (metres)

To counter the largely unfavourable conditions, Nordic farmers have developed intensive agricultural methods. Denmark has better conditions and is one of the world's most successful farming countries.

Map labels (Agriculture relief)
ARCTIC OCEAN
North Cape
Senja
Vesterålen
Lofoten
Hinnøy
Vest Fjorden
Kebnekaise 2111
Lapland
Torne
Lake Inari
Svartisen 1599
Arctic Circle
Kjölen Mountains
Luleå
Kemi
Norwegian Sea
Hornavan
Ångerman
Ume
Trondheim Fjord
Lake Oulu
NORWAY
Glittertind 2470
Jotunheimen
Storsjön
Ljusnan
Gulf of Bothnia
Pielinen
FINLAND
Sogne Fjord
Klar
Siljan
Kalla
Dal
Ori
Hauki
Mjøsa
Näsi
Hardanger Fjord
SWEDEN
Päijänne
Saimaa
Bokna Fjord
Vänern
Mälaren
Åland
Gulf of Finland
Skagerrak
Vättern
North Sea
Gotland
Kattegat
Bolmen
Jutland
Öland
DENMARK
Scania
Baltic Sea
Rømø
Fyn
Sjælland
Lolland
Bornholm
Falster

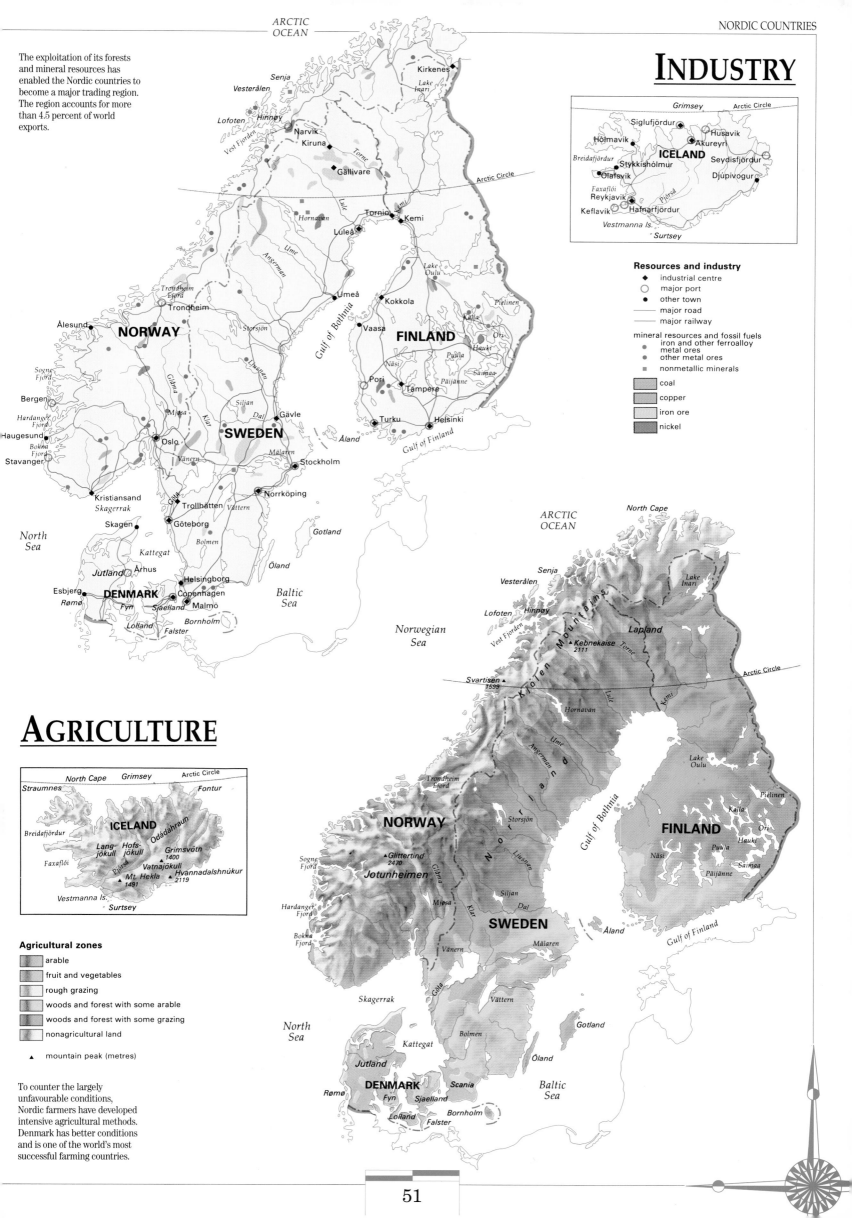

BRITISH ISLES

The British Isles contain a great variety of geology and a wide range of highland and lowland scenery that is unusual in such a small area. The climate is mild, mainly because of the influence of the North Atlantic Drift, the northern extension of the warm Gulf Stream. The weather is also distinguished by its variability, caused by the depressions that regularly cross the islands from west to east.

Celts settled in the region in about 450 B.C. But the population also owes its ancestry to invaders, such as the Romans, Vikings and Normans. There has recently been further diversification with the arrival of immigrants from Africa, Asia, and the West Indies.

The United Kingdom once ruled the largest empire in history. Though the imperial era has ended, the country remains a world power.

The British Isles consists of two large islands and more than 5,000 smaller ones, rising from the continental shelf off the coast of northwest Europe. It was cut off from the mainland about 7,500 years ago when melting ice sheets filled the North Sea and English Channel.

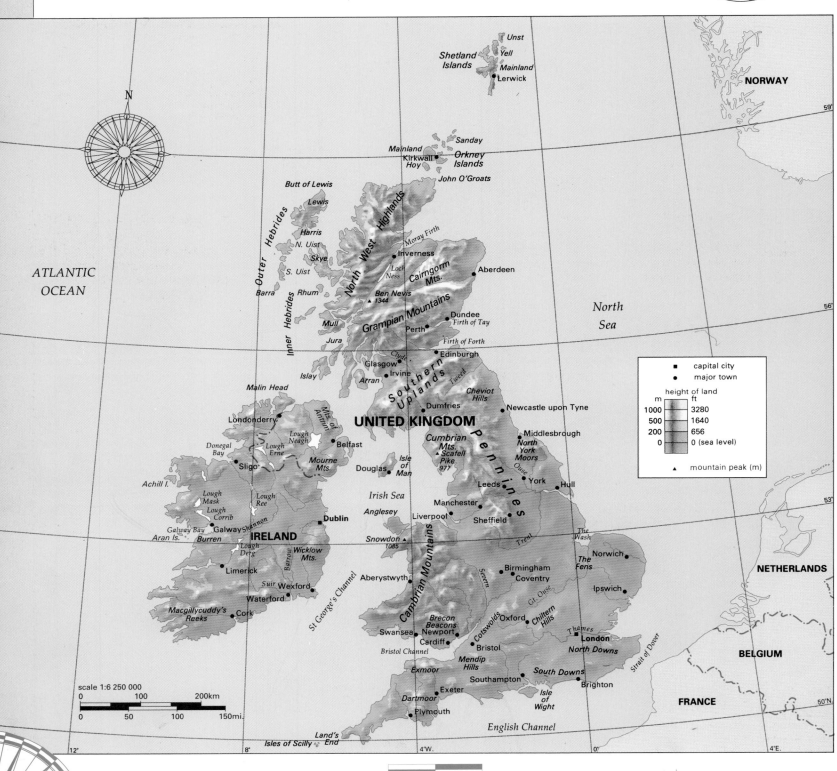

THE POLITICAL AND CULTURAL WORLD

The United Kingdom of Great Britain and Northern Ireland is often called Britain. Great Britain consists of England; Wales, which was absorbed by England in 1277; and Scotland, which was formally united with England under the Act of Union of 1707.

Ireland was united with Great Britain from 1801, but it became independent in 1921, with the exception of the six counties of Northern Ireland, which stayed in the United Kingdom.

The rest of Ireland is now a republic, while Britain is a constitutional monarchy. The Channel Islands and the Isle of Man are self-governing territories under the British Crown.

COUNTRIES IN THE REGION

Ireland, United Kingdom

Island territories Channel Islands, Isle of Man (U.K.)
Territories outside the region Anguilla, Ascension, Bermuda, British Indian Ocean Territory, British Virgin Islands, Cayman Islands, Falkland Islands, Gibraltar, Hong Kong (until 1997), Montserrat, St. Helena, South Georgia, South Sandwich Islands, Tristan da Cunha, Turks and Caicos Islands (U.K.)

MEMBERSHIP OF INTERNATIONAL ORGANIZATIONS

Council of Europe Ireland, U.K.
Colombo Plan U.K.
European Community Ireland, U.K.
North Atlantic Treaty Organization (NATO) U.K.
Organization for Economic Cooperation and Development (OECD) Ireland, U.K.

LANGUAGE

Country with one official language (English) U.K.
Country with two official languages (English, Irish) Ireland

Local minority languages are Gaelic, Irish and Welsh. Significant immigrant languages include Bengali, Chinese, Greek, Gujarati, Italian, Polish and Punjabi

RELIGION

Ireland Roman Catholic (93.1%), Anglican (2.8%), Protestant (0.4%), other (3.7%)
United Kingdom Anglican (56.8%), Roman Catholic (13.1%), Protestant (12.7%), nonreligious (8.8%), Muslim (1.4%), Jewish (0.8%), Hindu (0.7%). Sikh (0.4%)

STYLES OF GOVERNMENT

Republic Ireland
Monarchy United Kingdom
Multiparty states Ireland, U.K.
Two-chamber assembly Ireland, U.K.

ECONOMIC INDICATORS: 1990

	Ireland	U.K.
GDP (US$ billions)	42.54	975.15
GNP per capita (US$)	9,550	16,100
Annual rate of growth of GDP, 1980–1990	3.1%	3.1%
Manufacturing as % of GDP	3%	20%
Central government spending as % of GNP	55.0%	35.0%
Merchandise exports (US$ billions)	23.8	183.6
Merchandise imports (US$ billions)	20.7	222.6
% of GNP donated as development aid	0.16%	0.27%

WELFARE INDICATORS

Infant mortality rate (per 1,000 live births)		
1965	25	20
1990	7	8
Daily food supply available (calories per capita, 1989)	3,778	3,149
Population per physician (1984)	680	680
Teacher-pupil ratio (primary school, 1989)	1 : 28	1 : 20

■ capital city

Area 70,285 sq. km (27,137 sq. mi.)
Population 3,720,000
Capital Dublin
Currency 1 Irish pound (Ir$) = 100 new pence

Ireland

Shetland Islands

Orkney Islands

Lewis

Harris

Outer Hebrides

Skye

Rhum

Inner Hebrides

Mull

Jura

SCOTLAND

Edinburgh ■

Islay

Arran

Area 244,110 sq. km (94,251 sq. mi.)
Population 57,237,000
Capital London
Currency 1 pound sterling (£) = 100 new pence

United Kingdom

NORTHERN IRELAND
Belfast ■

Isle of Man

UNITED KINGDOM

Achill I.

IRELAND

Dublin ■

Aran Is.

Anglesey

ENGLAND

WALES

London ■

Cardiff ■

Isle of Wight

Regional loyalties are strong throughout the British Isles. Both Scotland and Wales have nationalist movements that have demanded a greater degree of home rule, and local parliaments.

HABITATS

The scenery of the British Isles is varied. There are areas of rocky and barren uplands; low, fertile plains, mostly on coasts; and soft, rolling hills resulting from glaciation, with some forests, moors and downland reserved from agricultural use.

LAND

Area 314,385 sq. km (121,353 sq. mi.)
Highest point Ben Nevis, 1,344 m (4,408 ft)
Lowest point Holme Fen, Great Ouse, −3 m (−9 ft)
Major features mountains chiefly in northern and western areas, with lower-lying areas in east and south

WATER

Longest river Shannon, 370 km (230 mi.)
Largest basin Severn, 21,000 sq. km (8,000 sq. mi.)
Highest average flow Shannon, 198 cu. m/sec (7,600 cu. ft/sec)
Largest lake Neagh, 400 sq. km (150 sq. mi.)

NOTABLE THREATENED NON-ENDEMIC SPECIES

Mammals Harbour porpoise (*Phocoena phocoena*)
Birds Red kite (*Milvus migrans*), White-tailed sea eagle (*Haliaeetus albicilla* – reintroduced), corncrake (*Crex crex*)
Others Kerry slug (*Geomalachus maculosus*), Chequered skipper butterfly (*Carterocephalus palaemon*), Freshwater pearl mussel (*Margaritifera margaritifera*), Ladybird spider (*Eresus niger*)

BOTANIC GARDENS

National Botanic Gardens, Dublin (25,000 taxa); Oxford (10,000 taxa); Royal Botanic Gardens, Edinburgh (12,000 taxa); Royal Botanic Gardens, Kew (30,000 taxa)

CLIMATE

The British Isles has a mild, moist climate which is ever-changing because the islands lie in the path of depressions. It is windier in the west. More stable conditions occur when the British Isles comes under the influence of anticyclones.

TEMPERATURE AND PRECIPITATION

	Temperature °C (°F) January	July	Altitude m (ft)
Aberdeen	2 (36)	14 (57)	59 (194)
Dublin	5 (41)	15 (59)	47 (154)
Valentia	7 (45)	15 (59)	9 (29)
Kew	4 (39)	18 (64)	5 (16)
Plymouth	6 (43)	16 (61)	27 (89)

	Precipitation mm (in) January	July	Year
Aberdeen	77 (3.0)	92 (3.6)	837 (33.0)
Dublin	67 (2.6)	70 (2.8)	758 (29.8)
Valentia	164 (6.5)	107 (4.2)	1,398 (55.0)
Kew	53 (2.1)	56 (2.2)	594 (23.4)
Plymouth	99 (3.9)	71 (2.8)	990 (39.0)

NATURAL HAZARDS

Storms, floods

ENVIRONMENTAL ISSUES

Britain was the first nation to industrialize and the rapid growth of mining, together with industries burning coal and oil, have caused much environmental damage. New development is currently threatening many habitats even in protected areas.

POPULATION AND WEALTH

	Ireland	UK
Population (millions)	3.7	57.2
Population increase (annual population growth rate, % 1960–90)	0.9	0.3
Energy use (gigajoules/person)	101	150
Real purchasing power (US$/person)	7,020	13,060

ENVIRONMENTAL INDICATORS

CO₂ emissions (million tonnes carbon/annum)	0.4	150
Municipal waste (kg/person/annum)	309	313
Nuclear waste (cumulative tonnes heavy metal)	0	30,900
Artificial fertilizer use (kg/ha./annum)	682	356
Cars (per 1,000 population)	199	353
Access to safe drinking water (% population)	100	100

MAJOR ENVIRONMENTAL PROBLEMS AND SOURCES

Air pollution: locally high, in particular urban; acid rain prevalent; high greenhouse gas emissions
River/lake pollution: local; *sources*: agricultural, sewage, acid deposition
Marine/coastal pollution: medium; *sources*: industrial, agricultural, sewage, oil
Land pollution: local; *sources*: industrial, agricultural, urban/household
Waste disposal problems: domestic; industrial; nuclear
Major events: *Torrey Canyon* (1967), oil tanker accident; Camelford (1989), chemical accident; river Mersey (1989), oil spill

HABITATS

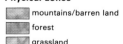

Generally the older highland regions are in the north and west. Younger, lower rocks, which produce more gentle landscapes of limestone and chalk ridges and clay vales, are found in the south and east.

Physical zones

- mountains/barren land
- forest
- grassland

▲ mountain peak (metres)
☀ climate station

ENVIRONMENTAL ISSUES

Problems include river and sea pollution, nuclear waste dumping, air pollution in cities caused by the increasing numbers of vehicles, and acid rain caused by industry and power plants.

Sanday
Mainland
Orkney Islands
Hoy
John O'Groats
Dounreay

Butt of Lewis
Lewis
Harris
Outer Hebrides
N. Uist
Skye
Moray Firth
S. Uist
North West Highlands
Barra
Rhum
Loch Ness
Cairngorm Mts.

Mull
Grampian Mountains
Firth of Tay
Jura

ATLANTIC OCEAN

Inner Hebrides
Firth of Forth
North Sea
Islay
Glasgow *Clyde*
Torness
Hunterston
Arran
Southern Uplands
Tweed
Cheviot Hills
Tyne
Chapelcross
Hartlepool

Malin Head
Mts. of Antrim
Lough Neagh
Belfast
UNITED KINGDOM
Cumbrian Mts.
Tees
North York Moors
Donegal Bay
Lough Erne
Calder Hall
Ouse
Mourne Mts.
Isle of Man
Sellafield
Pennines
Heysham
Achill I.
Lough Mask
Lough Ree
Lough Corrib
Manchester
Galway Bay
Shannon
Mersey
Liverpool
The Wash
Aran Is.
IRELAND
Dublin
Anglesey
Wylfa
Burren
Lough Derg
Wicklow Mts.
Barrow
Trawsfynydd
Trent
The Fens
Cambrian Mountains
Suir
Birmingham
Gt. Ouse
Sizewell
Severn
Chiltern Hills
Macgillycuddy's Reeks
St George's Channel
Brecon Beacons
Bradwell
Berkeley
Thames
Oldbury
London
Irish Sea
Bristol
Exmoor
Hinkley Point
Dungeness
Bristol Channel
Strait of Dover
Camelford
Winfrith
Dartmoor
Isle of Wight
Torrey Canyon
English Channel
Isles of Scilly

Shetland Islands
Unst
Yell
Mainland

Key environmental issues

- ● major town or city
- heavily polluted town or city
- major pollution event
- nuclear power station
- nuclear processing plant
- beach not complying with E.C. standard 1990
- heavily polluted river

acidity of rain (pH units)

- 4.6 (most acidic)
- 4.8
- 5.0 (least acidic)

CLIMATE

height above sea level of climate stations

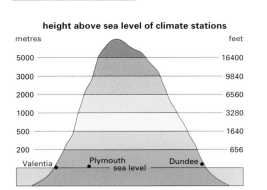

metres		feet
5000		16400
3000		9840
2000		6560
1000		3280
500		1640
200		656

Valentia   Plymouth   Dundee
sea level

Valentia
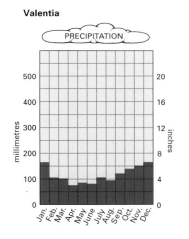
PRECIPITATION
millimetres / inches
Jan. Feb. Mar. Apr. May June July Aug. Sep. Oct. Nov. Dec.

Plymouth
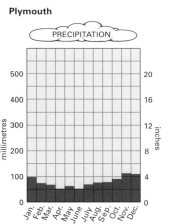
PRECIPITATION
millimetres / inches
Jan. Feb. Mar. Apr. May June July Aug. Sep. Oct. Nov. Dec.

Dundee
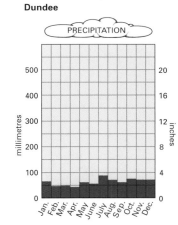
PRECIPITATION
millimetres / inches
Jan. Feb. Mar. Apr. May June July Aug. Sep. Oct. Nov. Dec.

Valentia
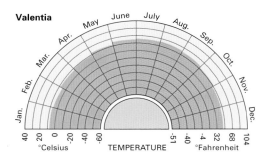
°Celsius TEMPERATURE Fahrenheit

Plymouth
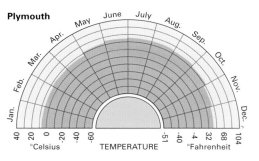
°Celsius TEMPERATURE Fahrenheit

Dundee
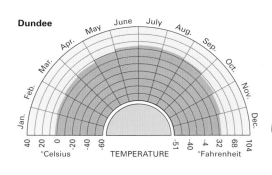
°Celsius TEMPERATURE Fahrenheit

POPULATION

Britain's population density is more than four times greater than the population density in Ireland. The chief centres of population are in England, central Scotland and south Wales, mainly in the older industrial cities. Fewer people live in rural areas.

POPULATION

Total population of region (millions)	60.6
Population density (persons per sq. km)	195.4
Population change (average annual percent 1960–1990)	
Urban	+0.7
Rural	-1.6

URBAN POPULATION

As percentage of total population	
1960	84.7
1990	91.8
Percentage in cities of more than 1 million	13.0

TEN LARGEST CITIES

	Country	Population
London †	United Kingdom	6,378,000
Manchester	United Kingdom	1,669,000
Birmingham	United Kingdom	1,400,000
Liverpool	United Kingdom	1,060,000
Dublin †	Ireland	921,000
Glasgow	United Kingdom	730,000
Newcastle upon Tyne	United Kingdom	617,000
Sheffield	United Kingdom	445,000
Leeds	United Kingdom	432,000
Edinburgh	United Kingdom	404,000

† denotes capital city

INDUSTRY

Since the 1960s, the extraction of North Sea natural gas and oil have made Britain the world's fifth largest energy producer. Until recently, Ireland's main source of energy was peat, but offshore gas deposits are now being exploited. Britain has large coal deposits.

MAJOR PRODUCTS (figures in brackets are percentages of world production)

Energy and minerals	Output	Change since 1960
Coal (mill tonnes)	100.0 (2.1%)	-49.2%
Oil (mill barrels)	673.6 (3.0%)	N/A
Natural gas (billion cu. metres)	43.7 (2.4%)	N/A
Nuclear power (mill tonnes coal equiv.)	22.2 (3.3%)	No data
Peat (mill tonnes)	4.4 (21.8%)	+20%
Chalk (mill tonnes)	14.5 (85.1%)	-10.8%

Manufactures		
Wool yarn (1,000 tonnes)	161.3 (7.2%)	-23%
Synthetic rubber (1,000 tonnes)	312.8 (3.1%)	-4.3%
Steel (mill tonnes)	18.9 (2.6%)	-23.5%
Cars (mill)	1.9 (2.0%)	+4.0%
Televisions (mill)	3.1 (2.8%)	+44.8%
Beer (mill hecolitres)	60.2 (5.8%)	-4.6%
Chocolate (1,000 tonnes)	480.1 (10.1%)	+12%

N/A means production had not begun in 1960

AGRICULTURE

Farming in both Britain and Ireland has become increasingly specialized since the countries joined the European Community. Arable farming is now concentrated in the drier eastern lowlands, with livestock farming in the wetter uplands and grazing on hillsides.

LAND (million hectares)

Total	Agricultural	Arable	Forest/woodland
31 (100%)	214 (78%)	8 (25%)	3 (9%)

FARMERS

793,000 employed in agriculture (3% of workforce)
10 hectares of arable land per person employed in agriculture

MAJOR CROPS

	Area mill ha.	Yield 100kg/ha.	Production mill tonnes	Change since 1963
Barley	2.1	51.4 (221)	10.8 (6)	+49%
Wheat	2.0	60.2 (258)	12.3 (2)	+220%
Rapeseed	0.4	34.8 (244)	1.4 (6)	+45,533%
Sugar beet	0.2	400.6 (116)	9.6 (3)	+40%
Potatoes	0.2	356.8 (227)	7.5 (3)	−19%
Oats	0.2	46.8 (254)	0.6 (1)	−71%
Vegetables	—	—	—	—
Dry peas	—	—	4.3 (1)	‡29%

MAJOR LIVESTOCK

	Number mill	Production mill tonnes	Change since 1963
Sheep	29.6 (3)	—	−14%
Cattle	18.1 (1)	—	+8%
Pigs	8.9 (1)	—	+10%
Milk	—	21.5 (5)	+41%
Fish catch	—	1.2 (1)	—

FOOD SECURITY (cereal exports minus imports)

mill tonnes	% domestic production	% world trade
+3.0	12	1

Numbers in brackets are percentages of world total

POPULATION

About 200 years ago, most Britons lived in small rural communities. Today, the United Kingdom is a highly urbanized country, though much of Wales, Scotland and northern Ireland retains a rural character.

Population density
city populations
(capital city is underlined)

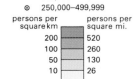

◆ over 5,000,000
■ 1,000,000–5,000,000
● 500,000–999,999
◉ 250,000–499,999

persons per square km		persons per square mi.
200		520
100		260
50		130
10		26

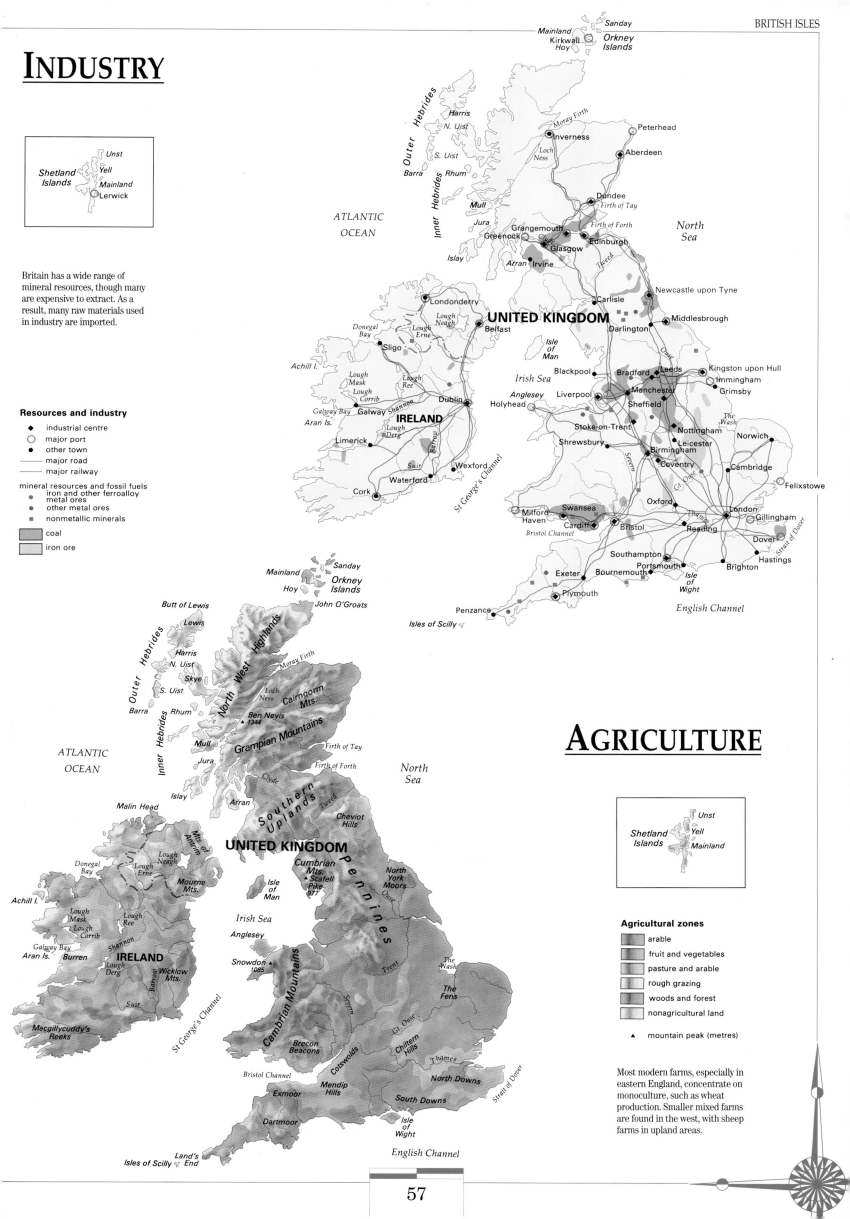

INDUSTRY

Britain has a wide range of mineral resources, though many are expensive to extract. As a result, many raw materials used in industry are imported.

Resources and industry

- ◆ industrial centre
- ◯ major port
- ● other town
- —— major road
- — major railway

mineral resources and fossil fuels
- ● iron and other ferroalloy metal ores
- ● other metal ores
- ■ nonmetallic minerals

▨ coal
▨ iron ore

AGRICULTURE

Agricultural zones

- arable
- fruit and vegetables
- pasture and arable
- rough grazing
- woods and forest
- nonagricultural land

- ▲ mountain peak (metres)

Most modern farms, especially in eastern England, concentrate on monoculture, such as wheat production. Smaller mixed farms are found in the west, with sheep farms in upland areas.

FRANCE

France is the largest country in Western Europe. Its varied landscapes include rolling plains, hills, beautiful river valleys, the remains of ancient volcanoes and dramatic mountain scenery in the Alps and Pyrenees.

The north has a cool temperate climate, while the south has the typical hot summers and mild, moist winters of Mediterranean lands. Other variations occur from west to east. While the west comes under the moderating influence of the Atlantic, to the east the climate becomes increasingly continental. Summers are hotter and winters are much colder.

The French have a strong sense of identity, a pride in their culture and a firm belief in the pre-eminence of their capital, Paris, as a world centre of art and learning. Yet the French owe their origins to many diverse groups, including Celts, Romans, Franks and Vikings. Recent immigration has been from North Africa, Southeast Asia and parts of Europe.

France is a major industrial power, with an increasingly urbanized population. It is also the largest producer of farm products in Western Europe. It is especially famous for its fine wines and wide range of cheeses.

Northern France lies at the western end of the North European Plain – an ancient pathway of human migrations – that extends from the Ural Mountains of Russia to southeastern England. The south and southeast lie in a zone where the African and Eurasian plates have collided, throwing up young ranges, including the snow-capped Pyrenees and Alps.

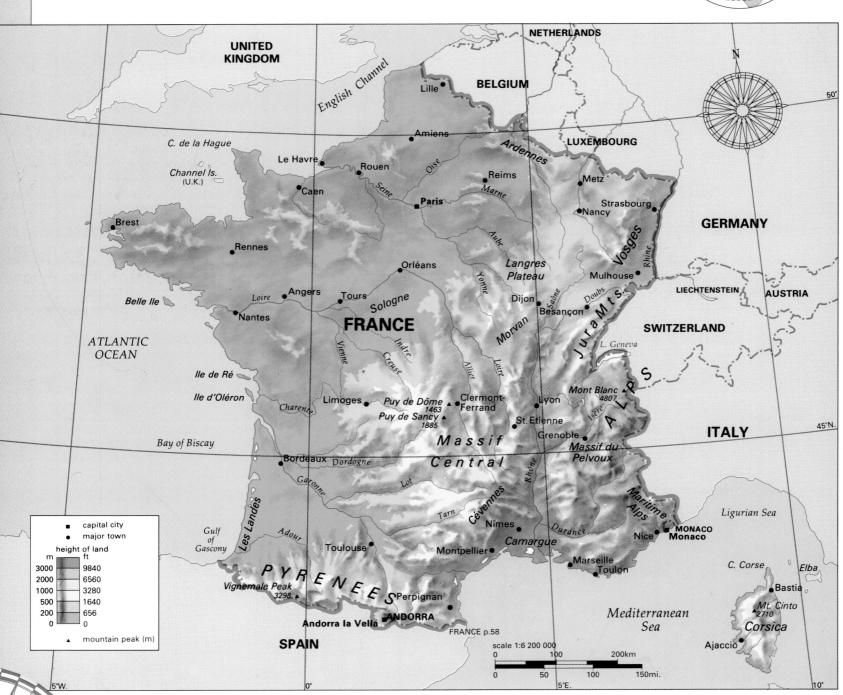

FRANCE p.58

scale 1:6 200 000

THE POLITICAL AND CULTURAL WORLD

Modern France owes its origins to the French Revolution of 1789 and its principles of liberty, equality and fraternity, which have been incorporated into the constitutions of many other countries. Today France is a parliamentary democracy, whose executive branch is headed by the president and the prime minister.

France has two of Europe's mini-states as neighbours. Nestling in the Pyrenees is the tiny state of Andorra, a principality whose heads of state are the President of France and the Bishop of Urgel in Spain. The other mini-state is Monaco, a principality ruled by the House of Grimaldi since 1308.

France

Area 543,965 sq. km
(210,026 sq. mi.)
Population 56,138,000
Currency 1 franc
(f) = 100 centimes

COUNTRIES IN THE REGION

Andorra, France, Monaco

Island territories Corsica (France)
Territories outside the region French Guiana, French Polynesia, Guadeloupe, Martinique, Mayotte, New Caledonia, Reunion, St Pierre and Miquelon, Wallis and Futuna (France)

LANGUAGE

Countries with one official language (Catalan) Andorra; (French) France, Monaco

Local minority languages in France are Basque, Breton, Catalan, Corsican, German (Alsatian) and Occitan. Significant immigrant languages include Arabic, Italian, Polish, Portuguese, Spanish and Turkish. English, Italian and Monegasque are spoken in Monaco; Spanish in Andorra.

RELIGION

Andorra Roman Catholic (99%)
France Roman Catholic (76%), Muslim (3%), nonreligious and atheist (3%), Protestant (2%), Jewish (1%)
Monaco Roman Catholic (91%), Anglican (1%), Eastern Orthodox (1%), Protestant (1%)

STYLES OF GOVERNMENT

Republic France
Principalities Andorra, Monaco
Multiparty state France
States without parties Andorra, Monaco
One-chamber assembly Andorra
Two-chamber assembly France, Monaco

MEMBERSHIP OF INTERNATIONAL ORGANIZATIONS

Council of Europe France
European Community (EC) France
North Atlantic Treaty Organization (NATO) France
Organization for Economic Cooperation and Development (OECD) France

France withdrew from NATO Military Command in 1966 but remains a member of the alliance

ECONOMIC INDICATORS: 1990

	France
GDP (US$ billions)	1,190.78
GNP per capita (US$)	19,490
Annual rate of growth of GDP, 1980–1990	2.2%
Manufacturing as % of GDP	21.0%
Central government spending as % of GNP	43.0%
Merchandise exports (US$ billions)	215.8
Merchandise imports (US$ billions)	233.8
% of GNP donated as development aid	0.79%

WELFARE INDICATORS

Infant mortality rate (per 1,000 live births)	
1965	22
1990	7
Daily food supply available (calories per capita, 1989)	3,465
Population per physician (1984)	320
Teacher-pupil ratio (primary school, 1989)	1 : 16

Andorra

Area 468 sq. km
(181 sq. mi.)
Population 47,000
Currency 1 French franc
(f) = 100 centimes
1 Spanish peseta
(Pts) = 100 centimos

Monaco

Area 1.95 sq. km
(0.75 sq. mi.)
Population 28,000
Currency 1 French franc
(f) = 100 centimes

- ■ capital city
- ● regional capital

France is divided into 22 metropolitan regions, each governed by an elected council, and its own president. The regions are responsible for their own economic planning. The regions are divided into 96 metropolitan departments, each with its own elected council. These councils are responsible for local social services.

HABITATS

Much of northern and western France consists of flat, fertile grassy plains or low, rolling hills. Much of this land is farmed. Wooded mountains rise in the east and south. The southern Massif Central with its spectacular river gorges contains largely poor soils.

LAND

Area 547,492 sq. km (211,272 sq. mi.)
Highest point Mont Blanc, 4,807 m (15,772 ft)
Lowest point sea level
Major features Pyrenees, Alps and Jura Mountains, Massif Central, Paris basin and basins of Garonne and Rhône

WATER

Longest river Loire, 1,020 km (630 mi.)
Largest basin Loire, 115,000 sq. km (44,377 sq. mi.)
Highest average flow Rhône, 1,500 cu. m/sec (53,000 cu. ft/sec)
Largest lake Geneva, 580 sq. km (224 sq. mi.)

NOTABLE THREATENED NON-ENDEMIC SPECIES

Mammals Long-fingered bat (Myotis capaccinii), Pond bat (Myotis dasycneme), Mouse-eared bat (Myotis myotis), Pyrenean desman (Galemys pyrenaicus), European mink (Mustela lutreola), Harbour porpoise (Phocoena phocoena), Fin whale (Balaenoptera physalus)
Birds Red kite (Milvus migrans), White-tailed sea eagle (Haliaeetus albicilla), corncrake (Crex crex), Little bustard (Tetrax tetrax), Audouin's gull (Larus audouinii)
Plants Aldrovanda vesiculosa; Angelica heterocarpa (Atlantic angelica); Caldensia parnassifolia; Hammarbya paludosa (bog orchid); Hormathophyllum pyrenaica (Pyrenean alyssum); Leucojum nicaeense; Lythrum thesioides; Primula allionii; Saxifraga florulenta; Viola hispida (raven violet)
Others Corsican swallowtail butterfly (Papilio hospiton), Quimper snail (Elona quimperiana), Shining macromia dragonfly (Macromia splendens), Longhorn beetle (Cerambyx cerdo)

CLIMATE

Western France is rainy, with cool summers and mild winters. The east is drier, with hotter summers and colder winters. The eastern mountains are snowy. The south has a Mediterranean climate, namely hot, dry summers and mild, moist winters.

TEMPERATURE AND PRECIPITATION

	Temperature °C (°F)		Altitude m (ft)
	January	July	
Brest	6 (43)	16 (61)	103 (338)
Paris	3 (37)	20 (68)	75 (173)
Strasbourg	0 (32)	19 (66)	154 (505)
Bordeaux	5 (41)	20 (68)	8 (26)
Marseille	6 (43)	23 (73)	4 (13)

	Precipitation mm (in)		
	January	July	Year
Brest	133 (5.2)	62 (2.4)	1,126 (44.3)
Paris	56 (2.2)	59 (2.3)	585 (23.0)
Strasbourg	39 (1.5)	77 (3.0)	607 (23.9)
Bordeaux	109 (4.3)	56 (2.2)	900 (35.4)
Marseille	43 (1.7)	11 (0.4)	546 (21.5)

NATURAL HAZARDS

Storms and floods, landslides, avalanches

ENVIRONMENTAL ISSUES

By 1992, about 75 percent of France's electricity was produced by the country's 55 nuclear power stations. Hence France is much less affected than most parts of Europe by the air pollution and acid rain caused by burning fossils fuels.

POPULATION AND WEALTH

Population (millions)	56.2
Population increase (annual population growth rate, % 1960–90)	0.7
Energy use (gigajoules/person)	109
Real purchasing power (US$/person)	13,590

ENVIRONMENTAL INDICATORS

CO_2 emissions (million tonnes carbon/annum)	120
Municipal waste (kg/person/annum)	272
Nuclear waste (cumulative tonnes heavy metal)	12,700
Artificial fertilizer use (kg/ha./annum)	299
Cars (per 1,000 population)	391
Access to safe drinking water (% population)	100

MAJOR ENVIRONMENTAL PROBLEMS AND SOURCES

Air pollution: locally high, in particular urban
Marine/coastal pollution: medium; sources: industrial, sewage, oil
Land pollution: medium; sources: industrial, nuclear
Waste disposal problems: domestic; industrial; nuclear
Population problems: tourism
Major events: Val d'Isere (1970), major avalanche; Amoco Cadiz (1978), oil tanker accident; Les Arcs (1981), landslide; le Grand Bornand (1987), major flood; Nîmes (1988), major flood; Protex plant, Tours (1988), fire at chemical plant

HABITATS

Northern and southwestern France are made up of plains and low hills. The uplands or massifs in the centre are divided from those in the east by the valley of the Rhône and Saône running north to south.

Physical zones
- mountains/barren land
- forest
- grassland

▲ mountain peak (metres)
climate station

ENVIRONMENTAL ISSUES

Tourism and industry have polluted coastal areas, while forest fires, avalanches and soil erosion are common hazards in the south. In recent years, the government has introduced many policies aimed at protecting the environment.

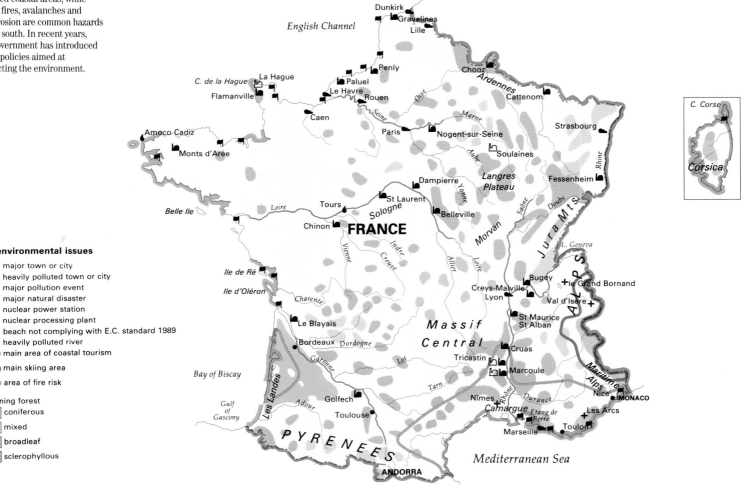

Key environmental issues

- • major town or city
- 🖋 heavily polluted town or city
- 🖋 major pollution event
- ➕ major natural disaster
- ⬛ nuclear power station
- ⬛ nuclear processing plant
- 🚩 beach not complying with E.C. standard 1989
- 〰 heavily polluted river
- main area of coastal tourism
- main skiing area
- area of fire risk

remaining forest
- coniferous
- mixed
- broadleaf
- sclerophyllous

English Channel

Dunkirk
Gravelines
Lille
Penly
Chooz
Ardennes
La Hague
C. de la Hague
Paluel
Cattenom
Flamanville
Le Havre
Rouen
Oise
Caen
Seine
Marne
Paris
Strasbourg
Amoco Cadiz
Nogent-sur-Seine
Monts d'Arée
Soulaines
Rhine
Dampierre
Yonne
Langres Plateau
Fessenheim
Belle Ile
Loire
Tours
St Laurent
Chinon
FRANCE
Sologne
Belleville
Morvan
Saône
Doubs
Jura Mts.
L. Geneva
Indre
Vienne
Creuse
Loire
Allier
Bugey
le Grand Bornand
Ile de Ré
Creys-Malville
Lyon
Val d'Isère
Ile d'Oléron
Charente
St Maurice
St Alban
A L P S
Le Blayais
Massif Central
Cruas
Bordeaux
Dordogne
Tricastin
Marcoule
Maritime Alps
Garonne
Lot
Nice
MONACO
Bay of Biscay
Golfech
Tarn
Nîmes
Rhône
Durance
Les Arcs
Les Landes
Toulouse
Camargue
Etang de Berre
Gulf of Gascony
Marseille
Toulon
Adour
P Y R E N E E S
Mediterranean Sea
ANDORRA

C. Corse
Corsica

CLIMATE

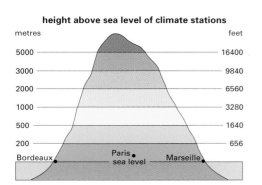

height above sea level of climate stations

metres		feet
5000		16400
3000		9840
2000		6560
1000		3280
500		1640
200		656

Bordeaux
Paris
sea level
Marseille

Bordeaux
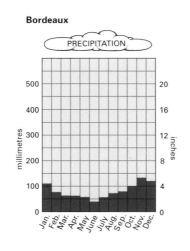
PRECIPITATION

Paris
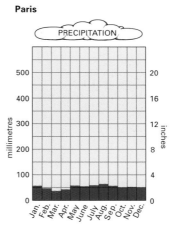
PRECIPITATION

Marseille
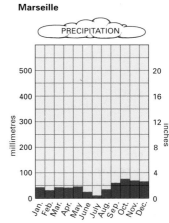
PRECIPITATION

Bordeaux
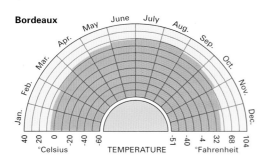

Paris
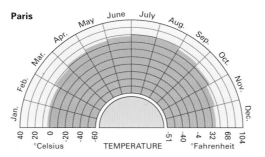

Marseille
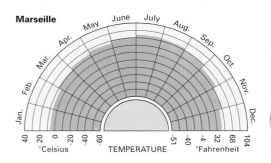

POPULATION

Before 1945, the movement of people from the countryside into urban areas was slower in France than in most parts of Europe. But urban areas now house about three-quarters of the people, largely in flats. Greater Paris is one of the world's largest conurbations.

POPULATION

Total population of region (millions)	56.2
Population density (persons per sq. km)	101.8
Population change (average annual percent 1960–1990)	
Urban	+1.3
Rural	-0.6

URBAN POPULATION

As percentage of total population	
1960	62.4
1990	74.1
Percentage in cities of more than 1 million	19.7

TEN LARGEST CITIES

	Population
Paris †	8,510,000
Lyon	1,170,000
Marseille	1,080,000
Lille	935,000
Bordeaux	628,000
Toulouse	523,000
Nantes	465,000
Nice	449,000
Toulon	410,000
Grenoble	392,000

† denotes capital city

INDUSTRY

France is a major manufacturing nation. Its traditional industries were originally built on local energy and mineral resources, mainly coal and iron. But it now has many dynamic high-tech industries, including aerospace and telecommunications.

INDUSTRIAL OUTPUT (US $ billion)

Total	Mining and Manufacturing	Average annual change since 1960
304.9	191.2	+3.1%

INDUSTRIAL WORKERS (millions)
(figures in brackets are percentages of total labour force)

Total	Mining and Manufacturing	Construction
5.7	4.1 (16.9%)	1.3 (5.3%)

MAJOR PRODUCTS (figures in brackets are percentages of world production)

Energy and minerals	Output	Change since 1960
Coal (mill tonnes)	13.5 (0.3%)	-76.8%
Oil (mill barrels)	27.1 (0.1%)	No data
Natural gas (billion cu. metres)	2.9 (0.1%)	-62%
Nuclear power (mill tonnes coal equiv.)	43.1 (13.3%)	N/A
Potash (mill tonnes)	1.6 (5.5%)	-24%
Bauxite (mill tonnes)	0.6 (0.7%)	-70.2%

Manufactures		
Cement (mill tonnes)	30.9 (2.8%)	+115%
Steel (mill tonnes)	18.9 (2.6%)	+9.4%
Cars (mill)	3.8 (8.0%)	+274.7%
Plastics and resins (mill tonnes)	3.4 (6.6%)	+57%
Fertilizers (mill tonnes)	5.8 (3.6%)	+57.6%
Vacuum cleaners (mill)	2.3 (6.4%)	+51.3%
Telecommunications equipment (US $ billion)	12.0 (12.9%)	No data

N/A means production had not begun in 1960

AGRICULTURE

France is a major producer of farm products. It is the second largest producer of wine and ranks among the world's top ten producers of milk, butter, meat, eggs, wheat, and barley. Only the United States exports more agricultural produce.

LAND (million hectares)

Total	Agricultural	Arable	Forest/woodland
55 (100%)	31 (57%)	18 (33%)	15 (27%)

FARMERS

1.4 million people employed in agriculture (6% of workforce)
12 hectares of arable land per person employed in agriculture

MAJOR CROPS

	Area mill ha.	Yield 100kg/ha.	Production mill tonnes	Change since 1963
Wheat	4.9	55.6 (238)	27.4 (5)	+119%
Barley	2.0	52.7 (226)	10.5 (6)	+59%
Maize	1.7	71.5 (197)	12.5 (3)	+352%
Sunflower seed	1.0	25.4 (178)	2.7 (13)	+10,979%
Grapes	1.0	88.7 (118)	9.2 (14)	−4%
Rapeseed	0.7	36.0 (253)	2.7 (12)	+1,255%

MAJOR LIVESTOCK

	Number mill	Production mill tonnes	Change since 1963
Cattle	22.8 (2)	—	+13%
Pigs	12.4 (1)	—	+38%
Sheep	10.6 (1)	—	+19%
Milk	—	28.6 (6)	+14%
Fish catch	—	0.8 (1)	—

FOOD SECURITY (cereal exports minus imports)

mill tonnes	% domestic production	% world trade
+26.0	49	12

Numbers in brackets are percentages of world total

POPULATION

Population density

city populations
(capital city is underlined)

◆	over 5,000,000
■	1,000,000–5,000,000
●	500,000–999,999
⊙	250,000–499,999
×	capital city less than 250,000

persons per square km	persons per square mi.
200	520
100	260
50	130
25	65

Areas of high population density occur around Paris and in the northern industrial areas. Migration to the south has created some high density areas in the Rhône valley and on the southeast coast.

INDUSTRY

The earliest industrial regions grew up in the northern mining districts. The recent decline in mining has led to the spread of industry to other areas.

Resources and industry

- ◆ industrial centre
- ○ major port
- • other town
- —— major road
- —— major railway

mineral resources and fossil fuels
- • iron and other ferroalloy metal ores
- • other metal ores
- ■ nonmetallic minerals

- bauxite
- coal
- iron ore
- lignite (brown coal)
- potash

AGRICULTURE

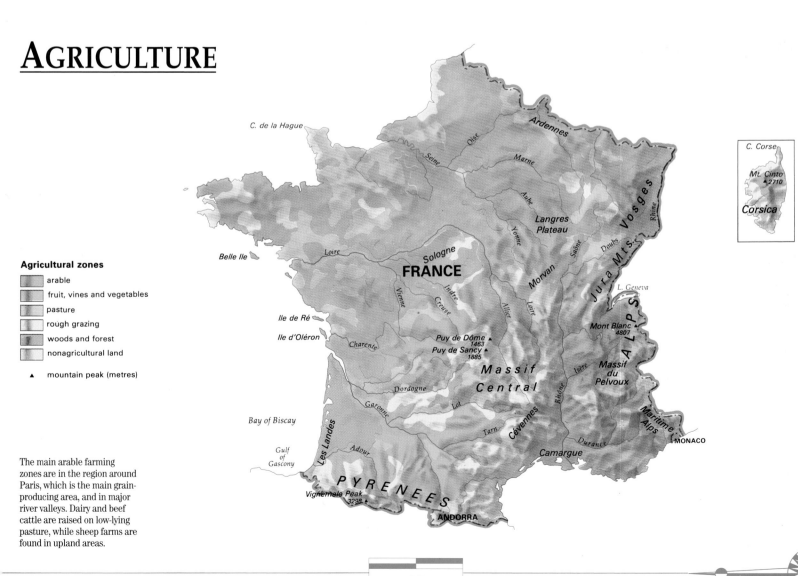

Agricultural zones

- arable
- fruit, vines and vegetables
- pasture
- rough grazing
- woods and forest
- nonagricultural land

- ▲ mountain peak (metres)

The main arable farming zones are in the region around Paris, which is the main grain-producing area, and in major river valleys. Dairy and beef cattle are raised on low-lying pasture, while sheep farms are found in upland areas.

Spain & Portugal

Spain, Portugal and the tiny British dependency of Gibraltar, which occupies a strategic position near the Strait of Gibraltar, form the Iberian Peninsula, isolated from the rest of Europe by the Pyrenees.

Much of the peninsula is a high plateau, called the Meseta. The Meseta is bordered not only by the Pyrenees, but also by the Cantabrian Mountains in the northwest and the Sierra Nevada in the southeast. Because of its altitude, the climate on the Meseta is severe, with hot summers and bitterly cold winters. The Meseta is arid and parts of the southeast are semidesert. Lowland Portugal's climate is moderated by moist Atlantic winds. Other lowlands include the Ebro and Guadalquivir river valleys in Spain.

From early times, Iberia was invaded by waves of colonizers, including Celts, Phoenicians, Greeks, Carthaginians, Romans and Visigoths, each of whom left their imprint on Iberian culture. The last invaders were the Moors (Muslim Arabs), who entered the peninsula in the year 711. Their last bastion, the Alhambra palace in Granada, did not fall until 1492, the year Columbus sailed from Spain.

Although Spain and Portugal were both leaders in terms of world exploration, both countries were, by the early 20th century, among Europe's poorest. Today, as members of the European Community, their economies have been expanding quickly and Spain, especially, is growing rapidly. Tourism plays a major part in the economies of both countries.

The Iberian Peninsula occupies the southwestern corner of Europe. Separated from North Africa by the Strait of Gibraltar, Iberia often seems to visitors to be almost as much African as European. Spain also includes the Balearic Islands in the Mediterranean and the Canary Islands in the Atlantic. Portugal has two autonomous regions, the Azores in the North Atlantic and the Madeira Islands off the northwest coast of Africa.

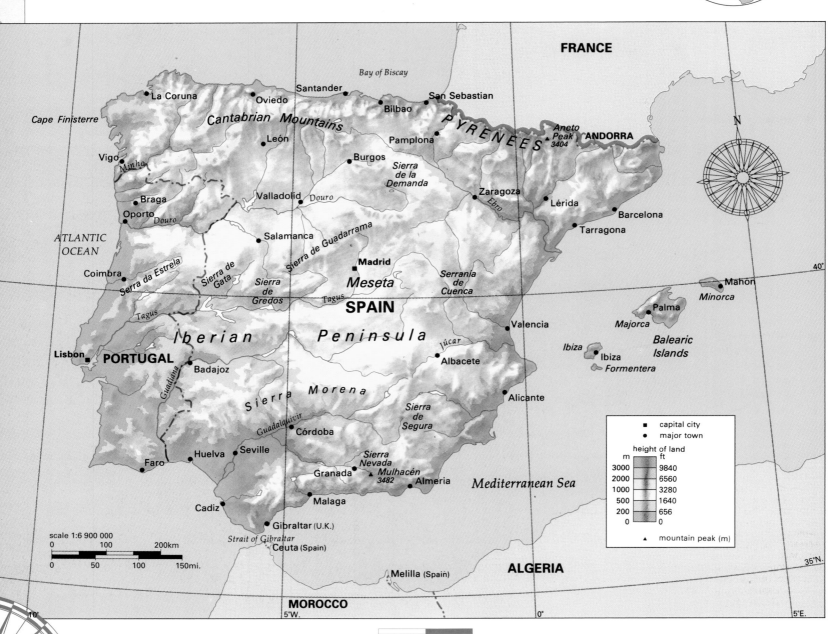

THE POLITICAL AND CULTURAL WORLD

Following the Civil War (1936–1939) Spain became a dictatorship under General Franco. After his death in 1975, the monarchy was restored and Spain became a parliamentary democracy. Between 1928 and 1974, Portugal was also a dictatorship. But after the overthrow of its military leaders, it became a democratic republic.

Spain claims Gibraltar, the world's smallest colony, but Britain justifies its control over the territory by arguing that the majority of Gibraltarians want to remain British. Despite the lack of agreement over sovereignty, cooperation over such matters as the shared use of Gibraltar's airport has increased.

Portugal

Area 92,389 sq. km (35, 672 sq. mi.)
Population 10,285,000
Capital Lisbon
Currency 1 escudo (Esc) = 100 centavos

Spain includes the Balearic Islands of Majorca, Minorca, Ibiza and Formentera. Portugal includes the islands of the Azores and Madeira in the Atlantic Ocean. Both Spain and Portugal are now democracies; Spain was governed by General Franco until 1973 and Portugal by the dictator Salazar until 1968. Spain's head of state is King Juan Carlos who came to the throne in 1975.

COUNTRIES IN THE REGION
Portugal, Spain

Island territories Azores, Madeira (Portugal); Balearic Islands, Canary Islands (Spain)
Territories outside the region Ceuta and Melilla (Spain); Macao (Portugal)

LAND
Highest point on mainland, Mulhacen, 3,482 m (11,424 ft); Pico de Teide on Tenerife, Canary Islands, 3,718 m (12,195 ft)
Lowest point sea level
Major features Meseta plateau in centre, Cantabrian Mountains and Pyrenees in north, Sierra Nevada in south

WATER
Longest river Tagus, 1,010 km (630 mi.)
Largest basin Douro, 98,000 sq. km (38,000 sq. mi.)
Highest average flow Douro, 312 cu. m/sec (11,000 cu. ft/sec)

CLIMATE

	Temperature °C (°F)		Altitude
	January	July	m (ft)
Oporto	9 (48)	20 (68)	95 (311)
Lisbon	11 (52)	22 (72)	77 (252)
Santander	9 (48)	19 (66)	66 (216)
Seville	10 (50)	28 (82)	9 (29)
Ibiza	11 (52)	24 (75)	7 (23)

	Precipitation mm (in)		
	January	July	Year
Oporto	159 (6.3)	20 (0.8)	1,150 (45.3)
Lisbon	111 (4.4)	3 (0.1)	708 (27.9)
Santander	119 (4.6)	54 (2.1)	1,208 (47.6)
Seville	66 (2.6)	1 (0.04)	559 (22.0)
Ibiza	42 (1.7)	5 (0.2)	444 (17.5)

LANGUAGE
Countries with one official language (Portuguese) Portugal; (Spanish) Spain

Local minority languages spoken in Spain are Basque, Catalan and Galician

RELIGION
Portugal Roman Catholic (94%), nonreligious (3.8%)
Spain Roman Catholic (97%), nonreligious and atheist (2.6%), Protestant (0.4%)

STYLES OF GOVERNMENT
Republic Portugal
Monarchy Spain
Multiparty states Portugal, Spain
One-chamber assembly Portugal
Two-chamber assembly Spain

ECONOMIC INDICATORS: 1990

	Spain	Portugal
GDP (US$ billions)	421.24	56.82
GNP per capita (US$)	11,020	4,900
Annual rate of growth of GDP, 1980–1990	3.1%	2.7%
Manufacturing as % of GDP	18.0%	9.0%
Central government spending as % of GNP	34.0%	43.0%
Merchandise exports (US$ billions)	56.3	16.3
Merchandise imports (US$ billions)	89.0	23.0
% of GNP donated as development aid	n/a	–

WELFARE INDICATORS
Infant mortality rate (per 1,000 live births)

1965	38	65
1990	8	12
Daily food supply available (calories per capita, 1989)	3,572	3,495
Population per physician (1984)	320	140
Teacher-pupil ratio (primary school, 1989)	1 : 25	1 : 17

■ capital city

Madrid

SPAIN

PORTUGAL

•Lisbon

Balearic Islands

Minorca

Majorca

Ibiza

Formentera

•Gibraltar (U.K.)

Area 504,750 sq. km (194,885 sq. mi.)
Population 39,187,000
Capital Madrid
Currency 1 peseta (Pta) = 100 centimos

Spain

ENVIRONMENTAL ISSUES

The Iberian Peninsula is one of the fastest changing parts of Europe, with new investment paying for rapid development. Tourism has led to the destruction of many coastal wildlife habitats, while the growth of cities has led to serious air and water pollution.

POPULATION AND WEALTH

	Portugal	Spain
Population (millions)	10.3	39.2
Population increase (annual population growth rate, % 1960–90)	0.5	0.8
Energy use (gigajoules/person)	39	62
Real purchasing power (US$/person)	4,190	8,250

ENVIRONMENTAL INDICATORS

CO$_2$ emissions (million tonnes carbon/annum)	17	73
Municipal waste (kg/person/annum)	221	275
Nuclear waste (cumulative tonnes heavy metal)	0	2,800
Artificial fertilizer use (kg/ha./annum)	103	99
Cars (per 1,000 population)	125	78
Access to safe drinking water (% population)	95	100

MAJOR ENVIRONMENTAL PROBLEMS AND SOURCES

Air pollution: urban high
Marine/coastal pollution: medium; *sources*: industrial, agricultural, sewage, oil
Land degradation: soil erosion; salinization; habitat destruction; *causes*: agriculture, industry, population pressure
Population problems: tourism
Major event: San Carlos de la Rapita (1978), transportation accident

POPULATION

Industrialization occurred later in the Iberian Peninsula than in other parts of Europe. But the industrial cities have grown steadily in the 20th century. Tourism has led to the development of an urban corridor around the coasts, while the interior is thinly populated.

POPULATION

Total population of region (millions)	49.6
Population density (persons per sq. km)	95.0
Population change (average annual percent 1960–1990)	
Urban	+1.9
Rural	-1.0

URBAN POPULATION

As percentage of total population	
1960	41.6
1990	59.0
Percentage in cities of more than 1 million	13.1

TEN LARGEST CITIES

	Country	Population
Madrid †	Spain	3,101,000
Barcelona	Spain	1,704,000
Lisbon†	Portugal	1,612,000
Oporto	Portugal	1,315,000
Valencia	Spain	732,000
Seville	Spain	655,000
Zaragoza	Spain	575,000
Malaga	Spain	566,000
Bilbao	Spain	382,000
Las Palmas	Spain	358,000

† denotes capital city

AGRICULTURE

Despite the growing importance of manufacturing, agriculture remains important in both Spain and Portugal. The main agricultural activities are the cultivation of citrus fruits, olives, vines and wheat, together with livestock rearing in the less fertile areas.

LAND (million hectares)

Total	Agricultural	Arable	Forest/woodland
59 (100%)	34 (58%)	18 (30%)	19 (33%)

FARMERS

2.5 million employed in agriculture (13%) of workforce
7 hectares of arable land per person employed in agriculture

MAJOR CROPS

	Area mill ha.	Yield 100kg/ha.	Production mill tonnes	Change since 1963
Barley	4.5	22.1 (95)	9.9 (5)	+391%
Wheat	2.5	24.9 (106)	6.3 (1)	+28%
Maize	0.8	52.4 (144)	4.2 (1)	+145%
Grapes	1.8	44.1 (59)	7.8 (12)	+29%
Oranges	—	—	2.5 (6)	+46%
Vegetables	—	—	2.5 (6)	+46%
Other fruit	—	—	5.9 (3)	+144%

MAJOR LIVESTOCK

	Number mill	Production mill tonnes	Change since 1963
Sheep/goats	26.4 (2)	—	−10%
Pigs	18.7 (2)	—	+156%
Milk	—	7.0 (2)	+93%
Fish catch	—	1.8 (2)	—

FOOD SECURITY (cereal exports minus imports)

mill tonnes	% domestic production	% world trade
−3.5	17	2

Numbers in brackets are percentages of world total

ENVIRONMENTAL ISSUES

Key environmental issues

- major town or city
- heavily polluted town or city
- major pollution event
- heavily polluted river
- main area of coastal tourism

soil degradation
- severe
- high
- moderate
- low

Soil erosion caused by farming, combined with drought and deforestation, has affected much of the Iberian Peninsula. Public debate about green issues and conservation is increasing.

POPULATION

Population density

city populations
(capital city is underlined)

- ■ 1,000,000–5,000,000
- ● 500,000–999,999
- ◉ 250,000–499,999

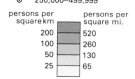

persons per square km.	persons per square mi.
200	520
100	260
50	130
25	65

The areas of high population density in the Iberian Peninsula are mainly situated along the coasts, especially around industrial cities such as Barcelona, Bilbao, Lisbon, Malaga, and Valencia.

AGRICULTURE

Agricultural zones

- arable
- fruit, vines and vegetables
- rough grazing
- woods and forest
- nonagricultural land

- ▲ mountain peak (metres)

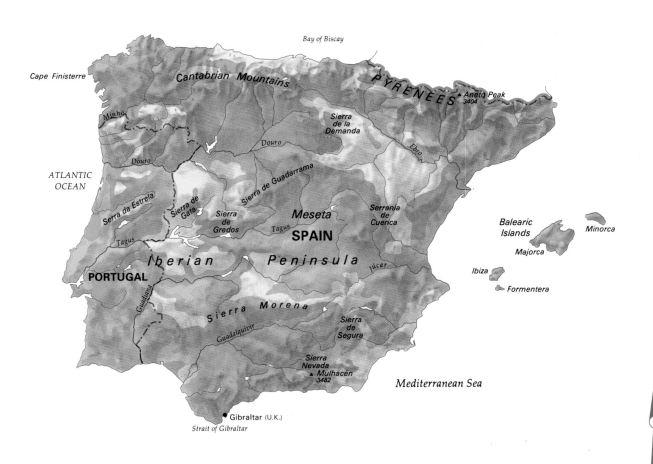

Fruit and vegetables are grown on the coasts, while dry parts of the Meseta are used to graze sheep. Many river valleys in the interior are cultivated.

ITALY & GREECE

Italy and Greece occupy a region where the Earth's crust is unstable; there are frequent earthquakes and spectacular volcanic eruptions, especially in southern Italy. The snow-capped Alps in northern Italy were raised up as the result of a collision between the northward-moving African plate and the Eurasian plate.

About two-fifths of the land is mountainous, the Po valley being the most extensive lowland.

The coastlands, with their hot, dry summers and mild, moist winters, are tourist magnets for north Europeans. But the mountains of southern Italy and Greece can be bitterly cold and snowy in the winter months.

The ancient ruins of Greece and Italy are testimony to two major civilizations, whose art, philosophy and politics lie at the heart of European culture.

Italy and Greece are two peninsulas that jut into the Mediterranean Sea. Both countries include many islands. Around 440 islands make up about one-fifth of Greece's area.

Malta is an island republic south of Sicily. Cyprus is another island republic in the east.

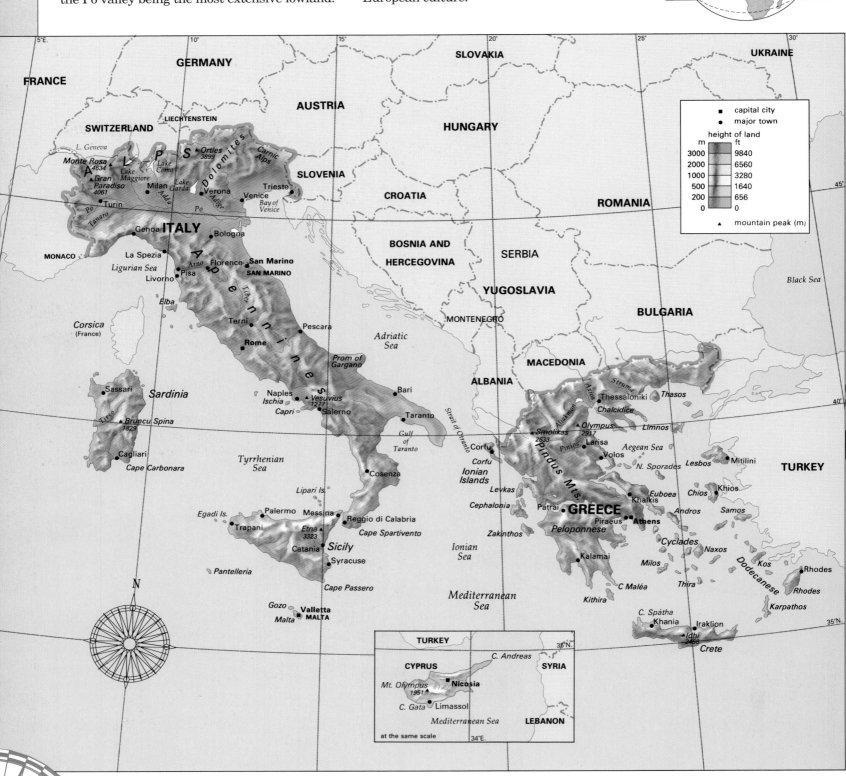

		capital city
		major town
	height of land	
m		ft
3000		9840
2000		6560
1000		3280
500		1640
200		656
0		0
	▲	mountain peak (m)

THE POLITICAL AND CULTURAL WORLD

Italy and Greece have both undergone periods of instability and dictatorship in the 20th century, though today they are democratic republics.

Greece has a long-standing dispute with Turkey over Cyprus, a Greek-speaking island with a Turkish minority. In 1974 Greece's military regime was implicated in moves to unite Cyprus, which had been independent since 1960, with Greece. Turkey invaded northern Cyprus and set up the Turkish Republic of Northern Cyprus, a state which is recognized only by Turkey.

Cyprus
Area 9,251 sq. km
(3,572 sq. mi.)
Population 701,000
Capital Nicosia
Currency 1 Cyprus pound
(C£) = 100 cents
[1 Turkish lira (LT) = 100 kurush]

Greece
Area 131,957 sq. km
(50,949 sq. mi.)
Population 10,047,000
Capital Athens
Currency 1 drachma
(Dr) = 100 lepta

■ capital city

COUNTRIES IN THE REGION
Cyprus, Greece, Italy, Malta, San Marino, Vatican City

Island territories Aegean Islands, Crete, Ionian Islands, (Greece); Elba, Capri, Ischia, Lipari Islands, Sardinia, Sicily (Italy)

LAND
Highest point Monte Rosa, 4,634 m (15,203 ft)
Lowest point sea level
Major features Alps, Apennines, Pindus Mountains, Po valley, islands including Sardinia, Crete, Greek archipelago and Cyprus

WATER
Longest river Po, 620 km (380 mi.)
Largest basin Po, 75,000 sq. km (29,000 sq. mi.)
Highest average flow Po, 1,540 cu. m/sec (54,000 cu. ft/sec)
Largest lake Garda, 370 sq. km (140 sq. mi.)

CLIMATE

	Temperature °C (°F)		Altitude
	January	July	m (ft)
Genoa	8 (46)	24 (75)	21 (69)
Venice	4 (39)	23 (73)	1 (3)
Messina	11 (52)	26 (79)	54 (117)
Salonika	6 (42)	27 (81)	25 (82)
Athens	9 (48)	28 (82)	107 (351)

	Precipitation mm (in)		
	January	July	Year
Genoa	79 (3.1)	40 (1.6)	1,270 (50)
Venice	37 (1.4)	69 (2.7)	854 (33.6)
Messina	146 (5.7)	19 (0.7)	974 (38.3)
Salonika	45 (1.7)	23 (0.9)	339 (13.3)
Athens	63 (2.4)	6 (0.2)	339 (13.3)

LANGUAGE
Countries with one official language (Greek) Greece; (Italian) Italy, San Marino
Countries with two official languages (English, Maltese) Malta; (Greek, Turkish) Cyprus; (Italian, Latin) Vatican City

Other languages spoken in the region include Albanian, Macedonian and Turkish (Greece); Albanian, Catalan, French, German, Greek, Ladin, Sard and Slovene (Italy)

Italy
Area 301,277 sq. km
(116,324 sq. mi.)
Population 57,061,000
Capital Rome
Currency 1 lira
(Lit) = 100 centesimi

Malta
Area 316 sq. km
(122 sq. mi.)
Population 353,000
Capital Valletta
Currency 1 Maltese lira
(Lm) = 100 cents = 1,000 mils

RELIGION
Cyprus Greek Orthodox (80%), Muslim (19%)
Greece Greek Orthodox (97.6%), Muslim (1.5%), other Christian (0.5%)
Italy Roman Catholic (83.2%), nonreligious and atheist (16.2%)
Malta Roman Catholic (97.3%), Anglican (1.2%), other (1.5%)
San Marino Roman Catholic (95%), nonreligious (3%)
Vatican City Roman Catholic (100%)

STYLES OF GOVERNMENT
Republics Cyprus, Greece, Italy, Malta, San Marino
City state Vatican City
Multiparty states Cyprus, Greece, Italy, Malta, San Marino
State without parties Vatican City
One-chamber assembly Cyprus, Greece, Malta, San Marino
Two-chamber assembly Italy

ECONOMIC INDICATORS: 1990

	Italy	Greece
GDP (US$ billions)	57.94	1,090.75
GNP per capita (US$)	5,990	16,830
Annual rate of growth of GDP, 1980–1990	1.8%	2.4%
Manufacturing as % of GDP	14.0%	23.0%
Central government spending as % of GNP	36.0%	49.0%
Merchandise exports (US$ billions)	6.4	182.2
Merchandise imports (US$ billions)	18.7	193.6
% of GNP donated as development aid	–	0.32%

WELFARE INDICATORS

Infant mortality rate (per 1,000 live births)		
1965	34	36
1990	11	9
Daily food supply available (calories per capita, 1989)	3,825	3,216
Population per physician (1984)	350	230
Teacher-pupil ratio (primary school, 1989)	1 : 22	1 : 12

San Marino
Area 61 sq. km
(24 sq. mi.)
Population 23,000
Capital San Marino
Currency 1 Italian lira
(Lit) = 100 centesimi

Vatican City
Area 0.44 sq. km
(0.17 sq. mi.)
Population 1,000
Currency 1 Vatican lira
(VL) = 1 Italian lira = 100 centesimi

Both Italy and Greece are republics that once had monarchies and abolished them. Both are highly centralized states. Malta has been a democratic republic within the British Commonwealth since 1964. San Marino claims to be the world's oldest republic.

ENVIRONMENTAL ISSUES

Deforestation in the past has caused extensive soil erosion and has increased the frequency of floods and avalanches. The growth of industrial areas in northern Italy and around Athens in Greece has caused large-scale air, river and sea pollution.

POPULATION AND WEALTH

	Greece	Italy	Malta
Population (millions)	10	57.1	0.4
Population increase (annual population growth rate, % 1960–90)	0.6	0.4	0.2
Energy use (gigajoules/person)	72	105	52
Real purchasing power (US$/person)	6,440	13,000	7,490

ENVIRONMENTAL INDICATORS

	Greece	Italy	Malta
CO$_2$ emissions (million tonnes carbon/annum)	20	120	0.2
Municipal waste (kg/person/annum)	259	263	n/a
Nuclear waste (cumulative tonnes heavy metal)	0	1,400	0
Artificial fertilizer use (kg/ha./annum)	171	190	46
Cars (per 1,000 population)	143	398	n/a
Access to safe drinking water (% population)	97	100	100

MAJOR ENVIRONMENTAL PROBLEMS AND SOURCES

Air pollution: locally high, in particular urban; acid rain prevalent; high greenhouse gas emissions
River pollution: medium; *sources*: agricultural, sewage
Marine/coastal pollution: medium/high; *sources*: industrial, agricultural, sewage, oil
Land degradation: *types*: soil erosion; *causes*: agriculture, industry, population pressure

POPULATION

During the Renaissance in the 15th–16th centuries, Italy had many wealthy cities which were centres of art and learning. But the population remained largely rural in both Italy and Greece until recent times, when industrial cities began to develop.

POPULATION

Total population of region (millions)	67.7
Population density (persons per sq. km)	161.1
Population change (average annual percent 1960–1990)	
Urban	+1.1
Rural	-0.5

URBAN POPULATION

As percentage of total population	
1960	55.2
1990	66.3
Percentage in cities of more than 1 million	14.9

TEN LARGEST CITIES

	Country	Population
Athens†	Greece	3,027,000
Rome †	Italy	2,817,000
Milan	Italy	1,464,000
Naples	Italy	1,203,000
Turin	Italy	1,012,000
Salonika	Greece	872,000
Palermo	Italy	731,000
Genoa	Italy	715,000
Bologna	Italy	422,000
Florence	Italy	417,000

† denotes capital city

AGRICULTURE

Mountainous terrain, summer droughts and poor soils have created many problems for farmers. To overcome these difficulties and achieve high agricultural yields, the people have terraced the slopes, drained marshes and built irrigation systems.

LAND (million hectares)

Total	Agricultural	Arable	Forest/woodland
43 (100%)	26 (61%)	12 (28%)	9 (22%)

FARMERS

2.9 million employed in agriculture (11% of workforce)
4 hectares of arable land per person employed in agriculture

MAJOR CROPS

	Area mill ha.	Yield 100kg/ha.	Production mill tonnes	Change since 1963
Wheat	4.0	29.2 (125)	11.6 (2)	+9%
Grapes	1.3	101.2 (135)	13.1 (20)	‡15%
Barley	0.7	32.7 (146)	2.4 (1)	+292%
Sugar beet	0.3	522.6 (151)	17.4 (6)	+112%
Vegetables	—	—	18.0 (4)	+58%
Peaches	—	—	2.1 (27)	+62%
Other fruit	—	—	8.2 (3)	+17%

MAJOR LIVESTOCK

	Number mill	Production mill tonnes	Change since 1963
Sheep/goats	27.9 (2)	—	+21%
Pigs	10.8 (1)	—	+101%
Cattle	9.7 (1)	—	-6%
Milk	—	11.6 (3)	+19%
Fish catch	—	0.7 (1)	—

Numbers in brackets are percentages of world total

ENVIRONMENTAL ISSUES

Tourism has caused much damage along the coasts and inland at ski resorts. These and other developments, such as the drainage of wetlands, have greatly reduced the area of wilderness in the region.

Key environmental issues

- • major town or city
- • heavily polluted town or city
- major pollution event
- + major natural disaster
- beach not complying with E.C. standard 1989
- heavily polluted river
- main area of coastal tourism
- main skiing area

remaining forest
- coniferous
- mixed
- broadleaf
- sclerophyllous

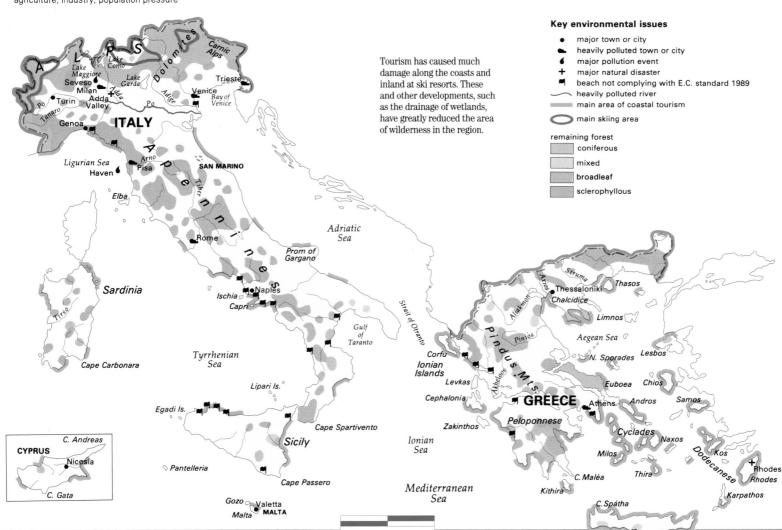

POPULATION

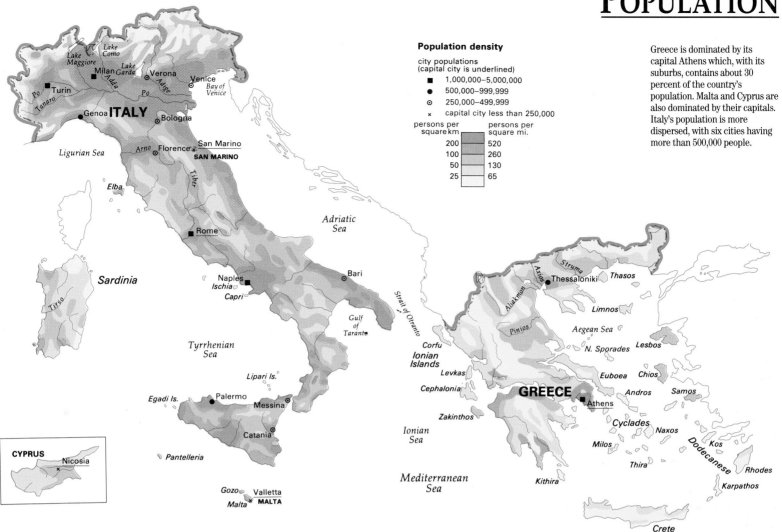

Population density

city populations
(capital city is underlined)

- ■ 1,000,000–5,000,000
- ● 500,000–999,999
- ◉ 250,000–499,999
- × capital city less than 250,000

persons per square km.	persons per square mi.
200	520
100	260
50	130
25	65

Greece is dominated by its capital Athens which, with its suburbs, contains about 30 percent of the country's population. Malta and Cyprus are also dominated by their capitals. Italy's population is more dispersed, with six cities having more than 500,000 people.

AGRICULTURE

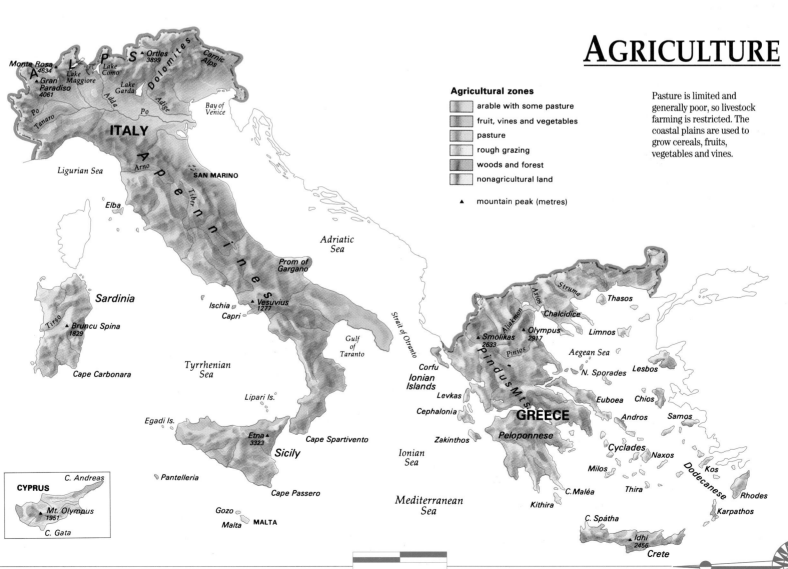

Agricultural zones

- arable with some pasture
- fruit, vines and vegetables
- pasture
- rough grazing
- woods and forest
- nonagricultural land

- ▲ mountain peak (metres)

Pasture is limited and generally poor, so livestock farming is restricted. The coastal plains are used to grow cereals, fruits, vegetables and vines.

Central Europe & the Low Countries

The Low Countries – Belgium, Luxembourg and the Netherlands – together with northern Germany, are part of the North European Plain, and are largely flat. The land contrasts with the mountainous Alpine scenery in the south, which includes Switzerland, Liechtenstein and Austria.

Most people speak Germanic languages, notably Dutch and German, though French is spoken in Belgium and Switzerland.

Highly efficient farms are found throughout the region. Manufacturing is the main source of wealth, and products include chemicals, electrical and electronic goods, and vehicles.

The Low Countries and their neighbours in Central Europe form part of the world's temperate zone. In the Low Countries, large areas are below sea level — much of the Netherlands has been reclaimed from the sea. The Alps in the south contain majestic peaks and sparkling lakes.

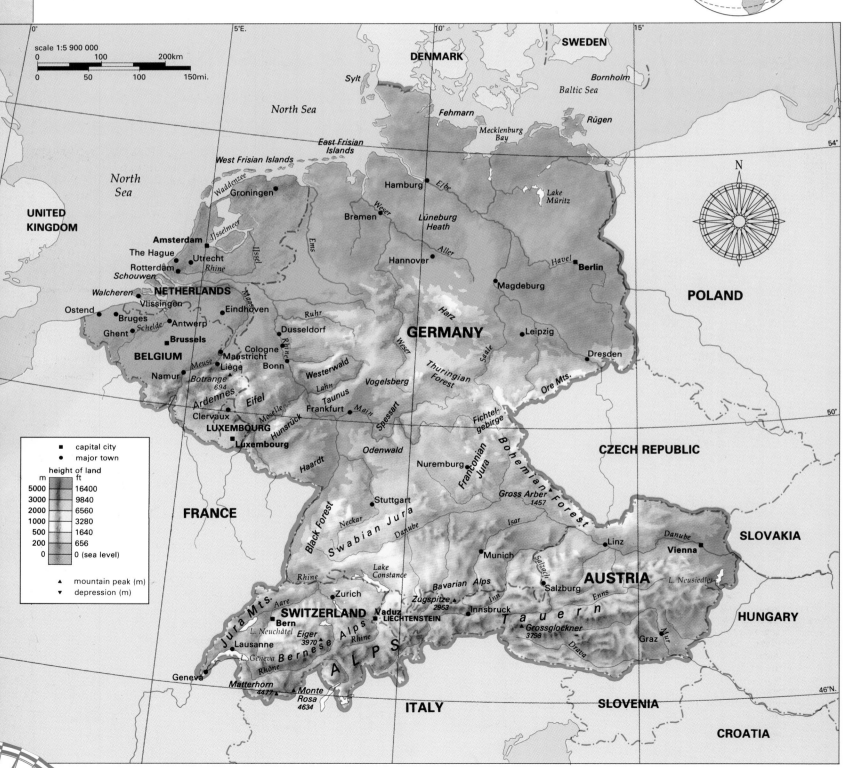

scale 1:5 900 000

■	capital city	
●	major town	

height of land

m	ft
5000	16400
3000	9840
2000	6560
1000	3280
500	1640
200	656
0	0 (sea level)

▲ mountain peak (m)
▼ depression (m)

THE POLITICAL AND CULTURAL WORLD

Of the seven countries in the region, four are parliamentary democracies with monarchs as heads of state. They are the kingdoms of Belgium and the Netherlands, the Grand Duchy of Luxembourg and the Principality of Liechtenstein. The other three countries – Austria, Germany and Switzerland – are federal republics.

After World War II, Central Europe played an important part in the cold war. But after the collapse of communism in Eastern Europe in 1990, West and East Germany, divided since 1945, were reunified politically. The task of economic integration, however, proved to be more costly than many Germans had expected.

COUNTRIES IN THE REGION
Austria, Belgium, Germany, Liechtenstein, Luxembourg, Netherlands, Switzerland

Territories outside the region
Aruba, Netherlands Antilles (Netherlands)

LANGUAGE
Countries with one official language (Dutch) Netherlands; (German) Austria, Germany, Liechtenstein
Countries with two official languages (French, German) Luxembourg
Countries with three official languages (Dutch, French, German) Belgium; (French, German, Italian) Switzerland

RELIGION
Austria Roman Catholic (85%), Protestant (6%), nonreligious (9%)
Belgium Roman Catholic (90%), nonreligious and atheist (8%), Muslim (1.1%), Protestant (0.4%)
Germany Protestant (47%), Roman Catholic (36%), other and nonaffiliated (11.3%), nonreligious (3.6%), Muslim (2.1%)
Luxembourg Roman Catholic (93%), nonreligious and atheist (5%), Protestant (1%)
Netherlands Roman Catholic (36.2%), nonreligious (34.7%), Protestant (26.4%), Hindu (1%), Muslim (1%)
Switzerland Roman Catholic (49%), Protestant (48%)

STYLES OF GOVERNMENT
Republics Austria, Germany, Switzerland
Monarchies Belgium, Liechtenstein, Luxembourg, Netherlands
Federal states Austria, Germany, Switzerland
Multiparty states Austria, Belgium, Germany, Liechtenstein, Luxembourg, Netherlands, Switzerland
One-chamber assembly Liechtenstein
Two-chamber assembly Austria, Belgium, Germany, Netherlands, Switzerland

ECONOMIC INDICATORS

	Belgium	Netherlands
GDP (US$ billions)	192.39	279.15
GNP per capita (US$)	15,540	17,320
Annual rate of growth of GDP, 1980–1990	2.0%	1.9%
Manufacturing as % of GDP	23.0%	20%
Central government spending as % of GNP	49.0%	53.0%
Merchandise exports (US$ billions)	118.1	131.4
Merchandise imports (US$ billions)	119.8	125.9
% of GNP donated as development aid	0.45%	0.94%

WELFARE INDICATORS

Infant mortality rate (per 1,000 live births)		
1965	24	14
1990	8	7
Daily food supply available (calories per capita, 1989)	3,679	3,151
Population per physician (1984)	330	450
Teacher-pupil ratio (primary school, 1989)	1 : 10	1 : 17

Austria
Area 83,857 sq. km (32,377 sq. mi.)
Population 7,583,000
Currency 1 Schilling (S) = 100 Groschen

Belgium
Area 30,518 sq. km (11,783 sq. mi.)
Population 9,845,000
Currency 1 Belgian franc (BF) = 100 centimes

■ capital city

Germany
Area 356,954 sq. km (137,820 sq. mi.)
Population 77,573,000
Currency 1 Deutschmark (DM) = 100 Pfennig

Liechtenstein
Area 160 sq. km (62 sq. mi.)
Population 28,000
Currency 1 Swiss franc (SwF) = 100 centimes

Luxembourg
Area 2,486 sq. km (999 sq. mi.)
Population 373,000
Currency 1 Luxembourg franc (LuxF) = 100 centimes

Netherlands
Area 41,863 sq. km (16,163 sq. mi.)
Population 14,951,000
Currency 1 Netherlands guilder (f) = 100 cents

Switzerland
Area 41,293 sq. km (15,943 sq. mi.)
Population 6,609,000
Currency 1 Swiss franc (SwF) = 100 centimes

Belgium, Luxembourg, the Netherlands and former West Germany were founder members in the 1950s of what is now the European Community. Both Switzerland and Leichtenstein were politically neutral during both world wars, while Austria was allied to Germany. After its defeat in 1945, Germany was divided and its eastern part came under Russian influence. The two parts of the country were reunited in October 1990.

HABITATS

There is a sharp contrast between the flat reclaimed and cultivated polders of the Netherlands and the rugged Alps, which contain some of Europe's finest scenery. Several rivers, including the Rhine, flow through scenic valleys, with forested mountains on each side.

LAND

Area 448,014 sq. km (172,934 sq. mi.)
Highest point Monte Rosa, 4,634 m (15,204 ft)
Lowest point in west Netherlands, −7 m (−22 ft)
Major features High Alps, Bohemian Forest, Black Forest, very low-lying areas in north Low Countries, Rhine rift valley

WATER

Longest river Rhine 1,320 km (820 mi.), Rhine basin 252,000 sq. km (97,000 sq. mi), also the upper part of the Danube.
Highest average flow Rhine, 2,490 cu. m/sec (88,000 cu. ft/sec)
Largest lake IJsselmeer, 1,210 sq. km (467 sq.mi.)

NOTABLE THREATENED NON-ENDEMIC SPECIES

Mammals Pond bat (*Myotis dasycneme*), Mouse-eared bat (*Myotis myotis*), Harbour porpoise (*Phocoena phocoena*)
Birds Red kite (*Milvus milvus*), White-tailed sea eagle (*Haliaeetus albicilla*), corncrake (*Crex crex*), Great bustard (*Otis tarda*), Aquatic warbler (*Acrocephalus paludicola*), Lesser kestrel (*Falco naumanni*), corncrake (*Crex crex*)
Plants *Agrostemma githago* (corncockle); *Echinodorus repens*; *Eriophorum gracile*; *Halimione pedunculata*; *Hammarbya paludosa* (bog orchid); *Luronium natans*; *Myosotis rehsteineri* (Lake Constance forget-me-not); *Oenanthe conioides* (Elb water dropwort); *Petroselinum segetum*; *Pilularia globulifera* (pillwort); *Salvinia natans*; *Spiranthes spiralis* (spiral orchid)

CLIMATE

The west of the region has a temperate, wet climate, with moderately warm summers and cool, mild winters. Eastern Germany has hotter summers and colder winters. Austria and Switzerland have permanently snow-capped mountains.

TEMPERATURE AND PRECIPITATION

	Temperature °C (°F) January	July	Altitude m (ft)
Hamburg	0 (32)	17 (63)	14 (46)
Zurich	−1 (30)	18 (64)	569 (1,886)
Lugano	2 (36)	21 (70)	276 (905)
Munich	−2 (28)	18 (64)	528 (1,732)
Vienna	−1 (30)	20 (68)	212 (695)
Ostend	3 (37)	16 (61)	10 (33)

	Precipitation mm (in) January	July	Year
Hamburg	57 (2.2)	84 (3.3)	720 (28.3)
Zurich	75 (2.9)	143 (5.6)	1,137 (44.8)
Lugano	63 (2.5)	185 (7.3)	1,744 (68.7)
Munich	59 (2.3)	140 (5.5)	964 (38.0)
Vienna	40 (1.6)	83 (3.3)	660 (26.0)
Ostend	41 (1.6)	62 (2.4)	598 (23.5)

NATURAL HAZARDS

Avalanches and landslides in mountains

ENVIRONMENTAL ISSUES

The Low Countries are among the world's most densely populated areas and this has had a great impact on the land. Deforestation and acid rain have damaged the entire region and industrial pollution has greatly affected eastern Germany.

POPULATION AND WEALTH

	Belgium	Germany	Netherlands
Population (millions)	9.9	77.7	15
Population increase (annual population growth rate, % 1960–90)	0.2	0.2	0.9
Energy use (gigajoules/person)	163	396	199
Real purchasing power (US$/person)	13,010	14,620	12,680

ENVIRONMENTAL INDICATORS

CO_2 emissions (million tonnes carbon/annum)	25	222	43
Municipal waste (kg/person/annum)	313	317	449
Nuclear waste (cumulative tonnes heavy metal)	700	3,300	200
Artificial fertilizer use (kg/ha/annum)	510	758	688
Cars (per 1,000 population)	349	412	346
Access to safe drinking water (% population)	100	100	100

MAJOR ENVIRONMENTAL PROBLEMS AND SOURCES

Air pollution: generally high, urban very high; acid rain prevalent
River/lake pollution: high; *sources*: agricultural, industrial, sewage
Marine/coastal pollution: high; *sources*: industrial, agricultural, sewage, oil
Land pollution: high; *sources*: industrial, agricultural, urban/household, nuclear
Waste disposal problems: domestic; industrial; nuclear
Resource problems: land use competition; coastal flooding; water level control and flooding
Major event: Lekkerkerk (1980), toxic waste dump discovered; Sandoz near Basel (1987), chemical spill

Glaciation has left its mark on the land. Northern Germany is covered by moraine left behind by the Scandinavian glaciers. Glaciers continue to shape the land in the Alps.

HABITATS

Physical zones
- mountains/barren land
- forest
- grassland
- ▲ mountain peak (metres)
- ☀ climate station

ENVIRONMENTAL ISSUES

Farming and industrialization have badly damaged many natural habitats in the region. Much of the air pollution originates in Germany. Tourism has badly affected some popular areas.

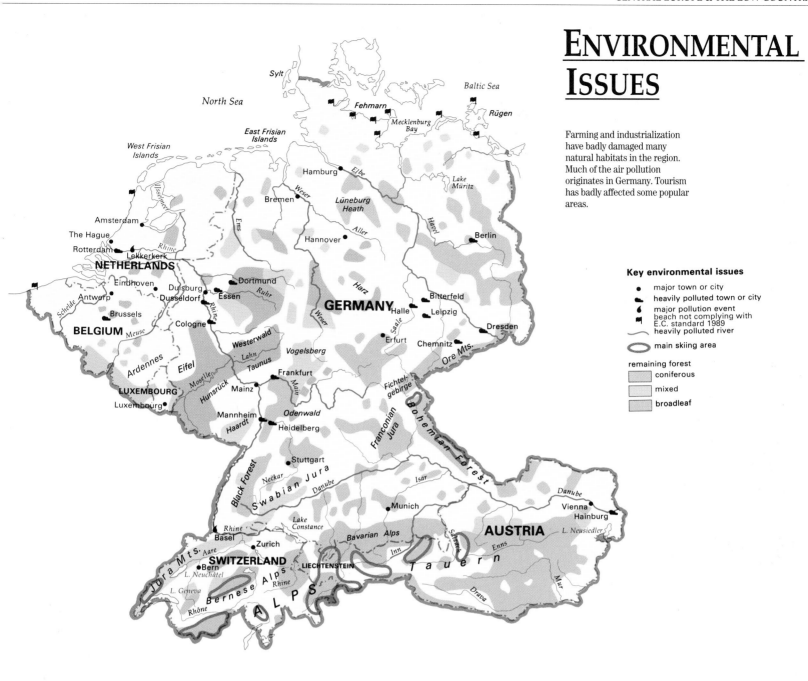

Key environmental issues
- major town or city
- heavily polluted town or city
- major pollution event
- beach not complying with E.C. standard 1989
- heavily polluted river
- main skiing area

remaining forest
- coniferous
- mixed
- broadleaf

CLIMATE

height above sea level of climate stations

Ostend
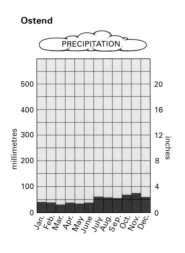

Lugano
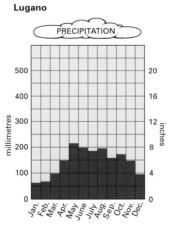

Munich
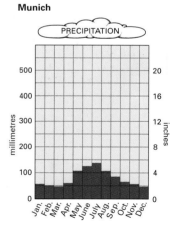

Ostend
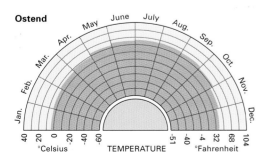

Lugano
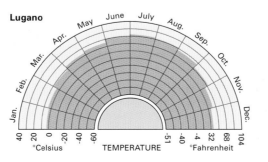

Munich
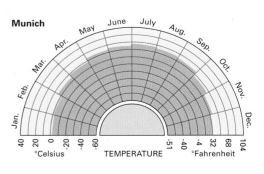

POPULATION

Industrialization led to a rapid increase in the region's population from the late 19th century. New cities grew up on coal or iron fields. Older cities, such as Berlin and Vienna, have also grown in the last 50 years. The Netherlands has towns on land reclaimed from the sea.

POPULATION

Total population of region (millions)	116.2
Population density (persons per sq. km)	276.1
Population change (average annual percent 1960–1990)	
Urban	+0.8
Rural	-1.2

URBAN POPULATION

As percentage of total population	
1960	81.8
1990	88.4
Percentage in cities of more than 1 million	4.1

TEN LARGEST CITIES

	Country	Population
Berlin †	Germany	3,301,000
Vienna †	Austria	2,044,000
Hamburg	Germany	1,594,000
Munich	Germany	1,189,000
Rotterdam	Netherlands	1,040,000
Amsterdam †	Netherlands	1,038,000
Brussels †	Belgium	976,000
Cologne	Germany	928,000
Zurich	Switzerland	839,000
The Hague	Netherlands	684,000

† denotes capital city

INDUSTRY

Germany is Europe's top industrial power. Its industries were based on local supplies of fuels and metals, but many raw materials are now imported. In some countries, such as Switzerland, much industry has been based on crafts, such as clock-making.

INDUSTRIAL OUTPUT (US $ billion)

Total	Mining	Manufacturing	Average annual change since 1960
882.0	56.9*	652.5**	+2.9%

* Figure relates to West Germany (pre-unification in 1990)
** Figure includes mining in Austria, East Germany (pre-unification in 1990) and Switzerland

MAJOR PRODUCTS (figures in brackets are percentages of world production)

Energy and minerals	Output	Change since 1960
Coal (mill tonnes)	498.0 (5.23%)	−83%
Natural gas (billion cu. metres)	76.2 (1.95%)	N/A
Nuclear power (mill tonnes coal equiv.)	15.2 (2.2%)	N/A

Manufactures		
Steel (mill tonnes)	58.0 (3.95%)	+9.7%
Cars (mill)	4.85 (10.2%)	+221%
Papermaking/printing machines (1,000)	299.7 (86.8%)	No data
Petroleum (mill tonnes)	78.5 (2.8%)	+95.9%
Plastics and resins (mill tonnes)	5.2 (10.3%)	+340%
Beer (mill hectolitres)	124.5 (12%)	+4%

N/A means production had not begun in 1960

AGRICULTURE

The farmers of the Low Countries produce some of the world's highest yields. Arable farming is important in northern and central Germany, but more than half of the land in Austria and three-quarters in Switzerland is too mountainous to be farmed.

LAND (million hectares)

Total	Agricultural	Arable	Forest/woodland
54 (100%)	28 (51.5%)	16 (27%)	16 (23%)

FARMERS

2.7 million people employed in agriculture (4% of workforce)
6 hectares of arable land per person employed in agriculture

MAJOR CROPS

Numbers in brackets are percentages of world average yield and total world production

	Area mill ha	Yield 100kg/ha	Production mill tonnes	Change since 1963
Barley	3.1	46.0 (198)	14.2 (8)	+162%
Wheat	3.1	57.9 (298)	17.7 (3)	+75%
Rye	1.2	36.6 (174)	42.1 (12)	−19%
Potatoes	0.9	368.8 (234)	30.5 (10)	+25%
Oats	0.7	42.8 (232)	2.9 (7)	−14%
Sugar beet	0.8	495.8 (143)	42.2 (14)	+82%
Rapeseed	0.6	28.3 (198)	1.7 (8)	+508%
Grapes	0.2	108.9 (145)	1.8 (3)	+74%
Other fruit	—	—	4.8 (1)	−10%
Vegetables	—	—	8.8 (10)	−56%

MAJOR LIVESTOCK

	Number mill	Production mill tonnes	Change since 1963
Cattle	16.8 (2)	—	+19%
Pigs	63.1 (3)	—	+174%
Milk	—	28.4 (6)	+34%
Fish catch	—	0.9 (1)	

FOOD SECURITY (cereal exports minus imports)

mill tonnes	% domestic production	% world trade
−4.7	92	5

POPULATION

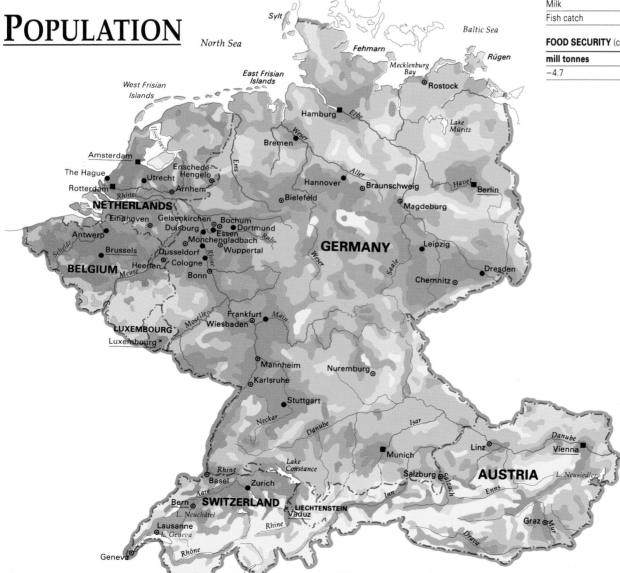

The Netherlands and Belgium, together with the Ruhr and Rhine valleys in Germany, have population densities of more than 200 per sq. km (500 per sq. mi.). Parts of Switzerland and Austria are thinly populated.

Population density

city populations
(capital city is underlined)

■	1,000,000–500,000
●	500,000–999,999
◉	250,000–499,999
×	capital city less than 250,000

persons per square km	persons per square mi.
200	520
100	260
50	130
25	65

INDUSTRY

Apart from Germany, most countries in the region have limited resources. They have concentrated on being highly efficient and specializing in high-cost products.

Resources and industry

- ◆ industrial centre
- ○ major port
- ● other town
- — major road
- — major railway

mineral resources and fossil fuels
- ● iron and other ferroalloy metal ores
- ● other metal ores
- ■ nonmetallic minerals

- coal
- iron ore
- lignite (brown coal)
- natural gas
- oil
- potash
- salt

Industry map labels:
North Sea, Sylt, Baltic Sea, Fehmarn, Rügen, Kiel, Stralsund, Mecklenburg Bay, Rostock, Lübeck, East Frisian Islands, West Frisian Islands, Emden, Bremerhaven, Hamburg, Elbe, Lake Müritz, Groningen, Bremen, Weser, Aller, Haarlem, Amsterdam, Ems, Berlin, The Hague, Europoort, Rhine, Utrecht, Enschede, Havel, Rotterdam, NETHERLANDS, Magdeburg, Ostend, Ruhr, Dortmund, Ghent, Antwerp, Essen, Leipzig, Brussels, Dusseldorf, Kassel, GERMANY, BELGIUM, Cologne, Meuse, Liège, Saale, Dresden, Charleroi, Lahn, Chemnitz, LUXEMBOURG, Moselle, Main, Luxembourg, Frankfurt, Esch, Mannheim, Karlsruhe, Neckar, Stuttgart, Danube, Isar, Danube, Vienna, Munich, AUSTRIA, L. Neusiedler, Basel, Rhine, Lake Constance, Inn, Salzach, Enns, Bern, SWITZERLAND, Aare, L. Neuchâtel, Vaduz, LIECHTENSTEIN, Mur, L. Geneva, Rhine, Drava, Rhône

AGRICULTURE

Arable farming predominates in low-lying areas in the Low Countries and northern Germany and in the sheltered valleys in the south. Forestry and livestock and dairy farming are more important in the uplands.

Agricultural zones

- arable and pasture
- fruit, vines, flowers and vegetables
- pasture
- rough grazing
- woods and forest
- nonagricultural land

- ▲ mountain peak (metres)

Agriculture map labels:
North Sea, Sylt, Baltic Sea, Fehmarn, Rügen, Mecklenburg Bay, East Frisian Islands, West Frisian Islands, Lake Müritz, Veluwe, NETHERLANDS, Elbe, Weser, Lüneburg Heath, Aller, Havel, Overflakkee, Rhine, IJssel, Ems, Kempenland, Schelde, Ruhr, BELGIUM, Rhine, Harz, GERMANY, Meuse, Botrange 694, Westerwald, Vogelsberg, Thuringian Forest, Ardennes, Eifel, Lahn, Ore Mts., Moselle, Taunus, Spessart, Fichtelgebirge, LUXEMBOURG, Hunsrück, Main, Odenwald, Franconian Jura, Bohemian Forest, Haardt, Gross Arber 1457, Neckar, Black Forest, Swabian Jura, Danube, Isar, Jura Mts., Lake Constance, Danube, Rhine, Bavarian Alps, Zugspitze 2963, AUSTRIA, SWITZERLAND, L. Neuchâtel, Eiger 3970, LIECHTENSTEIN, Inn, Tauern, L. Neusiedler, L. Geneva, Rhine, Bernese Alps, Grossglockner 3798, Mur, Matterhorn 4477, Monte Rosa 4634, ALPS, Drava

EASTERN EUROPE

Eastern Europe extends from the cool Baltic Sea region in the north to the Mediterranean lands in the south. Until 1989, Eastern Europe formed a buffer zone of communist states between Western Europe and the former Soviet Union.

Eastern Europe extends from the dune-lined Baltic Sea coast in the north, through part of the North European Plain in Poland and a series of uplands in the south, to the Adriatic Sea in the southwest, and the Black Sea, outlet of the River Danube, in the southeast. The region's plains include the Great Alföld in Hungary. The north is cold and dry, but the south has a subtropical climate.

The region is culturally complex. It contains several language groups, including Slavic, Germanic, Finno-Ugric and Romance languages. Religions, mainly Roman Catholicism, Orthodox Christianity and Islam, also divide the people.

Agriculture was the chief activity in the past. Under communism, however, great efforts were made to industrialize the region. This has caused extensive damage to the environment.

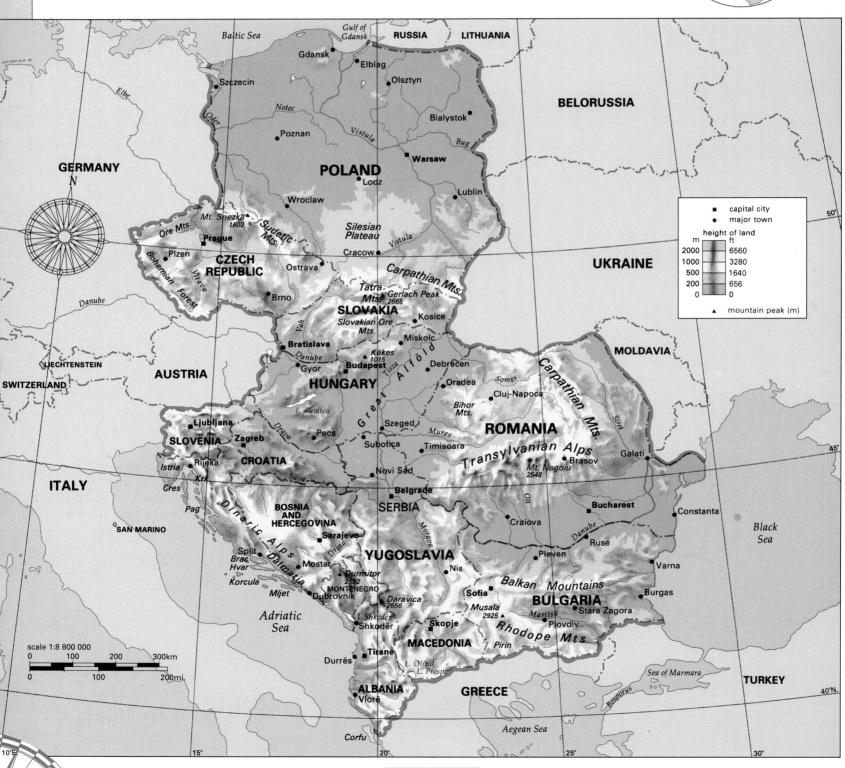

■	capital city
●	major town

height of land

m	ft
2000	6560
1000	3280
500	1640
200	656
0	0

▲ mountain peak (m)

scale 1:8 800 000

THE POLITICAL AND CULTURAL WORLD

Eastern Europe contains 12 countries. Of these, Bosnia and Hercegovina, Croatia, Macedonia, Slovenia and Yugoslavia (now consisting only of Serbia and Montenegro) made up Yugoslavia between 1918 and 1991. The Czech Republic and Slovakia came into being on 1 January 1993, when Czechoslovakia was divided into two parts.

This group of formerly communist countries has faced many problems since the collapse of their ideology in the late 1980s and early 1990s. Rivalries between ethnic groups have resurfaced, causing civil war in Yugoslavia. The countries have also faced many problems as they sought to re-establish free-enterprise economies.

COUNTRIES IN THE REGION

Albania, Bosnia and Hercegovina, Bulgaria, Croatia, Czech Republic, Hungary, Macedonia, Poland, Romania, Slovakia, Slovenia, Yugoslavia

LANGUAGE

Countries with one official language (Albanian) Albania; (Bulgarian) Bulgaria; (Czech) Czech Republic; (Hungarian) Hungary; (Macedonian) Macedonia; (Polish) Poland; (Romanian) Romania; (Serbo-Croat) Bosnia and Hercegovina, Croatia, Yugoslavia; (Slovak) Slovakia; (Slovene) Slovenia

Other languages spoken in the region include German (Czech Republic, Hungary), Greek (Albania), Romany (Bulgaria, Romania, Yugoslavia), Tatar (Romania), Turkish (Bulgaria), and Ukrainian (Czech Republic, Poland, Romania)

RELIGION

Countries with one major religion (BO) Bulgaria; (RC) Czech Republic, Hungary, Poland; (RO) Romania
Countries with more than one major religion (A,AO,M) Albania; (EO,M,O,RC) Yugoslavia

Key: A-Atheist, AO-Albanian Orthodox, BO-Bulgarian Orthodox, EO-Eastern Orthodox, M-Muslim, O-other, RC-Roman Catholic, RO-Romanian Orthodox

STYLES OF GOVERNMENT

Republics All countries in the region
Multiparty states All countries in the region
One-chamber assembly Albania, Bulgaria, Hungary, Macedonia, Yugoslavia
Two-chamber assembly Bosnia, Czech Republic, Poland, Romania, Slovakia, Slovenia
Three-chamber assembly Croatia

ECONOMIC INDICATORS: 1990

	Hungary	Poland	Romania
GDP(US$ billions)	32.92	63.59	34.73
GNP per capita (US$)	2,780	1,690	1,640
Annual rate of growth of GDP, 1980–1990	1.3%	1.8%	2.1%
Manufacturing as % of GDP	27%	20%	n/a
Central government spending as % of GNP	55%	40%	34%
Merchandise exports (US$ billions)	7.14	8.9	n/a
Merchandise imports (US$ billions)	6.1	7.4	n/a

WELFARE INDICATORS

Infant mortality rate (per 1,000 live births)

1965	39	42	44
1990	15	16	27

Daily food supply available (calories per capita, 1989)

	3,644	3,505	3,155
Population per physician (1984)	3,100	490	570
Teacher-pupil ratio (primary school, 1989)	1 : 13	1 : 16	1 : 21

Major changes occurred in Eastern Europe in the 1980s and 1990s. Those countries under communist rule emerged as struggling new democracies, while both Yugoslavia and Czechoslovakia refused to remain artificial unions of diverse nations, and separated, in the former case with great violence and bloodshed. All the region's nations face economic hardship.

- capital city

Albania
Area 28,748 sq. km. (11,100 sq. mi.)
Population 3,245,000

Bosnia and Hercegovina
Area 51,129 sq. km (19,741 sq. mi.)
Population 4,124,000

Bulgaria
Area 110,994 sq. km (42,855 sq. mi.)
Population 9,010,000

Croatia
Area 56,538 sq. km (21,829 sq. mi.)
Population 4,602,000

Czech Republic
Area 78,865 sq. km (30,450 sq. mi.)
Population 10,365,000

Hungary
Area 93,031 sq. km (35,919 sq. mi.)
Population 10,552,000

Macedonia
Area 25,713 sq. km (9,928 sq. mi.)
Population 1,909,000

Poland
Area 312,683 sq. km (120,727 sq. mi.)
Population 38,423,000

Romania
Area 237,500 sq. km (91,699 sq. mi.)
Population 23,272,000

Slovakia
Area 49,035 sq. km (18,932 sq. mi.)
Population 5,310,000

Slovenia
Area 20,251 sq. km (7,819 sq. mi.)
Population 1,892,000

Yugoslavia
Area 102,173 sq. km (39,449 sq. mi.)
Population 9,898,000

HABITATS

The region contains large farming areas, grasslands and wooded mountain ranges. The cool northern plains are drained by rivers that rise in the Sudetic and Carpathian mountains. The warmer southern plains are drained by the River Danube.

LAND

Area 1,275,191 sq. km (492,224 sq. mi.)
Highest point Musala, 2,925 m (9,597 ft)
Lowest point near Gulf of Gdansk, −10 m (−33 ft)
Major features northern lowlands, Carpathian Mountains, Balkan Mountains, Dinaric Alps, Great Alföld, Danube valley

WATER

Longest river Danube, 2,850 km (1,770 mi.)
Largest basin Danube, 773,000 sq. km (298,000 sq. mi.)
Highest average flow Danube, 6,430 cu. m/sec (227,000 cu. ft/sec)
Largest lake Balaton, 590 sq. km (230 sq. mi.)

NOTABLE THREATENED NON-ENDEMIC SPECIES

Mammals European bison (*Bison bonasus*), Grey wolf (*Canis lupus*), European mink (*Mustela lutreola*), Long-fingered bat (*Myotis capaccinii*), Mouse-eared bat (*Myotis myotis*)
Birds Dalmatian pelican (*Pelecanus crispus*), White-headed duck (*Oxyura leucocephala*), Lesser kestrel (*Falco naumanni*), Great bustard (*Otis tarda*), Aquatic warbler (*Acrocephalus paludicola*)
Plants *Astragalus ornacantha*; *Cochlearia polonica*; *Daphne arbuscula*; *Degenia velebitica*; *Dianthus uromoffii*; *Forsythia europaea*; *Lilium rhodopaeum*
Others olm (*Proteus anguinus*), Danube salmon (*Hucho hucho*), Scarce fritillary butterfly (*Euphydryas maturna*)

HABITATS

Physical zones

mountains/barren land

forest

grassland

▲ mountain peak (metres)

☀ climate station

The mountains include the young Carpathians and the old Sudetic Mountains. Some old ranges have been worn down to form plateaus. Lowlands occur in the north and centre.

CLIMATE

The northern parts of Eastern Europe have a continental climate, with rain throughout the year. The southern part of the region has warmer summers. Winters are cool and occasionally a strong, cold wind, called the bora, blows down from the north.

TEMPERATURE AND PRECIPITATION

	Temperature °C (°F)		Altitude m (ft)
	January	July	
Gdansk	−1 (30)	18 (64)	12 (39)
Dresden	0 (32)	19 (66)	129 (423)
Prague	−3 (27)	18 (64)	262 (861)
Tiranë	7 (45)	24 (75)	89 (292)
Bucharest	−3 (27)	23 (73)	92 (301)

	Precipitation mm (in)		
	January	July	Year
Gdansk	31 (1.2)	73 (2.9)	499 (19.6)
Dresden	42 (1.7)	120 (4.7)	680 (26.8)
Prague	18 (0.7)	68 (2.6)	508 (20.0)
Tiranë	135 (5.3)	32 (1.2)	1,189 (46.8)
Bucharest	46 (1.8)	53 (2.1)	578 (22.8)

NATURAL HAZARDS

Earthquakes, landslides and floods

ENVIRONMENTAL ISSUES

Deforestation, intensive farming and industrialization have caused much environmental damage in Eastern Europe in the last 40 years. Power stations have caused air pollution and acid rain, especially in Poland and the Czech Republic.

POPULATION AND WEALTH

	Highest	Middle	Lowest
Population (millions)	38.4 (Poland)	15.7 (Czecho)	3.3 (Albania)
Population increase (annual population growth rate, % 1960–90)	2.4 (Albania)	0.8 (Romania)	0.2 (Hungary)
Energy use (gigajoules/person)	185 (Czecho)	136 (Romania)	38 (Albania)
Real purchasing power (US$/person)	5,920 (Hungary)	4,860 (Yugoslavia)	4,190 (Poland)

ENVIRONMENTAL INDICATORS

CO₂ emissions (million tonnes carbon/annum)	56 (Poland)	25 (Romania)	1.2 (Albania)
Municipal waste (kg/person/annum)	756 (Bulgaria)	657 (Hungary)	212 (Poland)
Nuclear waste (cumulative tonnes heavy metal)	100 (Yugoslavia)	n/a	0 (Albania)
Artificial fertilizer use (kg/ha./annum)	303 (Czecho)	180 (Bulgaria)	130 (Romania)
Cars (per 1,000 population)	174 (Czecho)	122 (Bulgaria)	11 (Romania)
Access to safe drinking water (% population)	100 (Czecho)	97 (Hungary)	73 (Yugoslavia)

MAJOR ENVIRONMENTAL PROBLEMS AND SOURCES

Air pollution: generally high, urban very high; acid rain prevalent; high greenhouse gas emissions
River/lake pollution: high; *sources*: industrial, agricultural, sewage, acid deposition
Land pollution: high; *sources*: industrial, agricultural, urban/household, nuclear

Figures for Yugoslavia relate to the former Yugoslav Republic now divided into individual states.
Figures for Czechoslovakia are pre-partition in 1993.

ENVIRONMENTAL ISSUES

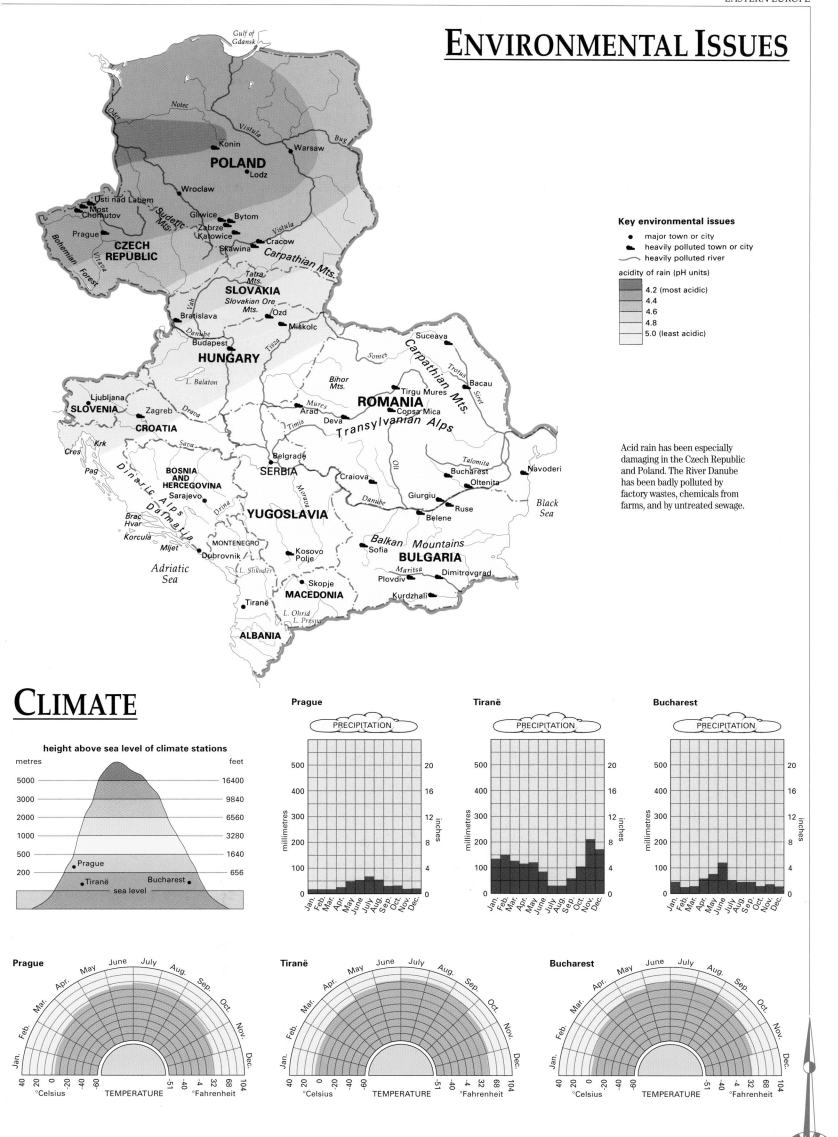

Key environmental issues

- major town or city
- heavily polluted town or city
- heavily polluted river

acidity of rain (pH units)

- 4.2 (most acidic)
- 4.4
- 4.6
- 4.8
- 5.0 (least acidic)

Acid rain has been especially damaging in the Czech Republic and Poland. The River Danube has been badly polluted by factory wastes, chemicals from farms, and by untreated sewage.

CLIMATE

height above sea level of climate stations

metres		feet
5000		16400
3000		9840
2000		6560
1000		3280
500		1640
200	Prague	656
	Tiranë	
	Bucharest	
	sea level	

Prague — PRECIPITATION

Tiranë — PRECIPITATION

Bucharest — PRECIPITATION

Prague — TEMPERATURE

Tiranë — TEMPERATURE

Bucharest — TEMPERATURE

POPULATION

Industrialization came later to Eastern Europe than it did in most other parts of the continent. Even today the proportion of people in rural areas is comparatively high, though urban areas now contain about two-thirds of the population.

POPULATION

Total population of region (millions)	124
Population density (persons per sq. km)	112.5
Population change (average annual percent 1960–1990)	
Urban	+1.7
Rural	−0.7

URBAN POPULATION

As percentage of total population	
1960	47.0
1990	64.3
Percentage in cities of more than 1 million	5.7

TEN LARGEST CITIES

	Country	Population
Budapest †	Hungary	2,115,000
Bucharest †	Romania	2,014,000
Warsaw †	Poland	1,674,000
Belgrade †	Serbia	1,470,000
Prague †	Czech Republic	1,209,000
Zagreb †	Croatia	1,175,000
Sofia †	Bulgaria	1,129,000
Lodz	Poland	852,000
Cracow	Poland	744,000
Wroclaw	Poland	640,000

† denotes capital city

POPULATION

Population density

city populations
(capital city is underlined)

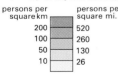

■   1,000,000–5,000,000
●   500,000–999,999
⊙   250,000–499,999
×   capital city less than 250,000

persons per square km	persons per square mi.
200	520
100	260
50	130
10	26

The main concentrations of population are in the industrial regions of the Czech Republic and Poland, and also around the region's capital cities.

INDUSTRY

Apart from Poland's rich coal deposits and some other minerals, the region lacks natural resources. Many industries were set up under communist rule and their managers are are now having great difficulties in converting to private enterprise.

MAJOR PRODUCTS (figures in brackets are percentages of world production)

Energy and minerals	Output	Change since 1960
Coal (mill tonnes)	559.2 (11.9%)	+165%
Copper (mill tonnes)	0.65 (7.6%)	+116.5%
Lead (mill tonnes)	0.28 (8.3%)	-16.4%
Sulphur (mill tonnes)	5.05 (33.7%)	N/A

Manufactures		
Linen fabrics (mill metres)	201.2 (19.7%)	No data
Knitted sweaters (mill)	416.7 (35.7%)	No data
Men's and boys' suits (mill)	7.75 (11.7%)	No data
Footwear (mill pairs)	571.7 (12.9%)	No data
Nitric acid (mill tonnes)	4.95 (18.2%)	+149%
Cement (mill tonnes)	60.9 (5.5%)	+196.5%
Steel (mill tonnes)	52.6 (7.2%)	+132.5%
Buses (1,000)	39.3 (11.9%)	No data
Railroad locomotives and rolling stock (1,000)	30.3 (16.5%)	No data

N/A means production had not begun in 1960

AGRICULTURE

While large tracts of Eastern Europe can be used for arable farming, irrigation is essential in the south because of the hot, dry summers. One-fifth of the land in this region is mountainous, and is only used for rough grazing.

LAND (million hectares)

Total	Agricultural	Arable	Forest/woodland
115 (100%)	69 (60%)	46 (40%)	36 (31%)

FARMERS

12.2 million people employed in agriculture (20% of workforce)
4 hectares of arable land per person employed in agriculture

MAJOR CROPS

	Area mill ha.	Yield 100kg/ha.	Production mill tonnes	Change since 1963
Wheat	9.8	40.3 (172)	39.6 (8)	+132%
Maize	7.1	53.5 (147)	38.0 (8)	+122%
Barley	3.4	39.7 (171)	13.5 (7)	+143%
Rye	3.0	25.6 (122)	7.7 (22)	−14%
Potatoes	2.8	177.9 (113)	50.6 (18)	−11%
Sunflower seed	1.4	20.1 (141)	2.9 (14)	+147%
Sugar beet	1.2	326.1 (94)	39.4 (13)	+39%

MAJOR LIVESTOCK

	Number mill	Production mill tonnes	Change since 1963
Pigs	61.5 (7)	—	+60%
Sheep	45.7 (4)	—	+12%
Cattle	31.7 (2)	—	+13%
Milk	—	36.7 (8)	+50%
Fish catch	—	1.2 (1)	—

FOOD SECURITY (cereal exports minus imports)

mill tonnes	% domestic production	% world trade
−1.3	1	1

Numbers in brackets are percentages of world average yield and total world production

INDUSTRY

Resources and industry

◆ industrial centre
○ major port
● other town
— major road
— major railway

mineral resources and fossil fuels
▲ iron and other ferroalloy metal ores
● other metal ores
■ nonmetallic minerals

coal
iron ore
lignite (brown coal)

Before 1945, industry was confined mainly to Poland and what is now the Czech Republic. Under communist rule, many natural resources were exploited and industries were set up throughout the region.

POLAND
Gulf of Gdansk
Gdynia
Gdansk
Szczecin
Stargard
Bydgoszcz
Notec
Oder
Poznan
Vistula
Bug
Warsaw
Lodz
Wroclaw
Prague
Katowice
Cracow
Plzen
CZECH REPUBLIC
Ostrava
Vltava
Brno
Zilina
Vah
Ruzomberok
SLOVAKIA
Miskolc
Danube
Budapest
Debrecen
HUNGARY
Tisza
Somes
Ljubljana
L. Balaton
ROMANIA
SLOVENIA
Zagreb
Drava
Arad
Mures
Sibiu
Brasov
Rijeka
CROATIA
Sava
Drava
Ploiesti
Sulina
Cres
Belgrade
SERBIA
Oltu
Pag
BOSNIA AND HERCEGOVINA
Sarajevo
Morava
Bucharest
Constanta
Split
Drina
Danube
Ruse
Brac
Hvar
Nis
Black Sea
Korcula
Mljet
MONTENEGRO
YUGOSLAVIA
Varna
Adriatic Sea
Sofia
BULGARIA
Burgas
Bar
L. Shkoder
Shkoder
Skopje
Maritsa
Plovdiv
Durres
MACEDONIA
Tirane
L. Ohrid
L. Prespa
ALBANIA

AGRICULTURE

Agricultural zones

arable and pasture
fruit and vegetables
pasture
rough grazing
woods and forest
nonagricultural land

▲ mountain peak (metres)

The most fertile regions are the North European Plain in Poland and the lowlands of Hungary, Romania, Croatia and northern Serbia. Livestock are raised in upland areas.

Gulf of Gdansk
Oder
Notec
Vistula
Bug
POLAND
Mt. Snezka 1603
Ore Mts.
Sudetic Mts.
Silesian Plateau
Vistula
Bohemian Forest
CZECH REPUBLIC
Vltava
Carpathian Mts.
Tatra Mts.
Gerlach Peak 2665
SLOVAKIA
Slovakian Ore Mts.
Vah
Danube
Kekes 1015
HUNGARY
Tisza
Great Alfold
Somes
Bihor Mts.
Carpathian Mts.
Siret
L. Balaton
ROMANIA
SLOVENIA
Drava
Mures
Transylvanian Alps
CROATIA
Krk
Sava
Mt. Negoiu 2548
Cres
Pag
Dinaric Alps
Dalmatia
BOSNIA AND HERCEGOVINA
Drina
SERBIA
Morava
Oltu
Danube
Black Sea
Brac
Hvar
YUGOSLAVIA
Korcula
Mljet
Durmitor 2522
MONTENEGRO
Daravica 2656
Balkan Mountains
Musala 2925
Maritsa
Adriatic Sea
L. Shkoder
Rhodope Mts.
Pirin
MACEDONIA
L. Ohrid
L. Prespa
ALBANIA

RUSSIA & ITS NEIGHBOURS

The region consists of the 15 republics which made up the Soviet Union, together with land-locked Mongolia. In the west is part of the North European plain, which extends from northern France to the Ural Mountains. East of the Urals is Siberia, a monotonous landscape of plains and plateaus, with uplands in the east. The far east contains the Kamchatka Peninsula, which has active volcanoes and forms part of the Pacific 'ring of fire'. The region also contains the Caucasus Mountain range between the Black and Caspian Seas, and two bleak deserts, the Kara Kum and the Kyzyl Kum. On the country's southern flanks are the Pamirs and the Altai Mountains, which extend into Mongolia. Mongolia contains part of the cold Gobi desert.

The former Soviet government recognized the existence of almost 100 nationalities within its borders. Slavs, including Belorussians, Russians and Ukrainians, form the largest group. Like most people in the western part of the region, including Latvians and Lithuanians, their languages belong to the Indo-European family.

During the cold war, the threat of the military strength of the Soviet Union was pitted against that of the West. But economic crises in the late 1980s, caused partly by the high expenditure on defence, led to the collapse of communism and the break-up of the country into 15 separate republics. The newly independent Baltic states restored cultural links with the neighbouring Nordic countries.

The region covers about one-sixth of the world's land area. It straddles two continents, including the eastern parts of Europe and the northern part of Asia. It contains Russia, which stretches from the Baltic Sea to the Bering Sea, a distance of about 9,650 km (6,000 mi). Russia is also divided between Europe and Asia. The boundary runs down the Ural Mountains, through the Caspian Sea, and along the crest of the Caucasus Mountains.

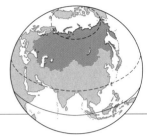

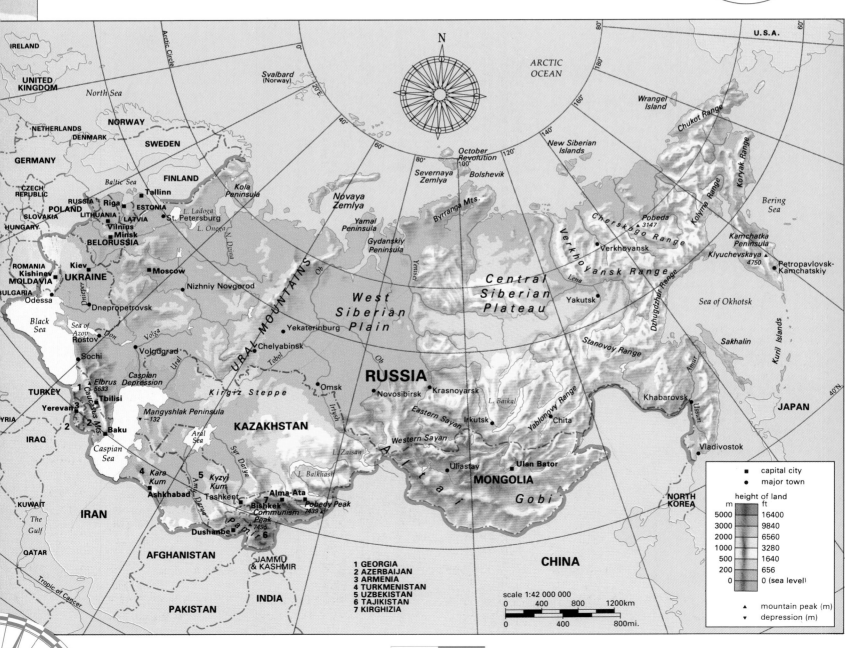

■	capital city
●	major town

height of land

m	ft
5000	16400
3000	9840
2000	6560
1000	3280
500	1640
200	656
0	0 (sea level)

▲ mountain peak (m)
▼ depression (m)

1 GEORGIA
2 AZERBAIJAN
3 ARMENIA
4 TURKMENISTAN
5 UZBEKISTAN
6 TAJIKISTAN
7 KIRGHIZIA

scale 1:42 000 000

THE POLITICAL AND CULTURAL WORLD

D ramatic changes occurred in the late 1980s, when the leaders of the Soviet Union introduced new policies which involved radical political changes and the introduction of free market trading and private ownership. Estonia, Latvia, and Lithuania, former republics of the Soviet Union, became independent nations in 1991 and, at the end of 1991, the Soviet Union was formally abolished. The remaining 12 republics became independent states, though all, except Georgia, joined a loose structure called the Commonwealth of Independent States. Mongolia followed the Soviet Union in abandoning communism in 1990.

COUNTRIES IN THE REGION

Armenia, Azerbaijan, Belorussia, Estonia, Georgia, Kazakhstan, Kirghizia, Latvia, Lithuania, Moldavia, Mongolia, Russia, Tajikistan, Turkmenistan, Ukraine, Uzbekistan

LANGUAGE

Countries with one official language (Armenian) Armenia; (Azeri) Azerbaijan; (Belorussian) Belorusssia; (Estonian) Estonia; (Georgian) Georgia; (Kasakh) Kazakhstan; (Kirghiz) Kirghizia; (Latvian) Latvia; (Lithuanian) Lithuania; (Moldavian) Moldavia; (Khalka Mongolian) Mongolia; (Russian) Russia; (Tadzhik) Tajikistan; (Turkmen) Turkmenistan; (Ukrainian) Ukraine; (Uzbec) Uzbekistan

Over 200 languages are spoken in the republics of the former Soviet Union. Russian is the second language in all the non-Russian republics. Other languages include Bashkir, Chuvash, German, Mordvian, Polish and Tatar.

RELIGION

Countries with one major religion (AAC) Armenia; (GO) Georgia; (M) Azerbaijan, Kazakhstan, Kirghizia, Tajikistan, Turkmenistan, Uzbekistan; (EO) Moldavia; (B) Mongolia
Countries with more than one major religion (EO,RC) Belorussia, Ukraine; (L,RO,P) Estonia, Latvia; (RC,L,RO) Lithuania; (RO,RC,P,M,J,B) Russia

Key: AAC-Armenian Apostolic Church, B-Buddhism, EO-Eastern Orthodox, GO-Georgian Orthodox, J-Jewish, L-Lutheran, M-Muslim, P-other Protestant, RC-Roman Catholic, RO-Russian Othodox

STYLES OF GOVERNMENT

Republics All the countries in the region
Multiparty states All the countries in the region
One-chamber assembly Mongolia
Two-chamber assembly (in 1990) all the former Soviet republics

```
1  GEORGIA
2  AZERBAIJAN
3  ARMENIA
4  TURKMENISTAN
5  UZBEKISTAN
6  TAJIKISTAN
7  KIRGHIZIA
```

The newly independent countries in the region include Estonia, Latvia, and Lithuania, in the northeast, and Belorussia and Ukraine in the west. Moldavia lies south of Ukraine. Between the Black Sea and the Caspian Sea lie Georgia, Azerbaijan and Armenia.

■ capital city

Area 17,075,400 sq. km
(6,592,800 sq. mi.)
Population 148,543,000
Capital Moscow **Russia**
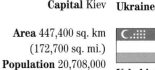

Area 45,100 sq. km
(17,400 sq. mi.)
Population 1,582,000
Capital Tallinn **Estonia**

Area 64,500 sq. km
(24,900 sq. mi.)
Population 2,681,000
Capital Riga **Latvia**

Area 143,100 sq. km
(55,300 sq. mi.)
Population 5,358,000
Capital Dushanbe **Tajikistan**
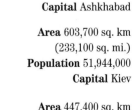

 Area 29,800 sq. km
(11,500 sq. mi.)
Population 3,376,000
Armenia **Capital** Yerevan

Area 69,700 sq. km
(26,900 sq. mi.)
Population 5,464,000
Capital Tbilisi **Georgia**

Area 65,200 sq. km
(25,200 sq. mi.)
Population 3,728,000
Capital Vilnius **Lithuania**

Area 488,100 sq. km
(188,500 sq. mi.)
Population 3,714,000
Capital Ashkhabad **Turkmenistan**

 Area 86,600 sq. km
(33,400 sq. mi.)
Population 7,137,000
Azerbaijan **Capital** Baku

Area 2,717,300 sq. km
(1,049,200 sq. mi.)
Population 16,793,000
Capital Alma-Ata
Kazakhstan **Moldavia**

Area 33,700 sq. km
(13,000 sq. mi.)
Population 4,367,000
Capital Kishinev

Area 603,700 sq. km
(233,100 sq. mi.)
Population 51,944,000
Capital Kiev **Ukraine**

 Area 207,600 sq. km
(80,200 sq. mi.)
Population 10,260,000
Belorussia **Capital** Minsk

Area 198,500 sq. km
(76,600 sq. mi.)
Population 4,422,000
Capital Bishkek **Kirghizia**   **Mongolia**

Area 1,566,500 sq. km
(604,800 sq. mi.)
Population 2,190,000
Capital Ulan Bator

Area 447,400 sq. km
(172,700 sq. mi.)
Population 20,708,000
Capital Tashkent **Uzbekistan**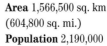

HABITATS

The north is tundra which merges into a vast belt of coniferous forest. Steppes occur in the southeastern parts of Russia and Kazakhstan, with desert in the Aral-Caspian lowland and Mongolia. There are mountains in much of the south.

LAND

Area 23,967,200 sq. km (9,251,339 sq. mi.), including largest country on Earth
Highest point Communism Peak, 7,495 m, (24,590 ft)
Lowest point Mangyshlak Peninsula, −132 m (−433 ft)
Major features plains and plateaus of north, Ural Mountains, Caucasus Mountains, Pamirs and Altai ranges, Kara Kum, Kyzyl Kum and Gobi deserts, Arctic islands

WATER

Longest river Yenisei, 5,870 km (3,650 mi.)
Largest lake Caspian Sea, 371,000 sq. km (143,240 sq. mi.), largest area of inland water in world; Lake Baikal is world's greatest in volume, at 22,000 cu. km (5,500 cu. mi.) and depth, at 1,940 m (6,365 ft)

NOTABLE THREATENED ENDEMIC SPECIES

Mammals Manzbier's marmot (*Marmota menzbieri*), Russian desman (*Desmana moschata*)
Plants *Astragalus tanaiticus*; *Elytrigia stipifolia*; *Eremurus korovinii*; *Fritillaria eduardii*; *Iris paradoxa*; *Lilium caucasicum*; *Potentilla volgarica*; *Rhododendron fauriei*; *Scrophularia cretacea*; *Tulipa kaufmanniana*
Others Amur sturgeon (*Acipenser schrencki*), Balkhash perch (*Perca schrenki*), Caucasian relict ant (*Aulacopone relicta*)

CLIMATE

A subarctic zone called the taiga stretches from northwest Russia to the Pacific Ocean. Summers are short but warm. Winters are long and cold. The west-central areas have a continental climate, while in the far south are deserts and semidesert areas.

TEMPERATURE AND PRECIPITATION

	Temperature °C (°F) January	July	Altitude m (ft)
Moscow	−13 (8.6)	18 (64)	156 (512)
Sochi	7 (45)	23 (73)	31 (102)
Krasnovodsk	2 (36)	28 (82)	21 (68)
Ulan Bator	−26 (−15)	16 (61)	1,325 (4,345)
Verkhoyansk	−51 (−60)	14 (57)	100 (328)
Vladivostok	−14 (7)	19 (66)	29 (95)

	Precipitation mm (in) January	July	Year
Moscow	31 (1.2)	88 (3.5)	575 (22.6)
Sochi	201 (7.9)	60 (2.4)	1,451 (57.1)
Krasnovodsk	13 (0.5)	5 (0.2)	92 (3.6)
Ulan Bator	1 (0.04)	76 (3.0)	209 (8.2)
Verkhoyansk	5 (0.2)	28 (1.1)	155 (6.1)
Vladivostok	8 (0.3)	84 (3.3)	824 (32.4)

ENVIRONMENTAL ISSUES

Rapid industrialization which began after the Russian Revolution of 1917 caused great ecological destruction. Siberia's Lake Baikal has been polluted by industrial wastes and the Aral Sea is shrinking because its water has been used for irrigation.

POPULATION AND WEALTH

	*Former USSR	Mongolia
Population (millions)	288.6	2.2
Population increase (annual population growth rate, % 1960–90)	1.0	2.8
Energy use (gigajoules/person)	194	53
Real purchasing power (US$/person)	n/a	n/a

ENVIRONMENTAL INDICATORS

CO₂ emissions (million tonnes carbon/annum)	690	1.9
Municipal waste (kg/person/annum)	n/a	n/a
Nuclear waste (cumulative tonnes heavy metal)	n/a	0
Artificial fertilizer use (kg/ha./annum)	118	18
Cars (per 1,000 population)	55	n/a
Access to safe drinking water (% population)	100	65

MAJOR ENVIRONMENTAL PROBLEMS AND SOURCES

Air pollution: generally high, urban very high; acid rain prevalent; high greenhouse gas emissions
River/lake pollution: high; *sources:* industrial, agricultural, sewage, acid deposition, nuclear
Land pollution: high; *sources:* industrial, agricultural, urban/household, nuclear
Land degradation: *types:* desertification, soil erosion, salinization, deforestation; *causes:* agriculture, industry
Waste disposal problems: domestic; industrial; nuclear
Major events: Chernobyl (1986) and Sosnovyy Bor (1992), nuclear accidents; Kyshtym (1957) hazardous waste spill; Novosibirsk (1979) catastrophic industrial accident

* All figures relate to the former Soviet Union

HABITATS

A band of subarctic tundra lies across the north, and huge forested taiga plains lie further south. In the west are broad regions of dry grasslands called steppes, while semideserts cover much of the south.

Physical zones

- tundra
- mountains/barren land
- forest
- grassland
- semidesert
- desert

▲ mountain peak (metres)
▼ depression (metres)
☀ climate station

1 GEORGIA
2 AZERBAIJAN
3 ARMENIA
4 TURKMENISTAN
5 UZBEKISTAN
6 TAJIKISTAN
7 KIRGHIZIA

ENVIRONMENTAL ISSUES

Air and water pollution are greatest in the industrialized west. The 1986 explosion at Chernobyl's nuclear power station was a disaster which polluted land over much of Europe.

Key environmental issues

- major town or city
- heavily polluted town or city
- major pollution event
- heavily polluted river
- area affected by permafrost
- dead lake

annual air pollution (tonnes per square km)

- 20
- 10
- 5
- 2

1 GEORGIA
2 AZERBAIJAN
3 ARMENIA
4 TURKMENISTAN
5 UZBEKISTAN
6 TAJIKISTAN
7 KIRGHIZIA

CLIMATE

height above sea level of climate stations

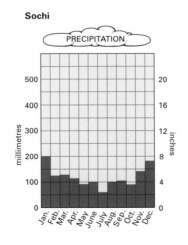

metres		feet
5000		16400
3000		9840
2000		6560
1000	Ulan Bator	3280
500		1640
200	Verkhoyansk	656
	Sochi	sea level

Sochi
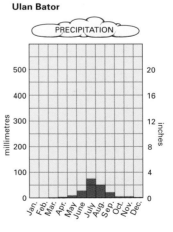
PRECIPITATION

Ulan Bator
PRECIPITATION

Verkhoyansk
PRECIPITATION

Sochi
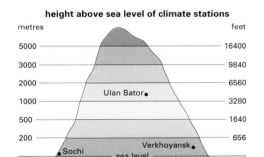
TEMPERATURE

Ulan Bator
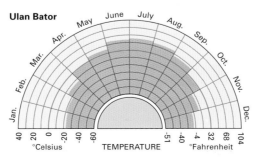
TEMPERATURE

Verkhoyansk
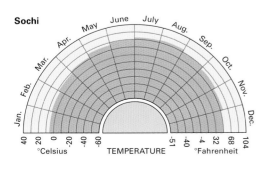
TEMPERATURE

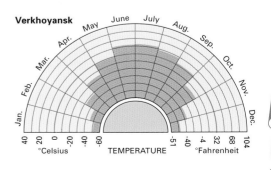

POPULATION

About two-thirds of the population of the region live in the European, western part rather than in the eastern, Asian part. However, under communist rule, the government encouraged the growth of industrial cities in the eastern part of the region, with some success.

POPULATION

Total population of region (millions)	290.7
Population density (persons per sq. km)	12.8
Population change (average annual percent 1960–1990)	
Urban	+2.1
Rural	−0.5

URBAN POPULATION

As percentage of total population	
1960	48.8
1990	67.5
Percentage in cities of more than 1 million	14.6

TEN LARGEST CITIES

	Country	Population
Moscow †	Russia	8,967,000
St. Petersburg (Leningrad)	Russia	5,020,000
Kiev †	Ukraine	2,587,000
Tashkent †	Uzbekistan	2,073,000
Baku †	Azerbaijan	1,757,000
Kharkov	Ukraine	1,611,000
Minsk †	Belorussia	1,589,000
Nizhny Novgorod	Russia	1,438,000
Novosibirsk	Russia	1,436,000
Yekaterinburg	Russia	1,367,000

† denotes capital city

INDUSTRY

The former Soviet Union built up a huge industrial sector based on its abundant natural resources. It invested in engineering and defence industries rather than the production of consumer goods. These newer industries are now being developed.

INDUSTRIAL OUTPUT (US $ billion)

Total	Mining and Manufacturing	Average annual change since 1960
752.6	752.6	+5.7%

INDUSTRIAL WORKERS (millions)
(figures in brackets are percentages of total labour force)

Total	Mining and Manufacturing	Construction
54.7	41.6 (31.8%)	13.1 (10%)

MAJOR PRODUCTS (figures in brackets are percentages of world production)

Energy and minerals	Output	Change since 1960
Coal (mill tonnes)	662.4 (14.1%)	+35.2%
Oil (mill barrels)	4452.9 (19.7%)	+311%
Natural gas (billion cu. metres)	711.7 (37.1%)	+1471%
Iron Ore (mill tonnes)	138.2 (24.3%)	+31%
Nickel (1,000 tonnes)	189.6 (23.5%)	+38.5%
Vanadium (1,000 tonnes)	9.6 (31.1%)	No data
Phosphate rock (mill tonnes)	12.0 (22.6%)	+83%

Manufactures		
Steel (mill tonnes)	163.0 (22.3%)	+149.6%
Cement (mill tonnes)	134.9 (12.3%)	+196.6%
Sulphuric acid (mill tonnes)	29.4 (20.5%)	+132.2%
Linen fabric (mill sq. metres)	788.8 (77.4%)	No data
Footwear (mill pairs)	819.1 (18.4%)	+141.2%
Refrigerators (mill)	6.2 (11.5%)	+167.3%

The tundra and taiga regions are sparsely populated, as also are the southern deserts and mountain areas. The greatest concentrations of population are in the southwestern part of the region.

AGRICULTURE

Only about 10 percent of the former Soviet Union is suitable for arable farming, while livestock rearing is the main occupation in Mongolia. Productivity on the communist state farms and collectives was generally low and food often has to be imported.

LAND (million hectares)

Total	Agricultural	Arable	Forest/woodland
2,384 (100%)	729 (31%)	230 (10%)	959 (40%)

FARMERS

20.7 million employed in agriculture (14% of workforce)
11 hectares of arable land per person employed in agriculture

MAJOR CROPS
Numbers in brackets are percentages of world average yield and total world production

	Area mill ha.	Yield 100kg/ha.	Production mill tonnes	Change since 1963
Wheat	47.2	17.8 (76)	83.9 (16)	+30%
Barley	30.8	19.0 (82)	58.5 (32)	+188%
Oats	11.8	15.7 (85)	18.5 (43)	+205%
Rye	9.7	18.6 (89)	18.1 (53)	+20%

MAJOR LIVESTOCK

	Number mill	Production mill tonnes	Change since 1963
Sheep	155.4 (14)	—	+6%
Cattle	124.6 (10)	—	+46%
Pigs	79.6 (9)	—	+38%
Milk	—	103.1 (22)	+61%
Fish catch	—	11.2 (12)	—

Population density

city populations
(capital city is underlined)

◆ over 5,000,000
■ 1,000,000–5,000,000
● 600,000–999,999
× capital city less than 600,000

persons per square km	persons per square mi.
100	260
50	130
10	26
1	2.6

POPULATION

1 GEORGIA
2 AZERBAIJAN
3 ARMENIA
4 TURKMENISTAN
5 UZBEKISTAN
6 TAJIKISTAN
7 KIRGHIZIA

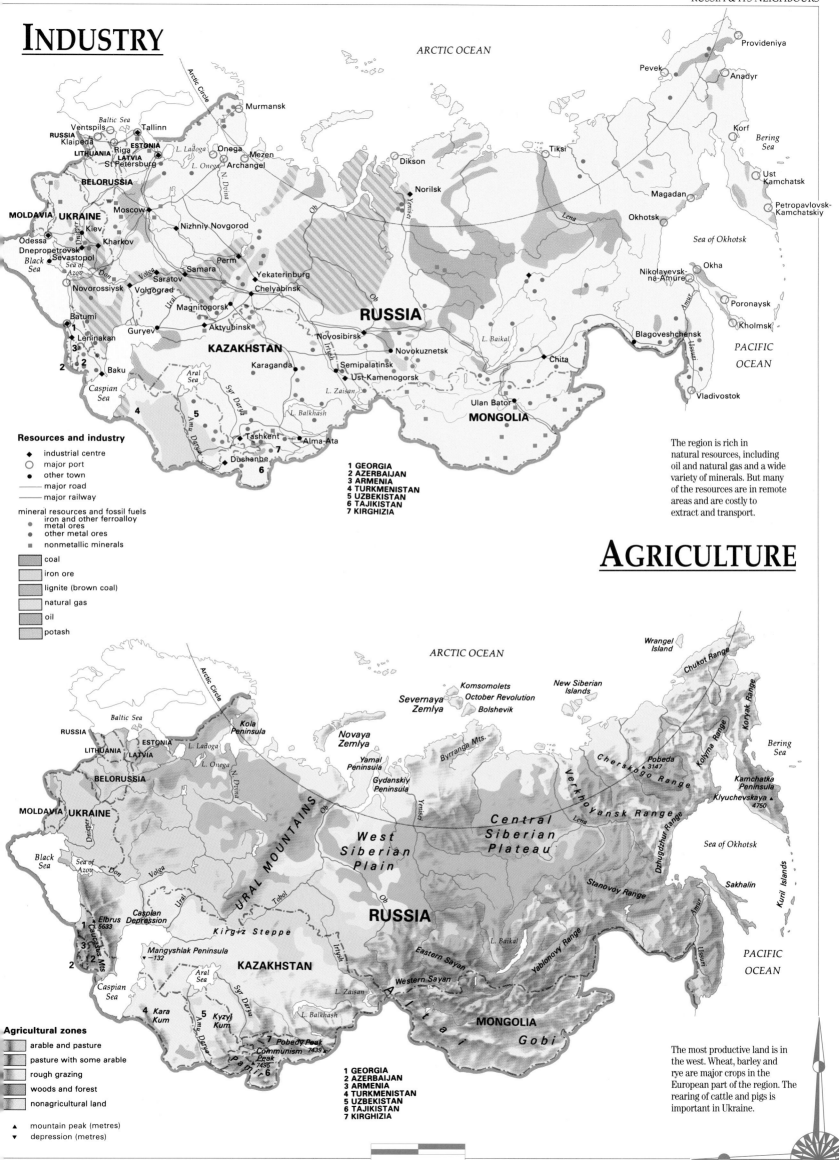

MIDDLE EAST

The Middle East contains some of the world's hottest and driest deserts. The two major rivers, the Tigris and Euphrates, rise in the well-watered mountains of Turkey and flow across the deserts of Syria and Iraq.

The mountains of Turkey are part of a long chain of fold mountains which extends across the northern Middle East to the Hindu Kush in northeastern Afghanistan.

The Middle East contains several oil-rich nations, but most of it is economically underdeveloped. It is the home of three religions – Judaism, Christianity and Islam – but religion has divided people and has been the cause of both international and civil wars. Politically, the Middle East is an unstable region, whose conflicts periodically involve the world community.

The Middle East is the meeting place of three continents. Here early peoples began to plant crops, build cities and found civilizations. Today the region is important economically and strategically because of its large reserves and production of oil and natural gas.

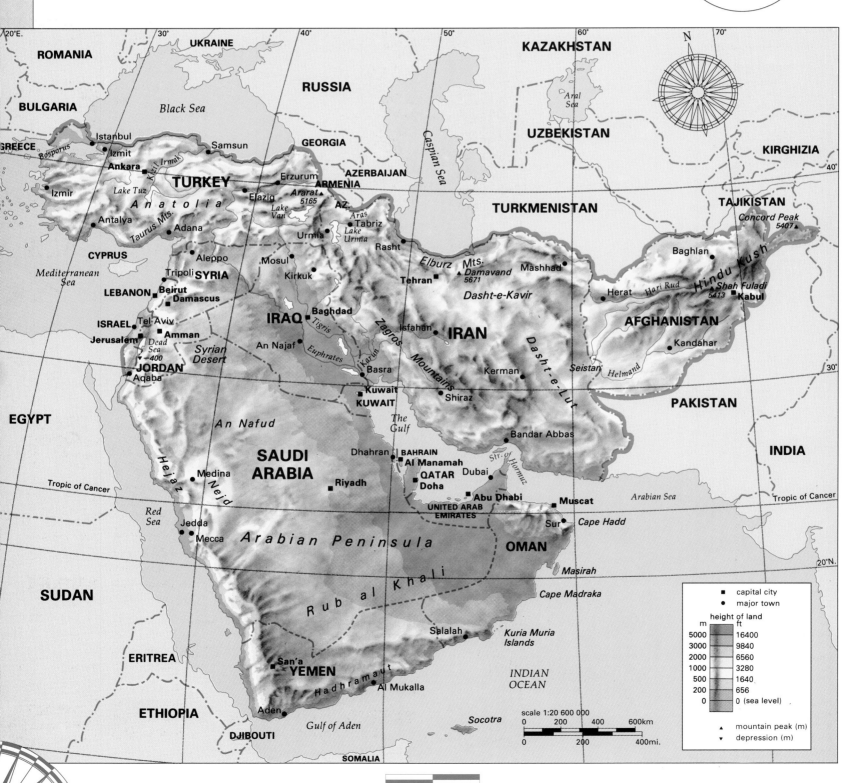

	height of land
m	ft
5000	16400
3000	9840
2000	6560
1000	3280
500	1640
200	656
0	0 (sea level)

■ capital city
● major town
▲ mountain peak (m)
▼ depression (m)

scale 1:20 600 000

0 200 400 600km
0 200 400mi.

THE POLITICAL AND CULTURAL WORLD

Islam, spread throughout the area by Arabs from the 7th century A.D., is the dominant religion in the Middle East. Israel, the only country where Muslims do not form a majority, has been in conflict with Arab nations since it was created as a homeland for Jews in 1948.

Other conflicts have arisen because of rivalries between ethnic, cultural and religious groups, as in Lebanon, and the aspirations of minorities, such as the Kurds who would like to establish their own country in parts of Iraq, Iran and Turkey. Territorial disputes have led to war between Iraq and Iran (1980–88) and Iraq's invasion of Kuwait (1990–91).

COUNTRIES IN THE REGION
Afghanistan, Bahrain, Iran, Iraq, Israel, Jordan, Kuwait, Lebanon, Oman, Qatar, Saudi Arabia, Syria, Turkey, United Arab Emirates, Yemen

LANGUAGE
Countries with one official language (Arabic) Bahrain, Iraq, Jordan, Kuwait, Lebanon, Oman, Qatar, Saudi Arabia, Syria, U.A.E., Yemen; (Farsi) Iran; (Turkish) Turkey
Countries with two official languages (Arabic, Hebrew) Israel; (Dari, Pushtu) Afghanistan

RELIGION
Countries with one major religion (M) Afghanistan, Bahrain, Iran, Iraq, Jordan, Kuwait, Oman, Qatar, Saudi Arabia, Syria, Turkey, U.A.E., Yemen
Countries with more than one major religion (C,J,M) Israel; (C,D,M and other) Lebanon

Key: C-various Christian, D-Druze, J-Jewish, M-Muslim

STYLES OF GOVERNMENT
Republics Afghanistan, Iran, Iraq, Israel, Lebanon, Syria, Turkey, U.A.E., Yemen
Monarchies Bahrain, Jordan, Kuwait, Oman, Qatar, Saudi Arabia
Federal state U.A.E.
Multiparty states Afghanistan, Israel, Lebanon, Turkey
One-party states Iran, Iraq, Syria
States without parties Bahrain, Jordan, Kuwait, Oman, Qatar, Saudi Arabia, U.A.E., Yemen

ECONOMIC INDICATORS: 1990

	U.A.E	Saudi Ar.	Jordan
GDP(US$ billions)	28.27	80.89	3.3329
GNP per capita (US$)	19,860	7,050	1,240
Annual rate of growth of GDP, 1980–1990	–4.5%	–1.8%	4.3%
Manufacturing as % of GDP	9%	9%	12%
Central government spending as % of GNP	13%	n/a	39%
Merchandise exports (US$ billions)	15.0	44.4	1.15
Merchandise imports (US$ billions)	9.6	24	2.66
% of GNP donated as development aid	2.65%	3.9%	–1%

WELFARE INDICATORS

Infant mortality rate (per 1,000 live births)			
1965	103	148	114
1990	23	65	51
Daily food supply available (calories per capita, 1989)			
	3,309	2,874	2,634
Population per physician (1984)	1,020	730	860
Teacher-pupil ratio (primary school, 1989)	1 : 18	1 : 16	1 : 28

Afghanistan
Area 652,225 sq. km (251,825 sq. mi.)
Population 16,557,000
Capital Kabul

Bahrain
Area 691 sq. km (267 sq. mi.)
Population 516,000
Capital Al Manamah

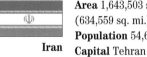
Iran
Area 1,643,503 sq. km (634,559 sq. mi.)
Population 54,607,000
Capital Tehran

Iraq
Area 438,317 sq. km (169,235 sq. mi.)
Population 18,920,000
Capital Baghdad

Israel
Area 20,700 sq. km (7,992 sq. mi.)
Population 4,600,000
Capital Jerusalem

Jordan
Area 89,206 sq. km (34,443 sq. mi.)
Population 4,009,000
Capital Amman

Kuwait
Area 17,818 sq. km (6,880 sq. mi.)
Population 2,039,000
Capital Kuwait

Lebanon
Area 10,230 sq. km (3,950 sq. mi.)
Population 2,701,000
Capital Beirut

Oman
Area 300,000 sq. km (116,000 sq. mi.)
Population 1,502,000
Capital Muscat

Qatar
Area 11,400 sq. km (4,400 sq. mi.)
Population 368,000
Capital Doha

Saudi Arabia
Area 2,240,000 sq. km (865,000 sq. mi.)
Population 14,134,000
Capital Riyadh

Syria
Area 185,180 sq. km (71,498 sq. mi.)
Population 12,530,000
Capital Damascus

Turkey
Area 779,452 sq. km (300 948 sq. mi.)
Population 58,687,000
Capital Ankara

United Arab Emirates
Area 77,700 sq. km (30,000 sq. mi.)
Population 1,589,000
Capital Abu Dhabi

Yemen
Area 472,099 sq. km (182,276 sq. mi.)
Population 11,282,000
Capital San'a

■ capital city

The Middle East has been in ferment since 1945. Israel has fought four wars against its Arab foes, while the Palestinians in Israel continue their protests against Israeli rule. The Iran-Iraq war was the longest in the 20th century, while the expulsion of Iraqi forces from Kuwait in 1991 involved many world powers.

HABITATS

Mountains, plateaus, and deserts dominate the Middle East. The Arabian Peninsula is almost completely surrounded by sea, yet much of the peninsula consists of desert and semidesert. The plains of the Tigris and Euphrates are fertile.

LAND

Highest point Concord Peak 5,407 m (17,740 ft)
Lowest point Dead Sea, −400 m (−1,312 ft), lowest point on land surface on Earth
Major features plateaus of Anatolia and Iran, Hindu Kush, Zagros and Elburz Mountains, deserts of Arabia and Iran

WATER

Longest river Euphrates, 2,720 km (1,700 mi.)
Largest lake Urmia 4,701 sq. km (1,815 sq. mi.) largest area of inland water in the world

NOTABLE THREATENED ENDEMIC SPECIES

Mammals Mountain gazelle *(Gazella gazella)*, Arabian oryx *(Oryx leucoryx)*, Arabian tahr *(Hemitragus jayakari)*
Birds Yemen thrush *(Turdus menachensis)*
Plants *Alkanna macrophylla*; *Anthemis brachycarpa*; *Ceratonia oreothauma* subsp. *oreothauma*; *Dionysia mira*; *Erodium subintegrifolium*; *Ferulago longistylis*; *Iris calcarea*; *Iris lortetii*; *Rumex rothschildianus*; *Wissmannia carinensis*
Others Latifi's viper *(Vipera latifi)*, cicek fish *(Acanthorutilus handlirschi)*

CLIMATE

The coasts of Turkey and the eastern Mediterranean have hot, dry summers and mild, moist winters. Inland is a hot desert region. The mountains and plateaus of the Turkish interior, Iran, and Afghanistan, are sub-tropical and dry, though it snows in the mountains.

TEMPERATURE AND PRECIPITATION

	Temperature °C (°F) January	July	Altitude m (ft)
Samsun	7 (45)	22 (71)	40 (131)
Haifa	14 (57)	27 (81)	10 (32)
Amman	8 (46)	25 (77)	777 (2,547)
Basra	12 (54)	34 (93)	2 (7)
Riyadh	15 (59)	34 (93)	590 (1,935)
Kandahar	6 (42)	29 (84)	1,055 (3,460)

	Precipitation mm (in) January	July	Year
Samsun	74 (2.9)	39 (1.5)	731 (28.8)
Haifa	175 (6.8)	0 (0)	499 (19.6)
Amman	68 (2.7)	0 (0)	273 (10.7)
Basra	36 (1.4)	0 (0)	164 (6.5)
Riyadh	3 (0.1)	0 (0)	82 (3.2)
Kandahar	79 (3.1)	3 (0.1)	225 (8.9)

ENVIRONMENTAL ISSUES

Soil erosion, and the build-up of salt in the soil caused by poor drainage of irrigated land, have damaged the area in the past. There is overgrazing and deforestation. Industrial and urban growth, together with oil extraction and war, have caused recent damage.

POPULATION AND WEALTH

	Highest	Middle	Lowest
Population (millions)	54.6 (Iran)	4.0 (Jordan)	0.4 (Qatar)
Population increase (annual population growth rate, % 1960–90)	10.0 (UAE)	3.4 (Iraq)	1.3 (Lebanon)
Energy use (gigajoules/person)	642 (Qatar)	39 (Lebanon)	4 (Afghanistan)
Real purchasing power (US$/person)	19,440 (Qatar)	9,290 (Oman)	710 (Afghanistan)

ENVIRONMENTAL INDICATORS

CO_2 emissions (million tonnes carbon/annum)	42 (S Arabia)	4.7 (Oman)	0.6 (Yemen)
Artificial fertilizer use (kg/ha./annum)	750 (Bahrain)	92 (Oman)	6 (Yemen)
Cars (per 1,000 population)	207 (Kuwait)	48 (Turkey)	2 (Yemen)
Access to safe drinking water (% population)	100 (Bahrain)	83 (Turkey)	21 (Afghanistan)

MAJOR ENVIRONMENTAL PROBLEMS AND SOURCES

Air pollution: urban high
Coastal pollution: medium/high; *sources:* oil; war
Land degradation: *types:* desertification, salinization; oil pollution, *causes:* agriculture; war
Resource problems: fuelwood shortage; inadequate drinking water and sanitation
Population problems: population explosion; war
Major events: Gulf (1991), oil spills and oil well fires during and after the Gulf War

HABITATS

Some of the world's hottest and driest deserts are found in the region. Here, the main sources of water are found at scattered oases or along such rivers as the Tigris and Euphrates.

Physical zones
- mountains/barren land
- forest
- grassland
- semidesert
- desert

▲ mountain peak (metres)
▼ depression (metres)
☼ climate station

ENVIRONMENTAL ISSUES

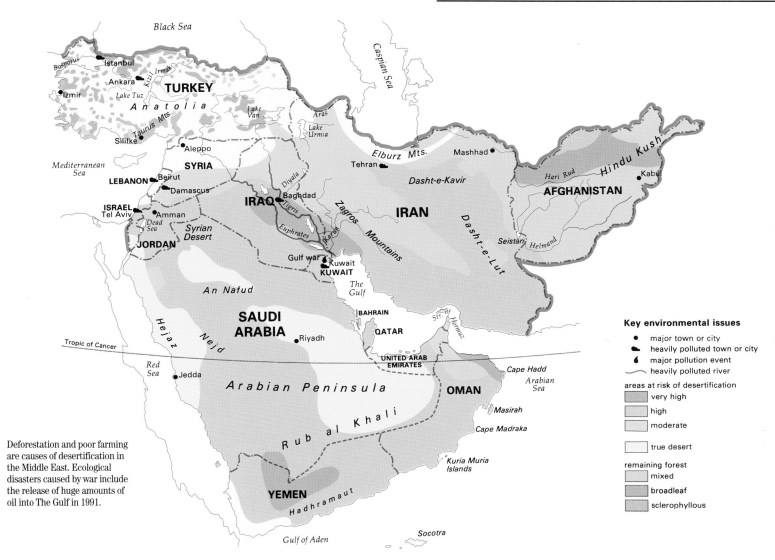

Key environmental issues

- ● major town or city
- ⌐ heavily polluted town or city
- ◗ major pollution event
- ～ heavily polluted river

areas at risk of desertification

- very high
- high
- moderate
- true desert

remaining forest

- mixed
- broadleaf
- sclerophyllous

Deforestation and poor farming are causes of desertification in the Middle East. Ecological disasters caused by war include the release of huge amounts of oil into The Gulf in 1991.

CLIMATE

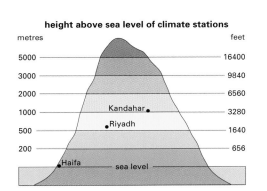

height above sea level of climate stations

metres		feet
5000		16400
3000		9840
2000		6560
1000	Kandahar	3280
500	Riyadh	1640
200		656
	Haifa sea level	

Haifa

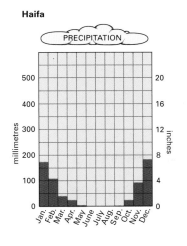

PRECIPITATION

Riyadh

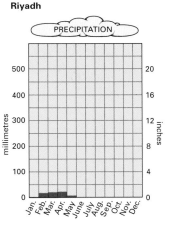

PRECIPITATION

Kandahar

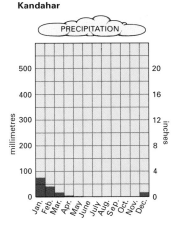

PRECIPITATION

Haifa

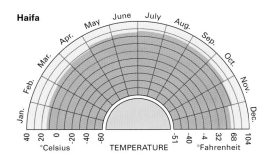

TEMPERATURE

Riyadh

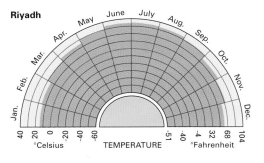

TEMPERATURE

Kandahar

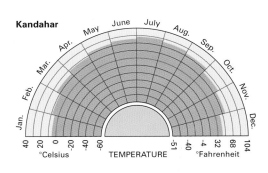

TEMPERATURE

POPULATION

Cities developed in the Middle East more than 5,000 years ago. Today, about half of the population is urban, and city populations are rising quickly because of natural increase and the movement of poor people from the countryside looking for work.

POPULATION

Total population of region (millions)	202.8
Population density (persons per sq. km)	31.2
Population change (average annual percent 1960–1990)	
Urban	+5.2
Rural	+0.8

URBAN POPULATION

As percentage of total population	
1960	36.8
1990	52.4
Percentage in cities of more than 1 million	16.8

TEN LARGEST CITIES

	Country	Population
Tehran †	Iran	6,043,000
Istanbul	Turkey	5,495,000
Baghdad †	Iraq	4,649,000
Ankara †	Turkey	2,252,000
Riyadh †	Saudi Arabia	2,000,000
Izmir	Turkey	1,490,000
Mashhad	Iran	1,464,000
Kabul †	Afghanistan	1,424,000
Jedda	Saudi Arabia	1,400,000
Damascus †	Syria	1,361,000

† denotes capital city

INDUSTRY

In the Middle East, only Israel and Turkey have built up broad-based manufacturing sectors. Foreign investment and expertise are now helping to build industries in the oil-rich nations, which are seeking to achieve more balanced economies.

INDUSTRIAL OUTPUT (US $ billion)

Total	Mining	Manufacturing	Average annual change since 1960
237.3	83.4	55.6	+4.9%

INDUSTRIAL WORKERS (millions)
(figures in brackets are percentages of total labour force)

Total	Mining	Manufacturing	Construction
11.77	1.33 (2.5%)	5.55 (10.6%)	4.9 (9.3%)

MAJOR PRODUCTS (figures in brackets are percentages of world production)

Energy and minerals	Output	Change since 1960
Oil (mill barrels)	5966.6 (26.3%)	+288.5%
Natural gas (billion cu. metres)	102.2 (5.3%)	+604%
Marble (mill cu. metres)	3.9 (40%)	No data
Magnesite (mill tonnes)	3.4 (18.8%)	No data
Borate (mill tonnes)	2.04 (52.8%)	No data

Manufactures		
Wool yarn (1,000 tonnes)	33.9 (10.3%)	-38.4%
Cement (mill tonnes)	66.5 (6.1%)	+1724%
Steel (mill tonnes)	9.8 (1.3%)	+2700%
Nitrogenous fertilizer (mill tonnes)	5.1 (5.5%)	N/A
Polyethylene (1,000 tonnes)	357 (1.6%)	N/A
Jet fuels (mill tonnes)	7.4 (5.2%)	N/A
Petroleum (mill tonnes)	26.0 (3.6%)	N/A
Liquefied petroleum gas (mill tonnes)	20.1 (13.1%)	N/A

N/A means production had not begun in 1960

AGRICULTURE

Much of the farming in the Middle East, when conditions make it possible, is still traditional in character. But new high-technology farming now exists in some places, notably Israel which has used large-scale irrigation systems and new technology to 'make the deserts bloom'.

LAND (million hectares)

Total	Agricultural	Arable	Forest/woodland
680 (100%)	265 (39%)	61 (9%)	47 (7%)

FARMERS

23.7 million employed in agriculture (38% of workforce)
3 hectares of arable land per person employed in agriculture

MAJOR CROPS

	Area mill ha.	Yield 100kg/ha.	Production mill tonnes	Change since 1963
Wheat	21.2	16.6 (71)	35.2 (7)	+119%
Barley	8.5	13.3 (57)	11.3 (6)	+76%
Lentils	1.1	9.4 (119)	1.1 (41)	+373%
Cotton lint	1.0	8.8 (153)	0.9 (5)	+45%
Grapes	1.1	60.2 (80)	6.5 (10)	+45%
Other fruit	—	—	12.7 (5)	+138%
Vegetables	—	—	31.3 (7)	+138%

MAJOR LIVESTOCK

	Number mill	Production mill tonnes	Change since 1963
Sheep/goats	170.2 (10)	—	+10%
Cattle	28.6 (2)	—	+15%
Milk	—	7.7 (2)	+80%
Fish catch	—	1.2 (1)	—

FOOD SECURITY (cereal exports minus imports)

mill tonnes	% domestic production	% world trade
−23.0	43	11

Numbers in brackets are percentages of world total

POPULATION

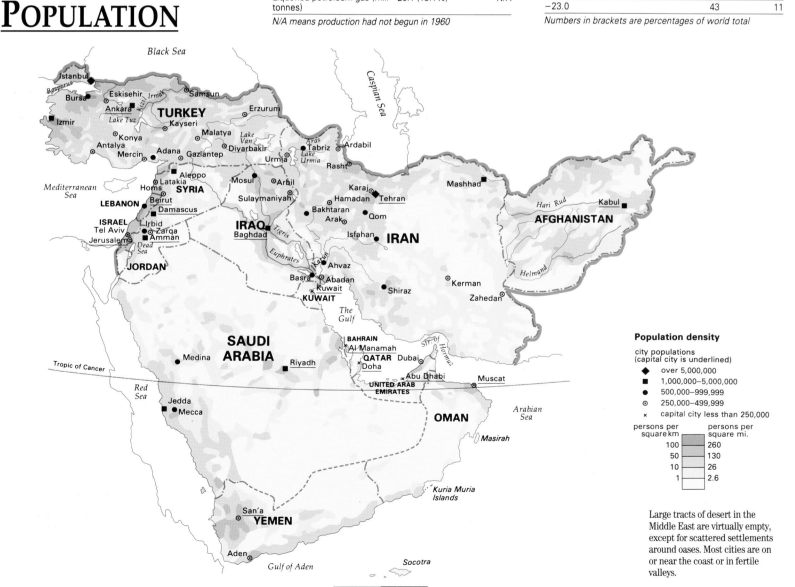

Population density

city populations
(capital city is underlined)

- ◆ over 5,000,000
- ■ 1,000,000–5,000,000
- ● 500,000–999,999
- ⊙ 250,000–499,999
- × capital city less than 250,000

persons per square km	persons per square mi.
100	260
50	130
10	26
1	2.6

Large tracts of desert in the Middle East are virtually empty, except for scattered settlements around oases. Most cities are on or near the coast or in fertile valleys.

INDUSTRY

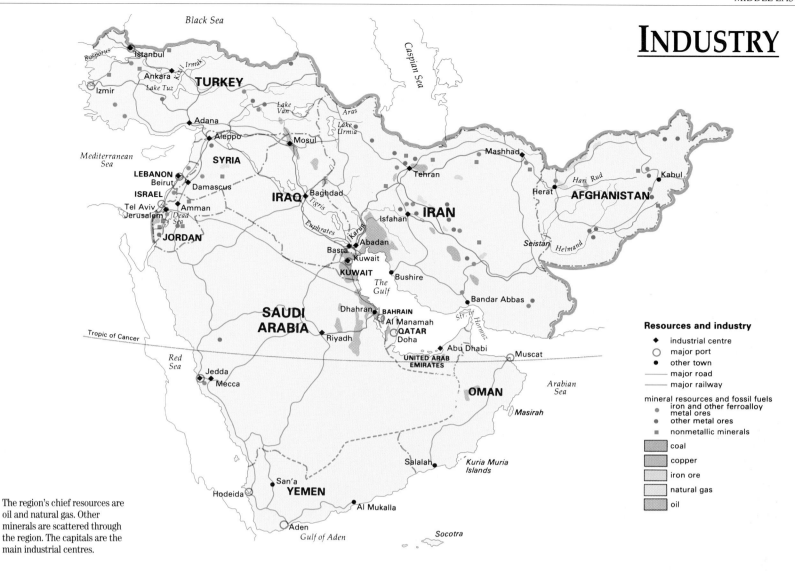

Resources and industry

- ◆ industrial centre
- ○ major port
- ● other town
- —— major road
- —— major railway

mineral resources and fossil fuels
- ● iron and other ferroalloy metal ores
- ● other metal ores
- ■ nonmetallic minerals

- coal
- copper
- iron ore
- natural gas
- oil

The region's chief resources are oil and natural gas. Other minerals are scattered through the region. The capitals are the main industrial centres.

AGRICULTURE

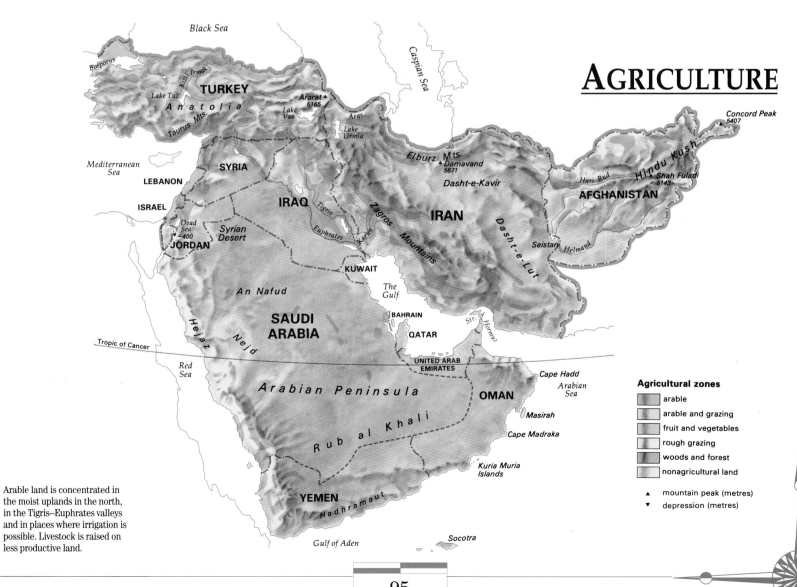

Agricultural zones

- arable
- arable and grazing
- fruit and vegetables
- rough grazing
- woods and forest
- nonagricultural land

- ▲ mountain peak (metres)
- ▼ depression (metres)

Arable land is concentrated in the moist uplands in the north, in the Tigris–Euphrates valleys and in places where irrigation is possible. Livestock is raised on less productive land.

NORTHERN AFRICA

The northern half of Africa consists largely of a low plateau broken by shallow basins and rugged volcanic highlands. The main land feature in the far northwest is the Atlas Mountain range. The other main highlands are in Ethiopia, though there are also mountain peaks in Algeria, Niger, Chad and Sudan. Running through these highlands is a section of the Great Rift Valley, the world's longest geological depression, which runs from Syria to Mozambique.

South of the Mediterranean coastlands and the Atlas Mountains lies the Sahara, the world's largest hot and dry region. Only two major rivers, the Nile and the Niger, flow across North Africa throughout the year. But North Africa is not completely arid. South of the Sahara is a dry grassland region called the Sahel, which merges into tropical grassland, or savanna, and forest.

North Africa contains two main groups of people: Arabs and Berbers in the north and Black Africans in the lands south of the Sahara. Nomadism is the traditional way of life in the Sahara, though it is now under threat. Most of the people are Muslims, though Christianity, introduced into the Horn of Africa between the 4th and 6th centuries A.D., survived the spread of Islam in the inaccessible highlands of Ethiopia. All the countries of the region except Ethiopia, which was only briefly conquered (by Italy, 1935—1941), came under colonial (mainly French) rule and this, too, has left its mark on the region's culture. Arabic is the official language in the northern states, though some people speak Berber dialects. By contrast, many languages are spoken in the lands south of the Sahara. The former colonial language is used in many countries as a means of communication.

Northern Africa is part of the ancient landmass of Gondwanaland, which broke up between 200 and 100 million years ago. About 70 million years ago, Africa consisted of two land plates; North Africa was tilted downwards, while Southern Africa was tilted upwards. This divided Africa into a high plateau in the south and a low plateau in the north, which was flooded by the sea. New rocks were formed on the sea bed. These rocks now contain water, oil and natural gas.

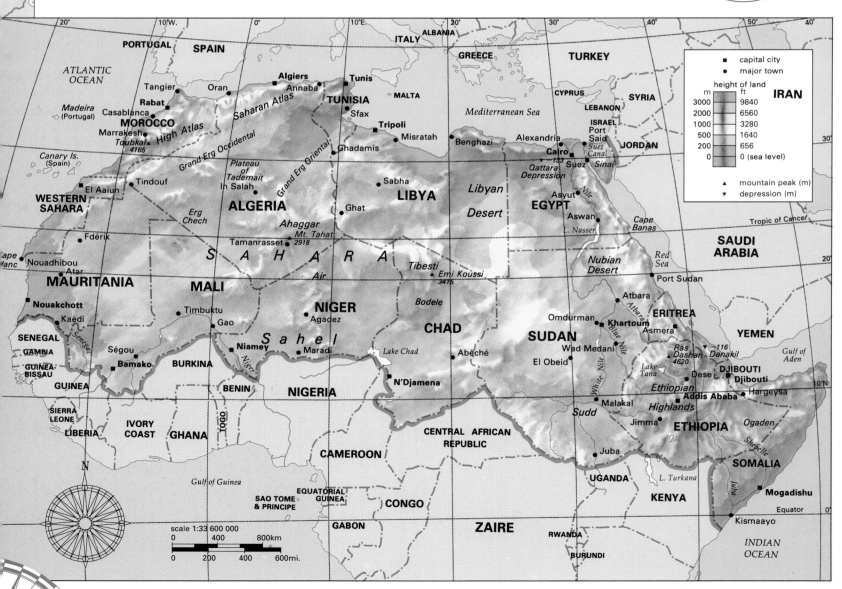

THE POLITICAL AND CULTURAL WORLD

L ike many other parts of the developing world, Northern Africa has faced many problems since the countries of the region became independent from colonial rule.

Egypt was in the front line of the Arab–Israeli wars until it agreed a peace treaty with Israel in 1979. To the south, Chad, Sudan, Ethiopia and Somalia have suffered bitter civil wars, while Libya has fought with Chad over their disputed border.

Western (formerly Spanish) Sahara, a thinly populated desert territory, was annexed by Morocco, in the face of opposition from nationalist Saharan guerrillas.

COUNTRIES IN THE REGION
Algeria, Chad, Djibouti, Egypt, Eritrea, Ethiopia, Libya, Mali, Mauritania, Morocco, Niger, Somalia, Sudan, Tunisia

MEMBERSHIP OF INTERNATIONAL ORGANIZATIONS
Arab League Algeria, Djibouti, Egypt, Libya, Mauritania, Morocco, Somalia, Sudan, Tunisia
Organization for African Unity (OAU) All countries except Eritrea and Morocco
Organization of Petroleum Exporting Countries (OPEC) Algeria, Libya

LANGUAGE
Countries with one official language (Amharic) Ethiopia; (Arabic) Algeria, Egypt, Libya, Morocco, Sudan, Tunisia; (French) Mali, Niger
Countries with two official languages (Arabic, French) Chad, Djibouti, Mauritania; (Arabic, Somali) Somalia

RELIGION
Countries with one major religion (M) Algeria, Djibouti, Libya, Mauritania, Morocco, Niger, Somalia, Tunisia
Countries with more than one major religion (M,C) Egypt; (M,C) Eritrea; (M,EO,I) Ethiopia; (M,I,C) Chad, Mali, Sudan

Key: C-various Christian, EO-Ethiopian Orthodox; I-indigenous religions, M-Muslim

SYTLES OF GOVERNMENT
Republics All countries in the region except Morocco
Monarchy Morocco
Federal state (since 1991) Sudan
Multiparty states Chad, Egypt, Ethiopia, Mali, Mauritania, Morocco, Sudan, Tunisia
One-party states Algeria, Djibouti, Libya, Somalia
State without parties Niger
Military influence Algeria, Libya, Mauritania, Niger, Sudan
State without effective government (since 1991) Somalia

ECONOMIC INDICATORS: 1990

	Algeria	Egypt	Ethiopia
GDP(US$ billions)	42.15	33.21	5.49
GNP per capita (US$)	2,060	600	120
Annual rate of growth of GDP, 1980–1990	3.1%	5.0%	1.8%
Manufacturing as % of GDP	12%	16%	11%
Central government spending as % of GNP	n/a	40	35
Merchandise exports (US$ billions)	9.5	10.3	1.08
Merchandise imports (US$ billions)	9.5	10.3	1.08
% of GNP received as development aid	0.4%	15.9%	14.6%
Total external debt as % of GNP	53.1%	126.5%	54.2%

WELFARE INDICATORS

Infant mortality rate (per 1,000 live births)			
1965	154	145	165
1990	67	66	132
Daily food supply available (calories per capita, 1989)	2,866	3,336	1,667
Population per physician (1984)	2,340	770	78,780
Teacher-pupil ratio (primary school, 1989)	1 : 28	1 : 24	1 : 43

Area 2,381,741 sq. km (919,595 sq. mi.)
Population 24,960,000
Algeria

Area 1,284,000 sq. km (496,000 sq. mi.)
Population 5,678,000
Chad

Area 23,200 sq. km (8,950 sq. mi.)
Population 409,000
Djibouti

Area 997,739 sq. km (385,229 sq. mi.)
Population 53,153,000
Egypt

Area 117,600 sq. km (45,405 sq. mi.)
Population 3,200,000
Eritrea

Area 1,223,500 sq. km (472,400 sq. mi.)
Population 49,240,000
Ethiopia

Area 1,757,000 sq. km (678,400 sq. mi.)
Population 4,545,000
Libya

Area 1,240,192 sq. km (478,841 sq. mi.)
Population 8,156,000
Mali

Area 458,730 sq. km (177,117 sq. mi.)
Population 25,061,000
Morocco

Area 1,186,408 sq. km (458,075 sq. mi.)
Population 7,731,000
Niger

Area 637,657 sq. km (246,201 sq. mi.)
Population 7,497,000
Somalia

Area 2,503,890 sq. km (966,757 sq. mi.)
Population 25,203,000
Sudan

Area 154,530 sq. km (59,664 sq. mi.)
Population 8,180,000
Tunisia

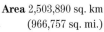

The boundaries of Northern Africa were drawn by the European colonial powers. The unwieldy shapes of many countries have caused friction in recent years. For example, the world's ninth largest country, Sudan, is divided into two cultural regions: the Arab north and the Black African south. Tensions between the cultures have led to civil war.

■ capital city

Area 1,030,700 sq. km (389,000 sq. mi.)
Population 2,024,000
Mauritania

Tunis · Algiers · Rabat · TUNISIA · Tripoli · MOROCCO · El Aaiun · WESTERN SAHARA · ALGERIA · LIBYA · Cairo · EGYPT · MAURITANIA · Nouakchott · MALI · NIGER · CHAD · Bamako · Niamey · N'Djamena · Khartoum · SUDAN · ERITREA · Asmera · DJIBOUTI · Djibouti · Addis Ababa · ETHIOPIA · SOMALIA · Mogadishu

HABITATS

The desert which dominates Northern Africa is spreading southwards into the Sahel region. This is the result of severe droughts and human misuse of the land, including overgrazing by livestock and the cutting down of trees and shrubs for fuel.

TEMPERATURE AND PRECIPITATION

	Temperature °C (°F) January	July	Altitude m (ft)
Ouarzazate	9 (48)	30 (86)	1,136 (3,726)
Timbuktu	22 (71)	32 (90)	301 (987)
Tripoli	12 (53)	26 (78)	22 (72)
Alexandria	15 (59)	26 (79)	32(104)
Wadi Halfa	13 (55)	32 (90)	155 (508)
Addis Ababa	16 (61)	15 (59)	2,450 (8,057)

	Precipitation mm (in) January	July	Year
Ouarzazate	6 (0.2)	2 (0.1)	123 (4.8)
Timbuktu	0 (0)	79 (3.1)	225 (8.9)
Tripoli	81 (3.2)	0 (0)	253 (10.0)
Alexandria	48 (1.8)	0 (0)	169 (6.7)
Wadi Halfa	0 (0)	1 (0.04)	3 (0.1)
Addis Ababa	13 (0.5)	279 (11.0)	1,089 (42.9)

World's highest recorded temperature, 58°C (136.4°F), Al Aziziyah, Libya; Wadi Halfa is one of the world's driest places

NATURAL HAZARDS

Drought, earthquakes in mountains of northwest

CLIMATE

Northern Africa contains the Sahara, and other deserts in the east. The northern coasts have a Mediterranean climate. To the south is the Sahel, a hot, semiarid zone. The far south has wet and dry seasons. Mountains in the far east have a moderate climate.

POPULATION AND WEALTH

	Highest	Middle	Lowest
Population (millions)	53.2 (Egypt)	8.2 (Tunisia)	0.41 (Djibouti)
Population increase (annual population growth rate, % 1960–90)	5.6 (Djibouti)	2.6 (Morocco)	2.1 (Chad)
Energy use (gigajoules/person)	83 (Libya)	10 (Morocco)	1 (Ethiopia)
Real purchasing power (US$/person)	3,170 (Tunisia)	970 (Sudan)	500 (Mali)

ENVIRONMENTAL INDICATORS

CO$_2$ emissions (million tonnes carbon/annum)	25 (Algeria)	3 (Tunisia)	below 0.1 (Djibouti)
Artificial fertilizer use (kg/ha./annum)	351 (Egypt)	14 (Mali)	below 1.0 (Niger)
Cars (per 1,000 population)	90 (Libya)	8 (Mauritania)	below 1.0 (Ethiopia)
Access to safe drinking water (% population)	97 (Libya)	61 (Morocco)	19 (Ethiopia)

MAJOR ENVIRONMENTAL PROBLEMS AND SOURCES

Air pollution: urban high
Land degradation: *types*: desertification, soil erosion, salinization; *causes*: agriculture, industry, population pressure
Resource problems: fuelwood shortage; inadequate drinking water and sanitation
Population problems: population explosion; urban overcrowding; famine; war

ENVIRONMENTAL ISSUES

The main environmental issue in the region is water. Intensive agriculture and the rapid expansion of city populations have added to the strain on Northern Africa's limited water resources. Desertification has already taken place in large areas.

LAND

Area 14,887,110 sq. km (5,747,919 sq. mi.)
Highest point Ras Dashan, 4,620 m (15,158 ft)
Lowest point Lake Assal, Djibouti, −150 m (−492 ft)
Major features Atlas ranges, Ethiopian Highlands, Sahara, world's greatest desert, northern part of East African Rift Valley

WATER

Longest river most of the Nile's 6,690 km (4,160 mi.) length, the world's greatest for a river, and 2,802,000 sq. km (1,082,000 sq. mi.) basin is in the region
Highest average flow Niger, 5,700 cu. m/sec (201,000 cu. ft/sec) on lower section
Largest lake Chad, 25,900 sq. km (10,000 sq. mi.)

NOTABLE THREATENED ENDEMIC SPECIES

Mammals Barbary macaque (*Macaca sylvanus*), Simien jackal (*Canis simensis*), Cuvier's gazelle (*Gazella cuvieri*), beira (*Dorcatragus megalotis*), addax (*Addax nasomaculatus*)
Birds Prince Ruspoli's turaco (*Tauraco ruspoli*), Djibouti francolin (*Francolinus ochropectus*), Algerian nuthatch (*Sitta ledanti*)
Plants *Allium crameri; Biscutella elbensis; Centaurea cyrenaica; Cordeauxia edulis* (ye-eb); *Cupressus dupreziana; Cyclamen rohlfsianum; Cyperus papyrus* subsp. *hadidii; Euphorbia cameronii; Gillettiodendron glandulosum; Olea laperrinei*

HABITATS

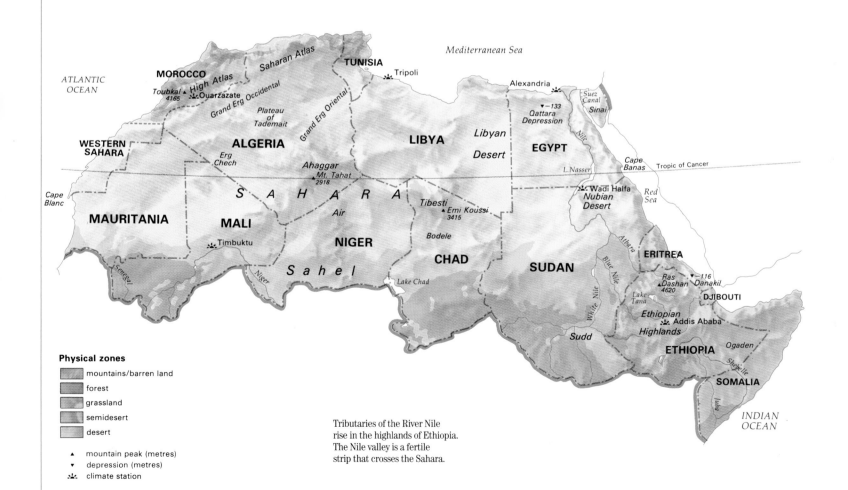

Tributaries of the River Nile rise in the highlands of Ethiopia. The Nile valley is a fertile strip that crosses the Sahara.

Physical zones
- mountains/barren land
- forest
- grassland
- semidesert
- desert

- ▲ mountain peak (metres)
- ▼ depression (metres)
- ⚶ climate station

ENVIRONMENTAL ISSUES

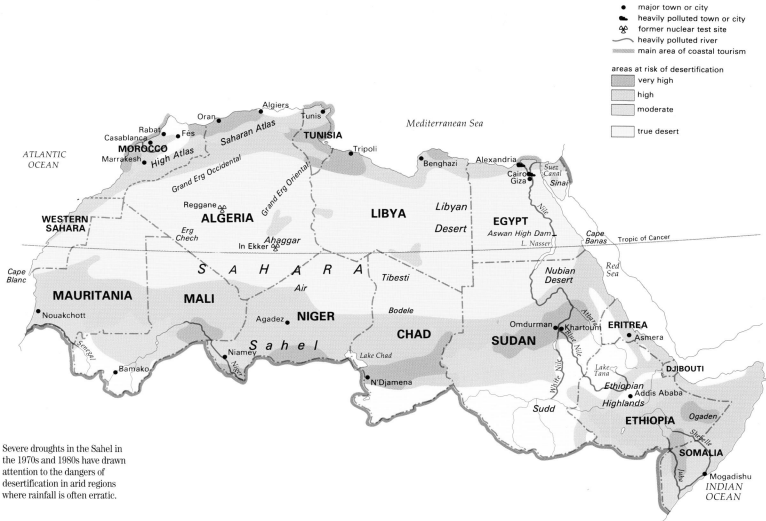

Key environmental issues
- • major town or city
- 🐦 heavily polluted town or city
- ☢ former nuclear test site
- 〰 heavily polluted river
- ▨ main area of coastal tourism

areas at risk of desertification
- very high
- high
- moderate
- true desert

Severe droughts in the Sahel in
the 1970s and 1980s have drawn
attention to the dangers of
desertification in arid regions
where rainfall is often erratic.

CLIMATE

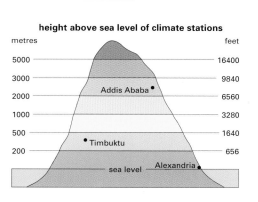

height above sea level of climate stations

Timbuktu

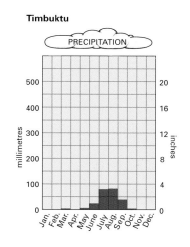

Addis Ababa

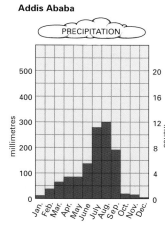

Alexandria

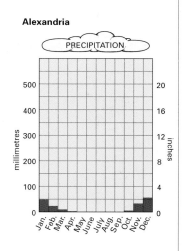

Timbuktu

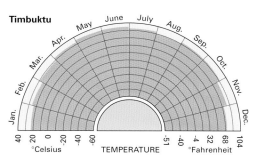

Addis Ababa

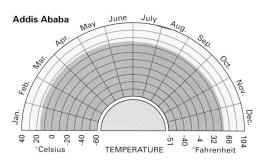

Alexandria

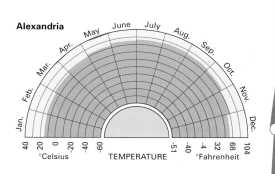

POPULATION

Much of Northern Africa is either uninhabited or sparsely populated. The population is mainly rural, though cities are growing quickly as people move into them from the countryside. Greater Cairo is one of the world's largest conurbations.

POPULATION

Total population of region (millions)	175.8
Population density (persons per sq. km)	13.2
Population change (average annual percent 1960–1990)	
Urban	+4.3
Rural	+1.6

URBAN POPULATION

As percentage of total population	
1960	31.2
1990	44.3
Percentage in cities of more than 1 million	8.1

TEN LARGEST CITIES

	Country	Population
Cairo †	Egypt	6,325,000
Alexandria	Egypt	2,893,000
Casablanca	Morocco	2,409,000
Giza	Egypt	1,858,000
Addis Ababa †	Ethiopia	1,739,000
Algiers †	Algeria	1,722,000
Tunis †	Tunisia	1,395,000
Mogadishu †	Somalia	1,000,000
Tripoli †	Libya	980,000
Rabat †	Morocco	893,000

† denotes capital city

INDUSTRY

Northern Africa's natural resources include oil and gas in Algeria, Egypt and Libya, uranium in Niger, phosphates in Morocco and Western Sahara and iron ore in Mauritania. The main industrial areas are in northern Egypt.

INDUSTRIAL OUTPUT (US $ billion)

Total	Mining	Manufacturing	Average annual change since 1960
59.8	19.4	30.1	2.6%

INDUSTRIAL WORKERS (millions)
(figures in brackets are percentages of total labour force)

Total	Mining	Manufacturing	Construction
7.34	0.62 (1.0%)	4.32 (7.1%)	2.4 (3.9%)

MAJOR PRODUCTS (figures in brackets are percentages of world production)

Energy and minerals	Output	Change since 1960
Oil (mill barrels)	1133.2 (5.0%)	+1193%
Natural gas (billion cu. metres)	50.0 (2.9%)	+333.3%
Iron Ore (mill tonnes)	9.5 (1.7%)	+42%
Natural phosphate (mill tonnes)	10.4 (19.6%)	+211%

Manufactures		
Cotton yarn (1,000 tonnes)	329 (2.1%)	+86%
Cotton woven fabrics (mill metres)	907 (1.8%)	+134%
Silk fabrics (mill sq. metres)	24.5 (1.0%)	No data
Manufactured tobacco (1,000 tonnes)	46.6 (20.7%)	No data
Footwear (mill pairs)	151.2 (3.4%)	+47%
Superphosphate fertilizer (mill tonnes)	1.5 (7.0%)	N/A
Liquefied petroleum gas (mill tonnes)	6.8 (4.4%)	N/A
Cement (million tonnes)	27.2 (0.25%)	+938%

N/A means production had not begun in 1960

AGRICULTURE

In the past, most people were subsistence farmers or nomadic herders. But today intensive farming is becoming common. Major products include cereals, citrus fruits, cotton, dates, groundnuts, potatoes and other vegetables, and rice.

LAND (million hectares)

Total	Agricultural	Arable	Forest/woodland
1,464 (100%)	383 (26%)	58 (4%)	133 (9%)

Farmers

39.3 million employed in agriculture (57% of workforce)
1.5 hectares of arable land per person employed in agriculture

MAJOR CROPS

	Area mill ha.	Yield 100kg/ha.	Production mill tonnes	Change since 1963
Millet/sorghum	13.0	5.1 (44)	6.6 (7)	+4%
Wheat	6.4	13.9 (60)	8.8 (2)	+67%
Barley	5.0	8.1 (35)	4.1 (2)	+17%
Maize	2.4	23.3 (64)	5.7 (1)	+76%
Cotton lint	1.2	5.8 (105)	0.7 (4)	+6%
Vegetables	—	—	17.6 (4)	+149%
Fruit	—	—	8.7 (3)	+49%

MAJOR LIVESTOCK

	Number mill	Production mill tonnes	Change since 1963
Sheep/goats	175.7 (11)	—	+36%
Cattle	77.9 (6)	—	+40%
Milk	—	6.3 (1)	+147%
Fish catch	—	1.2 (1)	—

FOOD SECURITY (cereal exports minus imports)

mill tonnes	% domestic production	% world trade
−20.3	63	9

Numbers in brackets are percentages of world total

POPULATION

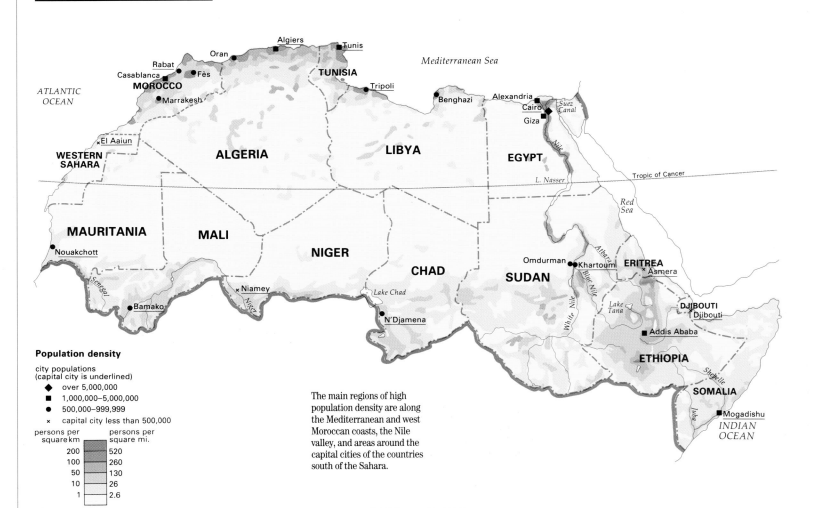

Population density

city populations
(capital city is underlined)

- ◆ over 5,000,000
- ■ 1,000,000–5,000,000
- ● 500,000–999,999
- × capital city less than 500,000

persons per square km	persons per square mi.
200	520
100	260
50	130
10	26
1	2.6

The main regions of high population density are along the Mediterranean and west Moroccan coasts, the Nile valley, and areas around the capital cities of the countries south of the Sahara.

INDUSTRY

Resources and industry

◆ industrial centre
◯ major port
● other town
— major road
— major railway
mineral resources and fossil fuels
● iron and other ferroalloy metal ores
● other metal ores
■ nonmetallic minerals

natural gas
oil
phosphates

Mediterranean Sea

ATLANTIC OCEAN

Tangier
Algiers
Annaba
Oran
Tunis
TUNISIA
Casablanca
Rabat
Sfax
MOROCCO
Tendrara
Touggourt
Tripoli
Benghazi
Marrakesh
Misratah
Tobruk
Alexandria
Port Said
Agadir
Hun
Al Jaghbub
Suez Canal
Suez
Cairo
El Aaiun
Boukra
WESTERN SAHARA
ALGERIA
LIBYA
EGYPT
El Kharga
Dakhla
L. Nasser
Aswan
Tropic of Cancer
Nouadhibou
Wadi Halfa
Red Sea
Port Sudan
Nouakchott
MAURITANIA
MALI
Karima
Timbuktu
NIGER
Khartoum
ERITREA
Mitsiwa
Agadez
CHAD
SUDAN
Asmera
Bamako
Niamey
Lake Tana
Aseb
DJIBOUTI
Berbera
N'Djamena
Nyala
Djibouti
Dire Dawa
Wau
Addis Ababa
ETHIOPIA
Juba
SOMALIA
Mogadishu
INDIAN OCEAN
Kismaayo

Manufacturing is increasing in the countries bordering the Mediterranean Sea. Tourism is also important in Egypt, Morocco and Tunisia.

AGRICULTURE

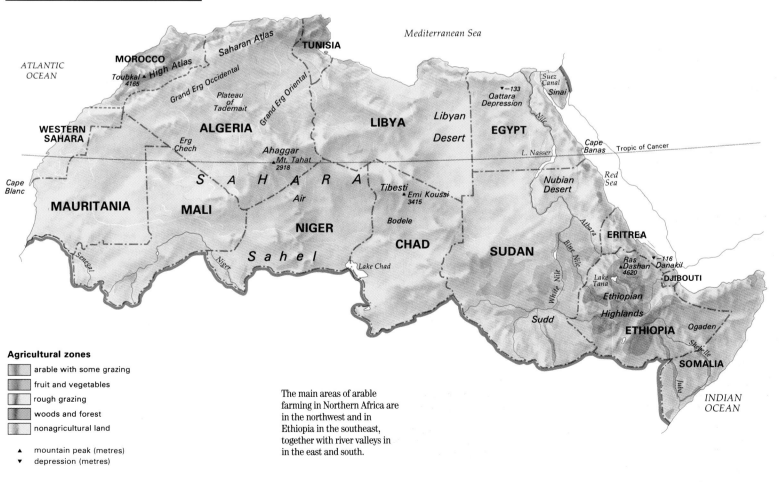

Mediterranean Sea

ATLANTIC OCEAN

MOROCCO
Saharan Atlas
TUNISIA
High Atlas
Toubkal 4165
Grand Erg Occidental
Suez Canal
Sinai
Plateau of Tademait
Grand Erg Oriental
▼ –133 Qattara Depression
WESTERN SAHARA
ALGERIA
LIBYA
Libyan Desert
EGYPT
Erg Chech
Ahaggar
Nile
Cape Banas
Tropic of Cancer
L. Nasser
Cape Blanc
Mt. Tahat 2918
S A H A R A
MAURITANIA
Air
MALI
Tibesti
Emi Koussi 3415
Red Sea
Nubian Desert
NIGER
Bodele
CHAD
SUDAN
Senegal
Sahel
Albara
ERITREA
Niger
Lake Chad
Ras Dashan 4620
▼ –116 Danakil
White Nile
Blue Nile
DJIBOUTI
Lake Tana
Sudd
Ethiopian Highlands
ETHIOPIA
Ogaden
Shebelle
SOMALIA
Juba
INDIAN OCEAN

Agricultural zones

arable with some grazing
fruit and vegetables
rough grazing
woods and forest
nonagricultural land

▲ mountain peak (metres)
▼ depression (metres)

The main areas of arable farming in Northern Africa are in the northwest and in Ethiopia in the southeast, together with river valleys in in the east and south.

CENTRAL AFRICA

Central Africa is made up of 26 countries, stretching from Cape Verde, an island nation in the Atlantic Ocean west of Senegal, to the Seychelles, another island nation, east of Kenya in the Indian Ocean.

West Africa, which extends from Senegal to Nigeria, consists of coastal plains that rise inland to low plateaus. Cameroon has some volcanic highlands, but the Zaire basin is a shallow depression in the central plateaus. Beyond the Zaire basin are mountains that overlook the Great Rift Valley, which contains Lakes Tanganyika, Edward and Albert. East of the Rift Valley lie the high plateaus of East Africa. This region contains Africa's largest lake, Victoria, the source of the White Nile. Ancient volcanic mountains include Kilimanjaro, Africa's highest peak. These volcanoes were formed while earth movements were fracturing the continent, creating the Rift Valley.

Central Africa straddles the Equator and the climate is generally hot and humid, though temperatures are much lower in the highlands. The world's second largest rainforest (after the Amazon basin) occupies parts of the Congo basin. But Central Africa also contains large areas of savanna, home of much wildlife, especially in the national parks on the plateaus of East Africa. Most of the people are Black Africans who are divided into many ethnic groups. Each group has its own language, art, customs and traditional religion, though Islam has made inroads into northern West Africa and also East Africa. Christianity was introduced by European missionaries during the colonial period in the 19th and 20th centuries.

Subsistence farming is the main activity and manufacturing is generally limited to producing basic items such as cement, clothes, and processed food and drink for the home market.

Central Africa is part of the vast plateau of extremely old rocks which makes up the African plateau. In places, the ancient rocks are overlain by young sedimentary rocks and, elsewhere, by volcanic rocks. The volcanic rocks in East Africa reached the surface 35 to 25 million years ago through cracks formed when the plateaus were stretched by earth movements. These movements tore open the Great Rift Valley which runs north-south through eastern Africa. The ancient rocks of Africa are rich in minerals.

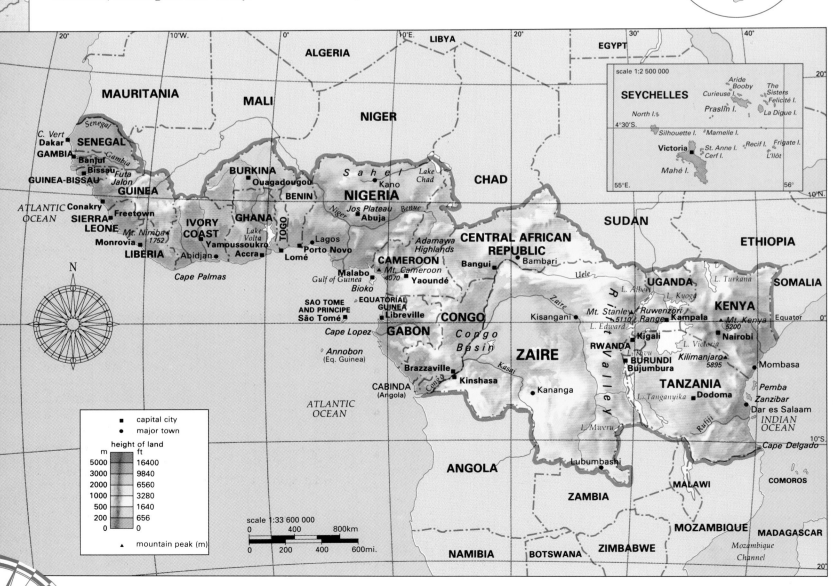

THE POLITICAL AND CULTURAL WORLD

The European colonizers drew Africa's boundaries with little regard for existing ethnic groups. One result of this policy is that the nations of Central Africa contain many cultural groups.

Nigeria, for example, has more than 200 ethnic groups and no local language is used widely enough for it to be the official language. Hence Nigeria, like most countries in the region, has adopted the former colonial language, in this case English, for official purposes. Several of the groups in Nigeria are rivals. In 1967, when one of these groups, the Ibo, tried to set up their own state, civil war ensued. Similar ethnic tensions are common in Central Africa.

COUNTRIES IN THE REGION

Benin, Burkina, Burundi, Cameroon, Cape Verde, Central African Republic, Congo, Equatorial Guinea, Gabon, Gambia, Ghana, Guinea, Guinea-Bissau, Ivory Coast, Kenya, Liberia, Nigeria, Rwanda, São Tomé and Príncipe, Senegal, Seychelles, Sierra Leone, Tanzania, Togo, Uganda, Zaire

Dependencies of other states British Indian Ocean Territory (U.K.)

MEMBERSHIP OF INTERNATIONAL ORGANIZATIONS

Economic Community of West African States (ECOWAS) Benin, Burkina, Cape Verde, Gambia, Ghana, Guinea, Guinea-Bissau, Ivory Coast, Kenya, Rwanda, Seychelles, Tanzania

RELIGION

Countries with one major religion (M) Gambia; (RC) Cape Verde, Equatorial Guinea
Countries with two major religions (M,P) Nigeria; (P,RC) São Tomé and Príncipe, Seychelles
Countries with three or more major religions (I,M,RC) Benin, Burkina, Gabon, Guinea, Guinea-Bissau, Ivory Coast, Liberia, Senegal; (C,I,M,P,RC) Kenya, Zaire; (I,M,P,RC) Cameroon, Burundi, Central African Republic, Congo, Ghana, Rwanda, Sierra Leone, Tanzania, Togo, Uganda

Key: C-various Christian, I-indigenous religions, M-Muslim, P-Protestant, RC-Roman Catholic

LANGUAGE

Countries with one official language (E) Gambia, Ghana, Liberia, Nigeria, Sierra Leone, Uganda; (F) Benin, Burkina, Central African Republic, Congo, Gabon, Guinea, Ivory Coast, Senegal, Togo, Zaire; (P) Cape Verde, Guinea-Bissau, São Tomé and Príncipe; (S) Equatorial Guinea
Countries with two official languages (E,F) Cameroon; (E,Sw) Kenya, Tanzania; (F,K) Burundi; (F,R) Rwanda
Country with three official languages (C,E,F) Seychelles

Key: C-Creole, E-English, F-French, K-Kirundi, P-Portuguese, R-Rwandan, S-Spanish, Sw-Swahili

Numerous indigenous languages are spoken in the region

STYLES OF GOVERNMENT

Republics All countries in the region
Federal state Nigeria
Multiparty states Benin, Burkina, Cameroon, Cape Verde, Congo, Gambia, Liberia, Nigeria, São Tomé and Príncipe, Senegal, Sierra Leone, Togo, Uganda, Zaire
One-party states Burundi, Central African Republic, Equatorial Guinea, Guinea-Bissau, Ivory Coast, Kenya, Rwanda, Seychelles, Tanzania
States without parties Ghana, Guinea
Military influence Burundi, Equatorial Guinea, Ghana, Guinea, Guinea-Bissau, Liberia, Nigeria, Sierra Leone, Togo

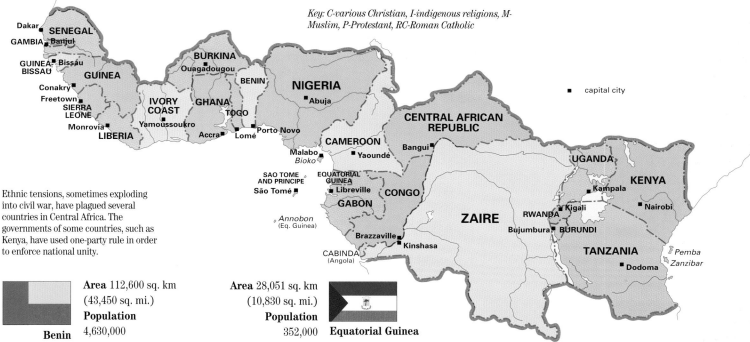

Ethnic tensions, sometimes exploding into civil war, have plagued several countries in Central Africa. The governments of some countries, such as Kenya, have used one-party rule in order to enforce national unity.

capital city

Benin
Area 112,600 sq. km (43,450 sq. mi.)
Population 4,630,000

Burkina
Area 274,200 sq. km (105,869 sq. mi.)
Population 8,996,000

Burundi
Area 25,967 sq. km (10,026 sq. mi.)
Population 5,472,000

Cameroon
Area 463,511 sq. km (178,963 sq. mi.)
Population 11,833,000

Cape Verde
Area 4,033 sq. km (1,557 sq. mi.)
Population 370,000

Central African Republic
Area 622,436 sq. km (240,324 sq. mi.)
Population 3,039,000

Congo
Area 342,000 sq. km (132,047 sq. mi.)
Population 2,271,000

Equatorial Guinea
Area 28,051 sq. km (10,830 sq. mi.)
Population 352,000

Gabon
Area 267,667 sq. km (103,347 sq. mi.)
Population 1,172,000

Gambia
Area 10,689 sq. km (4,127 sq. mi.)
Population 861,000

Ghana
Area 238,533 sq. km (92,098 sq. mi.)
Population 15,028,000

Guinea
Area 245,857 sq. km (941,926 sq. mi.)
Population 5,755,000

Guinea-Bissau
Area 36,125 sq. km (13,948 sq. mi.)
Population 964,000

Kenya
Area 571,416 sq. km (220,625 sq. mi.)
Population 24,031,000

Liberia
Area 99,067 sq. km (38,250 sq. mi.)
Population 2,575,000

Nigeria
Area 923,768 sq. km (356,669 sq. mi.)
Population 108,542,000

Rwanda
Area 26,338 sq. km (10,169 sq. mi.)
Population 7,237,000

São Tomé and Príncipe
Area 1,001 sq. km (386 sq. mi.)
Population 121,000

Senegal
Area 196,722 sq. km (75,955 sq. mi.)
Population 7,327,000

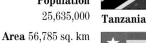
Seychelles
Area 453 sq. km (175 sq. mi.)
Population 68,700

Sierra
Area 71,740 sq. km (27,699 sq. mi.)
Population 4,151,000

Tanzania
Area 885,987 sq. km (342,081 sq. mi.)
Population 25,635,000

Togo
Area 56,785 sq. km (21,925 sq. mi.)
Population 3,531,000

Uganda
Area 197,040 sq. km (76,080 sq. mi.)
Population 18,794,000

Zaire
Area 2,345,095 sq. km (905,446 sq. mi.)
Population 35,568,000

HABITATS

Central Africa contains rainforests and grasslands called savanna. The savanna merges in the north into dry grassland. The altitude, especially on the high plateaus of East Africa, has a marked, moderating influence on the tropical climate.

LAND

Area 8,979,034 sq. km (3,465,907 sq. mi.)
Highest point Kilimanjaro, 5,895 m (19,341 ft)
Lowest point sea level
Major features Jos Plateau and Adamawa Highlands in west, Congo basin, Ruwenzori Range, mountains and Rift Valley in east

WATER

Longest river Congo (Zaire), 4,630 km (2,880 mi.)
Largest basin Congo, 3,822,000 sq. km (1,476,000 sq. mi.)
Highest average flow Congo, 39,000 cu. m/sec (1,377,000 cu. ft/sec)
Largest lake Victoria, 62,940 sq. km (24,300 sq. mi.)

NOTABLE THREATENED ENDEMIC SPECIES

Mammals Nimba otter-shrew (*Micropotamogale lamottei*), Mountain gorilla (*Gorilla gorilla beringei*), chimpanzee (*Pan troglodytes*), bonobo (*Pan paniscus*), drill (*Mandrillus leucophaeus*), Pygmy hippopotamus (*Choeropsis liberiensis*), Ader's duiker (*Cephalophus adersi*)
Birds White-breasted guinea fowl (*Agelastes meleagrides*), Bannerman's turaco (*Tauraco bannermani*), Sokoke scops owl (*Otus ireneae*), Seychelles magpie robin (*Copsychus sechellarum*)
Plants *Aeschynomene batekensis*; *Drypetes singroboensis*; *Justicia hepperi*; *Memecylon fragrans*; *Pitcairnia feliciana*; *Saintpaulia ionantha* (African violet); *Scleria sheilae*; *Temnopteryx sericea*; *Uvariodendron gorgonis*; *Vernonia sechellensis*
Others Goliath frog (*Conraua goliath*), Lake Victoria cichlid fish (250 species), African blind barbfish (*Caecobarbus geertsi*),

CLIMATE

Central Africa lies on the Equator and much of the region has a tropical rainy climate, though temperatures vary with altitude. To the east are the mountains, giving many places a pleasant, mild climate with moderate temperatures. To the north is a hot semiarid area.

TEMPERATURE AND PRECIPITATION

	Temperature °C (°F)		Altitude
	January	July	m (ft)
Dakar	22 (69)	27 (81)	40 (131)
Ngaoundéré	22 (72)	21 (70)	1,119 (3,670)
Lisala	25 (77)	24 (75)	460 (1,509)
Bukoba	21 (70)	20 (68)	1,137 (3,729)
Lodwar	29 (84)	28 (82)	506 (1,660)
Mombasa	28 (82)	24 (75)	16 (52)

	Precipitation mm (in)		
	January	July	Year
Dakar	0 (0)	88 (3.5)	578 (22.8)
Ngaoundéré	2 (0.1)	256 (10.1)	1,511 (59.5)
Lisala	63 (2.5)	190 (7.5)	1,626 (64.0)
Bukoba	151 (5.9)	49 (1.9)	2,043 (80.4)
Lodwar	8 (0.3)	15 (0.6)	162 (6.4)
Mombasa	25 (0.9)	89 (3.5)	1,163 (45.8)

NATURAL HAZARDS

Drought, floods, earthquakes

ENVIRONMENTAL ISSUES

Human adaptation of the environment of Central Africa has been going on for thousands of years. Today, the fast-increasing population and the devastation of wars are adding to the pressure on the region's fragile resources, such as soils and vegetation.

POPULATION AND WEALTH

	Highest	Middle	Lowest
Population (millions)	108.5 (Nigeria)	5.8 (Guinea)	0.4 (Equ Guinea)
Population increase (annual population growth rate, % 1960–90)	3.6 (Kenya)	2.8 (Zaire)	1.1 (Equ Guinea)
Energy use (gigajoules/person)	34 (Gabon)	2 (Guinea)	below 0.1 (C Verde)
Real purchasing power (US$/person)	3,960 (Gabon)	910 (Guinea)	410 (Uganda)

ENVIRONMENTAL INDICATORS

	Highest	Middle	Lowest
CO_2 emissions (million tonnes carbon/annum)	53 (Nigeria)	24 (Burkina)	9 (C Verde)
Deforestation ('000s ha./annum 1980s)	510 (Ivory C)	55 (CAR)	1 (Burundi)
Artificial fertilizer use (kg/ha./annum)	41 (Kenya)	4 (Ghana)	below 1.0 (Guinea)
Cars (per 1,000 population)	15 (Tanzania)	5 (Kenya)	below 1.0 (Rwanda)
Access to safe drinking water (% population)	75 (Gambia)	34 (Zaire)	12 (CAR)

MAJOR ENVIRONMENTAL PROBLEMS AND SOURCES

Land degradation: *types*: desertification, soil erosion, salinization, deforestation, habitat destruction; *causes*: agriculture, population pressure
Resource problems: fuelwood shortage; inadequate drinking water and sanitation; land use competition
Population problems: population explosion; urban overcrowding; inadequate health facilities; disease; famine; war
Major event: Lake Nyos (1986), gas cloud released

HABITATS

Physical zones

mountains/barren land
forest
grassland
semidesert

▲ mountain peak (metres)
⁂ climate station

West Africa contains low plateaus, which overlook the coastal plains. The high, rolling plateaus in East Africa are broken by huge volcanic massifs, while two arms of the Great Rift Valley run through the region.

ENVIRONMENTAL ISSUES

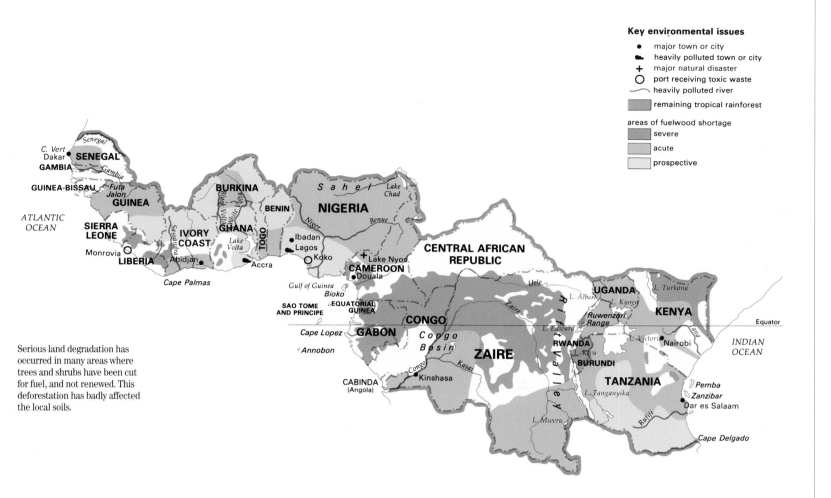

Key environmental issues

- ● major town or city
- ● heavily polluted town or city
- + major natural disaster
- ○ port receiving toxic waste
- ⌇ heavily polluted river
- ▓ remaining tropical rainforest

areas of fuelwood shortage
- ▓ severe
- ▒ acute
- ░ prospective

Serious land degradation has occurred in many areas where trees and shrubs have been cut for fuel, and not renewed. This deforestation has badly affected the local soils.

CLIMATE

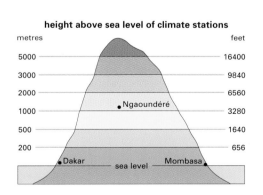

height above sea level of climate stations

metres		feet
5000		16400
3000		9840
2000		6560
1000	●Ngaoundéré	3280
500		1640
200		656
●Dakar	Mombasa●	
sea level		

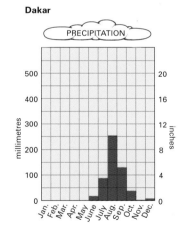

Dakar PRECIPITATION

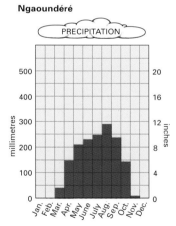

Ngaoundéré PRECIPITATION

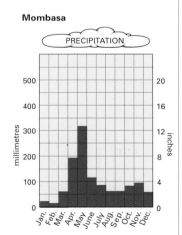

Mombasa PRECIPITATION

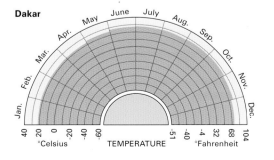

Dakar TEMPERATURE

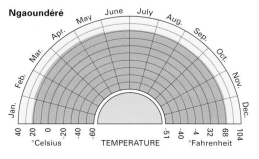

Ngaoundéré TEMPERATURE

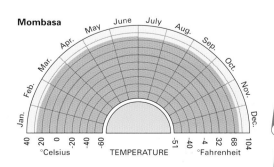

Mombasa TEMPERATURE

POPULATION

About three out of every four people in Central Africa live in rural areas, in scattered communities or in villages. But during this century, as the countries became independent, the cities have expanded rapidly as people have arrived looking for jobs and better education.

POPULATION

Total population of region (millions)	310.8
Population density (persons per sq. km)	75.6
Population change (average annual percent 1960–1990)	
Urban	+5.2
Rural	+1.9

URBAN POPULATION

As percentage of total population	
1960	15.2
1990	24.3
Percentage in cities of more than 1 million	2.1

TEN LARGEST CITIES

	Country	Population
Kinshasa †	Zaire	2,654,000
Abidjan	Ivory Coast	1,850,000
Nairobi †	Kenya	1,429,000
Dakar †	Senegal	1,382,000
Dar es Salaam	Tanzania	1,100,000
Lagos	Nigeria	1,097,000
Ibadan	Nigeria	1,060,000
Douala	Cameroon	1,030,000
Accra †	Ghana	965,000
Libreville †	Gabon	830,000

† denotes capital city

INDUSTRY

Central Africa's rich natural resources are mainly exported, because the region lacks manufacturing industries. Most industries are small-scale, except in Kenya and Nigeria, where larger-scale manufacturing is growing. Nigeria and Tanzania have coal deposits.

INDUSTRIAL OUTPUT (US $ billion)

Total	Mining	Manufacturing	Average annual change since 1960
22.8	10.6	12.2	+2.3%

INDUSTRIAL WORKERS (millions)

Total (mining, manufacturing, & utilities)	% of labour force
6.6	7.1%

MAJOR PRODUCTS (figures in brackets are percentages of total world production)

Energy and minerals	Output	Change since 1960
Oil (mill barrels)	700	+70%
Bauxite (mill tonnes)	18.0 (20%)	+350%
Copper (mill tonnes)	0.5 (6%)	+8%
Diamonds (mill carats)	25.9 (27%)	+28%

Manufactures		
Textiles (mill sq. meters)	677.3 (1.0%)	+123%
Palm oil (mill tonnes)	1.5 (8.1%)·	No data
Tobacco products (billion units)	9.7 (2.1%)	+79%

AGRICULTURE

Agriculture employs about seven-tenths of the people, with most farmers producing enough to meet the basic needs of their families. There is some nomadic herding. Commercial crops include cocoa, coffee, cotton, groundnuts, palm oil, rubber, and tea.

LAND (million hectares)

Total	Agricultural	Arable	Forest/woodland
823 (100%)	218 (27%)	75 (9%)	393 (48%)

FARMERS

84 million employed in agriculture (70% of workforce)
0.9 hectares of arable land per person employed in agriculture

MAJOR CROPS

	Area mill ha.	Yield 100kg/ha.	Production mill tonnes	Change since 1963
Millet/sorghum	15.2	9.9 (82)	15.0 (17)	+49%
Maize	8.0	11.7 (32)	9.4 (2)	+119%
Cassava	6.3	85.7 (92)	53.9 (40)	+100%
Groundnuts	3.7	9.0 (78)	3.4 (16)	−9%
Cocoa beans	3.7	3.2 (87)	1.2 (59)	+27%
Palm kernels	—	—	0.6 (22)	−21%
Palm oil	—	—	1.5 (18)	+59%
Bananas	—	—	21.2 (32)	+90%

MAJOR LIVESTOCK

	Number mill	Production mill tonnes	Change since 1963
Sheep/goats	110.5 (7)	—	+67%
Cattle	58.3 (5)	—	+50%
Milk	—	2.6 (1)	+36%
Fish catch	—	2.2 (2)	—

FOOD SECURITY (cereal exports minus imports)

mill tonnes	% domestic production	% world trade
−4.6	15	2

Numbers in brackets are percentages of world total

POPULATION

Population density

city populations
(capital city is underlined)

- ■ 1,000,000–5,000,000
- ● 500,000–999,999
- × capital city less than 500,000

persons per square km	persons per square mi.
200	520
100	260
50	130
10	26
1	2.6

Areas of high population density include the coastal regions of West Africa and the high plateaus of East Africa. The thinly populated areas are largely rainforests, where there are few towns, except for some river ports.

INDUSTRY

Resources and industry
- ◆ industrial centre
- ○ major port
- ● other town
- — major road
- — major railway

mineral resources and fossil fuels
- ● iron and other ferroalloy metal ores
- ● other metal ores
- ■ nonmetallic minerals

- bauxite
- coal
- copper
- diamonds
- gold
- iron ore
- oil and natural gas

The region is rich in mineral resources. Nigeria, Gabon and Congo produce oil. Ghana has gold mines, Zaire is rich in copper and diamonds, Guinea produces bauxite, and Liberia has large iron ore reserves.

AGRICULTURE

Agricultural zones
- arable and grazing
- fruit, vegetables and tree crops
- rough grazing
- woods and forest with some grazing
- nonagricultural land

- ▲ mountain peak (metres)

Arable farming is important in areas with abundant rainfall. Drier savanna areas are used for grazing. Many livestock and people died in the Sahel region of northern West Africa during long droughts in the 1970s and 1980s.

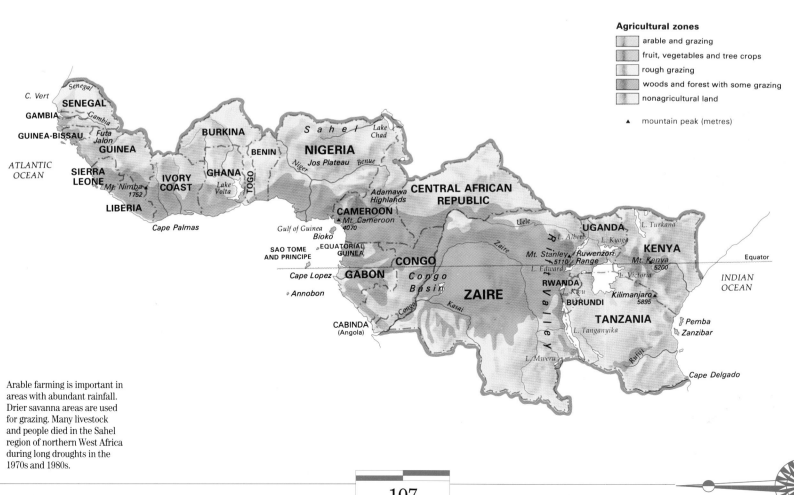

SOUTHERN AFRICA

Southern Africa consists of ten mainland countries, and three island nations, Madagascar, the Comoros and Mauritius. The mainland is a high, saucer-shaped plateau bordered by mostly narrow coastal plains. The Drakensberg contains the highest peaks. The region also contains the most southerly part of the Great Rift Valley, enclosing Lake Malawi.

Forests and savanna are found in the north, but the south is dry grassland, merging into the Kalahari, a semidesert, and the Namib Desert, one of the driest places on Earth.

Colonization, involving the introduction of commercial farming, the exploitation of natural resources and the setting up of manufacturing industries, has made a great impact on the Black African cultures of Southern Africa.

Nowhere has the impact been greater than in South Africa. Its history of racial conflict was one of the major international political issues. But in the early 1990s, talks began between the ethnic groups aimed at creating a society in which all adults could vote. The first multi-racial elections were held in the country in April 1994.

Southern Africa is a region of ancient, often mineral-rich rocks, which once formed part of the supercontinent of Gondwanaland. Younger rocks occur around the central plateau, which have been folded and faulted, notably in the southwest. Apart from the Atlas Mountains, these ranges are Africa's only recently formed fold mountains.

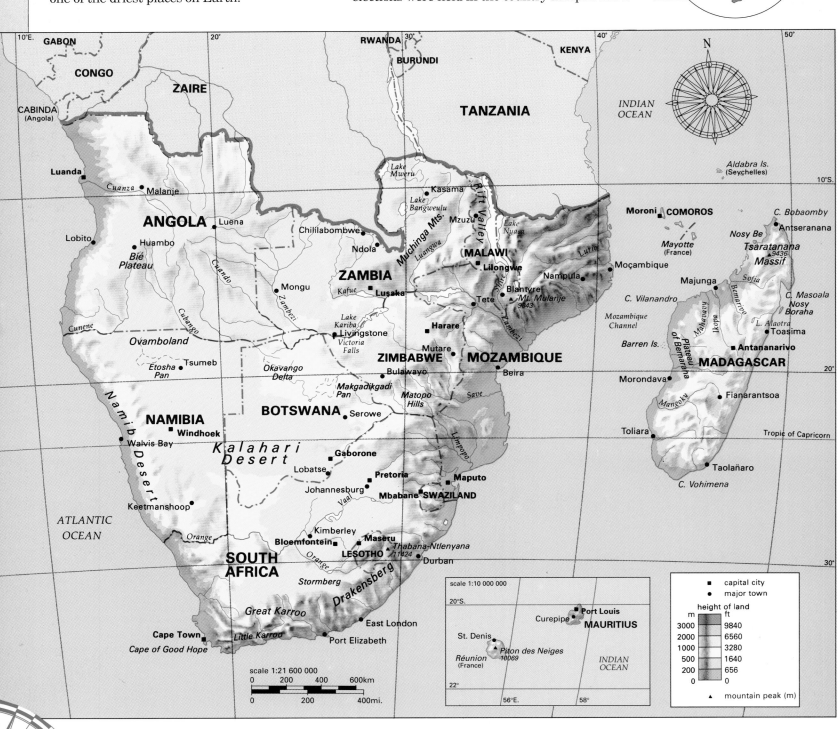

THE POLITICAL AND CULTURAL WORLD

Descendants of the region's earliest people, the Khoi-San (Hottentots and Bushmen), now make up extremely small groups. Most people are Black Africans, who speak one of the many Bantu languages, including Tswana and Zulu.

The other main groups are the descendants of European settlers, including the Afrikaaners (descendants of early Dutch settlers in South Africa) and the British. Relationships between European settlers and Black Africans have underlain the political problems of the region. In several countries, including Angola, Namibia, Mozambique and Namibia, independence was achieved only after long colonial wars.

COUNTRIES IN THE REGION

Angola, Botswana, Comoros, Lesotho, Madagascar, Malawi, Mauritius, Mozambique, Namibia, South Africa, Swaziland, Zambia, Zimbabwe

MEMBERSHIP OF INTERNATIONAL ORGANIZATIONS

Organization for African Unity (OAU) Angola, Botswana, Lesotho, Madagascar, Malawi, Mauritius, Mozambique, Namibia, Swaziland, Zambia, Zimbabwe
Southern Africa Development Coordination Conference (SADCC) Angola, Botswana, Lesotho, Malawi, Mozambique, Swaziland, Zambia, Zimbabwe

STYLES OF GOVERNMENT

Republics Angola, Botswana, Comoros, Madagascar, Malawi, Mozambique, Namibia, South Africa, Zambia, Zimbabwe
Monarchies Lesotho, Swaziland
Federal states Comoros
Multiparty states Angola, Botswana, Mauritius, Mozambique, Namibia, South Africa, Zambia, Zimbabwe
One-party states Comoros, Madagascar, Malawi, Swaziland
State without parties Lesotho
Military influence Lesotho

LANGUAGE

Countries with one official language (E) Botswana, Mauritius, Zambia, Zimbabwe; (M) Madagascar; (P) Angola, Mozambique
Countries with two official languages (A,F) Comoros; (Af,E) South Africa, Namibia; (C,E) Malawi; (E,Se) Lesotho; (E,Si) Swaziland

Other significant languages in the region include Afrikaans, Comorian, ChiSona, Kimbundu, Lunda, Makua, Setwana, Si Ndebele, Tombuka and Umbundu

Key: A-Arabic, Af-Afrikaans, C-Chichewa, E-English, F-French, M-Malagasy, P-Portuguese, Se-Sesotho, Si-siSwati

RELIGION

Countries with one major religion (C) Lesotho, Namibia; (H) Mauritius; (M) Comoros
Countries with two major religions (C,I) Angola, Botswana, Malawi, Swaziland, Zambia, Zimbabwe
Countries with three major religions (C,I,M) Madagascar, Mozambique
Country with more than three major religions (C,DR,H,I,M,RC) South Africa

Key: C-various Christian, DR-Dutch Reformed, H-Hindu, I-indigenous religions, M-Muslim, RC-Roman Catholic

Angola **Area** 1,246,700 sq. km (481,354 sq. mi.) **Population** 10,020,000

Botswana **Area** 581,730 sq. km (224,607 sq. mi.) **Population** 1,304,000

Comoros **Area** 1,862 sq. km (719 sq. mi.) **Population** 550,000

Lesotho **Area** 30,355 sq. km (11,720 sq. mi.) **Population** 1,774,000

Madagascar **Area** 587,041 sq. km (226,658 sq. mi.) **Population** 12,004,000

Malawi **Area** 94,276 sq. km (36,400 sq. mi.) **Population** 8,754,600

Mauritius **Area** 2,040 sq. km (788 sq. mi.) **Population** 1,082,000

Mozambique **Area** 799,379 sq. km (308,642 sq. mi.) **Population** 15,656,000

Namibia **Area** 823,144 sq. km (317,818 sq. mi.) **Population** 1,781,000

South Africa **Area** 1,225,815 sq. km (473,290 sq. mi.) **Population** 35,282,000

Swaziland **Area** 17,364 sq. km (6,704 sq. mi.) **Population** 788,000

Zambia **Area** 752,614 sq. km (290,586 sq. mi.) **Population** 8,452,000

Zimbabwe **Area** 390,759 sq. km (150,873 sq. mi.) **Population** 9,709,000

In the last 30 years, Southern Africa has been one of the world's most unstable regions. Civil wars occurred in Angola and Mozambique after independence and a long armed struggle took place in South Africa, with the African National Congress leading the fight against apartheid.

■ capital city

HABITATS

The plateau which forms the heart of Southern Africa is largely enclosed by mountain ranges. Some rivers, such as the Orange and Zambezi, cut through the rim and reach the sea. Others flow into inland drainage basins. In the southwest are desert areas.

LAND

Area 5,751,800 sq. km (2,220,194 sq. mi.)
Highest point Thabana Ntlenyana, 3,482 m (11,424 ft)
Lowest point sea level
Major features interior plateau, salt pans and deltas, Kalahari and Namib Deserts, Karoo tableland, Cape ranges in southwest, Drakensberg range, Madagascar

WATER

Longest river Zambezi, 2,650 km (1,650 mi.)
Largest basin Zambezi, 1,331,000 sq. km (514,000 sq. mi.)
Highest average flow Zambezi, 16,000 cu. m/sec (565,000 cu. ft/sec)
Largest lake Malawi, 29,600 sq. km (11,400 sq. mi.)

NOTABLE THREATENED ENDEMIC SPECIES

Mammals Juliana's golden mole (*Amblysomus julianae*), Golden bamboo lemur (*Hapalemur aureus*), indri (*Indri indri*), Brown hyena (*Hyaena brunnea*), Mauritian flying fox (*Pteropus niger*), Riverine rabbit (*Bunolagus monticularis*), Mountain zebra (*Equus zebra*)
Birds Madagascar serpent eagle (*Eutriorchis astur*), Cape vulture (*Gyps coprotheres*), Pink pigeon (*Nesoenas mayeri*)
Plants *Allophylus chirindensis*; *Aloe polyphylla* (spiral aloe); *Dasylepis burttdavyi*; *Encephalartos chimanimaniensis*; *Hyophorbe amaricaulis*; *Jubaeopsis caffra*; *Kniphofia umbrina*; *Nesiota elliptica* (St Helena olive); *Protea odorata*; *Ramosmania heterophylla*
Others Angonoka tortoise (*Geochelone yniphora*), Cape platana or clawed toad (*Xenopus gilli*), Fiery redfin (*Pseudobarbatus phlegethon*)

CLIMATE

The north of the region has a tropical climate, with dry and wet seasons. The southwest is largely desert. The southwestern tip has dry summers and mild, moist winters. The southeastern coasts of South Africa have hot, humid summers and mild, dry winters.

TEMPERATURE AND PRECIPITATION

	Temperature °C (°F) January	July	Altitude m (ft)
Lusaka	22 (72)	16 (61)	1,277 (4,188)
Bulawayo	21 (70)	14 (57)	1,341 (4,398)
Cape Town	21 (69)	12 (53)	17 (55)
Toliara	27 (81)	20 (68)	9 (30)
Antananarivo	21 (69)	15 (59)	1,372 (4,499)

	Precipitation mm (in) January	July	Year
Lusaka	231 (9.0)	0 (0)	829 (32.6)
Bulawayo	142 (5.6)	0 (0)	589 (23.2)
Cape Town	15 (0.5)	89 (3.5)	652 (25.7)
Toliara	71 (2.8)	4 (0.2)	342 (13.5)
Antananarivo	300 (11.8)	8 (0.3)	1,270 (50.0)

World's greatest recorded 24-hour rainfall, 1,870 mm (73.6 in), Réunion island

NATURAL HAZARDS

Drought

ENVIRONMENTAL ISSUES

Many problems in Southern Africa are related to the population explosion, which puts pressure on habitats and their wildlife. Pollution caused by urbanization and industry are evident in South Africa, while the ravages of war are widespread.

POPULATION AND WEALTH

	Highest	Middle	Lowest
Population (millions)	35.3 (S Africa)	8.5 (Zambia)	0.8 (Swaziland)
Population increase (annual population growth rate, % 1960–90)	3.4 (Botswana)	2.6 (Namibia)	1.7 (Mauritius)
Energy use (gigajoules/person)	83 (S Africa)	2 (Comoros)	1 (Madagascar)
Real purchasing power (US$/person)	5,480 (S Africa)	1,370 (Zimbabwe)	570 (Comoros)

ENVIRONMENTAL INDICATORS

CO₂ emissions (million tonnes carbon/annum)	47 (S Africa)	3.4 (Angola)	0.3 (Comoros)
Deforestation ('000s ha./annum 1980s)	156 (Madagascar)	80 (Zimbabwe)	0.5 (Mauritius)
Artificial fertilizer use (kg/ha./annum)	307 (Mauritius)	18 (Zambia)	below 1 (Botswana)
Cars (per 1,000 population)	3,079 (S Africa)	49 (Madagascar)	6 (Lesotho)
Access to safe drinking water (% population)	98 (Mauritius)	50 (Swaziland)	24 (Mozambique)

MAJOR ENVIRONMENTAL PROBLEMS AND SOURCES

Air pollution: locally high
Land degradation: *types*: desertification, soil erosion, deforestation, habitat destruction; *causes*: agriculture, population pressure
Resource problems: fuelwood shortage; inadequate drinking water and sanitation
Population problems: population explosion; urban overcrowding; inadequate health facilities; famine; war

HABITATS

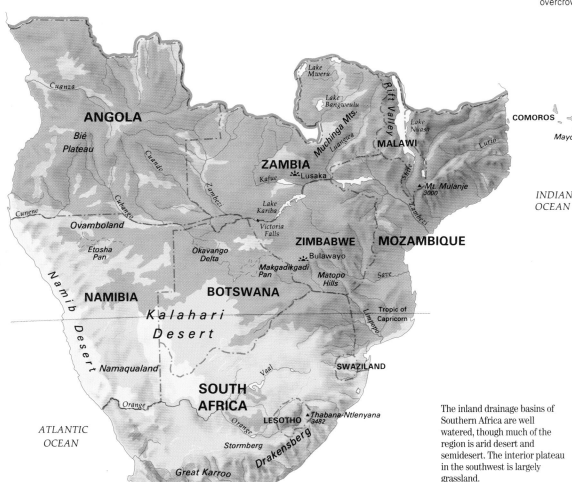

Physical zones
- mountains/barren land
- forest
- grassland
- semidesert
- desert

▲ mountain peak (metres)
☆ climate station

The inland drainage basins of Southern Africa are well watered, though much of the region is arid desert and semidesert. The interior plateau in the southwest is largely grassland.

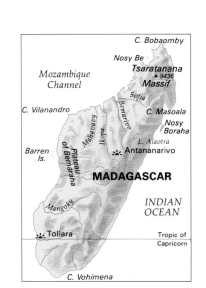

ENVIRONMENTAL ISSUES

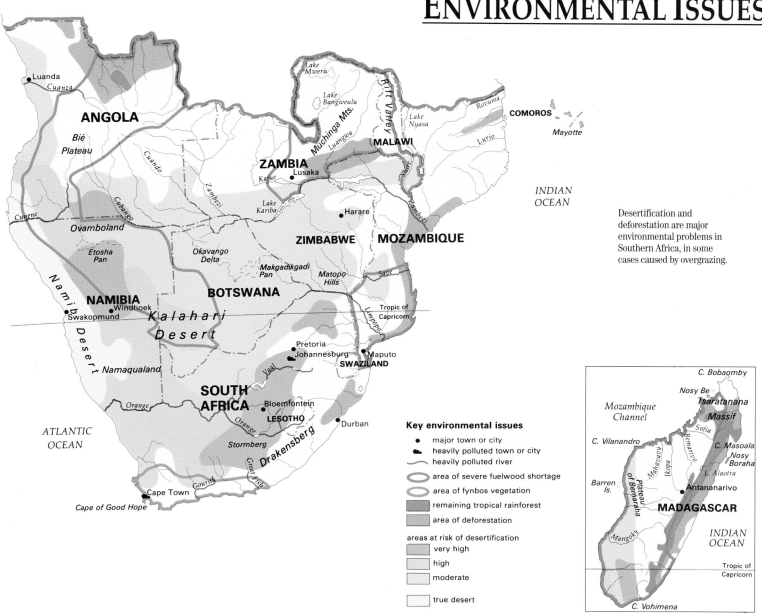

Desertification and deforestation are major environmental problems in Southern Africa, in some cases caused by overgrazing.

Key environmental issues

- • major town or city
- ◆ heavily polluted town or city
- ～ heavily polluted river
- ◯ area of severe fuelwood shortage
- ◯ area of fynbos vegetation
- ▨ remaining tropical rainforest
- ▨ area of deforestation

areas at risk of desertification
- ▨ very high
- ▨ high
- ▨ moderate
- ☐ true desert

CLIMATE

height above sea level of climate stations

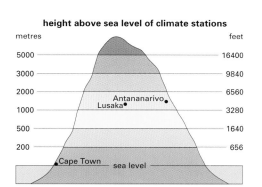

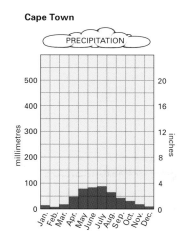

Cape Town

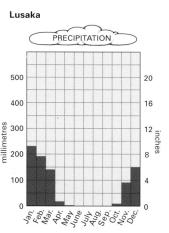

Lusaka

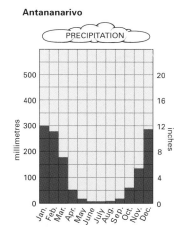

Antananarivo

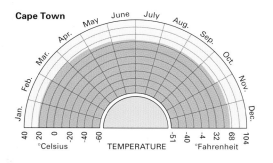

Cape Town

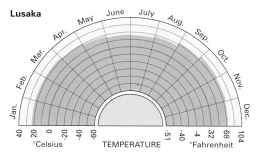

Lusaka

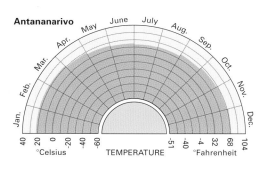

Antananarivo

111

POPULATION

Europeans founded most of the cities in Southern Africa. Today the cities are expanding quickly. They are magnets that attract people from the less populated rural areas who are seeking jobs and better health and education services for their families.

POPULATION

Total population of region (millions)	108.3
Population density (persons per sq. km)	21.6
Population change (average annual percent 1960–1990)	
Urban	+5.9
Rural	+1.6

URBAN POPULATION

As percentage of total population	
1960	22.1
1990	39.6
Percentage in cities of more than 1 million	4.1

TEN LARGEST CITIES

	Country	Population
Johannesburg	South Africa	3,411,000
Cape Town †	South Africa	1,912,000
Luanda †	Angola	1,200,000
Maputo †	Mozambique	1,070,000
Durban	South Africa	982,000
Lusaka †	Zambia	900,000
Pretoria †	South Africa	823,000
Antananarivo †	Madagascar	703,000
Harare †	Zimbabwe	681,000
Port Elizabeth	South Africa	652,000

† denotes capital city

INDUSTRY

South Africa is Africa's leading industrialized nation. It attracts migrant workers from the Black African states. Some countries, such as Madagascar, have little industry except commercial farming, though Namibia and Botswana export minerals.

INDUSTRIAL OUTPUT (US $ billion)

Total	Mining	Manufacturing	Average annual change since 1960
50.9	13.9	30.6	+2.3%

INDUSTRIAL WORKERS (millions)
(figures in brackets are percentages of total labour force)

Total	Mining	Manufacturing	Construction
4.7	1.0 (3.3%)	2.95 (9.8%)	0.73 (2.4%)

MAJOR PRODUCTS (figures in brackets are percentages of world production)

Energy and minerals	Output	Change since 1960
Bituminous coal (mill tonnes)	183.3 (5.3%)	+358%
Oil (mill barrels)	169.3 (0.7%)	N/A
Copper (1,000 tonnes)	770.0 (9.0%)	-22.3%
Nickel (1,000 tonnes)	69.5 (8.6%)	+124%
Chrome (mill tonnes)	2.17 (51.5%)	+153%
Vanadium (1,000 tonnes)	16.4 (53%)	N/A
Zirconium (1,000 tonnes)	154.5 (21.1%)	N/A
Gold (tonnes)	639.0 (35.9%)	-18%
Diamonds (mill carats)	25.6 (43.1%)	+86.2%

Manufactures		
Canned fruits (1,000 tonnes)	264.2 (5.1%)	No data
Ladies' dresses (mill)	19.1 (4.1%)	No data
Ferroalloys and chrome (mill tonnes)	3.4 (26.6%)	N/A
Household hardware (1,000 units)	10.3 (4.6%)	No data

N/A means production had not begun in 1960

AGRICULTURE

Subsistence farming is the main occupation in the region. Malawi exports sugar cane. In South Africa and Zimbabwe there is successful commercial farming. Both of these countries export food, while the other countries are food importers.

LAND (million hectares)

Total	Agricultural	Arable	Forest/woodland
650 (100%)	366 (56%)	34 (5%)	160 (25%)

FARMERS

23.3 million employed in agriculture (56% of workforce)
1.4 hectares of arable land per person employed in agriculture

MAJOR CROPS

	Area mill ha.	Yield 100kg/ha.	Production mill tonnes	Change since 1963
Maize	8.9	13.0 (36)	11.6 (3)	+36%
Wheat	2.0	17.0 (73)	3.4 (1)	+270%
Roots/tubers	2.0	55.5 (44)	11.0 (2)	+79%
Groundnuts	0.9	6.1 (52)	0.5 (3)	−17%
Sugar cane	0.6	724.3 (12)	42.9 (4)	+101%
Tobacco	0.2	11.8 (83)	0.2 (4)	+45%
Fruits	—	—	5.9 (2)	+105%

MAJOR LIVESTOCK

	Number mill	Production mill tonnes	Change since 1963
Sheep/goats	55.7 (3)	—	0%
Cattle	42.1 (3)	—	+24%
Milk	—	3.5 (1)	+13%
Fish catch	—	1.8 (2)	—

FOOD SECURITY (cereal exports minus imports)

mill tonnes	% domestic production	% world trade
−0.2	1	0.1

Numbers in brackets are percentages of world total

The lack of rainfall has greatly influenced the distribution of population in Southern Africa. Inland mining areas and coastal ports are the main zones of high population density.

POPULATION

Population density

city populations
(capital city is underlined)

■	1,000,000–5,000,000
●	500,000–999,999
◉	250,000–499,999
×	capital city less than 250,000

persons per square km	persons per square mi.
100	260
50	130
10	26
1	2.6

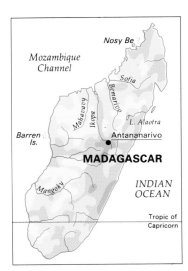

INDUSTRY

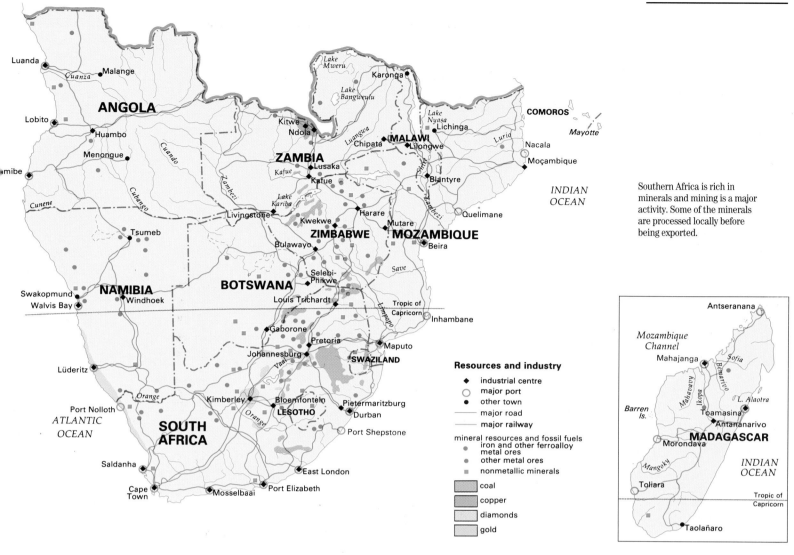

Southern Africa is rich in minerals and mining is a major activity. Some of the minerals are processed locally before being exported.

Resources and industry

◆ industrial centre
◯ major port
● other town
— major road
— major railway

mineral resources and fossil fuels
● iron and other ferroalloy metal ores
● other metal ores
■ nonmetallic minerals

▨ coal
▨ copper
▨ diamonds
▨ gold

AGRICULTURE

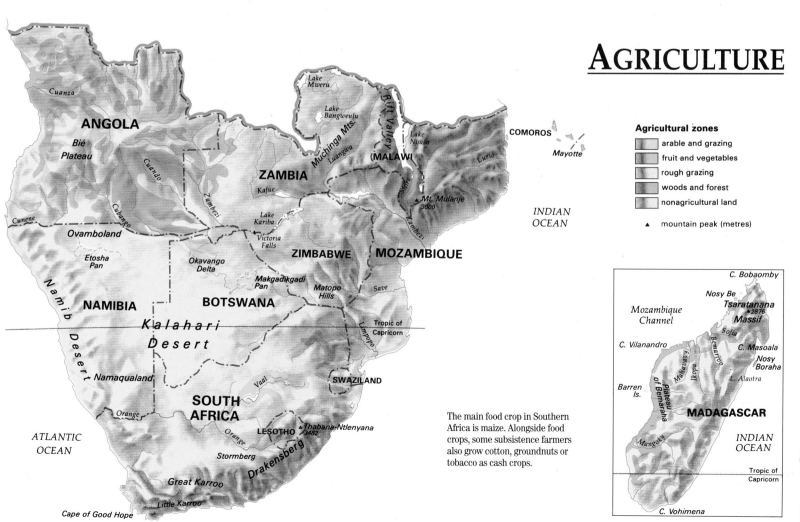

Agricultural zones

▨ arable and grazing
▨ fruit and vegetables
▨ rough grazing
▨ woods and forest
▨ nonagricultural land

▲ mountain peak (metres)

The main food crop in Southern Africa is maize. Alongside food crops, some subsistence farmers also grow cotton, groundnuts or tobacco as cash crops.

INDIAN SUBCONTINENT

The region is a pendant-shaped landmass, extending from the world's highest mountain ranges in the north to the islands of Sri Lanka and the Maldives in the south.

The climate ranges from polar conditions on the mountains to hot tropical weather on the plains. The influence of monsoon winds, which bring heavy rains in the summer, are felt throughout much of the region.

Over the centuries, many waves of migrants have settled in the subcontinent. Today the region has many languages and religions, reflecting its complex past. Cultural rivalries and religious differences sometimes cause conflict and violence. However, despite such pressures and the poverty in which many people live, India remains the world's largest parliamentary democracy.

The Indian subcontinent was once part of the ancient continent of Gondwanaland. Plate movements propelled the landmass north until it collided with Eurasia, throwing up the rocks on the intervening seabed into high fold mountains, the Himalayas, with the world's highest peak.

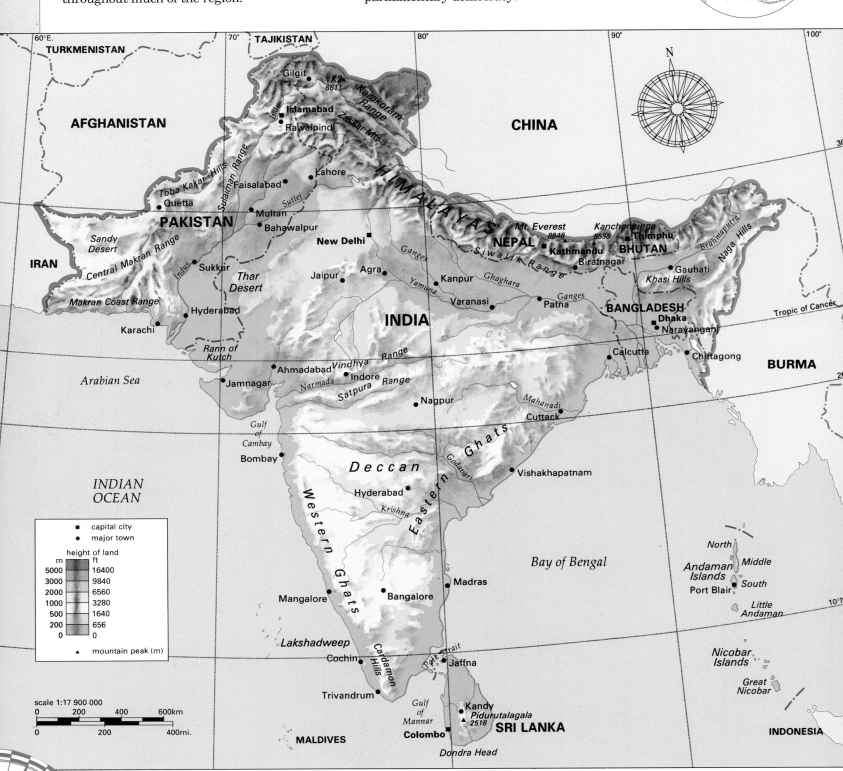

THE POLITICAL AND CULTURAL WORLD

In the mid-19th century, most of the Indian subcontinent, apart from the remote mountain kingdoms of Bhutan and Nepal, was under British rule. But when British India became independent in 1947, the region split into two countries: the mainly Hindu India and Muslim Pakistan. Pakistan consisted of two parts: West and East Pakistan. After a civil war, East Pakistan broke away from West Pakistan in 1971, and proclaimed its independence as Bangladesh.

Tensions between India and the Islamic Republic of Pakistan (formerly West Pakistan) continue and the boundaries in the Jammu and Kashmir region in the northwest are disputed.

COUNTRIES IN THE REGION

Bangladesh, Bhutan, India, Maldives, Nepal, Pakistan, Sri Lanka
Island territories
Andaman Islands, Nicobar Islands, Lakshadweep (India)

MEMBERSHIP OF INTERNATIONAL ORGANIZATIONS

Colombo Plan Bangladesh, Bhutan, India, Maldives, Nepal, Pakistan, Sri Lanka
South Asia Regional Cooperation Committee (SARC) All countries of the region

LANGUAGE

Countries with one official language (Bengali) Bangladesh; (Divehi) Maldives; (Nepali) Nepal; (Sinhalese) Sri Lanka; (Urdu) Pakistan
Country with two official languages (English, Hindi) India
Country with three official languages (Dzongkha, English, Lhotsam) Bhutan

India has 14 officially recognized languages. As well as Hindi and Urdu, the most significant languages in the region include Gujarati, Malayalam, Marathi, Punjabi, Tamil, and Telugu. There are hundreds of local languages and dialects.

RELIGION

Countries with one major religion (M) Maldives, Pakistan
Countries with two major religions (B,H) Bhutan; (H,M) Bangladesh
Countries with three or more major religions (B,H,M) Nepal; (B,C,H,M) Sri Lanka; (B,C,H,J,M,S) India

Key: B-Buddhist, C-various Christian, H-Hindu, J-Jain, M-Muslim, S-Sikh

ECONOMIC INDICATORS: 1990

	Bangladesh	India	Pakistan
GNP (US$ billions)	22.88	254.54	35.5
GNP per capita (US$)	210	350	380
Annual rate of growth of GDP, 1980-1990 (%)	4.3	5.3	6.3
Manufacturing as % of GDP	9	19	17
Central government spending as % of GNP	15	18	24
Merchandise exports (US$ billions)	1.49	16.1	4.95
Merchandise imports (US$ billions)	3.38	20.5	6.95
% of GNP received as development aid	9.2	0.6	2.9
Total external debt as % of GNP	53.8	25.0	52.1

WELFARE INDICATORS

Infant mortality rate (per 1,000 live births)			
1965	144	150	149
1990	105	92	103
Daily food supply available (calories per capita, 1989)	2,021	2,229	2,219
Population per physician (1984)	6,390	2,520	2,900
Teacher-pupil ratio (primary school, 1989)	1 : 60	1 : 61	1 : 41

Pakistan
Area 796,095 sq. km (307,374 sq. mi.)
Population 112,050,000
Capital Islamabad
Currency 1 Pakistan rupee (Pre; plural PRs) = 100 paisa

JAMMU & KASHMIR

Islamabad

PAKISTAN

New Delhi

NEPAL
Kathmandu

Thimphu
BHUTAN

BANGLADESH
Dhaka

INDIA

■ capital city

India is a non-aligned state, and did not take sides in the Cold War. It possesses nuclear weapons.
One family dominated Indian politics for many years. The country was led by the Nehru-Gandhi family from its independence in 1947 until prime minister Rajiv Gandhi was assassinated in May 1991.

Lakshadweep

North
Andaman Islands — Middle
— South
Little Andaman

Nicobar Islands
Great Nicobar

SRI LANKA
Colombo

MALDIVES

Bangladesh
Area 143,998 sq. km (55,598 sq. mi.)
Population 115,593,000
Capital Dhaka
Currency 1 Bangladesh taka (Yk) = 100 paisa

Bhutan
Area 47,000 sq. km (18,150 sq. mi.)
Population 1,516,000
Capital Thimphu
Currency 1 gnultrum (Nu) = 100 chetrum

India
Area 3,166,414 sq. km (1,222,559 sq. mi.)
Population 853,094,000
Capital New Delhi
Currency I Indian rupee (Re; plural Rs) = 100 paisa

Maldives
Area 298 sq km (115 sq. mi.)
Population 215,000
Capital Male
Currency 1 Maldivian rufiyaa (Rf) = 100 laair

Nepal
Area 147,181 sq. km (56,827 sq. mi.)
Population 19,143,000
Capital Kathmandu
Currency 1 Nepalese rupee (NRe; plural NRs) = 100 paisa

Sri Lanka
Area 65,610 sq. km (25,332 sq. mi.)
Population 17,217,000
Capital Colombo
Currency 1 Sri Lanka rupee (SL Re; plural SL Rs) = 100 cents

HABITATS

The mountains in the north and the deserts in the northwest are barren. The rivers that rise in the mountains, especially the Indus, Ganges, and Brahmaputra, drain the fertile river valleys and deltas south of the mountains.

LAND

Area 4,476,064 sq. km (1,727,276 sq. mi.)
Highest point Mount Everest, 8,848 m (29,030 ft), highest on Earth
Major features Himalayas, world's highest mountain range, plains and deltas in north, Thar Desert, Deccan plateau

WATER

Longest river Brahmaputra and Indus both 2,900 km (1,800 mi.)
Largest basin Ganges, 1,059,000 sq. km (409,000 sq. mi.)
Largest lake Manchhar, Pakistan, 260 sq. km (100 sq. mi.); reservoirs in India are larger

NOTABLE THREATENED ENDEMIC SPECIES

Mammals Lion-tailed macaque (*Macaca silenus*), Hispid hare (*Caprolagus hispidus*), Indus river dolphin (*Platanista minor*), Indian rhinoceros (*Rhinoceros unicornis*), Pygmy hog (*Sus salvanius*), Swamp deer (*Cervus duvauceli*)
Birds Lesser florican (*Sypheotides indica*), Jerdon's courser (*Cursorius bitorquatus*), Western tragopan (*Tragopan melanocephalus*), Forest owlet (*Athene blewitii*), Great Indian bustard (*Choriotis nigriceps*)
Plants *Cycas beddomei* (Beddomes cycad); *Dioscorea deltoidea* (kin); *Diospyros oppositifolia* (opposite-leaved ebony); *Frerea indica* (frerea); *Lilium macklineae* (Shirhoy lily); *Paphiopedilum druryi* (Drury's slipper orchid); *Prunus himalaica* (Himalayan cherry); *Saussurea roylei* (Royle's saussurea); *Ulmus wallichiana* (Wallich's elm); *Vanda coerulea* (blue vanda)

CLIMATE

South of the towering Himalayas, with their polar and subarctic climates, the Indian subcontinent is a warm tropical region. Dry climates include the hot Thar desert on the India—Pakistan border. Other areas have hot monsoon climates with heavy rains between late June and September.

TEMPERATURE AND PRECIPITATION

	Temperature °C (°F)		Altitude
	January	July	m (ft)
Jacobabad	15 (59)	37 (98)	57 (187)
Simla	19 (66)	5 (41)	2,022 (6,636)
New Delhi	14 (57)	32 (90)	218 (714)
Kathmandu	10 (50)	24 (75)	1,338 (4,388)
Chittagong	20 (68)	28 (82)	27 (88)
Trincomalee	26 (79)	30 (86)	7 (23)

	Precipitation mm (in)		
	January	July	Year
Jacobabad	5 (0.2)	23 (1.1)	88 (3.5)
Simla	61 (2.4)	424 (16.7)	1,577 (62.1)
New Delhi	23 (0.9)	180 (7.1)	715 (28.2)
Kathmandu	15 (0.6)	345 (13.5)	1,328 (52.3)
Chittagong	5 (0.2)	597 (23.5)	2,858 (112.5)
Trincomalee	173 (6.8)	51 (2.0)	1,727 (68.0)

World's highest recorded annual rainfall, 26,470 mm (1,042.1 in), Cherrapunji, northeast India

NATURAL HAZARDS

Cyclones, storm surges, flooding of great river deltas

ENVIRONMENTAL ISSUES

The Indian subcontinent is subject to such natural disasters as floods, drought, storms, and earthquakes. Population pressures have led to deforestation and soil erosion, while urban and industrial pollution are mounting problems.

POPULATION AND WEALTH

	Highest	Middle	Lowest
Population increase (annual population growth rate, % 1960–90)	3.0 (Pakistan)	2.4 (Nepal)	1.9 (Sri Lanka)
Energy use (gigajoules/person)	8 (India)	2 (Bangladesh)	1 (Nepal)
Real purchasing power (US$/person)	2,120 (Sri Lanka)	870 (Nepal)	720 (Bangladesh)

ENVIRONMENTAL INDICATORS

CO$_2$ emissions (million tonnes carbon/annum)	230 (India)	6.8 (Nepal)	0.2 (Bhutan)
Deforestation ('000s ha./annum 1980s)	1,500 (India)	58 (Sri Lanka)	1 (Bhutan)
Artificial fertilizer use (kg/ha./annum)	113 (Sri Lanka)	77 (Bangladesh)	1 (Bhutan)
Cars (per 1,000 population)	7 (Sri Lanka)	2 (India)	0.4 (Bangladesh)
Access to safe drinking water (% population)	57 (India)	41 (Sri Lanka)	36 (Nepal)

MAJOR ENVIRONMENTAL PROBLEMS AND SOURCES

Air pollution: generally high, urban very high; acid rain prevalent; high greenhouse gas emissions
River pollution: medium; *sources:* agricultural, sewage
Land degradation: *types:* desertification, soil erosion, salinization, deforestation, habitat destruction; *causes:* agriculture, industry, population pressure
Resource problems: fuelwood shortage; inadequate drinking water and sanitation; coastal flooding
Population problems: population explosion; urban overcrowding; inadequate health facilities; famine
Major events: Bhopal (1984), leak of poisonous chemicals; Bangladesh (1988, 1991), major floods

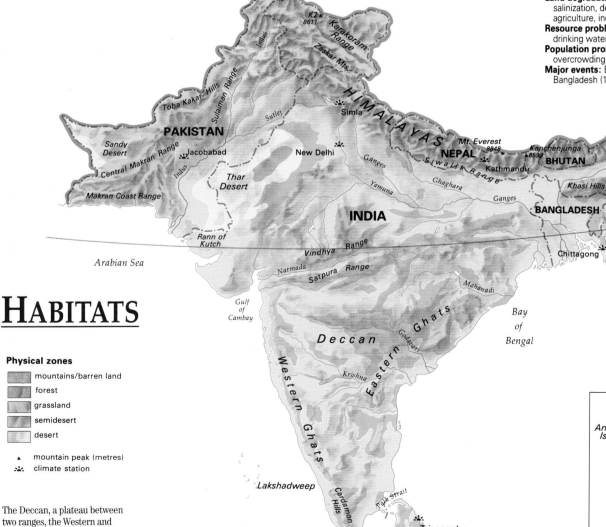

HABITATS

Physical zones

- mountains/barren land
- forest
- grassland
- semidesert
- desert

▲ mountain peak (metres)
⁂ climate station

The Deccan, a plateau between two ranges, the Western and Eastern Ghats, is an ancient landmass, unlike the young mountains in the north which are still rising. Between the two lie broad flood plains.

ENVIRONMENTAL ISSUES

The original forests of the Indian subcontinent have largely been destroyed. The arid northwest and the west-central Deccan plateau are at risk of desertification.

Key environmental issues

- • major town or city
- 🖤 heavily polluted town or city
- 🌢 major pollution event
- ✚ major natural disaster
- ⬭ heavily polluted river
- ⬭ area liable to flood
- ▓ remaining tropical rainforest
- ▒ area of deforestation

areas at risk of desertification
- ▓ very high
- ▒ high
- ░ moderate
- ☐ true desert

CLIMATE

height above sea level of climate stations

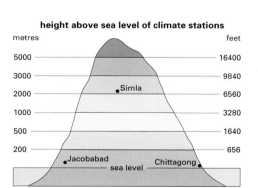

metres		feet
5000		16400
3000		9840
2000	Simla	6560
1000		3280
500		1640
200		656
	Jacobabad	Chittagong
	sea level	

Jacobabad

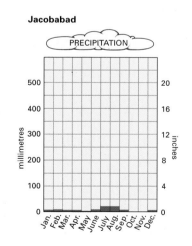
PRECIPITATION

Simla

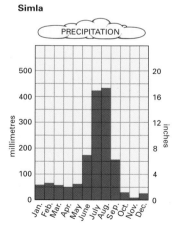
PRECIPITATION

Chittagong

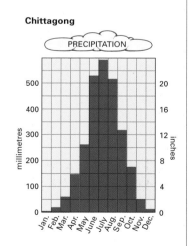
PRECIPITATION

Jacobabad

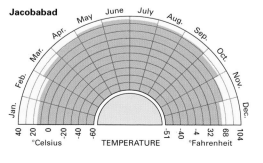
TEMPERATURE

Simla

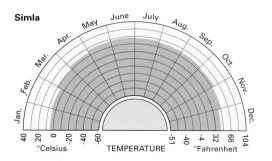
TEMPERATURE

Chittagong

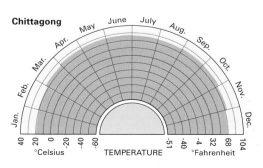
TEMPERATURE

POPULATION

The subcontinent is one of the world's most populous regions. Most people in the subcontinent live in rural areas, but there are many large cities, including some of the world's most crowded, with over 500 people per sq. km. India alone has more than 200 large cities.

POPULATION

Total population of region (millions)	1129.5
Population density (persons per sq. km)	289.6
Population change (average annual percent 1960–1990)	
Urban	+4.5
Rural	+2.3

URBAN POPULATION

As percentage of total population	
1960	19.2
1990	28.6
Percentage in cities of more than 1 million	4.8

TEN LARGEST CITIES

	Country	Population
Calcutta	India	9,194,000
Bombay	India	8,243,000
New Delhi †	India	5,729,000
Karachi	Pakistan	5,181,000
Dhaka †	Bangladesh	4,770,000
Madras	India	4,289,000
Lahore	Pakistan	2,953,000
Bangalore	India	2,922,000
Ahmadabad	India	2,548,000
Hyderabad	India	2,546,000

† denotes capital city

INDUSTRY

The countries of the Indian subcontinent are, according to the World Bank, 'low-income developing nations'. The region has plenty of resources and huge potential, but its industrial development has been extremely slow.

INDUSTRIAL OUTPUT (US $ billion)

Total	Mining	Manufacturing	Average annual change since 1960
86.33	7.53	68.0	+5%

MAJOR PRODUCTS (figures in brackets are percentages of world production)

Energy and minerals	Output	Change since 1960
Coal (mill tonnes)	205.3 (4.3%)	+271%
Oil (mill barrels)	266.8 (1.2%)	+7900%
Iron Ore (mill tonnes)	32.8 (5.8%)	+77%
Bauxite (mill tonnes)	4.0 (4.1%)	+255%

Manufactures		
Refined sugar (mill tonnes)	10.5 (16.4%)	+193%
Cotton woven fabrics (mill sq. metres)	16969 (14.2%)	+263%
Jute fabrics (mill sq. metres)	3735 (92%)	+48%
Footwear (mill pairs)	197.4 (4.4%)	+1368%
Broadleaved sawnwood (mill cu. metres)	15.1 (12.1%)	+647%
Nitrogenous fertilizer (mill tonnes)	7.9 (8.5%)	+652%
Cement (mill tonnes)	45.5 (4.1%)	+415%
Transistors (mill)	3560 (5.2%)	N/A
Bicycles (mill)	7.4 (7.3%)	+662%

N/A means production had not begun in 1960

AGRICULTURE

Farming is the main activity throughout the subcontinent. The best farmland is in the densely populated northern plains. Rice is the main food crop throughout the subcontinent, although wheat is also important in many areas.

LAND (million hectares)

Total	Agricultural	Arable	Forest/woodland
413 (100%)	223 (54%)	198 (48%)	80 (19%)

FARMERS

258.7 million people employed in agriculture (66% of workforce)
0.9 hectares of arable land per person employed in farming

MAJOR CROPS

	Area mill ha.	Yield 100kg/ha.	Production mill tonnes	Change since 1963
Paddy rice	52.7	22.3 (68)	117.7 (25)	+61%
Wheat	32.0	18.2 (78)	58.2 (11)	+274%
Millet/sorghum	30.3	6.3 (55)	19.1 (21)	+10%
Pulses	24.9	5.3 (66)	13.2 (24)	+3%
Cotton lint	9.1	2.8 (52)	2.6 (16)	+81%
Maize	7.2	10.9 (30)	7.8 (2)	+30%
Groundnuts	6.8	8.4 (73)	5.8 (27)	+11%
Sugar cane	4.1	539.5 (90)	222.4 (23)	+73%
Vegetables	—	—	53.0 (13)	+107%
Fruit	—	—	30.3 (9)	+94%

MAJOR LIVESTOCK

	Number mill	Production mill tonnes	Change since 1963
Cattle	247.4 (19)	—	+15%
Sheep/goats	235.8 (14)	—	+74%
Buffaloes	93.7 (68)	—	+48%
Milk	—	25.2 (5)	+158%
Fish catch	—	4.4 (5)	—

Numbers in brackets are percentages of world total

POPULATION

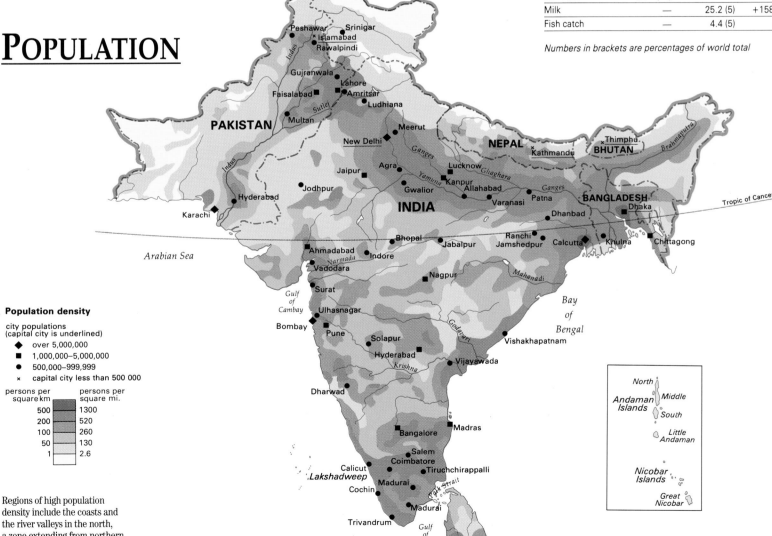

Population density

city populations
(capital city is underlined)
- ◆ over 5,000,000
- ■ 1,000,000–5,000,000
- ● 500,000–999,999
- × capital city less than 500 000

persons per square km	persons per square mi.
500	1300
200	520
100	260
50	130
1	2.6

Regions of high population density include the coasts and the river valleys in the north, a zone extending from northern Pakistan, through the plains of northern India, to the Ganges delta in Bangladesh.

INDUSTRY

India has coal and iron reserves; oil and gas fields are being developed. Pakistan and Bangladesh have large gas reserves.

Kalabagh

Lahore • Amritsar
Quetta • Multan • Simla
PAKISTAN
New Delhi
Karachi • Hyderabad
Bhuj
Arabian Sea
Ahmadabad

Resources and industry
◆ industrial centre
◯ major port
● other town
— major road
— major railway

mineral resources and fossil fuels
● iron and other ferroalloy metal ores
● other metal ores
■ nonmetallic minerals
▨ coal
▨ iron ore
▨ natural gas

Indus

Sutlej

Ganges
Kanpur
Jaipur
Yamuna
Varanasi
INDIA

NEPAL
Kathmandu
Ghaghara
Ganges
Jamalpur
BANGLADESH
Dhaka
Khulna
Jamshedpur
Calcutta
Chittagong

Thimphu
BHUTAN
Brahmaputra
Tropic of Cancer

Narmada
Nagpur
Mahanadi

Bay of Bengal

Gulf of Cambay
Bombay
Godavari

Hyderabad
Krishna

Marmagao

Mangalore
Bangalore • Madras

Lakshadweep
Cochin • Madurai
Trincomalee

Pak Strait

Gulf of Mannar
Colombo **SRI LANKA**

MALDIVES

North
Andaman Islands Middle
Port Blair • South
Little Andaman
Nicobar Islands
Great Nicobar

AGRICULTURE

K2 8611
Karakoram Range
Zaskar Mts.
Indus
Toba Kakar Hills
Sulaiman Range
PAKISTAN
Sandy Desert
Central Makran Range
Makran Coast Range
Thar Desert
Sutlej
HIMALAYAS
Mt. Everest 8848
NEPAL
Siwalik Range
Kanchenjunga 8598
BHUTAN
Naga Hills
Ganges
Yamuna
Ghaghara
Ganges
Khasi Hills
BANGLADESH
Tropic of Cancer
Brahmaputra

INDIA
Rann of Kutch
Arabian Sea
Vindhya Range
Narmada
Satpura Range
Mahanadi

Deccan
Krishna
Godavari
Eastern Ghats
Western Ghats

Bay of Bengal

Gulf of Cambay

Lakshadweep
Cardamom Hills
Gulf of Mannar
Pak Strait
Pidurutalagala 2518
SRI LANKA
MALDIVES
Dondra Head

Arable farming is important in most of the region, though irrigation is essential in dry areas. Fruits and fibre crops, including cotton and jute, are widely grown.

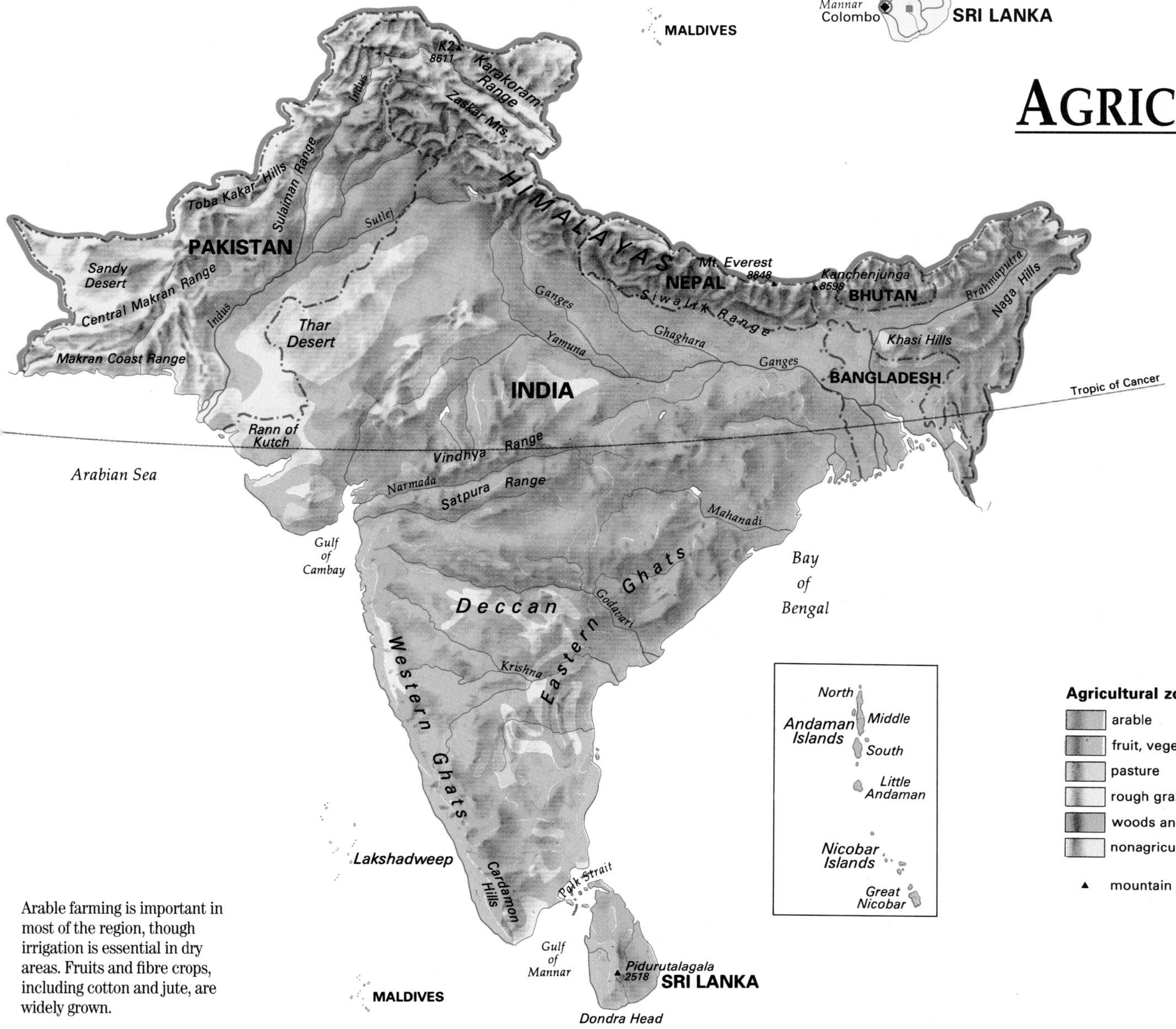

Agricultural zones
▨ arable
▨ fruit, vegetables and tree crops
▨ pasture
▨ rough grazing
▨ woods and forest
▨ nonagricultural land
▲ mountain peak (metres)

North
Andaman Islands Middle
South
Little Andaman
Nicobar Islands
Great Nicobar

CHINA & TAIWAN

China is the world's third largest country in area and the largest in population. It contains great mountain ranges, high plateaus, deserts, grasslands, and fertile valleys.

The climate in the southwest Plateau of Tibet is very harsh. The deserts in the northwest have an arid climate with temperatures that may soar to 38°C (100°F) in summer and plunge to −34°C (−29°F) during winter nights. Most people live in the east, where the climate ranges from temperate to subtropical.

About 93 percent of the people in China belong to the Han group, a name which comes from the Han dynasty (206 B.C.–A.D. 220). The other 7 percent belong to minority groups.

Civilization in China dates back around 5,000 years. The Chinese empire became weak in the 19th century and, in 1912, the country became a republic. A communist regime has ruled since 1949, though, from the late 1980s, the government began to introduce free enterprise economic policies.

China is bordered by Mongolia and Russia to the north and the Indian subcontinent and Southeast Asia in the south. It shares Everest, the world's highest mountain, with Nepal. It also has deep basins, one reaching 154 m (505 ft) below sea level. The great plains of China are drained by the great rivers Huang and Chang.

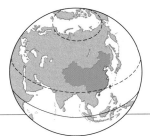

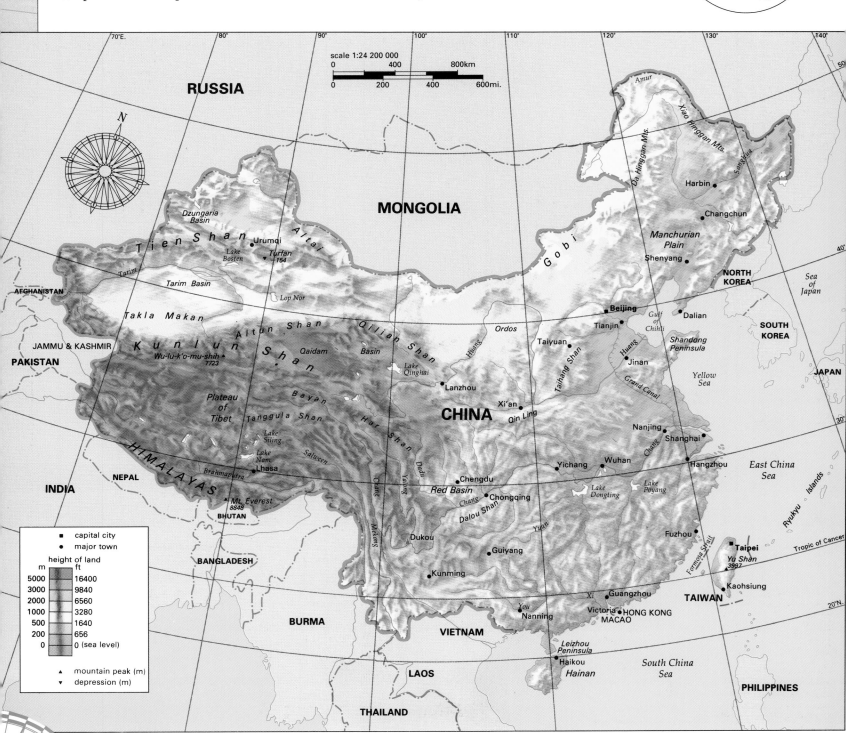

- ■ capital city
- ● major town

height of land

m	ft
5000	16400
3000	9840
2000	6560
1000	3280
500	1640
200	656
0	0 (sea level)

- ▲ mountain peak (m)
- ▼ depression (m)

THE POLITICAL AND CULTURAL WORLD

The region includes the small British territory of Hong Kong, a financial and industrial centre on the southeast coast of China, which Britain will return to China in 1997. Near Hong Kong is the even smaller Portuguese territory of Macao, which Portugal will return to China in 1999.

A third territory is the island of Taiwan, on which Chinese nationalist forces set up a rival government after the communists took power in 1949. China would also like to reunite with Taiwan, now a successful industrial economy, and has promised the Taiwanese a high degree of autonomy if they agree. But this seems unlikely until after the return of the dependencies of Hong Kong and Macao.

Since the death of China's communist leader Mao Zedong (1949–76), China's leadership has tried to make friendlier relations with other countries, notably the former Soviet Union. China was opened to foreign investment and free enterprise, and this led in the late 1980s to demands for political reform. Demonstrators for such changes were brutally suppressed.

COUNTRIES IN THE REGION
China, Taiwan

Island territories Hainan (China)
Dependencies of other states Hong Kong (U.K.: due to be returned to China in 1997); Macao (Portugal: due to be returned to China in 1999)

LANGUAGE
Countries with one official language (Mandarin Chinese) China, Taiwan

RELIGION
China Although religion is officially discouraged, many people practise a combination of Confucianist, Taoist and traditional folk belief. There are smaller groups of Buddhists, Muslims and Christians.
Taiwan Confucianist-Taoist-traditional (48.5%), Buddhist (43%), Christian (7.4%), Muslim (0.5%)

STYLES OF GOVERNMENT
Republics China, Taiwan
Federal state China
Multiparty state Taiwan
One-party state China
One-chamber assembly China, Taiwan

ECONOMIC INDICATORS

	China
GDP (US$ billions)	364.9
GNP per capita (US$)	370
Annual rate of growth of GDP, 1980–1990	9.5%
Manufacturing as % of GDP	38.0%
Central government spending as % of GNP	n/a
Merchandise exports (US$ billions)	61.3
Merchandise imports (US$ billions)	52.6
% of GNP received as development aid	0.6%
Total external debt as a % of GNP	14.4%

WELFARE INDICATORS

Infant mortality rate (per 1,000 live births)	
1965	90
1990	29
Daily food supply available (calories per capita, 1989)	2,639
Population per physician (1984)	1,010
Teacher-pupil ratio (primary school, 1989)	1 : 22

China
Area 9,526,900 sq. km (3,676,300 sq. mi.)
Population 1,139,060,000
Capital Beijing
Currency 1 yuan (Y) = 10 jiao = 100 fen

Taiwan
Area 36,000 sq. km (13,900 sq. mi.)
Population 20,100,000
Capital Taipei
Currency 1 new Taiwan dollar (NT$) = 100 cents

- ■ capital city
- • provincial or municipal capital
- □ province
- □ municipality
- □ autonomous region

HABITATS

The landscape of China falls into three main areas. In the west is the immense Plateau of Tibet, the 'roof of the world', the highest and largest plateau on Earth. Its average height is 4,000 m (13,000 ft). In the far south of the plateau are the Himalayas.

The next main area, to the north and east, is a vast region of plateaus and river basins. It includes the Gobi desert, and the basin of the River Tarim and the Red Basin. This area is bordered to the west by mountain ranges.

The great plains of China form the third main area, stretching east and southeast from the plateaus to the sea. They were formed from the deposited soils washed down by great rivers flowing from the higher land. The plains are generally below 500 m (1,600 ft), and broken by occasional hills.

The boundaries between these three main areas follow the lines of deepseated faults in the underlying crust of the Earth. Tectonic activity continues: there are frequent earthquakes, particularly in the mountains of the west and on the island of Taiwan.

LAND

Area 9,562,904 sq. km (3,690,246 sq. mi.)
Highest point Mount Everest, 8,848 m (29,030 ft) highest on earth
Lowest point Turfan depression, −154 m (−505 ft)
Major features Plateau of Tibet, Himalayas, world's highest mountain chain, Red and Tarim Basins, Takla Makan and Gobi deserts, river plains in east

WATER

Longest river Chang, 5,980 km (3,720 mi.)
Largest basin Chang, 1,827,000 sq. km (705,000 sq. mi.)
Highest average flow Chang, 32,190 cu. m/sec (1,137,000 cu. ft/sec)
Largest lake Qinghai, 4,460 sq. km (1,721 sq. mi.)

NOTABLE THREATENED ENDEMIC SPECIES

Mammals Kozlov's pika (*Ochotona koslowi*), Golden monkey (*Rhinopithecus roxellana*), Yunnan snub-nosed monkey (*Rhinopithecus bieti*), baiji (*Lipotes vexillifer*), Giant panda (*Ailuropoda melanoleuca*), Thorold's deer (*Cervus albirostris*)
Birds White-eared night heron (*Gorsachius magnificus*), Crested ibis (*Nipponia nippon*), Chinese monal (*Lophophorus lhuysii*)
Plants *Abies beshanzhuensis* (Baishanzhu mountain fir); *Burretiodendron hsienmu* (xianmu); *Camellia granthamiana*; *Coptis teeta*; *Cycas taiwaniana*; *Davidia involucrata* (dove tree); *Ginkgo biloba* (maidenhair tree); *Kirengeshoma palmata*; *Metasequoia glyptostroboides* (dawn redwood); *Panax ginseng* (ginseng)
Others Chinese alligator (*Alligator chinensis*), Chinese giant salamander (*Andrias davidianus*), Chinese paddlefish (*Psephurus gladius*), Chinese three-tailed swallowtail butterfly (*Bhutanitis thaidina*)

HABITATS

Physical zones

- mountains/barren land
- forest
- grassland
- semidesert
- desert

▲ mountain peak (metres)
▼ depression (metres)
☀ climate station

China contains barren regions of mountain, desert and semidesert. There are also grassy plains in the northwest, and fertile areas of valleys and plains in the southeast.

CLIMATE

There are three main climatic zones in the region, corresponding to the three major physical regions. The Plateau of Tibet has a harsh, cold, dry climate, and has been called the 'Earth's third pole'. The height of the mountains prevents warmer air from moving north. Above 4,000 m (13,000 ft) it is always freezing. The remote arid steppes and deserts of northwest China are far from the ocean and its rain-bearing winds, and have less than 100 mm (4 in) of rain a year.

The lowlands and hills of eastern China occupy almost half the country and have a great range of climates. The northeast lies in a temperate zone; farther south there are both warm temperate and subtropical zones, while southern Yunnan in the southwest and also the island of Hainan are tropical. Throughout eastern China the monsoon brings high rainfall in summer. Cold, dry, northerly winds (the winter monsoon) blow outward over much of China. When the land warms in spring, a great current of warm, humid air reaches inland from the south and east, bringing rain. This is the wet summer monsoon.

TEMPERATURE AND PRECIPITATION

	Temperature °C (°F)		Altitude
	January	July	m (ft)
Lhasa	−2 (28)	16 (60)	3,685 (12,088)
Hami	−12 (10)	28 (82)	738 (2,421)
Guangzhou	13 (56)	28 (82)	63 (201)
Beijing	−5 (23)	26 (79)	52 (170)
Shanghai	3 (38)	28 (82)	7 (22)
Harbin	−20 (−4)	23 (73)	172 (564)

	Precipitation mm (in)		
	January	July	Year
Lhasa	0.2 (0.01)	122 (4.8)	454 (17.9)
Hami	2 (0.1)	6 (0.2)	33 (1.3)
Guangzhou	39 (1.5)	220 (8.6)	1,681 (66.2)
Beijing	4 (0.1)	243 (9.5)	683 (26.9)
Shanghai	48 (1.8)	147 (5.8)	1,129 (44.4)
Harbin	4 (0.2)	127 (4.9)	554 (21.8)

NATURAL HAZARDS

Large rivers in flood, earthquakes in interior and on Taiwan, typhoons in coastal areas, landslides

CLIMATE

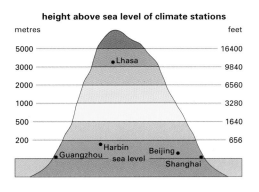

height above sea level of climate stations

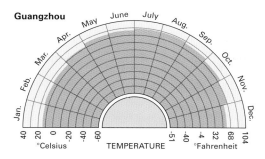

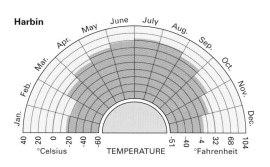

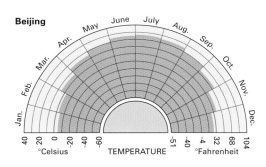

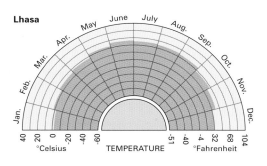

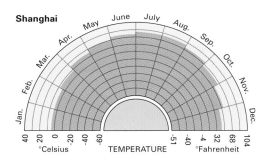

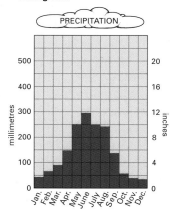

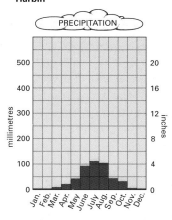

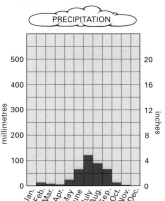

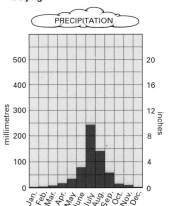

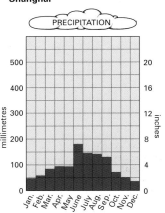

ENVIRONMENTAL ISSUES

The region's environmental problems arise largely from one factor—China's huge and still growing population. Attempts to tackle the problems are linked with the government's policy of reducing the overall population.

In recent decades pressure on the land from farming has contributed to the southward spread of the Gobi desert. Farming land has been terraced since prehistoric times, but over-irrigation in some areas has led to salinization and waterlogging, greatly reducing the productivity of the land. Only about 11 percent of China's forests remain. Also, the country has seen rapid growth of cities and industries since the 1970s, causing severe air and water pollution.

Those industries which still rely on fossil fuels also contribute to pollution. Coal-burning steam engines are still in production and use, and coal is still the chief source of power.

The village system of agriculture has encouraged the growth of small-scale environmental projects. These include the recycling of waste water and the conservation of naturally-produced methane for domestic use.

POPULATION AND WEALTH

Population (millions)	1,139.1
Population increase (annual population growth rate, % 1960–90)	1.8
Energy use (gigajoules/person)	22
Real purchasing power (US$/person)	2,470

ENVIRONMENTAL INDICATORS

CO_2 emissions (million tonnes carbon/annum)	380
Municipal waste (kg/person/annum)	n/a
Nuclear waste (cumulative tonnes heavy metal)	n/a
Artificial fertilizer use (kg/ha./annum)	23
Cars (per 1,000 population)	0.9
Access to safe drinking water (% population)	72

MAJOR ENVIRONMENTAL PROBLEMS AND SOURCES

Air pollution: generally high, urban very high; acid rain prevalent; high greenhouse gas emissions
River/lake pollution: local/medium; *sources*: agricultural, sewage, soil erosion
Land pollution: local/medium; *sources*: industrial, agricultural
Land degradation: *types*: desertification, soil erosion, salinization, deforestation; *causes*: agriculture, industry, population pressure
Waste disposal problems: domestic; industrial
Resource problems: inadequate sanitation; land use competition; coastal flooding
Population problems: population explosion; urban overcrowding; inadequate health facilities

Key environmental issues

- major town or city
- heavily polluted town or city
- heavily polluted river

soil degradation
- severe
- high
- moderate
- low

Over-intensive farming for centuries has caused severe soil erosion in many areas. China's drive to modernize its economy, together with the fast growth of cities, have led to air and water pollution.

POPULATION

China is the world's third largest country and the most populous. As early as 800 B.C. it had a population of nearly 14 million. Most of the people lived in country villages until the late 20th century. Peasant life was almost unchanged through several thousand years of political change, war, flood, famine, and invasion. European traders boosted the growth of the coastal cities in the 18th century, but the interior remained thinly populated. Changing patterns of settlement during the 20th century have been the result of government policy.

China's population doubled between 1949 and 1979 and, in the 1980s, it passed the 1,000 million mark. But as a result of government policies, the rate of population growth fell from 3 percent a year in the 1960s to 1.5 percent in the 1980s.

The heaviest concentrations of people, and most of the major cities, are found on the east coast and along the Huang and Chang rivers, especially around Shanghai. Western China remains sparsely settled because of its harsh climate and terrain.

POPULATION

Total population of region (millions)	1.162
Population density (persons per sq. km)	120.8
Population change (average annual percent 1960–1990)	
Urban	+2.2
Rural	+1.7

URBAN POPULATION

As percentage of total population	
1960	19.0
1990	21.4
Percentage in cities of more than 1 million	15.4

TEN LARGEST CITIES

	Population
Shanghai	12,320,000
Beijing †	9,750,000
Tianjin	7,790,000
Chongqing	6,511,000
Wenzhou	5,948,000
Guangzhou	5,669,000
Hangzhou	5,234,000
Shenyang	5,055,000
Dalian	4,619,000
Jinzhou	4,448,000

† *denotes capital city*

POPULATION

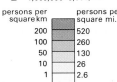

Population density

city populations
(capital city is underlined)
◆   over 5,000,000
■   1,000,000–5,000,000

persons per square km	persons per square mi.
200	520
100	260
50	130
10	26
1	2.6

Western China, with its harsh climate and rugged terrain, contains few people. The areas of highest population density are on the east coast and along the Huang and Chang rivers, especially around Shanghai.

INDUSTRY

China has huge resources of both fuel and minerals, and many industries. On a per capita basis, however, it is one of the world's poorer nations. Many of the resources are underdeveloped. They include coal, petroleum, natural gas, iron ore, bauxite, tin, antimony, and manganese in major reserves. There is great potential for hydroelectric power schemes as the country has many large rivers and a hilly landscape.

The economy is centrally planned, with all industries owned by the state until very recently. Some private enterprise is now being encouraged. Petrochemical products account for nearly one-quarter of China's exports. Other major industries include iron and steel, cement, vehicles, fertilizers, food processing, clothing, and textiles.

The most recent government plans have promoted modernization of industry and reform of its organization. Joint ventures with other countries and foreign loans have been encouraged. Much of this overseas investment went into light industry and textiles. Special Economic Zones were created to foster industrial contact with the west.

China's resources include coal, oil and natural gas, together with many metals and nonmetallic minerals. The smaller territories have few resources but are extremely important for manufacturing.

INDUSTRIAL OUTPUT (US $ billion)

Total	Mining and Manufacturing	Average annual change since 1960
255.8	255.8	+14.3%

INDUSTRIAL WORKERS (millions)
(figures in brackets are percentages of total labour force)

Total	Mining	Manufacturing	Construction
127.6	1.1 (0.2%)	100.4 (18.5%)	26.1 (4.7%)

MAJOR PRODUCTS (figures in brackets are percentages of world production)

Energy and minerals	Output	Change since 1960
Coal (mill tonnes)	1040.0 (22.1%)	+281%
Oil (mill barrels)	1013.7 (4.5%)	+2415%
Iron Ore (mill tonnes)	77.2 (13.7%)	+175.5%
Tungsten (1,000 tonnes)	21.0 (51.2%)	No data

Manufactures		
Cotton fabrics (mill sq. metres)	23258.0 (33.1%)	+179%
Silk fabrics (mill sq. metres)	2064.1 (82.1%)	+231%
Shirts (mill)*	189.1 (25%)	+88%
Nitrogenous fertilizers (mill tonnes)	13.8 (14.9%)	+452%
Cement (mill tonnes)	228.2 (20.8%)	+1567%
Steel (mill tonnes)	62.2 (8.5%)	+345%
Sewing machines (mill)	9.8 (55.5%)	+504%
Televisions (mill)	27.3 (24.9%)	N/A
Bicycles (mill)	44.4 (44.3%)	+685%

* Hong Kong only
N/A means production had not begun in 1960

Resources and industry

- ◆ industrial centre
- ○ major port
- ● other town
- —— major road
- —— major railway

mineral resources and fossil fuels
- ● iron and other ferroalloy metal ores
- ● other metal ores
- ■ nonmetallic minerals

- coal
- copper
- iron ore
- natural gas
- oil
- tin

AGRICULTURE

China covers only one-fifteenth of the world's land area, but succeeds in feeding its people, amounting to one-fifth of the world's population. Some 80 percent of its people belong to peasant or rural households, and traditional farming life continues, despite reforms introduced by communism since 1949.

Much of China, particularly in the north and west, will only grow scrub and provides poor pasture. Only 10 percent of the land can be used for growing crops, mainly in the valleys and plains in the east and south.

The main crops are wheat and rice. Small family plots have always been used to grow vegetables, a key part of the Chinese diet. Pigs, chickens and ducks are also raised in the villages. Water control is essential to prevent flooding and to provide irrigation in the plains, while in the foothills, terracing conserves both soil and water.

The northern plains also produce maize, millet, and potatoes. South of the Chang River, paddy rice predominates. Tea, tobacco, and mulberry trees (for silkworm production) are also commercially important.

LAND (million hectares)

Total	Agricultural	Arable	Forest/woodland
933 (100%)	414 (45%)	94 (10%)	117 (12%)

FARMERS

451 million people employed in agriculture (69% of workforce)
0.2 hectares of arable land per person employed in agriculture

MAJOR CROPS

	Area mill ha.	Yield 100kg/ha.	Production mill tonnes	Change since 1963
Paddy rice	32.7	54.1 (165)	177.0 (38)	+106%
Wheat	28.8	30.5 (131)	30.5 (131)	+295%
Maize	20.3	39.5 (109)	80.1 (17)	+254%
Roots/tubers	9.2	158.7 (126)	146.1 (25)	+32%
Soya beans	8.5	14.4 (76)	12.2 (12)	+14%
Rapeseed	5.3	12.5 (88)	6.6 (29)	+538%
Cotton lint	4.8	8.8 (160)	4.2 (26)	+246%
Millet/sorghum	4.6	22.0 (192)	10.1 (11)	−41%
Pulses	4.4	12.1 (150)	5.3 (10)	†27%
Vegetables	—	—	110.0 (26)	+134%

MAJOR LIVESTOCK

	Number mill	Production mill tonnes	Change since 1963
Pigs	344.6 (41)	—	+75%
Sheep/goats	166.5 (10)	—	+41%
Cattle	71.3 (6)	—	+16%
Milk	—	3.4 (1)	+25%
Fish catch	—	9.6 (10)	—

FOOD SECURITY (cereal exports minus imports)

mill tonnes	% domestic production	% world trade
−8.6	2	4

Numbers in brackets are percentages of world total

AGRICULTURE

Agricultural zones
- arable
- pasture with some arable
- rough grazing
- woods and forest
- nonagricultural land

▲ mountain peak (metres)
▼ depression (metres)

The rugged and arid west and north are suitable only for rearing livestock. The arable farming regions are in the east, where the densely populated valleys and plains are intensively farmed.

Southeast Asia

Southeast Asia includes a peninsula and a vast archipelago, comprising over 20,000 islands. The region contains two zones where volcanic eruptions and earthquakes are caused by collisions between the huge plates that form the Earth's outer shell. One zone runs east-west through southern Indonesia and the other from eastern Indonesia to the Philippines.

The region is humid and tropical. The south has rainfall throughout the year, but the north has a monsoon climate, with most rain coming in the summer months (June-August).

Small groups of Black Negritos, descendants of the earliest inhabitants, live in remote areas, but most Southeast Asians are of Malay or Chinese descent. The diversity of cultures shows how many outside influences have affected the region. Of the region's ten countries, only Thailand remained free of European rule. Wars marred the area's chances of independence and the post-colonial years have been marked by civil wars and political instability. Agriculture is the main activity. Industry is limited to a few cities, such as Manila and Singapore.

Southeast Asia lies between the eastern end of the Himalayan mountain chain and northern Australia. Most of the region lies on the southeastern edge of the huge Eurasian plate and is bordered by deep ocean trenches. As the plates descend, their edges melt, forming the molten rock that fuels Southeast Asia's volcanoes.

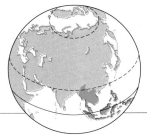

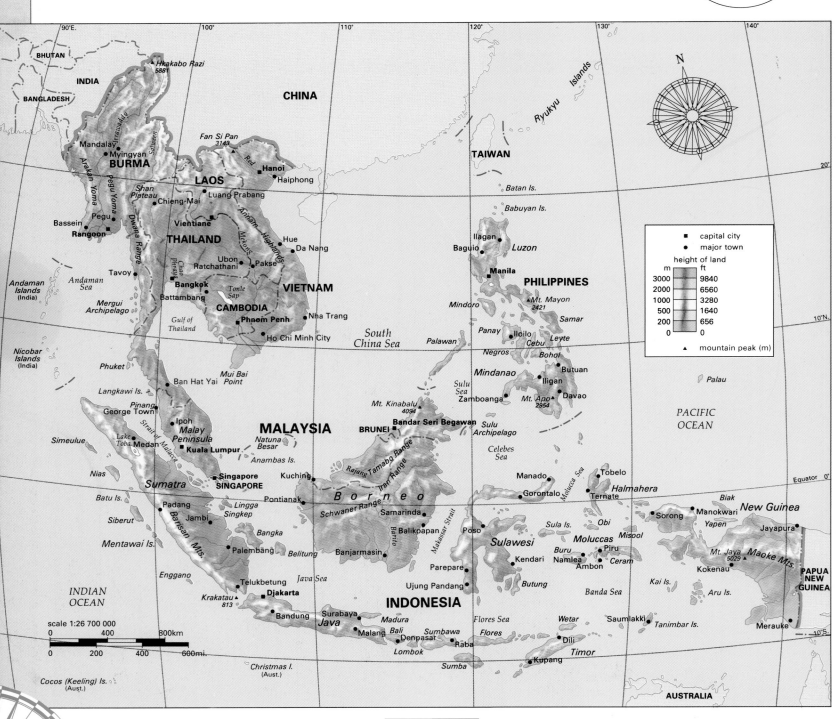

| | capital city |
| | major town |

height of land

m		ft
3000		9840
2000		6560
1000		3280
500		1640
200		656
0		0

▲ mountain peak (m)

scale 1:26 700 000

THE POLITICAL AND CULTURAL WORLD

After the defeat of Japan in 1945, communist forces began a long struggle for power in Southeast Asia. The British defeated them in Malaya, but after a long struggle in Vietnam, involving American troops, the communists emerged victorious in 1975. Cambodia and Laos also became communist countries.

In Burma (now renamed Myanmar), Indonesia and, for part of the time, Thailand, army rulers have suppressed political parties, while Brunei is an absolute monarchy, ruled by a sultan. The only countries which have preserved elements of parliamentary democracy are Malaysia, Singapore and the Philippines.

COUNTRIES IN THE REGION

Brunei, Burma, Cambodia, Indonesia, Laos, Malaysia, Philippines, Singapore, Thailand, Vietnam

LANGUAGE

Countries with one official language (Bahasa Indonesia) Indonesia; (Bahasa Malaysia) Malaysia; (Burmese) Burma; (Khmer) Cambodia; (Lao) Laos; (Thai) Thailand; (Vietnamese) Vietnam
Countries with two official languages (English, Malay) Brunei; (English, Pilipino) Philippines
Country with four official languages (Bahasa Malaysia, Chinese, English, Tamil) Singapore

RELIGION

Country with one major religion (B) Cambodia
Countries with two major religions (B,I) Laos; (B,M) Thailand
Countries with three or more major religions (B,C,T) Vietnam; (B,C,H,M) Indonesia; (B,C,I,M) Burma, Brunei; (B,M,P,RC) Philippines; (B,C,H,M,T) Singapore, Malaysia

Key: B-Buddhist, C-various Christian, H-Hindu, I-indigenous religions, M-Muslim, P-Protestant, RC-Roman Catholic, T-Taoist

ECONOMIC INDICATORS

	Singapore	Thailand	Indonesia
GDP(US$ billions)	34.6	80.17	107.29
GNP per capita (US$)	11,160	1,420	570
Annual rate of growth of GDP, 1980–1990	6.4%	7.6%	5.5%
Manufacturing as % of GDP	18%	26%	20%
Central government spending as % of GNP	23%	15%	20%
Merchandise exports (US$ billions)	52.6	22.9	25.7
Merchandise imports (US$ billions)	60.5	32.9	21.8
% of GNP received as development aid	–	1.0%	1.6%
Total external debt as % of GNP	–	32.6%	66.4%

WELFARE INDICATORS

	Singapore	Thailand	Indonesia
Infant mortality rate (per 1,000 live births)			
1965	26	145	128
1990	7	44	61
Daily food supply available (calories per capita, 1989)	3,198	3,121	2,750
Population per physician (1984)	1,410	2,150	9,410
Teacher-pupil ratio (primary school, 1989)	1 : 26	1 : 18	1 : 23

■ capital city

While the region has a volatile recent political history, the people continue to follow their traditional religious beliefs. The main religions are Buddhism, chiefly on the mainland peninsula, Islam in Indonesia, and Christianity in the Philippines. All these religious influences come from outside the region.

Area 5,765 sq. km (2,226 sq. mi.)
Population 266,000
Capital Bandar Seri Begawan — **Brunei**

Area 676,577 sq. km (261,228 sq. mi.)
Population 41,675,000
Capital Rangoon — **Burma**

Area 181,035 sq. km (69,898 sq. mi.)
Population 8,264,000
Capital Phnom Penh — **Cambodia**

Area 1,919,443 sq. km (741,101 sq. mi.)
Population 184,283,000
Capital Djakarta — **Indonesia**

Area 236,800 sq. km (91,400 sq. mi.)
Population 4,139,000
Capital Vientiane — **Laos**

Area 513,115 sq. km (198,115 sq. mi.)
Population 57,196,000
Thailand **Capital** Bangkok

Area 331,653 sq. km (128,052 sq. mi.)
Population 66,693,000
Vietnam **Capital** Hanoi

Area 622 sq. km (240 sq. mi.)
Population 2,723,000
Singapore **Capital** Singapore

Area 330,442 sq. km (127,584 sq. mi.)
Population 17,891,000
Capital Kuala Lumpur — **Malaysia**

Area 300,000 sq. km (115,800 sq. mi.)
Population 62,413,000
Capital Manila — **Philippines**

HABITATS

Rainforest flourishes in the south, with deciduous forest and tropical savanna grassland in the north. The fertile lowlands and broad deltas of the great rivers on the mainland peninsula, including the Irrawaddy, Mekong and Salween, are cultivated.

LAND

Major features mountain chains and flood plains, deltas of great rivers in north of region, mountainous and volcanic islands of Malaysia, Indonesia, Philippines, world's largest archipelago

WATER

Longest river Mekong, 4,180 km (2,600 mi.)
Largest lake Tonle Sap, 10,000 sq. km (3,860 sq. mi.)

NOTABLE THREATENED ENDEMIC SPECIES

Mammals Pileated gibbon (*Hylobates pileatus*), orang utan (*Pongo pygmaeus*), Flat-headed cat (*Felis planiceps*), Malayan tapir (*Tapirus indicus*), Javan rhinoceros (*Rhinoceros sondaicus*), kouprey (*Bos sauveli*), tamaraw (*Bubalus mindorensis*)
Birds Philippine eagle (*Pithecophaga jefferyi*), Giant ibis (*Pseudibis gigantea*), Gurney's pitta (*Pitta gurneyi*), Salmon-crested cockatoo (*Cacatua moluccensis*)
Plants *Allobunkillia* species; *Amorphopallus titanum* (titan arum); *Johannesteijsmannia lanceolata* (umbrella leaf palm); *Maingaya* species; *Maxburretia rupicola*; *Nepenthes* – Mount Kinabulu species (pitcher plant); *Paphiopedilum rothschildianum* (Rothschild's slipper orchid); *Phyllagathis magnifica*; *Rafflesia* species; *Strongylodon macrobotrys* (jade vine)
Others River terrapin (*Batagur baska*), False gharial (*Tomistoma schlegelii*), Komodo dragon (*Varanus komodoensis*)

CLIMATE

Malaysia and Indonesia, which straddle the Equator, have a tropical climate, also called a rainforest climate. The coastal areas in the north of the region have a marked summer monsoon. Other inland areas in the northwest have a distinct dry season in winter.

TEMPERATURE AND PRECIPITATION

	Temperature °C (°F)		Altitude
	January	July	m (ft)
Rangoon	25 (77)	27 (81)	6 (19)
Ho Chi Minh City	26 (79)	27 (81)	9 (29)
Manila	25 (77)	28 (82)	14 (45)
Cameron Highlands	18 (64)	18 (64)	1,449 (4,753)
Singapore	26 (79)	27 (81)	10 (33)
Djakarta	26 (79)	27 (81)	6 (19)

	Precipitation mm (in)		
	January	July	Year
Rangoon	3 (0.1)	580 (22.8)	2,618 (103.1)
Ho Chi Minh City	15 (0.5)	315 (12.3)	1,808 (71.2)
Manila	23 (0.9)	432 (17.0)	1,791 (70.5)
Cameron Highlands	168 (6.6)	122 (4.8)	2,640 (104.0)
Singapore	252 (9.9)	170 (6.7)	2,282 (89.8)
Djakarta	300 (11.8)	64 (2.5)	1,755 (69.1)

ENVIRONMENTAL ISSUES

Natural hazards include earthquakes, hurricanes (locally called typhoons), floods, and volcanic eruptions. But human activity, including the rapid destruction of forests, the population explosion, and urban expansion, are causing new problems.

POPULATION AND WEALTH

	Highest	Middle	Lowest
Population increase (annual population growth rate, % 1960–90)	2.8 (Philippines)	2.2 (Laos)	1.4 (Cambodia)
Energy use (gigajoules/person)	140 (Singapore)	8 (Philippines)	1 (Cambodia)
Real purchasing power (US$/person)	10,540 (Singapore)	2,170 (Philippines)	660 (Burma)

ENVIRONMENTAL INDICATORS

CO₂ emissions (million tonnes carbon/annum)	140 (Indonesia)	40 (Philippines)	5 (Cambodia)
Deforestation ('000s ha./annum 1980s)	920 (Indonesia)	173 (Vietnam)	30 (Cambodia)
Artificial fertilizer use (kg/ha./annum)	1,833 (Singapore)	63 (Vietnam)	0.2 (Cambodia)
Cars (per 1,000 population)	87 (Singapore)	6 (Philippines)	0.6 (Indonesia)
Access to safe drinking water (% population)	78 (Singapore)	51 (Malaysia)	30 (Burma)

MAJOR ENVIRONMENTAL PROBLEMS AND SOURCES

Air pollution: urban high; high greenhouse gas emissions
Marine/coastal pollution: medium; *sources:* industrial, agricultural, sewage, oil
Land degradation: *types:* soil erosion, deforestation, habitat destruction; *causes:* agriculture, industry, population pressure
Resource problems: fuelwood shortage; inadequate drinking water and sanitation
Population problems: population explosion; urban overcrowding; inadequate health facilities
Major events: Burkit Suharto (1982–83), fire in coal seams and peat; Bangkok (1991), chemical explosion and fire

HABITATS

Physical zones

- mountains/barren land
- forest
- grassland

▲ mountain peak (metres)
☀ climate station

Southeast Asia is a complex region with rugged peninsulas, islands swathed in forest, and active volcanoes. There are high mountains in the far north and in Borneo.

ENVIRONMENTAL ISSUES

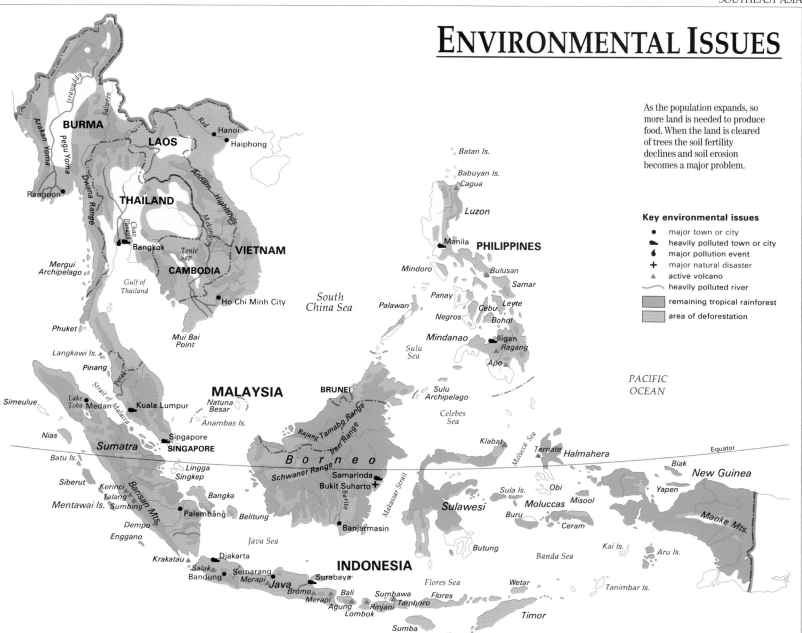

As the population expands, so
more land is needed to produce
food. When the land is cleared
of trees the soil fertility
declines and soil erosion
becomes a major problem.

Key environmental issues

- major town or city
- heavily polluted town or city
- major pollution event
- major natural disaster
- active volcano
- heavily polluted river
- remaining tropical rainforest
- area of deforestation

CLIMATE

height above sea level of climate stations

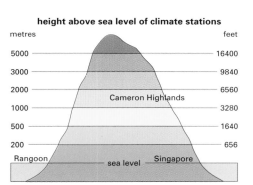

Rangoon
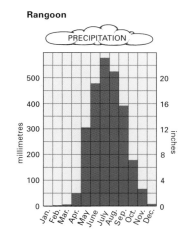

Cameron Highlands
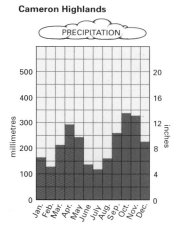

Singapore
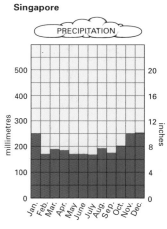

Rangoon
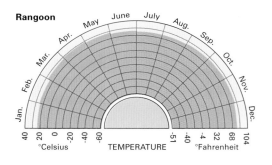

Cameron Highlands
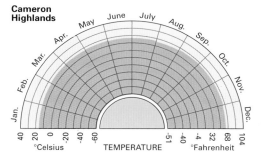

Singapore
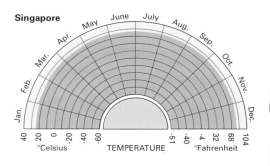

POPULATION

The mountains and forest areas are thinly populated and most people live on the cultivated lowlands and around the leading port cities. By world standards, the percentage of people living in urban areas is low, but the cities are growing at a rapid rate.

POPULATION

Total population of region (millions)	454.6
Population density (persons per sq. km)	181.8
Population change (average annual percent 1960–1990)	
Urban	+4.5
Rural	+2.0

TEN LARGEST CITIES

	Country	Population
Djakarta †	Indonesia	7,886,000
Manila †	Philippines	6,720,000
Bangkok †	Thailand	5,609,000
Ho Chi Minh City	Vietnam	3,420,000
Singapore †	Singapore	2,704,000
Hanoi †	Vietnam	2,571,000
Rangoon †	Burma	2,513,000
Surabaya	Indonesia	2,224,000
Medan	Indonesia	1,806,000
Quezon City	Philippines	1,546,000

† denotes capital city

The highest population densities are found on Java, Indonesia. Java contains about one-third of the population of Southeast Asia. The island contains Djakarta, the region's biggest city.

INDUSTRY

Political instability has restricted development in Southeast Asia. Some countries, such as Laos and Cambodia, are among the world's poorest. But Malaysia is developing quickly and Singapore has become a prosperous industrial centre.

INDUSTRIAL OUTPUT (US $ billion)

Total	Mining	Manufacturing	Average annual change since 1960
89.5	16.7	68.4	+7.2%

MAJOR PRODUCTS (figures in brackets are percentages of world production)

Energy and minerals	Output	Change since 1960
Coal (mill tonnes)	14.3 (0.3%)	+610%
Oil (mill barrels)	785.8 (3.5%)	+312%
Natural gas (billion cu. metres)	78.9 (4.1%)	+1073%
Tin (1,000 tonnes)	92.3 (46.0%)	-22.4%
Nickel (1,000 tonnes)	63.4 (7.8%)	+199%

Manufactures		
Processed palm and coconut oil 6.5 (35.3%) (mill tonnes)		+413%
Canned fruits (1,000 tonnes)	665.0 (12.9%)	+302%
Sawnwood (mill cu. metres)*	19.5 (15.6%)	+123%
Natural and synthetic rubber (mill tonnes)	3.9 (27.1%)	+54%
Rubber footwear (mill pairs)	47.2 (19.9%)	N/A
Jet fuels (mill tonnes)**	7.8 (5.5%)	N/A
Cement (mill tonnes)	36.3 (3.3%)	+1628%
Radios and sound recorders (mill)	57.7 (20.3%)	N/A

* Broadleaved timber only (coniferous excluded)
** Mainly Singapore
N/A means production had not begun in 1960

AGRICULTURE

Agriculture employs about half of the people of Southeast Asia. The region has large commercial plantations to grow such crops as oil palms, pineapples, rubber, and sugar cane, together with small plots worked by subsistence farmers to feed their families.

LAND (million hectares)

Total	Agricultural	Arable	Forest/woodland
436 (100%)	90 (21%)	59 (13%)	240 (55%)

FARMERS

97 million people employed in agriculture (54% of workforce)
0.6 hectares of arable land per person employed in agriculture

MAJOR CROPS

	Area mill ha.	Yield 100kg/ha.	Production mill tonnes	Change since 1963
Paddy rice	35.2	28.5 (87)	100.2 (22)	+103%
Maize	8.3	15.8 (44)	13.2 (3)	+140%
Cassara	3.4	116.3 (125)	39.3 (29)	+153%
Pulses	2.0	7.8 (97)	1.5 (3)	+126%
Soya beans	1.6	10.3 (54)	1.6 (2)	+255%
Sugar cane	1.3	547.9 (92)	71.2 (7)	+143%
Bananas	—	—	9.7 (15)	+128%
Other fruit	—	—	14.3 (6)	+196%

MAJOR LIVESTOCK

	Number mill	Production mill tonnes	Change since 1963
Cattle	28.9 (2)	—	+36%
Fish catch	—	9.0 (10)	

FOOD SECURITY (cereal exports minus imports)

mill tonnes	% domestic production	% world trade
+1.5	1	1

Numbers in brackets are percentages of world total

POPULATION

Population density

city populations
(capital city is underlined)

- ◆ over 5,000,000
- ■ 1,000,000–5,000,000
- ● 500,000–999,999
- × capital city less than 500,000

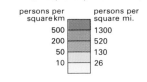

persons per square km	persons per square mi.
500	1300
200	520
50	130
10	26

Mandalay
Irrawaddy
Salween
BURMA
Hanoi
LAOS
Haiphong
Red
Rangoon
Vientiane
THAILAND
Da Nang
Chao Phraya
Bangkok
Mekong
Tonle Sap
VIETNAM
Mergui Archipelago
CAMBODIA
Gulf of Thailand
Phnom Penh
Ho Chi Minh City
Phuket
Langkawi Is.
Pinang
Lake Toba
Simeulue
Medan
Strait of Malacca
Kuala Lumpur
MALAYSIA
Natuna Besar
Anambas Is.
Nias
Singapore
SINGAPORE
Sumatra
Batu Is.
Lingga Singkep
Siberut
Bangka
Mentawai Is.
Belitung
Enggano
Java Sea
Palembang
Djakarta
Semarang
Bandung
Surabaya
Malang
Java
Madura
Bali
Sumbawa
Lombok
Sumba

Batan Is.
Babuyan Is.
Luzon
Caloocan
Quezon City
Manila
PHILIPPINES
Mindoro
Samar
Panay
Cebu
Leyte
Palawan
Negros
Cebu
Bohol
Mindanao
Sulu Sea
Davao
South China Sea
BRUNEI
Bandar Seri Begawan
Sulu Archipelago
Celebes Sea
Borneo
Rajang
Barito
Makassar Strait
Sulawesi
Ujung Pandang
INDONESIA
Flores Sea
Flores
Butung
Banda Sea
Sula Is.
Obi
Moluccas
Buru
Ceram
Misool
Molucca Sea
Halmahera
Equator
Biak
Yapen
New Guinea
Kai Is.
Aru Is.
Wetar
Tanimbar Is.
Timor

PACIFIC OCEAN

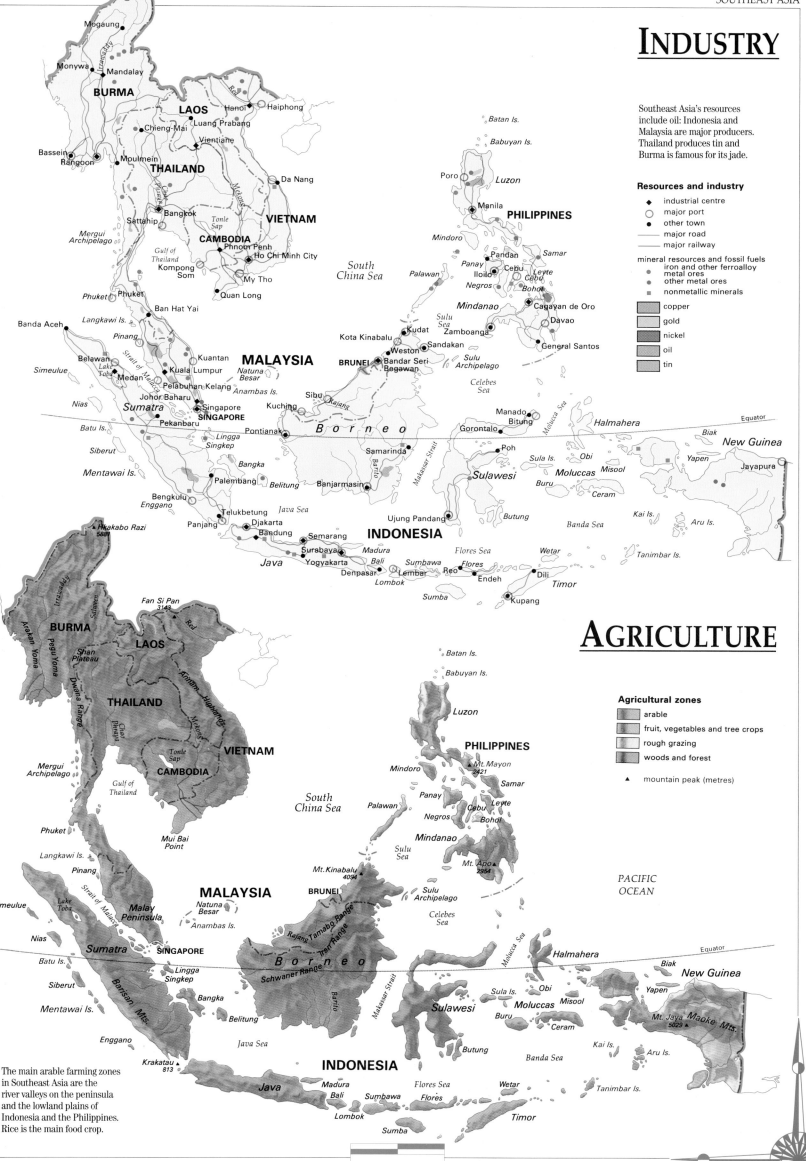

INDUSTRY

Southeast Asia's resources
include oil: Indonesia and
Malaysia are major producers.
Thailand produces tin and
Burma is famous for its jade.

Resources and industry

- ◆ industrial centre
- ○ major port
- ● other town
- —— major road
- — major railway

mineral resources and fossil fuels
- ● iron and other ferroalloy metal ores
- ● other metal ores
- ■ nonmetallic minerals

- copper
- gold
- nickel
- oil
- tin

BURMA
Mogaung
Monywa
Mandalay
LAOS
Hanoi · Haiphong
Luang Prabang
Chieng-Mai
Vientiane
Bassein
Rangoon
Moulmein
THAILAND
Da Nang
Sattahip · Bangkok
VIETNAM
Tonle Sap
CAMBODIA
Phnom Penh
Ho Chi Minh City
Mergui Archipelago
Gulf of Thailand
Kompong Som
My Tho
Phuket · Phuket
Quan Long
Ban Hat Yai
Langkawi Is.
Pinang
Banda Aceh
Belawan
Lake Toba
Kuantan
MALAYSIA
Simeulue
Medan
Kuala Lumpur
Natuna Besar
Pelabuhan Kelang
Anambas Is.
Nias
Johor Baharu
Sumatra
Singapore
Kuching
SINGAPORE
Sibu · Rajang
Batu Is.
Pekanbaru
Pontianak
Siberut
Lingga
Singkep
Bangka
Mentawai Is.
Palembang
Belitung
Bengkulu
Enggano
Telukbetung
Panjang
Djakarta
Bandung
Semarang
INDONESIA
Surabaya
Yogyakarta
Java
Bali
Denpasar
Lembar
Lombok

Batan Is.
Babuyan Is.
Poro
Luzon
Manila
PHILIPPINES
Mindoro
Pandan
Samar
Panay
Cebu
Iloilo
Leyte
Palawan
Negros
Cebu
Bohol
Mindanao
Cagayan de Oro
Sulu Sea
Davao
Kota Kinabalu
Kudat
Zamboanga
BRUNEI
Weston
Sandakan
General Santos
Bandar Seri Begawan
Sulu Archipelago
Celebes Sea
Borneo
Manado
Bitung
Halmahera
Equator
Gorontalo
Biak
New Guinea
Samarinda
Yapen
Bartito
Poh
Sula Is.
Obi
Misool
Jayapura
Banjarmasin
Sulawesi
Moluccas
Buru
Ceram
Kai Is.
Aru Is.
Ujung Pandang
Butung
Banda Sea
Madura
Flores Sea
Wetar
Tanimbar Is.
Sumbawa
Reo
Flores
Dili
Endeh
Timor
Sumba
Kupang

AGRICULTURE

Agricultural zones
- arable
- fruit, vegetables and tree crops
- rough grazing
- woods and forest
- ▲ mountain peak (metres)

Hkakabo Razi
5881
Fan Si Pan
3143
BURMA
Arakan Yoma
Pegu Yoma
LAOS
Shan Plateau
Red
Salween
Dwana Range
THAILAND
Annam Highlands
Chao Phraya
Mekong
Tonle Sap
VIETNAM
Mergui Archipelago
CAMBODIA
Gulf of Thailand
Mui Bai Point
Phuket
Langkawi Is.
Pinang
Lake Toba
MALAYSIA
Malay Peninsula
Natuna Besar
Simeulue
Anambas Is.
Nias
Strait of Malacca
Sumatra
SINGAPORE
Mt. Kinabalu
4094
BRUNEI
Sulu Archipelago
Celebes Sea
Batu Is.
Siberut
Lingga
Singkep
Borneo
Rajang Tamabo Range
Tran Range
Schwaner Range
Bartito
Bangka
Belitung
Makassar Strait
Barisan Mts.
Enggano
Mentawai Is.
Krakatau
813
Java Sea
INDONESIA
Java
Madura
Bali
Sumbawa
Lombok
Sumba

Batan Is.
Babuyan Is.
Luzon
PHILIPPINES
Mindoro
Mt. Mayon
2421
Samar
Panay
Leyte
Palawan
Cebu
Negros
Bohol
Mindanao
Mt. Apo
2954
Sulu Sea
South China Sea
PACIFIC OCEAN
Molucca Sea
Halmahera
Equator
Biak
New Guinea
Yapen
Sula Is.
Obi
Misool
Sulawesi
Moluccas
Buru
Ceram
Mt. Jaya
5029
Maoke Mts.
Butung
Banda Sea
Kai Is.
Aru Is.
Flores Sea
Wetar
Tanimbar Is.
Flores
Timor

The main arable farming zones
in Southeast Asia are the
river valleys on the peninsula
and the lowland plains of
Indonesia and the Philippines.
Rice is the main food crop.

JAPAN & KOREA

Rugged mountains, interspersed with lowlands, dominate the landscapes of Japan and Korea. The Korean mountains are old and stable, but most of Japan's highest peaks are volcanic. Japan lies in an unstable zone. Earthquakes and tsunamis (powerful sea waves triggered by earth movements) are constant threats. The region has a monsoon climate, with hot, wet summers and cold winters.

Until fairly recent times, Japan and Korea were cut off from the rest of the world. But from the mid-19th century, Japan began to modernize and become a world power. Its defeat in World War II proved a challenge. With help from the United States, it has become a major industrial power. Korea, occupied by Japan from 1910 to 1945, is split into free-enterprise South Korea and the communist North.

Japan and Korea occupy a frontier zone between Eurasia and the Pacific Ocean. Japan forms part of the Pacific 'ring of fire', a zone of crustal instability that encircles the Pacific Ocean. Japan has 60 active volcanoes and is struck by several thousand earthquakes every year.

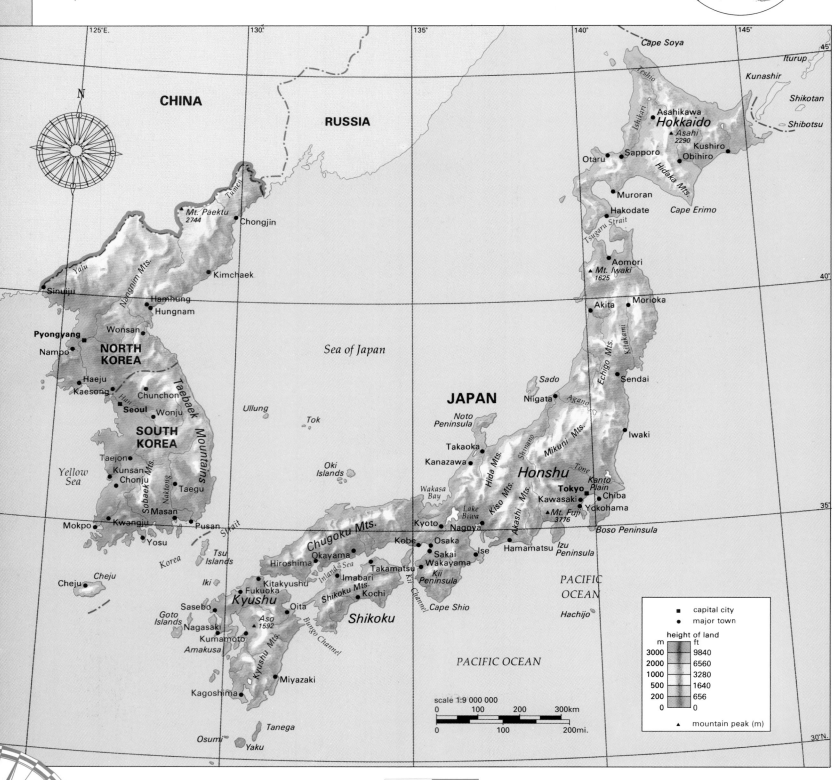

CHINA

RUSSIA

Cape Soya

Iturup

Kunashir

Teshio

Shikotan

Ishikari

Asahikawa

Hokkaido

Shibotsu

▲ Asahi 2290

Kushiro

Otaru • Sapporo

Obihiro

Hidaka Mts.

Muroran

Cape Erimo

Hakodate

Tsugaru Strait

▲ Mt. Paektu 2744

Chongjin

Yalu

Kimchaek

Mt. Iwaki 1625

Aomori

Naegrim Mts.

40°

Sinuiju

Hamhung

Hungnam

Akita

Morioka

Kitakami

Echigo Mts.

Pyongyang

Wonsan

Sea of Japan

Sado

Sendai

Nampo

NORTH KOREA

Haeju

Taebaek

Niigata

JAPAN

Mikuni Mts.

Kaesong

Chunchon

Mountains

Ullung

Tok

Noto Peninsula

Agano

Shinano

Iwaki

Seoul

Wonju

Takaoka

Hida Mts.

Honshu

Tone

SOUTH KOREA

Kanazawa

Kanto Plain

Taejon

Oki Islands

Tokyo

Chiba

Sobaek Mts.

Yellow Sea

Kunsan

Naktong

Wakasa Bay

Kiso Mts.

Kawasaki

Yokohama

Chonju

Taegu

Lake Biwa

Akashi Mts.

▲ Mt. Fuji 3776

Masan

Kyoto

Nagoya

35°

Mokpo

Kwangju

Pusan

Kobe

Osaka

Ise

Hamamatsu

Boso Peninsula

Yosu

Strait

Chugoku Mts.

Sakai

Wakayama

Izu Peninsula

Tsu Islands

Okayama

Inland Sea

Takamatsu

Kii Peninsula

PACIFIC OCEAN

Cheju

Cheju

Iki

Hiroshima

Imabari

Shikoku Mts.

Kochi

Kii Channel

Hachijo

Kitakyushu

Korea

Fukuoka

Sasebo

Oita

Cape Shio

Goto Islands

Kyushu

Shikoku

Nagasaki

Aso 1592

Kumamoto

Bungo Channel

Amakusa

Kyushu Mts.

PACIFIC OCEAN

Miyazaki

Kagoshima

scale 1:9 000 000

0   100   200   300km

0   100   200mi.

Tanega

Osumi

Yaku

30°N.

■ capital city
• major town

height of land

m		ft
3000		9840
2000		6560
1000		3280
500		1640
200		656
0		0

▲ mountain peak (m)

THE POLITICAL AND CULTURAL WORLD

Before World War II, Japan was a military dictatorship, whose emperor was thought to be a god. In 1947, a new constitution was adopted in which power was vested in a prime minister and cabinet, who were answerable to the Diet (parliament). Most Japanese embraced democracy, though corruption scandals in the late 1980s marred the image of elected leaders.

Korea was split into two parts in 1945. Separate governments for North and South Korea were set up in 1947 and this action triggered the Korean War (1948–1953). In recent years, talks have been held about reunification, but little progress has been made.

COUNTRIES IN THE REGION

Japan, North Korea, South Korea

MEMBERSHIP OF INTERNATIONAL ORGANIZATIONS

Colombo Plan Japan
Organization for Economic Cooperation and Development (OECD) Japan

LANGUAGE

Countries with one official language (Japanese) Japan; (Korean) North Korea, South Korea

RELIGION

Japan Most Japanese are adherents both of Shinto (93.1%) and Buddhism (73.9%); Christian (1.4%)
North Korea Nonreligious or atheist (67.9%), traditional beliefs (15.6%), Ch'ondogyo (13.9%), Buddhist (1.7%), Christian (0.9%)
South Korea Nonreligious or atheist (57.4%), Christian (20.7%), Buddhist (19.9%), Confucian (1.2%), Ch'ondogyo (0.1%)

STYLES OF GOVERNMENT

Republics North Korea, South Korea
Monarchy Japan
Multiparty states Japan, South Korea
One-party state North Korea
One-chamber assembly North Korea, South Korea
Two-chamber assembly Japan

ECONOMIC INDICATORS: 1990

	Japan	S. Korea
GDP (US$ billions)	2,942.89	236.4
GNP per capita (US$)	25,430	5,400
Annual rate of growth of GDP, 1980–1990	4.1%	9.7%
Manufacturing as % of GDP	29.0%	31.0%
Central government spending as % of GNP	17.0%	16.0%
Merchandise exports (US$ billions)	280.4	65.0
Merchandise imports (US$ billions)	216.8	69.8
% of GNP donated as development aid	0.31%	n/a

WELFARE INDICATORS

Infant mortality rate (per 1,000 live births)		
1965	18	62
1990	5	17
Daily food supply available (calories per capita, 1989)	2,956	2,852
Population per physician (1984)	660	1,160
Teacher-pupil ratio (primary school, 1989)	1 : 21	1 : 36

North Korea

Area 122,400 sq. km
(47,300 sq. mi.)
Population 21,773,000
Capital Pyongyang
Currency 1 won
(W) = 100 chon

South Korea

Area 99,173 sq. km
(38,291 sq. mi.)
Population 42,793,000
Capital Seoul
Currency 1 won
(W) = 100 chon

Area 377,815 sq. km
(145,875 sq. mi.)
Population 123,460,000
Capital Tokyo   **Japan**
Currency 1 yen
¥= 100 sen

NORTH KOREA

Pyongyang

Seoul

SOUTH KOREA

Ullung

Tok

Oki Islands

Tsu Islands

Cheju

Iki

Goto Islands

Amakusa

Kyushu

Shikoku

Sado

JAPAN

Honshu

Tokyo

Hokkaido

■ capital city

Japan is a constitutional monarchy. An emperor is the ceremonial head of state. The country is divided into 47 prefectures. South Korea is a republic, divided into nine provinces and five cities with the rank of province. North Korea is a communist state, divided into nine provinces and four city areas.

HABITATS

Both Japan and Korea are largely mountainous, with uplands extending to the sea and with few large coastal lowlands. There are extensive forests throughout the region on the mountain slopes, and cultivation of crops in the fertile valleys.

LAND

Area 601,241 sq. km (232,141 sq. mi.)
Highest point Mount Fuji, 3,776 m (12,389 ft)
Lowest point sea level
Major features mountains of moderate height cover most of Japan and Korea; over 3,900 islands in Japan

WATER

Longest river Yalu, 810 km (503 mi.)
Largest basin Yalu, 63,000 sq. km (24,000 sq. mi.)
Highest average flow Yalu, 526 cu. m/sec (19,000 cu. ft/sec)
Largest lake Biwa, 695 sq. km (268 sq. mi.)

NOTABLE THREATENED ENDEMIC SPECIES

Mammals Amami rabbit (Pentalagus furnessi), Iriomote cat (Felis iriomotensis)
Birds Short-tailed albatross (Diomeda albatrus), Okinawa rail (Rallus okinawae), Amami thrush (Zoothera amami)
Plants Abies koreana (Korean fir); Arisaema heterocephalum; Chrysanthemum zawadskii; Cyclobalanopsis hondae; Cymbidium koran; Euphrasia omiensis; Fritillaria shikokiana; Gentiana yakusimensis; Magnolia pseudokobus; Rhododendron mucronulatum
Others Japanese giant salamander (Andrias japonicus), Tokyo bitterling (Tanakia tanago)

CLIMATE

Concern about environmental issues is increasing, especially in Japan. Most problems, such as Minamata disease, caused by eating seafood which had absorbed mercury from toxic industrial wastes, are caused by overcrowding and the rapid development of industry.

TEMPERATURE AND PRECIPITATION

	Temperature °C (°F)		Altitude m (ft)
	January	July	
Wonsan	−4 (25)	23 (73)	37 (121)
Seoul	−5 (23)	25 (75)	86 (282)
Sapporo	−6 (21)	20 (68)	18 (59)
Niigata	2 (36)	24 (75)	4 (13)
Tokyo	3 (37)	25 (77)	6 (20)

	Precipitation mm (in)		
	January	July	Year
Wonsan	31 (1.2)	273 (10.7)	1,310 (51.6)
Seoul	31 (1.2)	376 (14.7)	1,258 (49.5)
Sapporo	111 (4.4)	100 (3.9)	1,136 (44.7)
Niigata	194 (7.6)	193 (7.6)	1,841 (72.5)
Tokyo	48 (1.9)	142 (5.6)	1,563 (61.5)

NATURAL HAZARDS

Earthquakes and associated sea waves (tsunami) in Japan, floods, typhoons, landslides

ENVIRONMENTAL ISSUES

During the winter, North Korea and northern Japan are cooled by polar air giving low temperatures and heavy snow falls. In summer, moist monsoon winds bring hot and humid weather, especially in the south. Typhoons, or hurricanes, often strike eastern Japan.

POPULATION AND WEALTH

	Japan	N Korea	S Korea
Population increase (annual population growth rate, % 1960–90)	0.9	2.4	1.8
Energy use (gigajoules/person)	110	79	52

ENVIRONMENTAL INDICATORS

CO$_2$ emissions (million tonnes carbon/annum)	220	20	29
Municipal waste (kg/person/annum)	344	n/a	396
Nuclear waste (cumulative tonnes heavy metal)	5,600	0	700
Artificial fertilizer use (kg/ha./annum)	433	312	422

MAJOR ENVIRONMENTAL PROBLEMS AND SOURCES

Air pollution: locally high, urban high; acid rain prevalent; high greenhouse gas emissions
River/lake pollution: medium; *sources*: industrial, agricultural, sewage
Marine/coastal pollution: medium; *sources*: industrial, agricultural, sewage, oil
Population problems: urban overcrowding

HABITATS

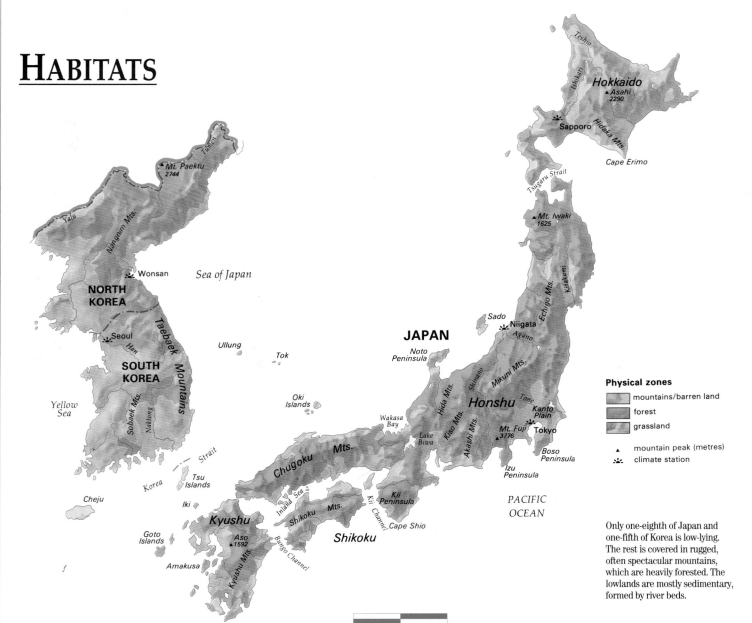

Physical zones
- mountains/barren land
- forest
- grassland
- ▲ mountain peak (metres)
- ☀ climate station

Only one-eighth of Japan and one-fifth of Korea is low-lying. The rest is covered in rugged, often spectacular mountains, which are heavily forested. The lowlands are mostly sedimentary, formed by river beds.

ENVIRONMENTAL ISSUES

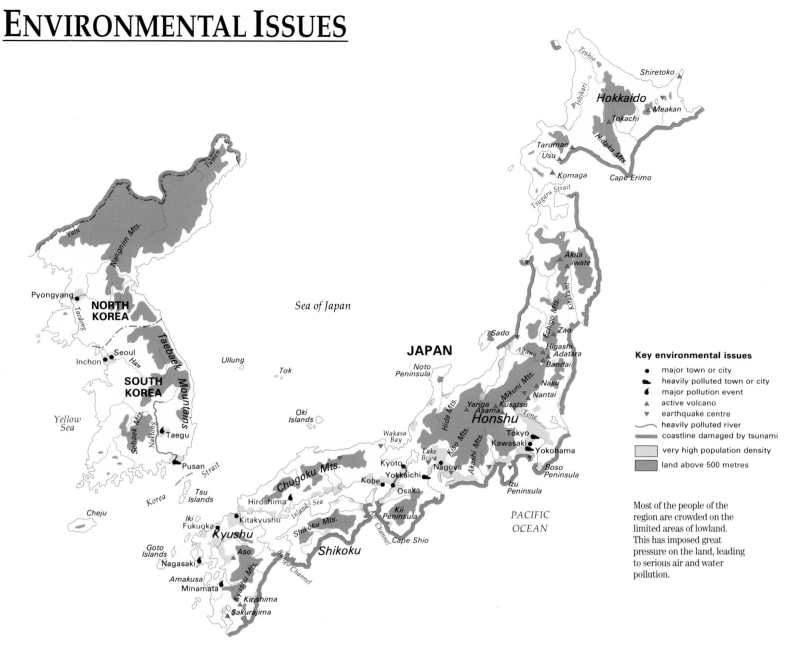

Key environmental issues

- ● major town or city
- ◖ heavily polluted town or city
- ◗ major pollution event
- ▲ active volcano
- ▽ earthquake centre
- ∿ heavily polluted river
- ▬ coastline damaged by tsunami
- very high population density
- land above 500 metres

Most of the people of the region are crowded on the limited areas of lowland. This has imposed great pressure on the land, leading to serious air and water pollution.

Sea of Japan

JAPAN

Honshu

Hokkaido

NORTH KOREA

SOUTH KOREA

Yellow Sea

PACIFIC OCEAN

Kyushu

Shikoku

CLIMATE

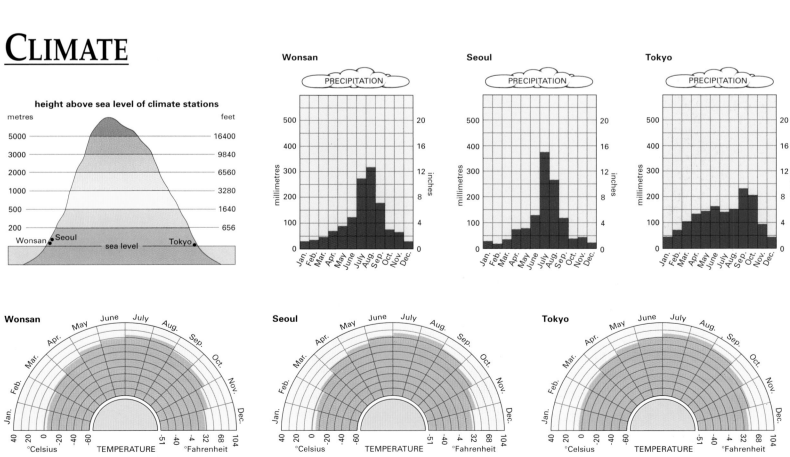

POPULATION

Between 1870 and 1970, Japan's population rose from 30 million to over 100 million. The annual growth rate has now dropped, averaging 0.5 percent between 1980 and 1991. The growth rate in North and South Korea is also below the world average of 1.7 percent.

POPULATION

Total population of region (millions)	190
Population density (persons per sq. km)	322.0
Population change (average annual percent 1960–1990) Urban	+2.1
Rural	-0.2

URBAN POPULATION

As percentage of total population	
1960	62.5
1990	74.2
Percentage in cities of more than 1 million	14.2

TEN LARGEST CITIES

	Country	Population
Tokyo †	Japan	11,936,000
Seoul †	South Korea	9,646,000
Pusan	South Korea	3,517,000
Yokohama	Japan	3,220,000
Pyongyang †	North Korea	2,639,000
Osaka	Japan	2,624,000
Nagoya	Japan	2,155,000
Taegu	South Korea	2,031,000
Sapporo	Japan	1,672,000
Kyoto	Japan	1,461,000

† denotes capital city

INDUSTRY

The region has limited natural resources and the countries import many raw materials. But through ingenuity and hard work, they have become world leaders in manufacturing. Their technical expertise ensures the quality and saleability of their products.

INDUSTRIAL OUTPUT (US $ billion)

Total	Mining	Manufacturing	Average annual change since 1960
1100.9	19.4	1081.5	+8.0%

INDUSTRIAL WORKERS (millions)
(figures in brackets are percentages of total labour force)

Total	Mining	Manufacturing	Construction
29.6	0.2 (0.23%)	22.6 (25.6%)	6.8 (7.7%)

MAJOR PRODUCTS (figures in brackets are percentages of world production)

Energy and minerals	Output	Change since 1960
Coal (mill tonnes)	86.9 (1.8%)	+29.5%
Limestone (mill tonnes)	231.0 (9%)	+407%
Graphite (1,000 tonnes)	129.8 (12.7%)	+36%

Manufactures		
Steel (mill tonnes)	129.1 (17.7%)	+481.3%
Cars (mill)	17.2 (36.2%)	+2163%
Ships (mill gross tonnes)	24.1 (57.7%)	+590%
Excavators (1,000)	115.3 (65.2%)	No data
Clocks and watches (mill)	382.9 (31.8%)	No data
Semiconductors/transistors (mill)	60455.0 (88.9%)	N/A
Calculators (mill)	72.3 (85%)	N/A
Televisions (mill)	28.1 (25.7%)	+540%
Radios and sound recorders/players (mill)	88.4 (29.5%)	+534%
Pianos and organs (1,000)	543.0 (53.8%)	No data
Industrial robots (1,000)	55.8 (70%)	N/A

N/A means production had not begun in 1960

AGRICULTURE

Because only 14 percent of the land can be cultivated, farming is generally intensive and scientific, using irrigation, fertilizers, farm machinery, and improved seeds. Mountainous land is terraced along traditional lines to control soil erosion from rain and wind.

LAND (million hectares)

Total	Agricultural	Arable	Forest/woodland
60 (100%)	10 (17%)	10 (17%)	8 (14%)

MAJOR CROPS

	Area mill ha.	Yield 100kg/ha.	Production mill tonnes	Change since 1963
Paddy rice	4.3	63.2 (193)	27.1 (6)	+14%
Soya beans	0.6	14.7 (77)	0.9 (1)	+43%
Barley	0.6	25.9 (111)	1.5 (1)	−46%
Pulses	0.5	10.2 (126)	0.5 (1)	−2%
Wheat	0.5	34.6 (148)	1.7 (—)	+5%
Maize	0.5	63.3 (175)	3.0 (1)	+105%
Millet	0.4	12.6 (165)	0.6 (2)	+39%
Vegetables	—	—	26.8 (6)	+71%
Fruit	—	—	8.8 (3)	+117%

MAJOR LIVESTOCK

	Number mill	Production mill tonnes	Change since 1963
Pigs	17.8 (2)	—	+182%
Cattle	8.7 (1)	—	+66%
Milk	—	8.8 (2)	+222%
Fish catch	—	16.4 (18)	—

POPULATION

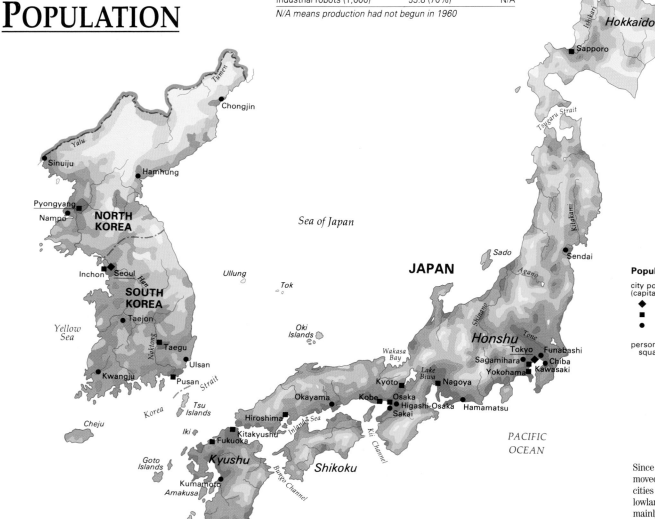

Population density

city populations
(capital city is underlined)

♦ over 5,000,000
■ 1,000,000–5,000,000
● 500,000–999,999

persons per square km	persons per square mi.
500	1300
200	520
100	260
50	130
25	65

Since 1950, many people have moved from rural areas into the cities and towns on the coastal lowlands. This movement arose mainly because of the many jobs available in the new manufacturing industries.

INDUSTRY

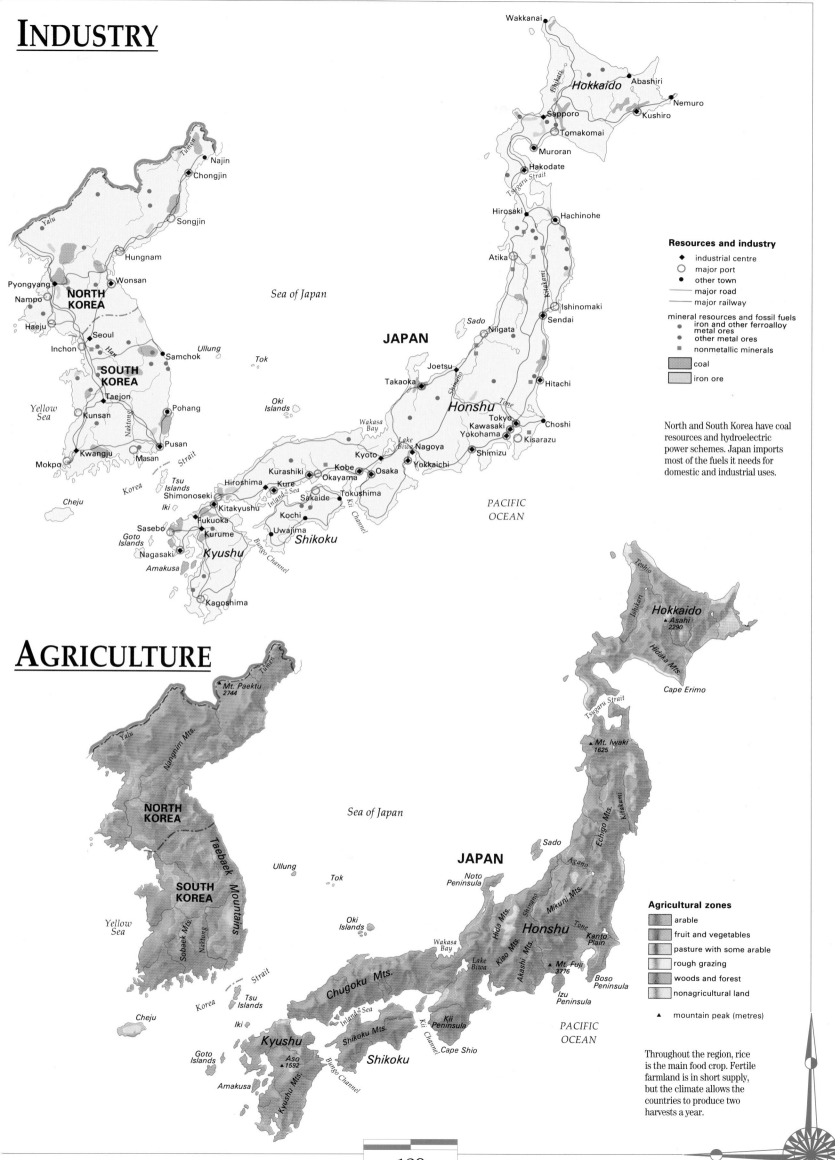

Wakkanai

Hokkaido

Abashiri

Ishikari

Nemuro

Sapporo

Kushiro

Tomakomai

Muroran

Hakodate

Tsugaru Strait

Hirosaki

Hachinohe

Najin

Atika

Chongjin

Kitakami

Songjin

Ishinomaki

Hungnam

Sendai

NORTH KOREA

Sea of Japan

Sado

Niigata

Pyongyang

Wonsan

JAPAN

Nampo

Haeju

Joetsu

Shinano

Takaoka

Seoul

Hitachi

Inchon

SOUTH KOREA

Ullung

Han

Samchok

Tone

Honshu

Tok

Tokyo

Taejon

Naktong

Pohang

Kawasaki

Choshi

Oki Islands

Yokohama

Yellow Sea

Kunsan

Wakasa Bay

Lake Biwa

Nagoya

Kisarazu

Kyoto

Pusan

Kwangju

Masan

Yokkaichi

Shimizu

Strait

Osaka

Mokpo

Kurashiki

Kobe

Tsu Islands

Hiroshima

Kure

Okayama

Tokushima

Cheju

Shimonoseki

Sakaide

Iki

Kitakyushu

Inland Sea

Kochi

PACIFIC OCEAN

Sasebo

Fukuoka

Uwajima

Kii Channel

Shikoku

Nagasaki

Kurume

Goto Islands

Kyushu

Amakusa

Bungo Channel

Kagoshima

Resources and industry

- ◆ industrial centre
- ○ major port
- ● other town
- major road
- major railway

mineral resources and fossil fuels
- ● iron and other ferroalloy metal ores
- ● other metal ores
- ■ nonmetallic minerals
- coal
- iron ore

North and South Korea have coal resources and hydroelectric power schemes. Japan imports most of the fuels it needs for domestic and industrial uses.

AGRICULTURE

Teshio

Hokkaido

Ishikari

▲ Asahi 2290

Hidaka Mts.

Cape Erimo

▲ Mt. Paektu 2744

Tumen

Tsugaru Strait

Yalu

Nangnim Mts.

▲ Mt. Iwaki 1625

NORTH KOREA

Echigo Mts.

Sea of Japan

Sado

Kitakami

Taebaek Mountains

JAPAN

Agano

Mikuni Mts.

SOUTH KOREA

Noto Peninsula

Ullung

Shinano

Kanto Plain

Tok

Hida Mts.

Honshu

Sobaek Mts.

Yellow Sea

Naktong

Oki Islands

Kiso Mts.

Tone

Akashi Mts.

▲ Mt. Fuji 3776

Boso Peninsula

Wakasa Bay

Izu Peninsula

Chugoku Mts.

Lake Biwa

Strait

Korea

Tsu Islands

Inland Sea

Kii Peninsula

Iki

Shikoku Mts.

Kii Channel

Cape Shio

Cheju

Kyushu

Aso 1592

Shikoku

PACIFIC OCEAN

Goto Islands

Amakusa

Kyushu Mts.

Bungo Channel

Agricultural zones

- arable
- fruit and vegetables
- pasture with some arable
- rough grazing
- woods and forest
- nonagricultural land

▲ mountain peak (metres)

Throughout the region, rice is the main food crop. Fertile farmland is in short supply, but the climate allows the countries to produce two harvests a year.

AUSTRALIA & ITS NEIGHBOURS

Australia is the world's sixth largest country and the smallest continent. Most of the land is flat—plains or level plateaus make up nine-tenths of Australia. Papua New Guinea is more mountainous, but has large lowlands.

The climate in Australia ranges from tropical in the north to Mediterranean in the south, though the interior is semiarid or desert. Tasmania has a mild temperate climate.

Australia's Aboriginal people arrived from Southeast Asia at least 40,000 years ago. A nomadic people, they developed complex cultural and religious traditions. Most Australians today are of European descent, especially from Britain, though recent arrivals include people from Asia. The economy is based on farming and mining, but most people work in manufacturing and service industries.

Australia is an ancient landmass which once formed part of the supercontinent of Gondwanaland. Australia has been a stable continent for at least 300 years and its scenery is now the result of constant erosion and deposition rather than great land movements.

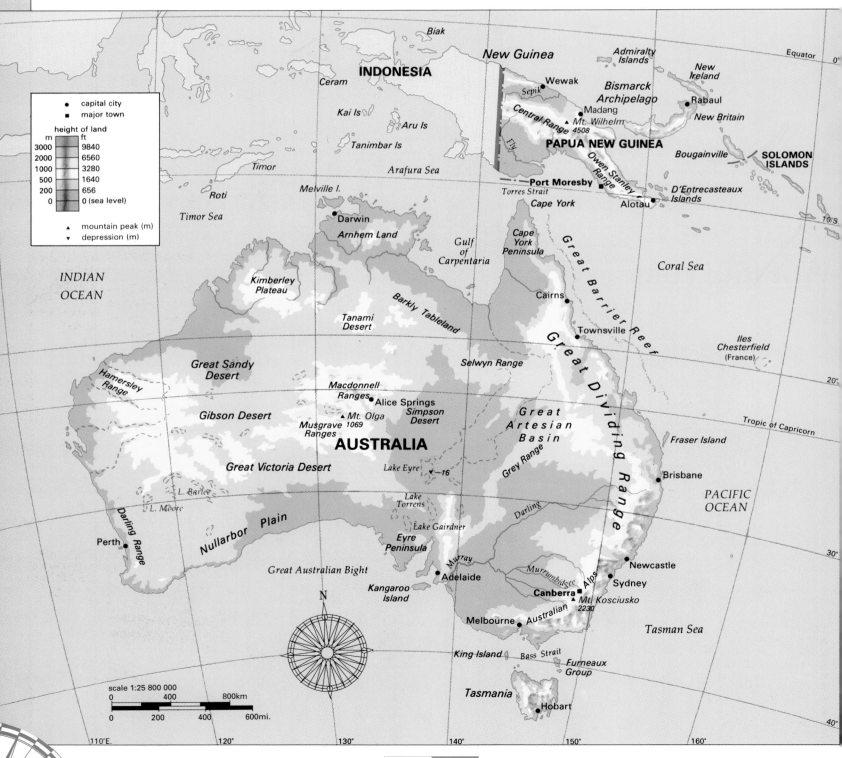

Map key

- ● capital city
- ■ major town

height of land

m	ft
3000	9840
2000	6560
1000	3280
500	1640
200	656
0	0 (sea level)

- ▲ mountain peak (m)
- ▼ depression (m)

scale 1:25 800 000

0   400   800km
0 200 400 600mi.

Map labels

Biak · New Guinea · Admiralty Islands · Equator · 0° · INDONESIA · Ceram · Wewak · New Ireland · Sepik · Bismarck Archipelago · Rabaul · Kai Is · Madang · New Britain · Central Range · Mt. Wilhelm 4508 · Aru Is · Tanimbar Is · PAPUA NEW GUINEA · Bougainville · SOLOMON ISLANDS · Timor · Arafura Sea · Fly · Owen Stanley Range · Port Moresby · D'Entrecasteaux Islands · 10°S · Roti · Melville I. · Torres Strait · Alotau · Cape York · Timor Sea · Timor Sea · Darwin · Gulf of Carpentaria · Cape York Peninsula · Coral Sea · INDIAN OCEAN · Arnhem Land · Kimberley Plateau · Barkly Tableland · Cairns · Iles Chesterfield (France) · Tanami Desert · Townsville · Hamersley Range · Great Sandy Desert · Selwyn Range · 20° · Macdonnell Ranges · Alice Springs · Simpson Desert · Great Artesian Basin · Fraser Island · Gibson Desert · Mt. Olga 1069 · Musgrave Ranges · Tropic of Capricorn · AUSTRALIA · Great Victoria Desert · Lake Eyre ▼ -16 · Grey Range · Brisbane · L. Barlee · PACIFIC OCEAN · L. Moore · Lake Torrens · Darling · Nullarbor Plain · Lake Gairdner · 30° · Perth · Darling Range · Eyre Peninsula · Murray · Newcastle · Great Australian Bight · Adelaide · Murrumbidgee · Alps · Sydney · Kangaroo Island · Canberra · Mt. Kosciusko 2230 · Melbourne · Australian · Tasman Sea · N · King Island · Bass Strait · Furneaux Group · Tasmania · Hobart · 40° · 110°E · 120° · 130° · 140° · 150° · 160°

THE POLITICAL AND CULTURAL WORLD

In 1901, the former British colonies of New South Wales, Queensland, South Australia, Tasmania, Victoria and Western Australia became states and were federated to become the independent federal Commonwealth of Australia. Northern Territory was transferred from South Australia as a territory in 1911.

Today Australia remains a constitutional monarchy—its head of state is the British monarch who is represented by a Governor-General. Papua New Guinea, which was ruled by Australia during the colonial period, is another constitutional monarchy, which, with Australia, is a member of the Commonwealth.

COUNTRIES IN THE REGION
Australia, Papua New Guinea

Island territories
Cocos Islands, Christmas Island, Norfolk Island, Heard and McDonald Islands (Australia)

MEMBERSHIP OF INTERNATIONAL ORGANIZATIONS
Colombo Plan Australia, Papua New Guinea
Organization for Economic Cooperation and Development (OECD) Australia
South Pacific Forum Australia, Papua New Guinea

LANGUAGE
Countries with one official language (English)
Australia, Papua New Guinea

RELIGION
Australia Roman Catholic (26%), Anglican (24%), other Protestant (17%), nonreligious (13%), other Christian (6%), others (14%)
Papua New Guinea Protestant (64%), Roman Catholic (33%), traditional beliefs (2%), Baha'i (0.6%), others (0.3%)

STYLES OF GOVERNMENT
Monarchies Australia, Papua New Guinea
Federal state Australia
Multiparty states Australia, Papua New Guinea

ECONOMIC INDICATORS
	Australia
GDP (US$ billions)	296.3
GNP per capita (US$)	17,000
Annual rate of growth of GDP, 1980–1990	3.4%
Manufacturing as % of GDP	15.0%
Central government spending as % of GNP	26.0%
Merchandise exports (US$ billions)	41.2
Merchandise imports (US$ billions)	38.4
% of GNP donated as development aid	0.34%

WELFARE INDICATORS
Infant mortality rate (per 1,000 live births)	
1965	19
1990	8
Daily food supply available (calories per capita, 1989)	3,216
Population per physician (1984)	440
Teacher-pupil ratio (primary school, 1989)	1 : 17

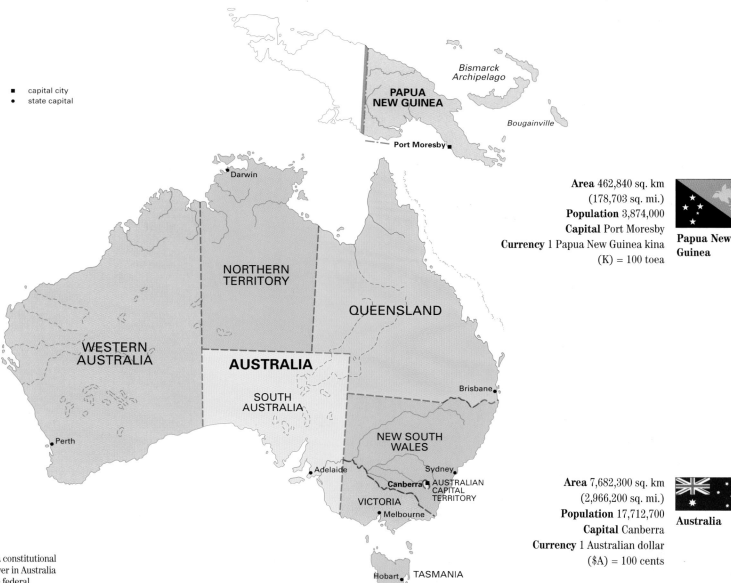

■ capital city
● state capital

PAPUA NEW GUINEA

Bismarck Archipelago

Bougainville

Port Moresby ■

Darwin

NORTHERN TERRITORY

QUEENSLAND

WESTERN AUSTRALIA

AUSTRALIA

SOUTH AUSTRALIA

Brisbane

NEW SOUTH WALES

Perth

Adelaide

Sydney

Canberra AUSTRALIAN CAPITAL TERRITORY

VICTORIA

Melbourne

Hobart TASMANIA

Area 462,840 sq. km (178,703 sq. mi.)
Population 3,874,000
Capital Port Moresby
Currency 1 Papua New Guinea kina (K) = 100 toea

Papua New Guinea

Area 7,682,300 sq. km (2,966,200 sq. mi.)
Population 17,712,700
Capital Canberra
Currency 1 Australian dollar ($A) = 100 cents

Australia

Although it is a constitutional monarchy, power in Australia is vested in the federal government, led by the prime minister. Each state also has its own parliament, which deals with such matters as education and public welfare. Some Australians would like to see constitutional changes to make their country a republic.

HABITATS

Northern Australia is tropical, with much savanna grassland that merges into the country's arid heart. The east coast has tropical forests, with a range of mountains extending north to south. There are large grassland areas in the southwest and southeast.

LAND

Area (Australia/Papua New Guinea) 8,145,140 sq. km (3,144,903 sq. mi.)
Highest points Mount Kosciusko, Australia 2,230 m (7,317 ft); Mount Wilhelm, Papua New Guinea 4,508 m (14,790 ft)
Lowest point Lake Eyre, Australia, −16 m (−52 ft)
Major features Australia, 7,686,848 sq. km (2,967,909 sq. mi.) is the world's lowest continent

WATER

Longest river Murray–Darling, 3,780 km (2,330 mi.)
Largest basin Murray–Darling, 1,072,000 sq. km (414,100 sq. mi.)
Highest average flow Murray, 400 cu. m/sec (14,000 cu. ft/sec)
Largest lake Eyre, 9,500 sq. km (3,668 sq. mi.)

NOTABLE THREATENED ENDEMIC SPECIES

Mammals Northern hairy-nosed wombat (*Lasiorhinus krefftii*), numbat (*Myrmecobius fasciatus*), Great bilby (*Macrotis lagotis*)
Birds Paradise parrot (*Psephotus pulcherrimus*)
Plants *Banksia goodii* (Good's banksia), *Dacrydium franklinii* (Huon pine), *Eucalyptus caesia* (caesia), *Platycerium grande* (Stag's horn fern)
Others Western swamp turtle (*Pseudemydura umbrina*), Baw baw frog (*Philoria frosti*)

CLIMATE

Papua New Guinea and northern Australia have a tropical climate. The interior of Australia is very dry. Mediterranean climates occur in the south. The east is subtropical, while the southeast, and Tasmania, have warm summers and cool winters.

CLIMATE

	Temperature °C (°F) January	July	Altitude m (ft)
Darwin	28 (82)	25 (77)	30 (98)
Perth	23 (73)	13 (55)	60 (197)
Alice Springs	28 (82)	12 (54)	579 (1,900)
Sydney	22 (72)	12 (54)	42 (138)
Port Moresby	28 (82)	25 (77)	38 (126)

	Precipitation mm (in) January	July	Year
Darwin	386 (15.1)	0 (0)	1,661 (65.4)
Perth	8 (0.3)	180 (7.1)	873 (34.4)
Alice Springs	43 (1.7)	8 (0.3)	252 (9.9)
Sydney	89 (3.5)	117 (4.6)	1,214 (47.3)
Port Moresby	178 (7.0)	28 (1.1)	1,175 (46.3)

NATURAL HAZARDS

Drought, storms and flooding, bush fires

ENVIRONMENTAL ISSUES

While the Aboriginal people generally lived in harmony with nature, the rapid population increase in the last 200 years and the spread of livestock farming has led to a depletion of plants and animals. Introduced species, such as rabbits, have caused much damage.

POPULATION AND WEALTH

	Australia
Population (millions)	17.7
Population increase (annual population growth rate, % 1960–90)	1.7
Energy use (gigajoules/person)	201
Real purchasing power (US$/person)	14,530

ENVIRONMENTAL INDICATORS

CO₂ emissions (million tonnes carbon/annum)	71
Deforestation ('000s ha/annum 1980s)	679
Artificial fertilizer use (kg/ha./annum)	29
Cars (per 1,000 population)	220
Access to safe drinking water (% population)	90

MAJOR ENVIRONMENTAL PROBLEMS AND SOURCES

Air pollution: urban high
Marine/coastal pollution: medium; *sources:* industrial, agricultural, sewage
Land degradation: *types:* desertification, soil erosion, salinization, deforestation, coastal degradation, habitat destruction; *causes:* agriculture, industry, population pressure
Resource problems: inadequate drinking water; inadequate sanitation; coastal flooding

HABITATS

Physical zones
- mountains/barren land
- forest
- grassland
- semidesert
- desert

▲ mountain peak (metres)
▼ depression (metres)
☀ climate station

Behind the narrow coastal plain in the east lies the Great Dividing Range of mountains. Beyond lie the grasslands which merge to the west into the semideserts and deserts of the vast western plateaus.

ENVIRONMENTAL ISSUES

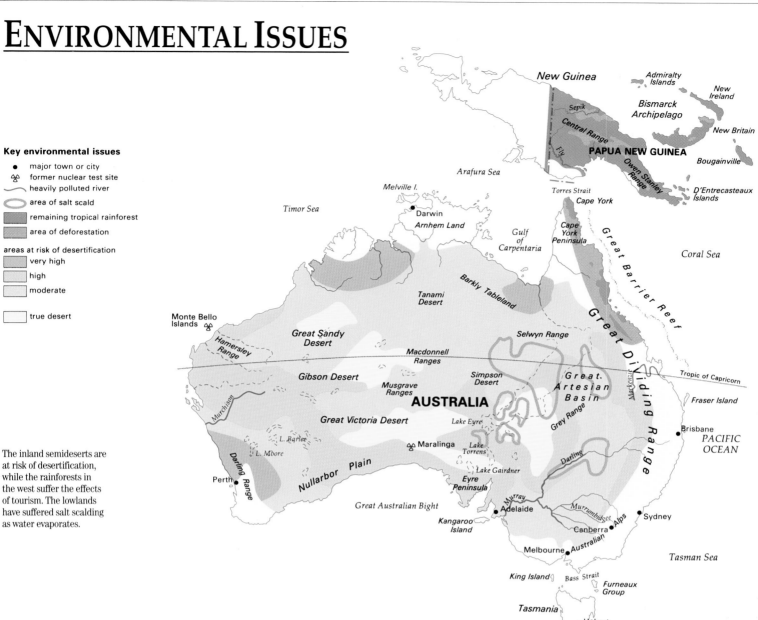

Key environmental issues

- ● major town or city
- ⚛ former nuclear test site
- ∿ heavily polluted river
- ◯ area of salt scald
- ▨ remaining tropical rainforest
- ▨ area of deforestation

areas at risk of desertification

- ▨ very high
- ▨ high
- ▨ moderate
- ☐ true desert

The inland semideserts are at risk of desertification, while the rainforests in the west suffer the effects of tourism. The lowlands have suffered salt scalding as water evaporates.

CLIMATE

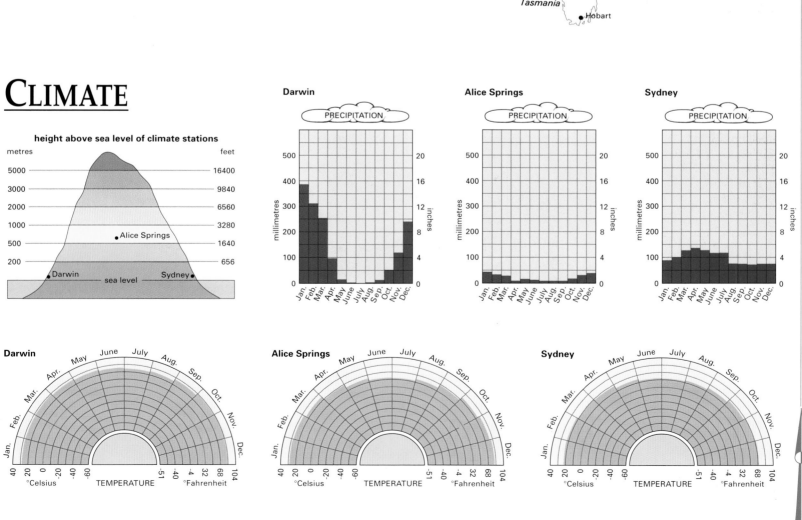

height above sea level of climate stations

metres		feet
5000		16400
3000		9840
2000		6560
1000		3280
500	Alice Springs	1640
200		656
	Darwin sea level Sydney	

POPULATION

Australia has one of the world's lowest average population densities, but 86 percent of its people live in cities and towns on the coasts, making it one of the more urbanized countries. In Papua New Guinea, 84 percent of the people live in rural areas.

POPULATION

Total population of the region (millions)	21.4
Population density (Australia) (persons per sq. km)	2
Population change (average annual percent 1960–1990)	−4%

URBAN POPULATION

As percentage of total population	
1970	47.5
1990	50

TEN LARGEST CITIES

	Country	Population
Melbourne	Australia	3,080,900
Sydney	Australia	3,656,500
Brisbane	Australia	1,301,700
Perth	Australia	1,193,100
Adelaide	Australia	1,049,800
Canberra †	Australia	310,100
Gold Coast	Australia	285,000
Newcastle	Australia	255,787
Hobart	Australia	183,500
Port Moresby †	Papua New Guinea	152,000

† denotes capital city

INDUSTRY

Mining is a major industry in Australia. Some raw materials are exported to Japan and elsewhere, but other materials are used in local manufacturing industries. Australia's industries concentrate on producing consumer goods both for domestic use and for export.

INDUSTRIAL OUTPUT (US$ billion)

Total	Mining	Manufacturing
40.50	7.9	32.5

INDUSTRIAL WORKERS ('000s)

Total	Mining	Manufacturing
1,559	419	1,140

MAJOR PRODUCTS

Energy and minerals	output
Coal (mill tonnes)	162
Iron ore (mill tonnes)	96.7
Copper (1,000 tonnes)	375.8
Nickel (1,000 tonnes)	42
Bauxite (1,000 tonnes)	38.88
Uranium (1,000 tonnes)	3.5
Gold (tonnes)	284
Diamonds (mill carats)	36

Manufactures	
Wool carpets (mill sq. m)	41.46
Cement (mill tonnes)	7.0
Steel (mill tonnes)	6.6
Aluminium (mill tonnes)	1.3

AGRICULTURE

Australia's prosperity was based on farming. Cattle, wheat and wool are major products, together with dairy products, fruit and sugar cane. Australia now exports mainly in the Pacific region since its trade with Britain, its main trading partner, declined in the 1970s.

LAND (million hectares)

	Australia	Papua New Guinea
Total	768.2 (100%)	46.2 (100%)
Agricultural	453.2 (59%)	0.36 (0.8%)
Arable	33.03 (4.3%)	0.09 (0.2%)
Forest/woodland	–	39.17 (84.8%)

MAJOR CROPS

	Area mill ha.	Yield kg/ha.	Production mill tonnes
Wheat	11.5	748	8.6
Sugar cane	0.32	61,906	25.9
Fruit	–	–	3.23
Cereals, total	16.26	887	14.62

Major livestock

	Number mill	Production mill tonnes
Sheep	137.9	–
Cattle	24.68	–
Pigs	–	252
Milk	–	5.19
Fish catch	–	0.15

POPULATION

Population density

city populations
(capital city is underlined)
- ■ 1,000,000–5,000,000
- ● 500,000–999,999
- ◉ 250,000–499,999
- ○ 100,000–249,999

persons per square km		persons per square mi.
100		260
50		130
10		26
1		2.6

The cities of Sydney, Melbourne, Brisbane, Perth and Adelaide together contain about 60 percent of Australia's population. Most of the interior is uninhabited. Papua New Guinea is also thinly populated.

INDUSTRY

New Guinea

Admiralty Islands

Wewak

New Ireland

Sepik Pagwi

Rabaul

Bismarck Archipelago

Porgera Usino

New Britain

Mendi

PAPUA NEW GUINEA

Arafura Sea

Bereina

Bougainville

Torres Strait

Port Moresby

D'Entrecasteaux Islands

Australia has many valuable reserves of metals, coal, oil, and precious stones, including opals. Papua New Guinea has some gold and copper.

Melville I.

Darwin

Timor Sea

Wyndham

Gulf of Carpentaria

Cooktown

Coral Sea

Cairns

Port Hedland

Townsville

Dampier

Mount Isa

Newman

Alice Springs

Tropic of Capricorn

Gladstone

Fraser Island

AUSTRALIA

Lake Eyre

Brisbane

PACIFIC OCEAN

Geraldton

L. Barlee

Lake Torrens

Darling

L. Moore Kalgoorlie

Port Augusta

Perth

Murray

Newcastle

Fremantle

Murrumbidgee Sydney

Great Australian Bight

Adelaide

Port Kembla

Bunbury

Kangaroo Island

Canberra

Albany

Geelong Melbourne

Tasman Sea

King Island *Bass Strait*

Furneaux Group

Launceston

Tasmania

Hobart

Resources and industry

◆ industrial centre
○ major port
● other town
— major road
— major railway

mineral resources and fossil fuels
● iron and other ferroalloy metal ores
● other metal ores
■ nonmetallic minerals

	bauxite
	coal
	diamonds
	iron ore
	lignite (brown coal)
	natural gas
	oil

AGRICULTURE

New Guinea

Admiralty Islands

New Ireland

Sepik

Bismarck Archipelago

Central Range ▲ Mt. Wilhelm 4508

New Britain

PAPUA NEW GUINEA

Owen Stanley Range

Bougainville

Arafura Sea

Fly

Torres Strait

D'Entrecasteaux Islands

Cape York

Melville I.

Timor Sea

Arnhem Land

Gulf of Carpentaria

Cape York Peninsula

Coral Sea

Kimberley Plateau

Great Barrier Reef

Tanami Desert

Barkly Tableland

Great Sandy Desert

Selwyn Range

Hamersley Range

Macdonnell Ranges

Tropic of Capricorn

Gibson Desert

Simpson Desert

Great Artesian Basin

Musgrave Ranges ▲ Mt. Olga 1069

Fraser Island

AUSTRALIA

Great Victoria Desert

Lake Eyre ▼ −16

PACIFIC OCEAN

Grey Range

Lake Torrens

Darling

L. Barlee

Lake Gairdner

Darling Range

L. Moore

Eyre Peninsula

Nullarbor Plain

Murray

Great Australian Bight

Murrumbidgee

Kangaroo Island

Australian Alps ▲ Mt. Kosciusko 2230

Tasman Sea

King Island *Bass Strait*

Furneaux Group

Tasmania

Agricultural zones

	arable and pasture
	fruit, vines and vegetables
	pasture with some arable
	rough grazing
	woods and forest
	nonagricultural land

▲ mountain peak (metres)
▼ depression (metres)

The main farming zones are in the southeast and southwest, including the Murray-Darling River basin. Sheep and cattle are reared in the Great Artesian Basin.

NEW ZEALAND & ITS NEIGHBOURS

New Zealand is a beautiful island nation, with snow-capped mountains, fertile green plains, forested hills and volcanic regions famous for their bubbling hot springs and explosive geysers. The climate varies from subtropical in the North Island to wet temperate on the South Island. The Southern Alps on the South Island have a severe mountain climate.

The Maoris, a Polynesian people, settled in New Zealand, or Aotearoa ('land of the long white cloud'), in about A.D. 750. Dutch sailors reached the islands in 1642, but European settlement did not begin until the early 19th century. New Zealand has a strongly British character. Its economy was founded on farming and foreign trade, but manufacturing is now important.

New Zealand lies in the southwestern Pacific Ocean, 1,600 km (994 mi.) southeast of Australia. It lies in an unstable zone, marked by earthquakes and, on the North Island, volcanic eruptions. Glacial action has carved scenic fjords into the southwest coast of the South Island.

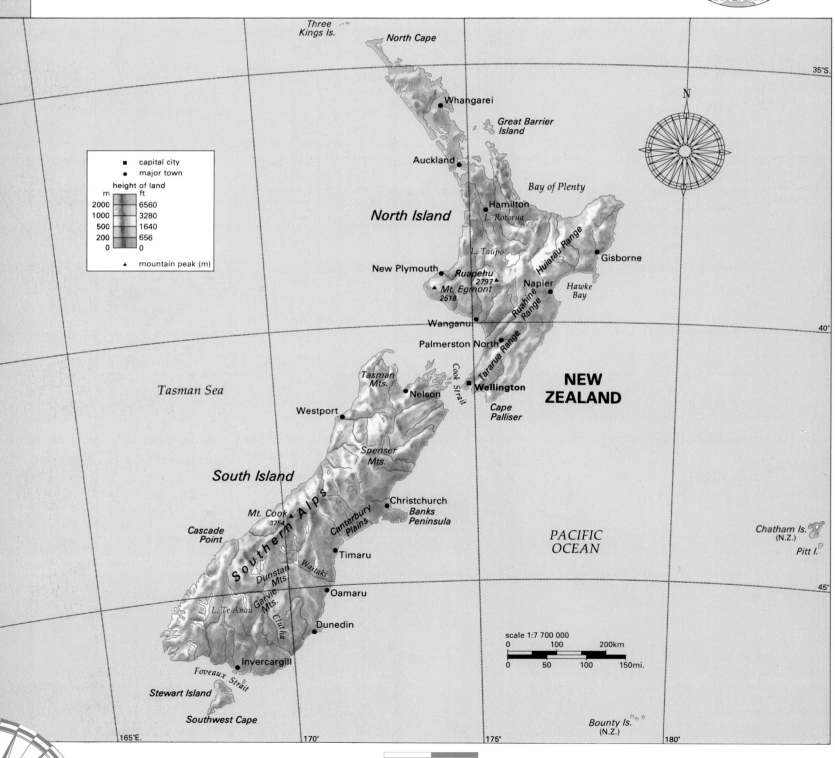

THE POLITICAL AND CULTURAL WORLD

With its Maori population, New Zealand is regarded as part of Polynesia, which also includes the independent island nations of Kiribati, Tonga, Tuvalu, and Western Samoa, as well as the American state of Hawaii. Kiribati contains both Polynesians and Micronesians.

Micronesia lies mainly in the North Pacific and includes Nauru, the Marshall Islands and the Federated States of Micronesia. Melanesia includes Papua New Guinea, the Solomon Islands, Vanuatu and Fiji.

COUNTRIES IN THE REGION

Fiji, Kiribati, Marshall Islands, Nauru, New Zealand, Solomon Islands, Tonga, Tuvalu, Vanuatu, Western Samoa

Island territories Cook Islands, Niue
Dependencies of other states American Samoa, Guam, Johnston Atoll, Midway Islands, Northern Marianas, U.S. Trust Territory of the Pacific Islands (Federated States of Micronesia, Belau) Wake Island (U.S.A.); French Polynesia, New Caledonia, Wallis and Futuna Islands (France)

LANGUAGE

Countries with one official language (E) Fiji, Kiribati, New Zealand, Solomon Islands; (N) Nauru
Countries with two official languages (E,Ma) Marshall Islands; (E,T) Tonga; (E,Sa) Western Samoa
Countries with three or more official languages (B,E,F) Vanuatu
Country with no official language Tuvalu

Key: B-Bislama, E-English, F-French, Ma-Marshallese, N-Nauruan, Sa-Samoan, T-Tongan

Other significant languages in the region include French, and a great variety of indigenous Melanesian and Polynesian languages

RELIGION

Countries with one major religion (P) Marshall Islands, Tuvalu
Countries with two major religions (P,RC) Kiribati, Nauru, Tonga, Western Samoa; (C,I) Vanuatu
Countries with three or more major religions (C,H,M) Fiji; (A,I,P,RC) Solomon Islands; (A,N,P,RC) New Zealand

Key: A-Anglican, C-various Christian, H-Hindu, I-indigenous religions, M-Muslim, N-nonreligious, P-Protestant, RC-Roman Catholic

ECONOMIC INDICATORS

	New Zealand
GDP (US$ billions)	42.76
GNP per capita (US$)	12,680
Annual rate of growth of GDP, 1980–1990	1.9%
Manufacturing as % of GDP	19.0%
Central government spending as % of GNP	35.0%
Merchandise exports (US$ billions)	9.5
Merchandise imports (US$ billions)	7.12
% of GNP donated as development aid	0.23%

WELFARE INDICATORS

Infant mortality rate (per 1,000 live births)	
1965	20
1990	10
Daily food supply available (calories per capita, 1989)	3,362
Population per physician (1984)	580
Teacher-pupil ratio (primary school, 1989)	1 : 19

Fiji
Area 18,274 sq. km (7,056 sq. mi.)
Population 764,000
Capital Suva

Kiribati
Area 849 sq. km (328 sq. mi.)
Population 66,000
Capital Bairiki

Marshall Islands
Area 181 sq. km (70 sq. mi.)
Population 30,870
Capital Dalap-Uliga-Darrit

Nauru
Area 21 sq. km (8 sq. mi.)
Population 9,000
Capital Yaren

New Zealand
Area 267,515 sq. km (103,288 sq. mi.)
Population 3,392,000
Capital Wellington

Solomon Islands
Area 28,370 sq. km (10,954 sq. mi.)
Population 320,000
Capital Honiara

Tonga
Area 780 sq. km (310 sq. mi)
Population 95,000
Capital Nuku'alofa

Tuvalu
Area 24 sq. km (9 sq. mi.)
Population 9,000
Capital Fongafale

Vanuatu
Area 12,190 sq. km (4,707 sq. mi.)
Population 158,000
Capital Port-Vila

Western Samoa
Area 2,831 sq. km (1,093 sq. mi.)
Population 168,000
Capital Apia

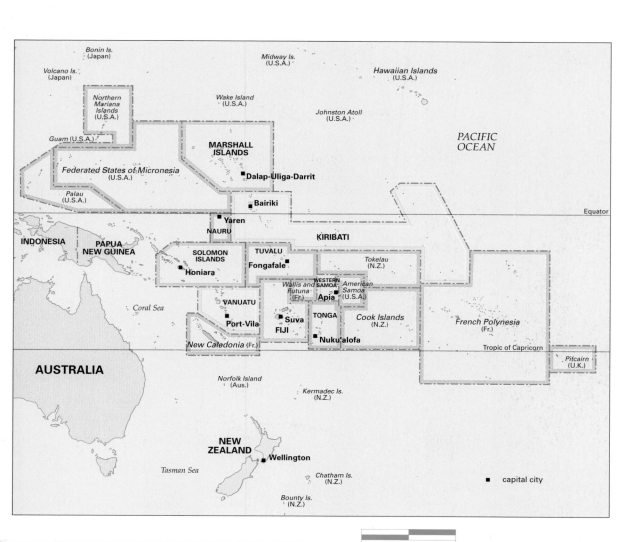

Oceania contains thousands of islands scattered across the Pacific Ocean. Some are mountainous and volcanic, while others are made up of coral which has accumulated on the tops of submerged volcanoes.

HABITATS

Scenic mountains and wilderness cover much of the country, providing habitats for New Zealand's wildlife. Forests run the length of the country from northeast to southwest. There are volcanoes, fjords and geysers. The island countries have a range of tropical habitats.

LAND

Area 330,854 sq. km (127,744 sq. mi.)
Highest point Mount Cook, New Zealand 3,754 m (12,317 ft)
Major features Mountain ranges of New Zealand; coral, volcanic and continental islands in the Pacific Ocean

WATER

Longest river Waikato, New Zealand 434 km (270 mi.)
Largest lake Lake Taupo, New Zealand 606 sq. km (234 sq. mi.)

NOTABLE THREATENED ENDEMIC SPECIES

Mammals Woodland Island cuscus (*Phalanger lullulae*), Pohnpei flying fox (*Pteropus molossinus*), Samoan flying fox (*Pteropus samoensis*)
Birds kagu (*Rhynochetos jubatus*), Black stilt (*Himantopus novaezelandiae*), Rapa fruit-dove (*Ptilinopus huttoni*), kakapo (*Strigops habroptilus*), Guam flycatcher (*Myiagra freycineti*)
Plants *Argyroxiphium kauense* (Kau silverwood), *Clianthus puniceus* (lobster claw), *Hibiscus insularis* (Philip Island hibiscus), *Myosotium hortensia* (Chatham Island forget-me-not), *Noeveitchia storckii* (vuleito), *Sophora toromiro* (toromiro), *Tecomanthe speciosa*
Others tuatara (*Sphenodon punctatus*), short Samoan tree snail (*Samoana abbreviata*), Stephens Island weta beetle (*Deinacrida rugosa*), Queen Alexandra's birdwing butterfly (*Ornithoptera alexandrae*)

CLIMATE

New Zealand has a mild, wet climate. The North Island is warm and humid in the north, but the central plateau has frosts. The South Island is cooler and the Southern Alps contain large snow-fields and glaciers. The west is rainy, while the eastern plains are much drier.

CLIMATE

	Temperature °C (°F) January	July	Altitude m (ft)
Auckland	19 (66)	10 (51)	26 (85)
Hokitika	15 (59)	7 (45)	4 (12)
Wellington	17 (62)	9 (47)	127 (415)
Dunedin	14 (58)	6 (42)	73 (240)
Christchurch	16 (61)	6 (42)	10 (32)

	Precipitation mm (in) January	July	Year
Auckland	79 (3.1)	145 (5.7)	1,249 (49.1)
Hokitika	262 (10.3)	218 (8.6)	2.907 (114.4)
Wellington	81 (3.2)	137 (5.4)	1,205 (47.4)
Dunedin	86 (3.4)	79 (3.1)	936 (36.9)
Christchurch	56 (2.2)	69 (2.7)	637 (25.1)

ENVIRONMENTAL ISSUES

New Zealanders are concerned that local trees are being replaced by imported species. The country has its own supply of energy from hot water geysers. Many people oppose the testing of nuclear weapons on Pacific islands, where deforestation also occurs.

POPULATION AND WEALTH

	New Zealand	Fiji	Solomon Is
Population (millions)	3.4	0.7	
Population increase (annual population growth rate, % 1960–1990)	1.2		
Energy use (gigajoules/person)		11	7
Real purchasing power (US$/person)	3,900		

ENVIRONMENTAL INDICATORS

CO₂ emissions (million tonnes carbon/annum)		0.2	
Artificial fertilizer use (kg/ha./annum)	709	89	
Cars (per 1,000 population)		44	
Access to safe drinking water (% population)			75

MAJOR ENVIRONMENTAL PROBLEMS AND SOURCES

Air pollution: urban high
Marine/coastal pollution: medium; *sources:* industrial, agricultural, sewage
Land degradation: *types:* desertification, soil erosion, salinization, deforestation, coastal degradation, habitat destruction; *causes:* agriculture, industry, population pressure
Resource problems: inadequate drinking water; inadequate sanitation; coastal flooding

HABITATS

Physical zones

- mountains/barren land
- forest
- grassland

- ▲ mountain peak (metres)
- ⁂ climate station

The North Island contains the long, mountainous northern peninsula, and a volcanic region around lakes Taupo and Rotorua. The mountain range extends southwest across the South Island, though both islands have fertile coastal plains.

ENVIRONMENTAL ISSUES

Key environmental issues

- ● major town or city
- ▲ active volcano
- ▬ main area of coastal erosion
- ⬭ main area affected by soil erosion
- ▨ remaining forest
- ▨ area of deforestation

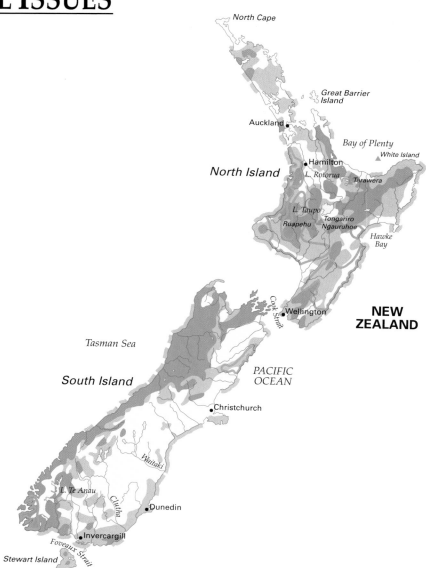

North Cape

Great Barrier Island

Auckland

Bay of Plenty

White Island

North Island

Hamilton

L. Rotorua

Tarawera

L. Taupo

Tongariro

Ruapehu

Ngauruhoe

Hawke Bay

Cook Strait

Wellington

NEW ZEALAND

Tasman Sea

South Island

PACIFIC OCEAN

Christchurch

Waitaki

L. Te Anau

Clutha

Dunedin

Invercargill

Foveaux Strait

Stewart Island

New Zealand has strong conservationist groups concerned with protecting national parks and nature reserves. Plans to build hydroelectric projects have been opposed because they may damage the environment.

CLIMATE

height above sea level of climate stations

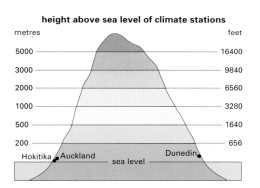

Hokitika   Auckland   Dunedin

Hokitika — PRECIPITATION

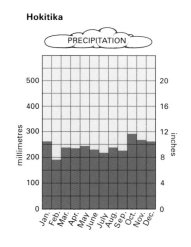

Auckland — PRECIPITATION

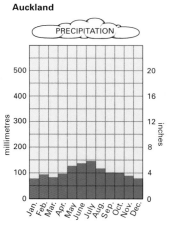

Dunedin — PRECIPITATION

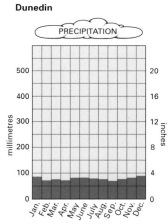

Hokitika

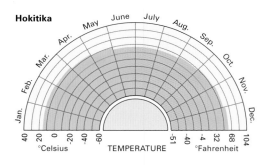

TEMPERATURE

Auckland

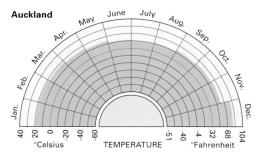

TEMPERATURE

Dunedin

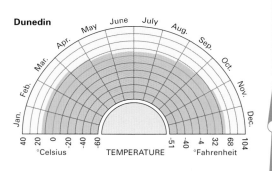

TEMPERATURE

POPULATION

The North Island has more than 70 percent of the population of New Zealand and the two largest cities, Auckland and Wellington. The South Island has attracted fewer people, most of them living on the east coast, especially around Christchurch and Dunedin.

POPULATION

Total population of the region (millions)	4.9
Population density (persons per sq. km)	95
Population change (average annual percent 1960–1990)	−20.4%

URBAN POPULATION

As percentage of total population	
1970	31.0
1990	35.5
Percentage in cities of more than 1 million	n/a

TEN LARGEST CITIES

	Country	Population
Auckland	New Zealand	982,000
Wellington †	New Zealand	326,900
Christchurch	New Zealand	307,000
Suva †	Fiji	141,000
Hamilton	New Zealand	126,000
Dunedin	New Zealand	111,200
Palmerston North	New Zealand	74,100
Tauranga	New Zealand	73,800
Hastings	New Zealand	58,200
Rotorua	New Zealand	54,200

† *denotes capital city*

INDUSTRY

Water power from hydroelectric power stations is the main source of electricity. Many industries process agricultural products, but New Zealand's cities have a wide range of other industries. Auckland is the leading industrial city. There is a little industry elsewhere.

INDUSTRIAL OUTPUT (US$ billion)

Total	Mining	Manufacturing
21.6	5.93	15.32

INDUSTRIAL WORKERS ('000s)

Total	Mining	Manufacturing
334	7	327

MAJOR PRODUCTS

Energy and minerals	output
Gold (tonnes)	6.9

Manufactures	
Cement (mill tonnes)	0.8
Aluminium (mill tonnes)	0.26

AGRICULTURE

New Zealand has plenty of grazing land, and sheep and cattle farming are still the chief agricultural activities. But forestry, fruit growing and other kinds of farming have become increasingly important in recent years. The other countries export few farm products.

LAND (million hectares)

Total	Agricultural	Arable	Forest/woodland
33.0 (100%)	4.4 (13%)	8.1 (24%)	10.7 (32%)

MAJOR CROPS

	Area mill ha.	Yield 100 kg/ha.	Production mill tonnes
Wheat	0.076	42.1	0.32
Oats	0.015	38.0	0.057
Pulses	0.028	15.77	0.064
Sorghum	0.002	25.83	0.004
Sugar cane	0.069	58.97	4.2
Fruit	–	–	0.44

MAJOR LIVESTOCK

	Number mill	Production mill tonnes
Sheep	74.30	–
Pigs	–	42
Cattle	8.5	–
Fish catch	–	0.18
Milk	–	6.7

POPULATION

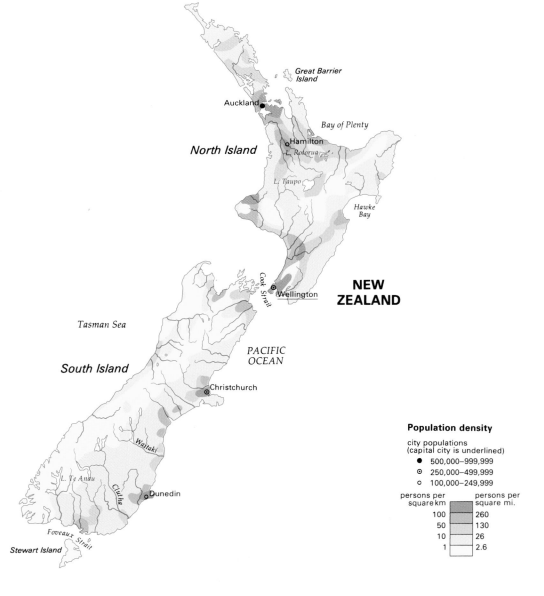

More than 80 percent of the people of New Zealand live in urban areas. Nearly half of the people live in one of three cities: Auckland, Wellington and Christchurch. Large areas are thinly populated.

Population density

city populations
(capital city is underlined)
- ● 500,000–999,999
- ◉ 250,000–499,999
- ○ 100,000–249,999

persons per square km	persons per square mi.
100	260
50	130
10	26
1	2.6

INDUSTRY

New Zealand's mineral resources include coal, natural gas, iron ore, and gold. Steam from geysers in the North Island's volcanic area is used as a source of power.

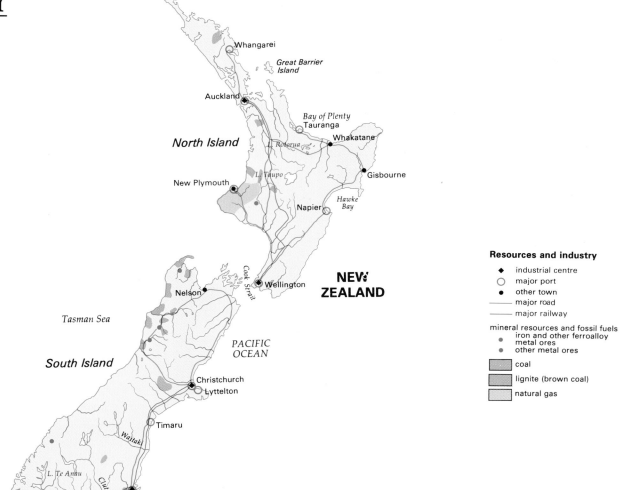

Whangarei

Great Barrier Island

Auckland

Bay of Plenty
Tauranga
Whakatane

North Island

Rotorua

Gisborne

L. Taupo

New Plymouth

Napier

Hawke Bay

NEW ZEALAND

Wellington

Cook Strait

Nelson

Tasman Sea

South Island

PACIFIC OCEAN

Christchurch
Lyttelton

Timaru

Waitaki

L. Te Anau

Clutha

Dunedin

Invercargill
Bluff
Foveaux Strait

Stewart Island

Resources and industry

- ◆ industrial centre
- ○ major port
- ● other town
- —— major road
- —— major railway

mineral resources and fossil fuels
- ● iron and other ferroalloy metal ores
- ● other metal ores

coal

lignite (brown coal)

natural gas

AGRICULTURE

Agricultural zones

- arable and pasture
- fruit and vegetables
- pasture with some arable
- pasture
- rough grazing
- woods and forest
- nonagricultural land

- ▲ mountain peak (metres)

The Canterbury Plains are the chief grain-growing region. Livestock farming is important in the southeast corner of the South Island. Sheep are bred on both the South and the North Island.

North Cape

Great Barrier Island

Bay of Plenty

North Island

L. Rotorua

L. Taupo

Ruapehu
2797 ▲
▲ Mt. Egmont
2518

Hulalau Range

Ruahine Range

Tararua Range

Hawke Bay

Cape Farewell

Tasman Mts.

NEW ZEALAND

Cook Strait

Cape Palliser

Tasman Sea

Spenser Mts.

PACIFIC OCEAN

South Island

Mt. Cook ▲
3754

Southern Alps

Canterbury Plains

Banks Peninsula

Cascade Point

Dunstan Mts.

Waitaki

L. Te Anau

Garvie Mts.

Clutha

Foveaux Strait

Stewart Island

Southwest Cape

ANTARCTICA

Antarctica is the coldest place on Earth. It is a mountainous and mostly ice-covered continent surrounding the South Pole. It is also the driest continent, though it holds almost nine-tenths of the planet's ice. Much of the region is poorly mapped because it is difficult to reach, and has a very harsh climate. But research on Antarctica has helped in the understanding of the way the southern continents have reached their present positions. Its climate influences weather systems all over the world. The ice sheet over Antarctica holds a record of recent climatic change and of pollution, including the presence of 'greenhouse gases'. The ice sheet comprises so much of the world's ice and snow, that were it to melt under the influence of global warming, the world mean sea level would rise by 65 m (210 ft).

Although scientists carry out research in Antarctica, the continent has no permanent population. In 1982, scientists located a depletion, or hole, in the ozone layer over Antarctica. The ozone layer screens out 90 percent of the Sun's ultraviolet radiation and damage to it has been put down to chlorofluorocarbons, chemicals used, for example, as propellants in aerosol spray cans. They are also used in industry and in the coolant system of refrigerators. The ozone hole is seasonal, developing only in the Antarctic winter and spring, and its size also changes. An increase in ultraviolet radiation would decrease the yield of farmers' crops, change climates around the world, and increase the number of cases of skin cancer.

Antarctica was once part of the ancient supercontinent of Gondwanaland, which also comprised Australia, New Zealand, and the southwest Pacific islands. About 500 million years ago it was near the Equator, and had a warm, wet climate. Coal deposits give evidence of this. As Gondwanaland broke up, the part which became Antarctica drifted towards the South Pole and remained there when the other continents drifted away to the warmer north.

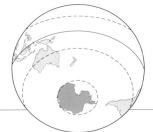

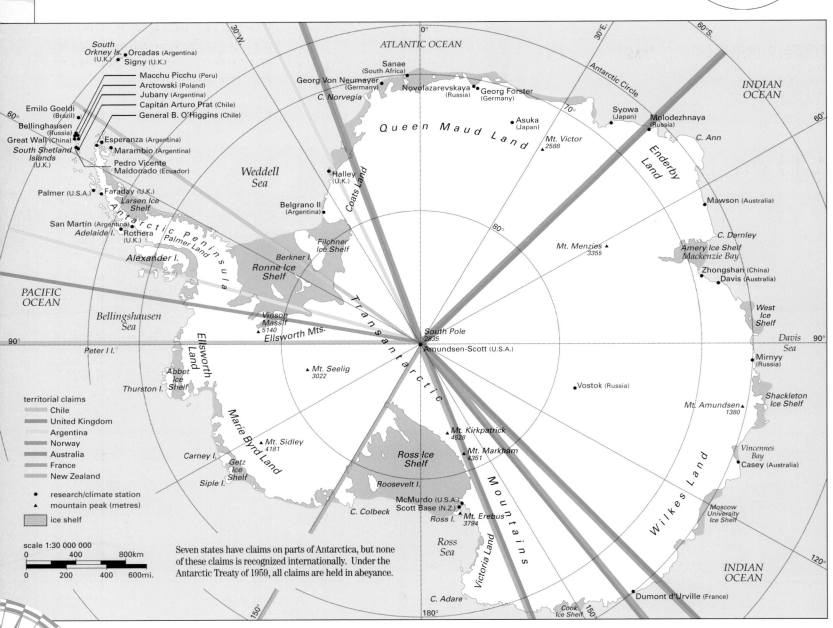

territorial claims
- Chile
- United Kingdom
- Argentina
- Norway
- Australia
- France
- New Zealand

- • research/climate station
- ▲ mountain peak (metres)
- ▢ ice shelf

scale 1:30 000 000

Seven states have claims on parts of Antarctica, but none of these claims is recognized internationally. Under the Antarctic Treaty of 1959, all claims are held in abeyance.

THE POLITICAL AND CULTURAL WORLD

Despite claims to parts of Antarctica by various nations, people from any part of the world can go anywhere in Antarctica, providing their purpose is peaceful, because under international agreement, Antarctica is a demilitarized, nuclear-free zone.

Under recent agreements, restrictions have been placed on the development of the continent. Under the 1991 Environmental Protocol, for example, mining was banned for a period of 50 years. Some campaigning conservationists would like to go further and declare that Antarctica should become a World Park, dedicated to science and the preservation of this fragile wilderness. Early this century several expeditions set out to reach the South Pole at the heart of the interior. The Norwegian, Roald Amundsen (1872-1928), was the first to arrive on 14 December 1911. He was followed a month later by British explorers led by Robert Falcon Scott (1868-1912) who perished in a blizzard on the return journey. In 1929 the American Richard Evelyn Byrd (1888-1957) became the first man to fly over the South Pole.

LAND

Area of exposed rock 48,310 sq.km (18,650 sq. mi.)
Highest point Vinson Massif 4,897 m (16,066 ft)
Height of surface at South Pole 2,800 m (9,186 ft)
Maximum thickness of ice 4,776 m (15,669 ft)

HABITATS

The long Transantarctic Mountain chain runs across the whole of Antarctica, passing close to the South Pole and dividing the continent into two unequal parts: Lesser Antarctica and the massive semicircle of Greater Antarctica. From Lesser Antarctica the mountainous Antarctic Peninsula snakes northeast towards the southern tip of South America to the west of the Weddell Sea. The Ross Sea is a smaller gulf south of New Zealand. The southern end of both these seas is covered by permanent ice shelves.

The hostile conditions in Antarctica, combined with long months of darkness, limit plant life to lichens, mosses, algae, and moulds in the few ice-free areas. There are no land mammals in Antarctica, but whales and seals feed on masses of tiny, shrimp-like krill, while porpoises and dolphins are attracted by shoals of fish, especially Atlantic perch. With no land predators, the Antarctic coast is a haven for birds. Emperor penguins, Antarctic petrels, and South polar skuas breed here and nowhere else, and more than 40 other species of bird live in Antarctica.

CLIMATE

Temperatures in Antarctica rarely rise above 0°C in summer and they plummet in winter to –40 to –70°C (–40 to –94°F). Strong winds sweep outwards from the plateau at 70 km/h (43 mph), with gusts reaching 190 km/h (118 mph). The wind chill factor makes conditions even worse. On the Antarctic Peninsula, milder winds from neighbouring oceans raise summer temperatures a little. High atmospheric pressure, giving clear winter skies, dominates the interior of the continent.

The winds blow loose snow across the surface, creating blinding blizzards. But Antarctica has little precipitation, and with about 50 mm (2 in) of snow a year, it is classed as a desert. Only trace amounts of precipitation are recorded at climate stations in the region. By the end of March, the sun has set on Antarctica, and the continent is in freezing darkness for six months. Although the summer is very short, the land receives more sunlight than equatorial regions do throughout the year. However, the ice sheet reflects most of the Sun's energy back into the atmosphere.

CLIMATE

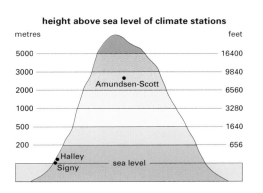

height above sea level of climate stations

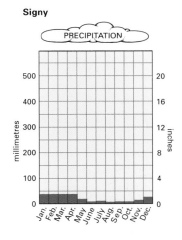

Signy — PRECIPITATION

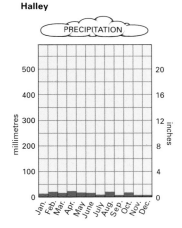

Halley — PRECIPITATION

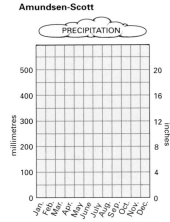

Amundsen-Scott — PRECIPITATION

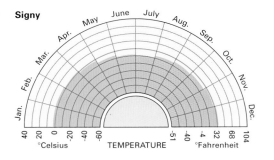

Signy

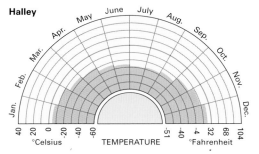

Halley

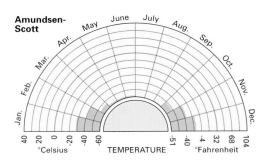

Amundsen-Scott

GAZETTEER

This gazetteer lists places and features, such as rivers or mountains, found on the topographic map in each region. The first number (in **bold** type) is the page number then coordinates give the latitude (distance north or south of 0°, the Equator) and longitude (distance east or west of 0°, the Greenwich Meridian).

Abbreviations:
b. bay, *c.* country, *d.* district, *des.* desert, *est.* estuary, *f.* feature, *i.* island, *isls.* islands, *l.* lake, *mt.* mountain, *mts.* mountains, *pen.* peninsula, *r.* river, *str.* strait

Aare (*r.*), **72**, 47.37N 8.13E
Abéché, **96**, 13.49N 20.49E
Aberdeen, **52**, 57.08N 2.07W
Aberystwyth, **52**, 52.25N 4.06W
Abidjan, **102**, 2.19N 4.01W
Abu Dhabi, **90**, 24.27N 54.23E
Abuja, **102**, 9.12N 7.11E
Acapulco, **30**, 16.51N 99.56W
Accra, **102**, 5.33N 0.15W
Achill Island, **52**, 53.57N 10.00W
Acklins Island, **31**, 22.30N 74.10W
Aconcagua (*mt.*), **38**, 32.37S 70.00W
Adamawa Highlands, **102**, 7.05N 12.00E
Adana, **90**, 37.00N 35.19E
Adda (*r.*), **68**, 45.08N 9.55E
Addis Ababa, **96**, 9.03N 38.42E
Adelaide, **140**, 34.56S 138.36E
Aden, **90**, 12.50N 45.00E
Aden, Gulf of, **90**, 13.00N 47.00E
Adige (*r.*), **68**, 45.10N 12.20E
Admiralty Islands, **140**, 2.00S 147.20E
Adour (*r.*), **58**, 43.32N 1.32W
Afghanistan (*c.*), **90**, 33.00N 65.30E
Agadez, **96**, 17.00N 7.56E
Agano (*r.*), **134**, 37.58N 139.02E
Agra, **114**, 27.09N 78.00E
Ahaggar (*mts.*), **96**, 24.00N 5.50E
Ahmadabad, **114**, 23.03N 72.40E
Air (*mts.*), **96**, 20.00N 8.30E
Ajaccio, **58**, 41.55N 8.43E
Akashi Mts., **134**, 35.20N 138.10E
Akita, **134**, 39.44N 140.05E
Akureyri, **46**, 65.41N 18.04W
Al Manamah, **90**, 26.12N 50.36E
Al Mukalla, **90**, 14.34N 49.09E
Åland (*isls.*), **46**, 60.15N 20.00E
Alaotra, Lake, **108**, 17.30S 48.30E
Alaska (*d.*), **22**, 66.00N 153.00W
Alaska Peninsula, **22**, 56.00N 160.00W
Alaska Range, **22**, 62.10N 152.00W
Albacete, **64**, 39.00N 1.52W
Albania (*c.*), **78**, 41.00N 20.00E
Albany (*r.*), **16**, 52.10N 82.00W
Albert, Lake, **102**, 1.45N 31.00E
Ålborg, **46**, 57.03N 9.56E
Albuquerque, **22**, 35.05N 106.40W
Aldabra Islands, **108**, 9.00S 47.00E
Aleppo, **90**, 36.14N 37.10E
Aleutian Is., **22**, 52.00N 170.00W
Alexander Archipelago, **22**, 56.30N 134.30W
Alexandria, **96**, 31.13N 29.55E
Algeria (*c.*), **96**, 25.00N 3.00E
Algiers, **96**, 36.50N 3.00E
Aliakmon (*r.*), **68**, 40.30N 22.38E
Alicante, **64**, 38.21N 0.29W
Alice Springs, **140**, 23.42S 133.52E
Allegheny Mts., **22**, 40.00N 80.00W
Aller (*r.*), **72**, 52.57N 9.11E
Allier (*r.*), **58**, 46.58N 3.30E
Alma-Ata, **84**, 43.19N 76.55E
Almeria, **64**, 36.50N 2.26W
Alotau, **140**, 10.20S 150.23E
Alps (*mts.*), **72**, 46.00N 6.50E
Altai (*mts.*), **84**, 46.30N 93.30E
Altun Shan (*mts.*), **120**, 38.10N 87.50E
Amakusa (*i.*), **134**, 32.30N 130.00E
Amazon (*r.*), **38**, 2.00S 50.00W
Ambon, **128**, 3.50S 128.10E
Amiens, **58**, 49.54N 2.18E
Amman, **90**, 31.57N 35.56E
Amsterdam, **72**, 52.22N 4.54E
Amu Darya (*r.*), **84**, 43.50N 59.00E
Amur (*r.*), **120**, 53.17N 140.00E
An Nafud (*des.*), **90**, 28.40N 41.30E
An Najaf, **90**, 31.59N 44.19E
Anambas Islands, **128**, 3.00N 106.10E
Anatolia (*f.*), **90**, 38.00N 35.00E
Anchorage, **22**, 61.10N 150.00W
Andaman Islands, **114**, 12.00N 93.00E
Andes (*mts.*), **38**, 15.00S 72.00W
Andorra (*c.*), **58**, 42.30N 1.32E
Andorra la Vella, **58**, 42.30N 1.31E
Andreas, Cape, **68**, 35.40N 34.35E
Andros (*i.*), **30**, 24.30N 78.00W
Andros (*i.*), **68**, 37.50N 24.50E
Aneto Peak, **64**, 42.38N 0.40W
Angerman (*r.*), **46**, 63.00N 17.43E
Angers, **58**, 47.29N 0.32W
Anglesey (*i.*), **52**, 53.16N 4.25W
Angola (*c.*), **108**, 11.45S 18.00E
Ankara, **90**, 39.55N 32.50E
Annaba, **96**, 36.55N 7.47E
Annam Highlands, **128**, 17.40N 105.30E
Annobon (*i.*), **102**, 1.25S 5.36E
Antalya, **90**, 36.53N 30.42E
Antananarivo, **108**, 18.55S 47.31E
Antigua (*i.*), **31**, 17.09N 61.49W
Antigua and Barbuda (*c.*), **31**, 17.30N 61.49W
Antofagasta, **38**, 23.40S 70.23W
Antrim, Mts. of, **52**, 55.00N 6.10W
Antseranana, **108**, 12.19S 49.17E
Antwerp, **72**, 51.13N 3.14E
Aomori, **134**, 40.50N 140.43E
Apennines (*mts.*), **68**, 42.00N 13.30E
Apo, Mt., **128**, 6.58N 125.17E
Appalachian Mts., **22**, 39.30N 80.00W
Aqaba, **90**, 29.32N 35.00E
Arabian Peninsula, **90**, 21.20N 46.44E
Araguaia (*r.*), **38**, 5.30S 48.05W
Arakan Yoma (*mts.*), **128**, 20.00N 94.00E
Aran Is., **52**, 53.07N 9.38W
Ararat (*mt.*), **90**, 39.45N 44.15E
Aras (*r.*), **90**, 40.00N 48.28E
Ardennes (*mts.*), **58**, 49.40N 5.00E
Arequipa, **38**, 17.58S 63.14W
Argentina (*c.*), **38**, 35.00S 65.00W
Århus, **46**, 56.09N 10.13E
Arica, **38**, 18.30S 70.20W
Arkansas (*r.*), **22**, 33.50N 91.00W
Armenia (*c.*), **84**, 40.00N 45.00E
Arnhem Land (*f.*), **140**, 13.10S 134.30E
Arno (*r.*), **68**, 43.43N 10.17E
Arran (*i.*), **52**, 55.35N 5.14W
Aru Islands, **128**, 6.00S 134.30E
Aruba (*i.*), **31**, 12.30N 70.00W
Asahi (*mt.*), **134**, 43.42N 142.54E
Asahikawa, **134**, 43.46N 142.23E
Ashkhabad, **84**, 37.58N 58.24E
Asmera, **96**, 15.20N 38.58E
Aso (*mt.*), **134**, 32.55N 131.02E
Aswan, **96**, 24.05N 32.56E
Asyut, **96**, 27.14N 31.07E
Atacama Desert, **38**, 21.00S 69.00W
Atar, **96**, 20.32N 13.08W
Atbara, **96**, 17.42N 34.00E
Atbara (*r.*), **96**, 17.47N 34.00E
Athabasca (*r.*), **16**, 58.40N 110.50W
Athabasca Lake, **16**, 59.07N 110.00W
Athens, **68**, 37.59N 23.42E
Atlanta, **22**, 33.45N 84.23W
Aube (*r.*), **58**, 48.34N 3.43E
Auckland, **146**, 36.55S 174.45E
Australia (*c.*), **140**, 27.00S 135.00E
Australian Alps, **140**, 36.30S 148.30E
Austria (*c.*), **72**, 47.30N 14.00E
Axios (*r.*), **68**, 40.31N 22.43E
Azerbaijan (*c.*), **84**, 40.10N 47.50E

Babuyan Islands, **128**, 19.20N 121.30E
Back (*r.*), **16**, 66.37N 96.00W
Badajoz, **64**, 38.53N 6.58W
Baffin Bay, **16**, 72.00N 63.00W
Baffin Island, **16**, 68.05N 70.00W
Baghdad, **90**, 33.20N 44.26E
Baghlan, **90**, 36.11N 68.44E
Baguio, **128**, 16.25N 120.37E
Bahamas (*c.*), **31**, 23.30N 75.00W
Bahawalpur, **114**, 29.24N 71.36E
Bahía Blanca, **38**, 38.45S 62.15W
Bahrain (*c.*), **90**, 26.00N 50.35E
Baikal, Lake, **84**, 53.30N 108.00E
Baja California (*pen.*), **30**, 25.00N 112.00W
Baku, **84**, 40.22N 49.53E
Balaton, Lake, **78**, 46.55N 17.50E
Balearic Islands, **64**, 39.30N 2.30W
Bali (*i.*), **128**, 8.30S 115.05E
Balikpapan, **128**, 1.15S 116.50E
Balkan Mountains, **78**, 42.50N 24.30E
Balkhash, Lake, **84**, 46.40N 75.00E
Balsas (*r.*), **30**, 18.10N 102.05W
Baltimore, **22**, 39.17N 76.37W
Bamako, **96**, 12.40N 7.59W
Bambari, **102**, 5.45N 20.40E
Ban Hat Yai, **128**, 7.00N 100.28E
Banas, Cape, **96**, 23.54N 35.48E
Bandar Abbas, **90**, 27.10N 56.15E
Bandar Seri Begawan, **128**, 4.56N 114.58E
Bandung, **128**, 6.57S 107.34E
Bangalore, **114**, 12.58N 77.35E
Bangka (*i.*), **128**, 2.20S 106.10E
Bangkok, **128**, 13.45N 100.35E
Bangladesh (*c.*), **114**, 24.00N 90.00E
Bangui, **102**, 4.23N 18.37E
Bangweulu, Lake, **108**, 11.15S 29.45E
Banjarmasin, **128**, 3.22S 114.36E
Banjul, **102**, 13.28N 16.39W
Banks Island, **16**, 73.00N 122.00W
Banks Peninsula, **146**, 43.45S 173.10E
Barbados (*c.*), **31**, 13.20N 59.40W
Barbuda (*i.*), **31**, 17.41N 61.48W
Barcelona, **64**, 41.25N 2.10E
Bari, **68**, 41.08N 16.52E
Barisan Mts., **128**, 3.30S 102.30E
Barito (*r.*), **128**, 3.35S 114.35E
Barkly Tableland (*f.*), **140**, 19.00S 136.40E
Barlee, Lake, **140**, 29.30S 119.30E
Barra (*i.*), **52**, 56.59N 7.28W
Barranquilla, **38**, 11.00N 74.50W
Barren Islands, **108**, 18.55S 44.15E
Barrow, **22**, 71.16N 156.50W
Barrow (*r.*), **52**, 52.17N 7.00W
Basra, **90**, 30.33N 47.50E
Bass Strait, **140**, 39.45S 146.00E
Bassein, **128**, 16.45N 94.30E
Basseterre, **31**, 17.17N 62.43W
Bastia, **58**, 42.41N 9.26E
Batan Islands, **128**, 20.50N 121.55E
Battambang, **128**, 13.06N 103.13E
Batu Islands, **128**, 0.30S 98.20E
Bavarian Alps (*mts.*), **72**, 47.38N 11.30E
Bayan Har Shan (*mts.*), **120**, 34.00N 97.20E
Beijing, **120**, 39.55N 116.25E
Beira, **108**, 19.49S 34.52E
Beirut, **90**, 33.52N 35.30E
Belém, **38**, 1.27S 48.29W
Belfast, **52**, 54.36N 5.57W
Belgium (*c.*), **72**, 51.00N 4.30E
Belgrade, **78**, 44.49N 20.28E
Belitung (*i.*), **128**, 3.00S 108.00E
Belize (*c.*), **30**, 17.00N 88.30W
Belle Ile (*i.*), **58**, 47.20N 3.10W
Belmopan, **30**, 17.25N 88.46W
Belo Horizonte, **38**, 19.45S 43.53W
Belorussia (*c.*), **84**, 53.00N 27.00E
Bemaraha, Plateau of, **108**, 20.00S 45.15E
Bemarivo (*r.*), **108**, 15.27S 47.40E
Ben Nevis (*mt.*), **52**, 56.48N 5.00W
Bengal, Bay of, **114**, 13.00N 85.00E
Benghazi, **96**, 32.07N 20.05E
Benin (*c.*), **102**, 9.00N 2.30E
Benue (*r.*), **102**, 7.52N 6.45E
Bergen, **46**, 60.23N 5.20E
Berlin, **72**, 52.31N 13.24E
Bermuda (*i.*), **31**, 32.18N 65.00W
Bern, **72**, 46.57N 7.26E
Bernese Alps (*mts.*), **72**, 46.30N 7.37E
Besançon, **58**, 47.14N 6.02E
Bhutan (*c.*), **114**, 27.25N 90.00E
Biak (*i.*), **128**, 0.55S 136.00E
Bialystok, **78**, 53.09N 23.01E
Bié Plateau, **108**, 13.00S 16.00E
Bihor Mts., **78**, 46.26N 22.43E
Bilbao, **64**, 43.15N 2.56W
Bioko (*i.*), **102**, 3.25N 8.45E
Biratnagar, **114**, 26.18N 87.17E
Birmingham, **52**, 52.30N 1.55W
Biscay, Bay of, **58**, 45.00N 3.00W
Bishkek, **84**, 42.53N 74.46E
Bismarck Archipelago, **140**, 3.35S 147.00E
Bissau, **102**, 11.52N 15.39W
Bitterroot Range, **22**, 47.06N 115.00W
Biwa, Lake, **134**, 35.20N 136.10E
Black Forest, **72**, 48.00N 8.00E
Black Hills, **22**, 44.17N 103.28W
Blanc, Cape, **96**, 20.44N 17.05W
Blanc, Mont, **58**, 45.50N 6.52E
Blantyre, **108**, 15.46S 35.00E
Bloemfontein, **108**, 29.07S 26.14E
Blönduós, **46**, 65.39N 20.18W
Blue Ridge Mts., **22**, 36.30N 80.15W
Bobaomby, Cape, **108**, 11.48S 49.19E
Bodele (*f.*), **96**, 16.50N 17.10E
Bogotá, **38**, 4.38N 74.05W
Bohemian Forest, **72**, 49.20N 13.10E
Bohol (*i.*), **128**, 9.45S 124.10E
Bokna Fjord, **46**, 59.10N 5.35E
Bolivia (*c.*), **38**, 17.00S 65.00W
Bolmen (*l.*), **46**, 56.55N 13.40E
Bologna, **68**, 44.30N 11.20E
Bolshevik (*i.*), **84**, 78.30N 102.00E
Bombay, **114**, 18.56N 72.51E
Bonaire (*i.*), **31**, 12.15N 68.27W
Bonn, **72**, 50.44N 7.05E
Boothia Peninsula, **16**, 70.30N 95.00W
Borås, **46**, 57.43N 12.55E
Borborema, Plateau of, **38**, 7.00S 38.30W
Bordeaux, **58**, 44.50N 0.34W
Borneo (*i.*), **128**, 1.00N 114.00E
Bornholm (*i.*), **46**, 55.10N 15.00E
Bosnia and Hercegovina (*c.*), **78**, 44.20N 17.50E
Boso Peninsula, **134**, 35.20N 140.00E
Bosporus (*str.*), **90**, 41.07N 29.04E
Bosten, Lake, **120**, 42.00N 87.00E
Boston, **22**, 42.21N 71.04W
Bothnia, Gulf of, **46**, 63.30N 20.30E
Botrange (*mt.*), **72**, 50.30N 6.04E
Botswana (*c.*), **108**, 21.00S 24.00E
Bougainville (*i.*), **140**, 6.00S 155.00E
Bounty Islands, **146**, 48.20S 179.00E
Brac (*i.*), **78**, 43.20N 16.38E
Braga, **64**, 41.32N 8.26W
Brahmaputra (*r.*), **114**, 23.50N 89.45E
Brasília, **38**, 15.54S 47.50W
Brasov, **78**, 45.40N 25.35E
Bratislava, **78**, 48.10N 17.10E
Brazil (*c.*), **38**, 10.00S 52.00W
Brazil, Plateau of, **38**, 14.00S 45.00W
Brazzaville, **102**, 4.14S 15.14E
Brecon Beacons (*mts.*), **52**, 51.53N 3.27W
Breidafjördur, **46**, 65.15N 23.00W
Bremen, **72**, 53.05N 8.49E
Brest, **58**, 48.24N 4.29W
Bridgetown, **31**, 13.06N 59.37W
Brighton, **52**, 50.50N 0.09W
Brisbane, **140**, 27.30S 153.00E
Bristol, **52**, 51.26N 2.35W
Bristol Channel, **52**, 51.17N 3.20W
Brno, **78**, 49.11N 16.39E
Brooks Range, **22**, 68.50N 152.00W
Bruges, **72**, 51.13N 3.14E
Bruncu Spina (*mt.*), **68**, 40.00N 9.07E
Brunei (*c.*), **128**, 4.56N 114.58E
Brussels, **72**, 50.50N 4.23E
Bucharest, **78**, 44.25N 26.06E
Budapest, **78**, 47.30N 19.03E
Buenos Aires, **38**, 34.40S 58.30W
Bug (*r.*), **78**, 52.29N 21.11E
Bujumbura, **102**, 3.22S 29.21E
Bulawayo, **108**, 20.10S 28.43E
Bulgaria (*c.*), **78**, 42.30N 25.00E
Bungo Channel, **134**, 32.52N 132.30E
Burgas, **78**, 42.30N 27.29E
Burgos, **64**, 42.21N 3.41W
Burkina (*c.*), **102**, 12.15N 1.30W
Burma (*c.*), **128**, 21.00N 95.00E
Burren, **52**, 53.00N 9.00W
Buru (*i.*), **128**, 3.30S 126.30E
Burundi (*c.*), **102**, 3.30S 30.00E
Butuan, **128**, 8.56N 125.31E
Butung (*i.*), **128**, 5.00S 122.50E
Byrranga Mts., **84**, 74.50N 100.00E

Cabinda (*d.*), **102**, 5.34S 12.12E
Cadiz, **64**, 36.32N 6.18W
Caen, **58**, 49.11N 0.22W
Cagliari, **68**, 39.14N 9.07E
Caicos Islands, **31**, 21.30N 72.00W
Cairngorm Mts., **52**, 57.04N 3.30W
Cairns, **140**, 16.51S 145.43E
Cairo, **96**, 30.03N 31.15E
Calcutta, **114**, 22.35N 88.21E
Calgary, **16**, 51.00N 114.10W
Cali, **38**, 3.24N 76.30W
California, Gulf of, **30**, 28.30N 111.00W
Camagüey, **30**, 21.25N 77.55W
Camargue (*f.*), **58**, 43.40N 4.35E
Cambay, Gulf of, **114**, 20.30N 72.00E
Cambodia (*c.*), **128**, 12.00N 105.00E
Cambrian Mountains, **52**, 52.33N 3.33W
Cameroon (*c.*), **102**, 6.00N 12.30E
Cameroon, Mt., **102**, 4.20N 9.05E
Campeche, Bay of, **30**, 20.58N 94.00W
Canada (*c.*), **16**, 55.00N 100.00W
Canadian (*r.*), **22**, 35.20N 95.40W
Canadian Shield (*f.*), **16**, 54.00N 82.00W
Canary Islands, **96**, 29.00N 15.00W
Canberra, **140**, 35.18S 149.08E
Cantabrian Mountains, **64**, 42.55N 5.10W
Canterbury Plains, **146**, 43.50S 171.40E
Cape Breton Island, **16**, 46.00N 60.30W
Cape Town (*town*), **108**, 33.56S 18.28E
Cape York Peninsula, **140**, 12.40S 142.20E
Capri (*i.*), **68**, 40.33N 14.13E
Caprivi Strip (*f.*), **108**, 17.50S 23.10E
Caracas, **38**, 10.35N 66.56W
Carbonara, Cape, **68**, 39.06N 9.32E
Cardamon Hills, **114**, 9.30N 76.55E
Cardiff, **52**, 51.28N 3.11W
Carnic Alps, **68**, 46.40N 12.48E
Carpathian Mts., **78**, 46.20N 25.40E
Carpentaria, Gulf of, **140**, 14.00S 139.00E
Casablanca, **96**, 33.39N 7.35W
Cascade Point, **146**, 44.01S 168.22E
Cascade Range, **22**, 44.00N 121.30W
Caspian Depression, **84**, 47.00N 48.00E
Castries, **31**, 14.01N 60.59W
Catania, **68**, 37.31N 15.05E
Caucasus Mts., **84**, 43.00N 44.00E
Cayenne, **38**, 4.55N 52.18W
Cayman Islands, **30**, 19.00N 81.00W
Cebu (*i.*), **128**, 10.15N 123.45E
Central African Republic (*c.*), **102**, 6.30N 20.00E
Central Makran Range, **114**, 26.30N 65.00E
Central Range, **140**, 6.00S 144.00E
Central Siberian Plateau, **84**, 66.00N 108.00E
Cephalonia (*i.*), **68**, 38.15N 20.33E
Ceram (*i.*), **128**, 3.10S 129.30E
Ceuta, **64**, 35.53N 5.19W
Cévennes (*mts.*), **58**, 44.00N 3.30E
Chad (*c.*), **96**, 13.00N 19.00E
Chad, Lake, **96**, 13.30N 14.00E
Chalcidice (*i.*), **68**, 40.30N 23.40E
Chang (*r.*), **120**, 31.40N 121.15E
Changchun, **120**, 43.50N 125.20E
Channel Islands, **58**, 49.28N 2.13E
Chao Phraya (*r.*), **128**, 13.34N 100.35E
Charente (*r.*), **58**, 45.57N 1.05W
Chatham Islands, **146**, 44.00S 176.40W
Cheju, **134**, 33.31N 126.32E
Cheju (*i.*), **134**, 33.30N 126.35E
Chelyabinsk, **84**, 55.10N 61.25E
Chengdu, **120**, 30.37N 104.06E
Cherskogo Range, **84**, 65.50N 143.00E
Chesapeake Bay, **22**, 38.00N 76.00W
Chesterfield, Iles (*isls.*), **140**, 19.30S 158.00E
Cheviot Hills, **52**, 55.22N 2.24W
Chiba, **134**, 35.38N 140.07E
Chicago, **22**, 41.50N 87.45W
Chiclayo, **38**, 6.47S 79.47W
Chieng-Mai, **128**, 18.48N 98.59E
Chihli, Gulf of, **120**, 38.30N 119.30E
Chile (*c.*), **38**, 26.00S 71.00W
Chililabombwe, **108**, 12.29S 27.53E
Chiloe Island, **38**, 43.00S 73.00W
Chiltern Hills, **52**, 51.40N 0.53W
China (*c.*), **120**, 33.00N 105.00E
Chios (*i.*), **68**, 38.23N 26.04E
Chirripo (*mt.*), **30**, 9.31N 83.30W
Chita, **84**, 52.03N 113.35E
Chittagong, **114**, 22.20N 91.48E
Chongjin, **134**, 41.55N 129.50E
Chongqing, **120**, 29.31N 106.35E
Chonju, **134**, 36.39N 127.31E
Chonos Archipelago, **38**, 45.00S 73.00W
Christchurch, **146**, 43.32S 172.37E
Christmas Island, **128**, 10.30S 105.40E
Chugoku Mts., **134**, 35.00N 133.00E
Chukot Range, **84**, 68.13N 179.55E
Chunchon, **134**, 37.52N 127.43E
Churchill, **16**, 58.46N 94.10W
Churchill (*r.*), **16**, 58.47N 94.12W
Cincinnati, **22**, 39.10N 84.30W
Cinto, Mt., **58**, 42.23N 8.56E
Citlaltépetl (*mt.*), **30**, 19.00N 97.20W
Ciudad Bolívar, **38**, 8.06N 1.59W
Ciudad Juárez, **30**, 31.42N 106.29W
Clermont-Ferrand, **58**, 45.47N 3.05E
Clervaux, **72**, 50.04N 6.01E
Cleveland, **22**, 41.30N 81.41W
Clipperton Island, **30**, 10.17N 109.13W
Cluj-Napoca, **78**, 46.47N 23.37E
Clutha (*r.*), **146**, 46.18S 169.05E
Clyde (*r.*), **52**, 55.58N 4.53W
Coast Mountains, **16**, 55.00N 129.00W
Coast Range, **22**, 40.00N 123.00W
Cochin, **114**, 9.56N 76.15E
Coco (*r.*), **30**, 14.58N 83.15W
Cocos (*isls.*), **30**, 5.32N 87.04W
Cocos Islands, **128**, 12.10S 96.55E
Cod, Cape, **22**, 42.08N 70.01W
Coimbra, **64**, 40.12N 8.25W
Cologne, **72**, 50.56N 6.59E
Colombia (*c.*), **38**, 5.00N 75.00W
Colombo, **114**, 6.55N 79.52E
Colorado (*r.*), **38**, 39.50S 62.02W
Colorado (*r.*), **22**, 31.45N 114.40W
Colorado (*r.*), **22**, 28.36N 95.58W
Colorado Plateau, **22**, 36.00N 112.00W
Columbia (*r.*), **22**, 46.15N 124.05W

Communism Peak, **84**, 38.39N 72.01E
Como, Lake, **68**, 46.05N 9.17E
Comoros *(c.)*, **108**, 12.15S 44.00E
Conakry, **102**, 9.30N 13.43W
Concepción, **38**, 36.50S 73.03W
Conchos *(r.)*, **30**, 29.34N 104.30W
Concord Peak, **90**, 37.35N 73.38E
Congo *(c.)*, **102**, 0.30N 16.00E
Congo *(r.)*, **102**, 6.04S 12.24E
Congo Basin, **102**, 0.30S 17.00E
Constance, Lake, **72**, 47.40N 9.30E
Constanta, **78**, 44.10N 28.31E
Cook, Mt., **146**, 43.45S 170.12E
Cook Strait, **146**, 41.15S 174.30E
Copenhagen, **46**, 55.40N 12.35E
Cordillera Occidental *(mts.)*, **38**, 5.00S 76.15W
Cordillera Oriental *(mts.)*, **38**, 5.00S 74.30W
Córdoba, **38**, 31.25S 64.11W
Córdoba, **64**, 37.53N 4.46W
Corfu, **68**, 39.37N 19.50E
Corfu *(i.)*, **68**, 39.37N 19.50E
Cork, **52**, 51.54N 8.28W
Corrib, Lough, **52**, 53.26N 9.14W
Corrientes, Cape, **30**, 20.37N 105.38W
Corse, Cape, **58**, 43.00N 9.25E
Corsica *(i.)*, **58**, 42.00N 9.10E
Cosenza, **68**, 39.17N 16.14E
Costa Rica *(c.)*, **30**, 10.00N 84.00W
Cotopaxi *(mt.)*, **38**, 0.40S 78.30W
Cotswolds, **52**, 51.50N 2.00W
Coventry, **52**, 52.38N 1.17W
Cracow, **78**, 50.03N 19.55E
Craiova, **78**, 44.18N 23.46E
Cres *(i.)*, **78**, 44.50N 14.20E
Crete *(i.)*, **68**, 35.15N 25.00E
Creuse *(r.)*, **58**, 47.00N 0.35E
Croatia *(c.)*, **78**, 45.20N 16.30E
Cuando *(r.)*, **108**, 18.30S 23.30E
Cuanza *(r.)*, **108**, 9.22S 13.09E
Cuba *(c.)*, **30**, 22.00N 79.00W
Cubango *(r.)*, **108**, 18.30S 22.04E
Cuiabá, **38**, 15.32S 56.05W
Cumbrian Mts., **52**, 54.32N 3.05W
Cunene *(r.)*, **108**, 17.15S 11.50E
Curaçao *(i.)*, **31**, 12.15N 69.00W
Curepipe, **108**, 30.16S 57.36E
Cuttack, **114**, 20.26N 85.56E
Cuzo, **38**, 13.32S 72.10W
Cyclades *(isls.)*, **68**, 37.00N 25.00E
Cyprus *(c.)*, **68**, 35.00N 33.00E
Czech Republic *(c.)*, **78**, 49.30N 15.30E

D'Entrecasteaux Islands, **140**, 9.30S 150.40E
Da Hinggan Mts., **120**, 49.30N 122.00E
Da Nang, **128**, 16.04N 108.14E
Dadu *(r.)*, **120**, 28.47N 104.40E
Dakar, **102**, 14.38N 17.27W
Dal *(r.)*, **46**, 60.38N 17.27E
Dalian, **120**, 38.53N 121.37E
Dallas, **22**, 32.47N 96.48W
Dalmatia *(f.)*, **78**, 43.30N 17.00E
Dalou Shan *(mts.)*, **120**, 28.25N 107.15E
Damascus, **90**, 33.30N 36.19E
Damavand *(mt.)*, **90**, 35.47N 52.04E
Danakil Depression, **96**, 13.00N 41.00E
Danube *(r.)*, **78**, 45.26N 29.38E
Dar es Salaam, **102**, 6.51S 39.18E
Daravica *(mt.)*, **78**, 42.32N 20.08E
Darling *(r.)*, **140**, 34.05S 141.57E
Darling Range, **140**, 32.00S 116.30E
Dartmoor *(f.)*, **52**, 50.33N 3.55W
Darwin, **140**, 12.23S 130.44E
Dasht-e-Kavir *(des.)*, **90**, 34.40N 55.00E
Dasht-e-Lut *(des.)*, **90**, 31.30N 58.00E
Davao, **128**, 7.05N 125.38E
Davis Strait, **16**, 66.00N 58.00W
Death Valley, **22**, 36.30N 117.00W
Debrecen, **78**, 47.30N 21.37E
Deccan *(f.)*, **114**, 18.00N 77.30E
Delgado, Cape, **102**, 10.45S 40.38E
Denmark *(c.)*, **46**, 56.05N 10.00E
Denpasar, **128**, 8.40S 115.14E
Denver, **22**, 39.43N 105.01W
Derg, Lough, **52**, 52.57N 8.18W
Dese, **96**, 11.05N 39.40E
Detroit, **22**, 42.20N 83.03W
Devon Island, **16**, 75.00N 86.00W
Dhahran, **90**, 26.18N 50.08E
Dhaka, **114**, 23.42N 90.22E
Dijon, **58**, 47.20N 5.02E
Dili, **128**, 8.35S 125.35E
Dinaric Alps *(mts.)*, **78**, 44.00N 16.30E
Djakarta, **128**, 6.08N 106.45E
Djibouti, **96**, 11.35N 43.11E
Djibouti *(c.)*, **96**, 12.00N 42.50E
Djúpivogur, **46**, 64.41N 14.16W
Dnepropetrovsk, **84**, 48.29N 35.00E
Dnieper *(r.)*, **84**, 46.30N 32.25E
Dodecanese *(isls.)*, **68**, 36.00N 27.00E
Dodoma, **102**, 6.10S 35.40E
Doha, **90**, 25.15N 51.34E
Dolomites *(mts.)*, **68**, 46.25N 11.50E
Dôme, Puy de *(mt.)*, **58**, 45.47N 2.58E
Dominica *(c.)*, **31**, 15.30N 61.30W
Dominican Republic *(c.)*, **31**, 18.00N 70.00W
Don *(r.)*, **84**, 47.06N 39.16E
Dondra Head, **114**, 5.55N 80.20E
Donegal Bay, **52**, 54.32N 8.18W
Dongting, Lake, **120**, 29.40N 113.00E
Dordogne *(r.)*, **58**, 45.02N 0.35W
Doubs *(r.)*, **58**, 46.54N 5.02E
Douglas, **52**, 54.09N 4.29W
Douro *(r.)*, **64**, 41.10N 8.40W
Dover, Strait of, **52**, 51.00N 1.30E
Downs, North *(f.)*, **52**, 51.18N 0.40W
Downs, South *(f.)*, **52**, 50.54N 0.34W
Drakensberg *(mts.)*, **108**, 30.00S 29.00E
Drava *(r.)*, **78**, 45.34N 18.56E
Dresden, **72**, 51.03N 13.44E
Drina *(r.)*, **78**, 44.53N 19.20E
Dubai, **90**, 25.13N 55.17E
Dublin, **52**, 53.21N 6.18W
Dubrovnik, **78**, 42.40N 18.07E
Dukou, **120**, 26.33N 101.44E
Dumfries, **52**, 55.04N 3.37W
Dundee, **52**, 56.28N 3.00W
Dunedin, **146**, 45.53S 170.31E
Dunstan Mts., **146**, 44.45S 169.45E
Durance *(r.)*, **58**, 43.55N 4.44E
Durban, **108**, 29.53S 31.00E
Durmitor *(mt.)*, **78**, 43.08N 19.03E
Durrës, **78**, 41.19N 19.27E
Dushanbe, **84**, 38.38N 68.51E
Dusseldorf, **72**, 51.12N 6.47E
Dvina, North *(r.)*, **84**, 64.40N 40.50E
Dwana Range, **128**, 17.30N 98.00E
Dzhugdzhur Range, **84**, 57.30N 138.00E
Dzungaria Basin, **120**, 44.30N 83.07E

East Frisian Islands, **72**, 53.45N 7.00E
East London, **108**, 33.00S 27.54E
Ebro *(r.)*, **64**, 40.43N 0.54W
Echigo Mts., **134**, 38.30N 140.30E
Ecuador *(c.)*, **38**, 2.00S 78.00W
Edinburgh, **52**, 55.57N 3.13W
Edmonton, **16**, 53.30N 113.30W
Edward, Lake, **102**, 0.30S 29.30E
Edwards Plateau, **22**, 31.20N 101.00W
Egadi Islands, **68**, 38.00N 12.10E
Egmont, Mt., **146**, 39.20S 174.05E
Egypt *(c.)*, **96**, 26.30N 29.30E
Eifel *(f.)*, **72**, 50.10N 6.45E
Eiger *(mt.)*, **72**, 46.34N 8.01E
Eindhoven, **72**, 51.26N 5.30E
El Aaiun, **96**, 27.09N 13.12W
El Obeid, **96**, 13.11N 30.10E
El Paso, **22**, 45.00N 93.10W
El Salvador *(c.)*, **30**, 13.30N 89.00W
Elazig, **90**, 38.41N 39.14E
Elba *(i.)*, **68**, 42.47N 10.17E
Elbe *(r.)*, **72**, 53.33N 10.00E
Elbert, Mt., **22**, 39.07N 106.27W
Elblag, **78**, 54.10N 19.25E
Elbrus *(mt.)*, **84**, 43.21N 42.29E
Elburz Mts., **90**, 36.00N 52.00E
Eleuthera *(i.)*, **30**, 25.00N 76.00W
Ellesmere Island, **16**, 78.00N 82.00W
Emi Koussi *(mt.)*, **96**, 19.58N 18.30E
Ems *(r.)*, **72**, 53.14N 7.25E
Enggano *(i.)*, **128**, 5.20S 102.15E
English Channel, **52**, 50.15N 1.00W
Enns *(r.)*, **72**, 48.14N 14.22E
Equatorial Guinea *(c.)*, **102**, 1.30N 10.30E
Erg Chech *(des.)*, **96**, 24.30N 2.30W
Erie, Lake, **16**, 42.15N 81.00W
Erimo, Cape, **134**, 41.55N 143.13E
Eritrea *(c.)*, **96**, 16.30N 38.00E
Erne, Lough, **52**, 54.28N 7.48W
Erzurum, **90**, 39.57N 41.17E
Esbjerg, **46**, 55.28N 8.27E
Estonia *(c.)*, **84**, 58.45N 25.30E
Ethiopia *(c.)*, **96**, 7.30N 40.00E
Ethiopian Highlands, **96**, 10.00N 38.45E
Etna *(mt.)*, **68**, 37.43N 14.59E
Etosha Pan *(f.)*, **108**, 18.50S 16.30E
Euboea *(i.)*, **68**, 38.30N 23.50E
Euphrates *(r.)*, **90**, 31.00N 47.27E
Everest, Mt., **114**, 27.59N 86.56E
Exeter, **52**, 50.43N 3.31W
Exmoor *(f.)*, **52**, 51.08N 3.45W
Eyre, Lake, **140**, 28.30S 137.25E
Eyre Peninsula, **140**, 34.00S 135.45E

Faeroe Islands, **46**, 62.00N 7.00W
Fairbanks, **22**, 64.50N 147.50W
Faisalabad, **114**, 31.25N 73.09E
Falkland Islands, **38**, 58.00S 60.00W
Falster *(i.)*, **46**, 54.48N 11.58E
Fan Si Pan *(mt.)*, **128**, 22.30N 104.00E
Farewell, Cape, **16**, 60.00N 44.20W
Faro, **64**, 37.01N 7.56W
Faxaflói *(b.)*, **46**, 64.30N 22.50W
Fdérik, **96**, 22.30N 12.30W
Fehmarn *(i.)*, **72**, 54.30N 11.05E
Fens, The, **52**, 52.30N 0.40E
Fernando de Noronha *(i.)*, **38**, 3.50S 32.25W
Fianarantsoa, **108**, 21.26S 47.05E
Fichtelgebirge *(mts.)*, **72**, 50.00N 11.50E
Finisterre, Cape, **64**, 42.54N 9.16W
Finland *(c.)*, **46**, 62.30N 26.00E
Finland, Gulf of, **46**, 59.30N 24.00E
Florence, **68**, 43.46N 11.15E
Flores *(i.)*, **128**, 8.40S 121.20E
Fly *(r.)*, **140**, 8.22S 142.23E
Fontur, **46**, 66.23N 14.30W
Formentera *(i.)*, **64**, 38.41N 1.30E
Formosa Strait, **120**, 25.00N 120.00E
Fort Albany, **16**, 52.15N 81.35W
Fortaleza, **38**, 3.45S 38.45W
Forth, Firth of *(est.)*, **52**, 56.05N 3.00W
Foveaux Strait, **146**, 46.40S 168.00E
France *(c.)*, **58**, 47.00N 2.00E
Franconian Jura *(mts.)*, **72**, 49.30N 11.10E
Frankfurt, **72**, 50.07N 8.40E
Fraser *(r.)*, **16**, 49.07N 123.11W
Fraser Island, **140**, 25.15S 153.10E
Freetown, **102**, 8.30N 13.17W
French Guiana, **38**, 3.40N 53.00W
Fuji, Mt., **134**, 35.23N 138.42E
Fukuoka, **134**, 33.39N 130.21E
Furneaux Group *(isls.)*, **140**, 40.15S 148.15E
Futa Jalon *(f.)*, **102**, 11.30N 12.30W
Fuzhou, **120**, 26.01N 119.20E
Fyn *(i.)*, **46**, 55.20N 10.30E

Gabon *(c.)*, **102**, 0.00 12.00E
Gaborone, **108**, 24.45S 25.55E
Gairdner, Lake, **140**, 31.30S 136.00E
Galapagos Islands, **38**, 0.30S 90.30W
Galati, **78**, 45.27N 27.59E
Galway, **52**, 53.17N 9.04W
Galway Bay, **52**, 53.12N 9.07W
Gambia *(c.)*, **102**, 13.30N 15.00W
Gambia *(r.)*, **102**, 13.28N 15.55W
Ganges *(r.)*, **114**, 23.30N 90.25E
Gao, **96**, 16.19N 0.09W
Garda, Lake, **68**, 45.40N 10.40E
Gargano, Prom. of, **68**, 41.49N 16.12E
Garonne *(r.)*, **58**, 45.02N 0.36W
Garvie Mts., **146**, 45.15S 169.00E
Gascony, Gulf of, **58**, 44.00N 2.40W
Gata, Cape, **68**, 34.33N 33.03E
Gatun Lake, **30**, 9.20N 80.00W
Gauhati, **114**, 26.05N 91.55E
Gdansk, **78**, 54.22N 18.38E
Gdansk, Gulf of, **78**, 54.45N 19.15E
Geneva, **72**, 46.12N 6.09E
Geneva, Lake, **72**, 46.25N 6.30E
Genoa, **68**, 44.24N 8.54E
George Town, **128**, 5.30N 100.16E
Georgetown, **38**, 6.48N 58.08W
Georgia *(c.)*, **84**, 42.00N 43.30E
Gerlach Peak, **78**, 49.10N 20.10E
Germany *(c.)*, **72**, 52.00N 10.00E
Ghadamis, **96**, 30.10N 9.30E
Ghaghara *(r.)*, **114**, 25.45N 84.50E
Ghana *(c.)*, **102**, 8.00N 1.00W
Ghat, **96**, 24.59N 10.11E
Ghats, Eastern *(mts.)*, **114**, 16.30N 80.30E
Ghats, Western *(mts.)*, **114**, 15.30N 74.30E
Ghent, **72**, 51.02N 3.42E
Gibraltar, **64**, 36.07N 5.22W
Gibraltar, Strait of, **64**, 36.00N 5.25W
Gibson Desert, **140**, 24.00S 125.00E
Gilgit, **114**, 35.54N 74.20E
Gisborne, **146**, 38.39S 178.01E
Glåma *(r.)*, **46**, 59.12N 10.57E
Glasgow, **52**, 55.52N 4.15W
Glittertind *(mt.)*, **46**, 61.39N 8.33E
Gobi *(des.)*, **120**, 43.30N 114.00E
Godavari *(r.)*, **114**, 16.40N 82.15E
Godthåb, **16**, 64.10N 51.40W
Good Hope, Cape of, **108**, 34.20S 18.25E
Gorontalo, **128**, 0.33N 123.05E
Göta *(r.)*, **46**, 57.42N 11.52E
Göteborg, **46**, 57.43N 11.58E
Gotland *(i.)*, **46**, 57.30N 18.33E
Goto Islands, **134**, 32.43N 128.36E
Gozo *(i.)*, **68**, 36.03N 14.16E
Gracias a Dios, Cape, **30**, 15.00N 83.10W
Grampian Mountains, **52**, 56.55N 4.00W
Gran Chaco *(f.)*, **38**, 23.30S 60.00W
Gran Paradiso *(mt.)*, **68**, 45.31N 7.15E
Granada, **64**, 37.10N 3.35W
Grand Bahama *(i.)*, **30**, 26.35N 78.00W
Grand Canal, **120**, 39.10N 117.12E
Grand Canyon, **22**, 36.10N 112.45W
Grand Erg Occidental *(des.)*, **96**, 30.10N 0.00
Grand Erg Oriental *(des.)*, **96**, 30.00N 7.00E
Graz, **72**, 47.05N 15.27E
Great Abaco *(i.)*, **30**, 26.30N 77.00W
Great Alföld *(f.)*, **78**, 47.20N 20.30E
Great Artesian Basin *(f.)*, **140**, 26.30S 143.02E
Great Australian Bight *(b.)*, **140**, 33.10S 129.30E
Great Barrier Island, **146**, 36.15S 175.30E
Great Barrier Reef *(f.)*, **140**, 16.30S 146.30E
Great Basin, **22**, 40.35N 116.00W
Great Bear Lake, **16**, 66.00N 120.00W
Great Dividing Range, **140**, 29.00S 152.00E
Great Inagua *(i.)*, **31**, 21.00N 73.20W
Great Karroo *(f.)*, **108**, 32.50S 22.30E
Great Nicobar *(i.)*, **114**, 7.00N 93.50E
Great Ouse *(r.)*, **52**, 52.47N 0.23E
Great Plains, **22**, 40.00N 103.00W
Great Salt Lake, **22**, 41.10N 112.30W
Great Sandy Desert, **140**, 20.30S 123.35E
Great Slave Lake, **16**, 61.23N 115.38W
Great Victoria Desert, **140**, 29.00S 127.30E
Greater Antilles *(isls.)*, **30**, 17.00N 70.00W
Greece *(c.)*, **68**, 38.00N 22.30E
Greenland *(i.)*, **16**, 75.00N 40.00W
Grenada *(c.)*, **31**, 12.15N 61.45W
Grenoble, **58**, 45.11N 5.43E
Grey Range, **140**, 27.30S 143.59E
Grimsey *(i.)*, **46**, 66.33N 18.00W
Grimsvötn *(mt.)*, **46**, 64.30N 17.10W
Groningen, **72**, 53.13N 6.35E
Gross Arber *(mt.)*, **72**, 49.07N 13.07E
Grossglockner *(mt.)*, **72**, 47.05N 12.50E
Guadalajara, **30**, 20.30N 103.20W
Guadalquivir *(r.)*, **64**, 36.50N 6.20W
Guadeloupe *(i.)*, **31**, 16.20N 61.40W
Guadiana *(r.)*, **64**, 37.10N 7.36W
Guangzhou, **120**, 23.20N 113.30E
Guantánamo, **31**, 20.09N 75.14W
Guatemala, **30**, 14.38N 90.22W
Guatemala *(c.)*, **30**, 15.40N 90.00W
Guayaquil, **38**, 2.13S 79.54W
Guiana Highlands, **38**, 4.00N 59.00W
Guinea *(c.)*, **102**, 10.30N 10.30W
Guinea, Gulf of, **102**, 3.00N 3.00E
Guinea-Bissau *(c.)*, **102**, 12.00N 15.30W
Guiyang, **120**, 26.35N 106.40E
Gulf, The, **90**, 27.00N 50.00E
Guyana *(c.)*, **38**, 5.00N 59.00W
Gydanskiy Peninsula, **84**, 70.00N 78.30E
Gyor, **78**, 47.41N 17.40E

Haardt *(mts.)*, **72**, 49.21N 7.55E
Hachijo *(i.)*, **134**, 33.10N 139.45E
Hadd, Cape, **90**, 22.32N 59.49E
Hadhramaut *(f.)*, **90**, 16.30N 49.30E
Haeju, **134**, 38.04N 125.40E
Hafnarfjördur, **46**, 64.04N 21.58W
Hague, Cap de la, **58**, 49.44N 1.56W
Hague, The, **72**, 52.05N 4.16E
Haifa, **90**, 32.49N 34.59E
Haikou, **120**, 20.05N 110.25E
Hainan *(i.)*, **120**, 18.30N 109.40E
Haiphong, **128**, 20.58N 106.41E
Haiti *(c.)*, **31**, 19.00N 73.00W
Hakodate, **134**, 41.46N 140.44E
Halifax, **16**, 44.39N 63.36W
Halmahera *(i.)*, **128**, 0.45N 128.00E
Hamamatsu, **134**, 34.42N 137.42E
Hamburg, **72**, 53.33N 9.59E
Hamersley Range, **140**, 22.00S 118.00E
Hamhung, **134**, 39.54N 127.35E
Hamilton, **146**, 37.47S 175.17E
Han *(r.)*, **134**, 37.30N 127.00E
Hangzhou, **120**, 30.10N 120.07E
Hannover, **72**, 52.24N 9.44E
Hanoi, **128**, 21.01N 105.52E
Harare, **108**, 17.49S 31.04E
Harbin, **120**, 45.45N 126.41E
Hardanger Fjord, **46**, 60.10N 6.00E
Hargeysa, **96**, 9.31N 44.02E
Hari Rud *(r.)*, **90**, 35.42N 61.12E
Harney Basin, **22**, 43.15N 120.40W
Harris *(i.)*, **52**, 57.50N 6.55W
Harz *(mts.)*, **72**, 51.43N 10.40E
Hatteras, Cape, **22**, 35.14N 75.31W
Hauki *(l.)*, **46**, 62.10N 28.30E
Havana, **30**, 23.07N 82.25W
Havel *(r.)*, **72**, 52.53N 11.58E
Hawaii *(i.)*, **22**, 19.30N 155.30W
Hawaiian Islands, **22**, 21.00N 157.00W
Hawke Bay, **146**, 39.18S 177.15E
Hay River (town), **16**, 60.51N 115.44W
Hebrides, Inner *(isls.)*, **52**, 57.00N 7.00W
Hebrides, Outer *(isls.)*, **52**, 58.00N 7.45W
Hejaz *(f.)*, **90**, 25.00N 39.00E
Hekla, Mt., **46**, 64.00N 19.45W
Helmand *(r.)*, **90**, 31.10N 61.20E
Helsingborg, **46**, 56.05N 12.45E
Helsinki, **46**, 60.08N 25.00E
Herat, **90**, 34.21N 62.10E
Heulva, **64**, 37.15N 6.56W
Hida Mts., **134**, 36.35N 137.00E
Hidaka Mts., **134**, 42.50N 143.00E
High Atlas *(mts.)*, **96**, 32.00N 5.50W
Himalayas *(mts.)*, **114**, 29.00N 84.00E
Hindu Kush *(mts.)*, **90**, 36.40N 70.00E
Hinnøy *(i.)*, **46**, 68.35N 15.50E
Hiroshima, **134**, 34.30N 132.27E
Hispaniola *(i.)*, **31**, 19.00N 71.00W
Hkakabo Razi *(mt.)*, **128**, 28.17N 97.46E
Ho Chi Minh City, **128**, 10.46N 106.43E
Hobart, **140**, 42.54S 147.18E
Hofsjökull *(mt.)*, **46**, 64.50N 19.00W
Hokkaido *(i.)*, **134**, 43.00N 144.00E
Honduras *(c.)*, **30**, 14.30N 87.00W
Hong Kong, **120**, 22.30N 114.10E
Honolulu, **22**, 21.19N 157.50W
Honshu *(i.)*, **134**, 36.00N 138.00E
Hormuz, Strait of, **90**, 26.35N 56.20E
Horn, Cape, **38**, 55.47S 67.00W
Hornavan *(l.)*, **46**, 66.10N 17.30E
Houston, **22**, 29.46N 95.22W
Hoy *(i.)*, **52**, 58.51N 3.17W
Huambo, **108**, 12.47S 15.44E
Huang *(r.)*, **120**, 37.55N 118.46E
Huascarán *(mt.)*, **38**, 9.20S 77.36W
Hudson *(r.)*, **22**, 40.42N 74.02W
Hudson Bay, **16**, 58.00N 86.00W
Hudson Strait, **16**, 62.00N 70.00W
Hue, **128**, 16.28N 107.35E
Huiarau Range, **146**, 38.20S 177.15E
Hull, **52**, 53.45N 0.20W
Hungary *(c.)*, **78**, 47.20N 19.00E
Hungnam, **134**, 39.49N 127.40E
Hunsrück *(mts.)*, **72**, 49.45N 7.00E
Huron, Lake, **16**, 44.30N 82.15W
Hvannadalshnúkur *(mt.)*, **46**, 64.02N 16.35W
Hvar *(i.)*, **78**, 43.10N 16.45E
Hyderabad, **114**, 17.22N 78.26E
Hyderabad, **114**, 25.23N 68.24E

Iberian Peninsula, **64**, 39.00N 5.00W
Ibiza, **64**, 38.55N 1.30E
Ibiza *(i.)*, **64**, 39.00N 1.23E
Iceland *(c.)*, **46**, 64.45N 18.00W
Idhi *(mt.)*, **68**, 35.13N 24.45E
Iguaçu Falls, **38**, 25.35S 54.22W
IJssel *(r.)*, **72**, 52.34N 5.50E
IJsselmeer *(l.)*, **72**, 52.45N 5.20E
Iki *(i.)*, **134**, 33.50N 129.38E
Ikopa *(r.)*, **108**, 16.29S 46.43E
Ilagan, **128**, 17.07N 121.53E
Iligan, **128**, 8.12N 124.13E
Iloilo, **128**, 10.45N 122.33E
Imabari, **134**, 34.04N 132.59E
In Salah, **96**, 27.13N 2.28E
Inari, Lake, **46**, 69.00N 28.00E
Indals *(r.)*, **46**, 62.30N 17.20E
India *(c.)*, **114**, 24.00N 78.00E
Indianapolis, **22**, 39.45N 86.10W
Indonesia *(c.)*, **128**, 6.00S 118.00E
Indore, **114**, 22.42N 75.54E
Indre *(r.)*, **58**, 47.16N 0.19E
Indus *(r.)*, **114**, 24.00N 67.33E
Inn *(r.)*, **72**, 48.35N 13.28E
Innsbruck, **72**, 47.16N 11.24E
Invercargill, **146**, 46.25S 168.21E
Inverness, **52**, 57.27N 4.15W
Ionian Islands, **68**, 38.45N 19.40E
Ipoh, **128**, 4.36N 101.02E
Ipswich, **52**, 52.04N 1.09E
Iquitos, **38**, 3.51S 73.13W
Iraklion, **68**, 35.20N 25.08E
Iran *(c.)*, **90**, 32.00N 54.30E
Iran Range, **128**, 3.20N 115.00E
Iraq *(c.)*, **90**, 33.00N 44.00E
Ireland *(c.)*, **52**, 53.00N 7.00W
Irkutsk, **84**, 52.18N 104.15E

Mutare, **108**, 18.58S 32.40E
Mweru, Lake, **102**, 9.00S 28.40E
Myingyan, **128**, 21.25N 95.20E
Mzuzu, **108**, 11.50S 33.39E

Naga Hills, **114**, 26.10N 94.30E
Nagasaki, **134**, 32.45N 129.52E
Nagoya, **134**, 35.08N 136.53E
Nagpur, **114**, 21.10N 79.12E
Nairobi, **102**, 1.17S 36.50E
Naktong *(r.)*, **134**, 35.10N 128.18E
Nam, Lake, **120**, 30.40N 90.30E
Namib Desert, **108**, 22.50S 14.40E
Namibia *(c.)*, **108**, 22.00S 17.00E
Namlea, **128**, 3.15S 127.07E
Nampo, **134**, 38.40N 125.30E
Nampula, **108**, 15.09S 39.14E
Namur, **72**, 50.28N 4.52E
Nancy, **58**, 48.42N 6.12E
Nangnim Mts., **134**, 40.30N 127.00E
Nanjing, **120**, 32.00N 118.40E
Nanning, **120**, 22.50N 108.19E
Nantes, **58**, 47.14N 1.35W
Napier, **146**, 39.30S 176.54E
Naples, **68**, 40.50N 14.14E
Narayanganj, **114**, 23.36N 90.28E
Narmada *(r.)*, **114**, 21.40N 73.00E
Narvik, **46**, 68.26N 17.25E
Näsi *(l.)*, **46**, 61.58N 23.57E
Nassau, **30**, 25.05N 77.20W
Nasser, Lake, **96**, 22.40N 32.00E
Natuna Besar *(i.)*, **128**, 3.00N 108.50E
Naxos *(i.)*, **68**, 37.03N 25.30E
Ndola, **108**, 13.00S 28.39E
Neagh, Lough, **52**, 54.36N 6.26W
Neblina Peak *(mt.)*, **38**, 0.45N 66.01W
Neckar *(r.)*, **72**, 49.31N 8.26E
Negoiu, Mt., **78**, 45.36N 24.32E
Negro *(r.)*, **38**, 3.00S 59.55W
Negros *(i.)*, **128**, 10.00N 123.00E
Nejd *(des.)*, **90**, 25.00N 43.00E
Nelson, **146**, 41.16S 173.15E
Nelson *(r.)*, **16**, 57.04N 92.30W
Nepal *(c.)*, **114**, 28.00N 84.00E
Ness, Loch, **52**, 57.16N 4.30W
Netherlands *(c.)*, **72**, 52.00N 5.00E
Neuchâtel, Lake, **72**, 46.52N 6.50E
Neusiedler, Lake, **72**, 47.52N 16.45E
New Britain *(i.)*, **140**, 6.00S 150.00E
New Delhi, **114**, 28.37N 77.13E
New Guinea *(i.)*, **140**, 5.00S 140.00E
New Ireland *(i.)*, **140**, 2.30S 151.30E
New Orleans, **22**, 29.58N 90.07W
New Plymouth, **146**, 39.04S 174.04E
New Providence *(i.)*, **30**, 25.03N 77.25W
New Siberian Islands, **84**, 76.00N 144.00E
New York, **22**, 40.43N 74.01W
New Zealand *(c.)*, **146**, 41.35S 175.00E
Newcastle, **140**, 32.55S 151.46E
Newcastle upon Tyne, **52**, 54.58N 1.36W
Newfoundland *(i.)*, **16**, 48.30N 56.00W
Newport, **52**, 51.34N 2.59W
Nha Trang, **128**, 12.15N 109.10E
Niagara Falls, **22**, 43.06N 79.04W
Niamey, **96**, 13.32N 2.05E
Nias *(i.)*, **128**, 1.05N 97.30E
Nicaragua *(c.)*, **30**, 13.00N 85.00W
Nicaragua, Lake, **30**, 11.30N 85.30W
Nice, **58**, 43.42N 7.16E
Nicobar Islands, **114**, 8.00N 94.00E
Nicosia, **68**, 35.11N 33.23E
Niger *(c.)*, **96**, 17.00N 10.00E
Niger *(r.)*, **102**, 4.15N 6.05E
Nigeria *(c.)*, **102**, 9.00N 9.00E
Niigata, **134**, 37.58N 139.02E
Niihau *(i.)*, **22**, 21.55N 160.10W
Nile *(r.)*, **96**, 31.30N 30.25E
Nile, Blue *(r.)*, **96**, 15.45N 32.25E
Nile, White *(r.)*, **96**, 15.45N 32.25E
Nimba, Mt., **102**, 7.35N 8.28W
Nîmes, **58**, 43.50N 4.21E
Nis, **78**, 43.20N 21.54E
Nizhniy Novgorod, **84**, 56.20N 44.00E
Norfolk, **22**, 36.54N 76.18W
Norrköping, **46**, 58.36N 16.11E
Norrland *(f.)*, **46**, 63.00N 17.00E
North *(i.)*, **114**, 13.14N 94.00E
North Cape, **46**, 71.11N 25.48E
North Cape, **46**, 66.30N 23.00W
North Cape, **146**, 34.28S 173.00E
North Island, **146**, 39.00S 175.00E
North Korea *(c.)*, **134**, 38.30N 127.00E
North West Highlands, **52**, 57.30N 5.15W
North York Moors, **52**, 54.21N 0.50W
Norway *(c.)*, **46**, 63.00N 10.00E
Norwich, **52**, 52.38N 1.17E
Nosy Be *(i.)*, **108**, 13.20S 48.15E
Nosy Boraha *(i.)* **108**, 16.50S 49.55E
Notec *(r.)*, **78**, 52.44N 15.26E
Noto Peninsula, **134**, 37.30N 137.00E
Notodden, **46**, 59.34N 9.17E
Nouadhibou, **96**, 20.54N 17.01W
Nouakchott, **96**, 18.09N 15.58W
Nova Scotia, **16**, 45.00N 63.30W
Novaya Zemlya *(i.)*, **84**, 74.00N 56.00E
Novi Sad, **78**, 45.16N 19.52E
Novosibirsk, **84**, 55.04N 82.55E
Nubian Desert, **96**, 21.00N 34.00E
Nuevo Laredo, **30**, 27.30N 99.30W
Nullarbor Plain, **140**, 31.30S 125.00E
Nunivak Island, **22**, 60.00N 166.30W
Nuremburg, **72**, 49.27N 11.04E
Nyasa, Lake, **108**, 12.00S 34.30E
N'Djamena, **96**, 12.10N 14.59E

Oahu *(i.)*, **22**, 21.30N 158.00W
Oamaru, **146**, 45.05S 170.59E
Ob *(r.)*, **84**, 66.50N 69.00E
Obi *(i.)*, **128**, 1.45S 127.30E
Obihiro, **134**, 42.55N 143.00E
October Revolution *(i.)*, **84**, 79.30N 96.00E
Odádahraun *(mts.)*, **46**, 65.00N 17.30W
Odense, **46**, 55.24N 10.23E
Odenwald *(mts.)*, **72**, 49.35N 9.05E
Oder *(r.)*, **78**, 53.30N 14.36E
Odessa, **84**, 46.30N 30.46E
Ogaden *(f.)*, **96**, 7.50N 45.40E
Ohio *(r.)*, **22**, 36.59N 89.08W
Ohrid, Lake, **78**, 41.06N 20.48E
Oise *(r.)*, **58**, 49.00N 2.04E
Oita, **134**, 33.15N 131.40E
Okavango Delta, **108**, 19.30S 23.00E
Okayama, **134**, 34.40N 133.54E
Okeechobee, Lake, **22**, 27.00N 80.45W
Oki Islands, **134**, 36.10N 133.10E
Öland *(i.)*, **46**, 56.45N 16.38E
Oléron, Ile d', **58**, 45.56N 1.15W
Olga, Mt., **140**, 25.18S 130.44E
Olsztyn, **78**, 53.48N 20.29E
Olt *(r.)*, **78**, 44.13N 24.28E
Olympus *(mt.)*, **68**, 40.04N 22.20E
Olympus, Mt., **68**, 34.55N 32.52E
Oman *(c.)*, **90**, 22.30N 57.30E
Omdurman, **96**, 15.37N 32.59E
Omsk, **84**, 55.00N 73.22E
Onega, Lake, **84**, 62.00N 35.30E
Ontario, Lake, **16**, 43.45N 78.00W
Oporto, **64**, 41.09N 8.37W
Oradea, **78**, 47.03N 21.55E
Oran, **96**, 35.45N 0.38W
Orange *(r.)*, **108**, 28.38S 16.38E
Ordos *(des.)*, **120**, 40.00N 109.00E
Ore Mts., **72**, 50.34N 13.00E
Örebro, **46**, 59.17N 15.13E
Ori *(l.)*, **46**, 62.21N 29.34E
Orinoco *(r.)*, **38**, 9.00N 61.30W
Orkney Islands, **52**, 59.00N 3.00W
Orléans, **58**, 47.54N 1.54E
Örnskoldsvik, **46**, 63.17N 18.50E
Ortles *(mt.)*, **68**, 46.31N 10.33E
Osaka, **134**, 34.40N 135.30E
Oslo, **46**, 59.55N 10.45E
Ostend, **72**, 51.13N 2.55E
Östersund, **46**, 63.10N 14.40E
Ostrava, **78**, 49.50N 18.15E
Osumi *(i.)*, **134**, 30.30N 130.30E
Otaru, **134**, 43.14N 140.59E
Otranto, Strait of, **68**, 40.10N 19.00E
Ottawa, **16**, 45.25N 75.42W
Ouagadougou, **102**, 12.20N 1.40W
Oulu, **46**, 65.01N 25.28E
Oulu, Lake, **46**, 64.20N 27.15E
Ouse *(r.)*, **52**, 53.41N 0.42W
Ovamboland *(f.)*, **108**, 17.45S 16.00E
Oviedo, **64**, 43.21N 5.50W
Owen Stanley Range, **140**, 9.30S 148.00E
Oxford, **52**, 51.45N 1.15W
Ozark Plateau, **22**, 37.00N 93.00W

Padang, **128**, 0.55S 100.21E
Paektu, Mt., **134**, 42.00N 128.17E
Pag *(i.)*, **78**, 44.28N 15.00E
Päijänne *(l.)*, **46**, 61.22N 25.37E
Pakistan *(c.)*, **114**, 30.00N 70.00E
Pakse, **128**, 15.05N 105.50E
Palau *(i.)*, **128**, 7.00N 134.25E
Palawan *(i.)*, **128**, 9.30N 118.30E
Palembang, **128**, 2.59S 104.50E
Palermo, **68**, 38.09N 13.22E
Palk Strait, **114**, 10.00N 79.40E
Palliser, Cape, **146**, 41.35S 175.15E
Palma, **64**, 39.36N 2.39E
Palmas, Cape, **102**, 4.30N 7.55W
Palmerston North, **146**, 40.21S 175.37E
Pamir *(mts.)*, **84**, 37.50N 73.30E
Pampas *(f.)*, **38**, 35.00S 64.00W
Pamplona, **64**, 42.49N 1.39W
Panama, **30**, 8.57N 79.30W
Panama *(c.)*, **30**, 9.00N 80.00W
Panama Canal, **30**, 9.21N 79.54W
Panay *(i.)*, **128**, 11.10N 122.30E
Pantelleria *(i.)*, **68**, 36.48N 12.00E
Papua New Guinea *(c.)*, **140**, 6.00S 144.00E
Paraguay *(c.)*, **38**, 23.00S 57.00W
Paraguay *(r.)*, **38**, 27.30S 58.50W
Paramaribo, **38**, 5.52N 55.14W
Paraná *(r.)*, **38**, 34.00S 58.30W
Parepare, **128**, 4.03S 119.40E
Paris, **58**, 48.52N 2.20E
Passero, Cape, **68**, 36.40N 15.09E
Patagonia *(f.)*, **38**, 42.20S 67.00W
Patna, **114**, 25.37N 85.12E
Patrai, **68**, 38.15N 21.45E
Peace *(r.)*, **16**, 59.00N 111.25W
Pecs, **78**, 42.40N 20.17E
Pegu, **128**, 17.18N 96.31E
Pegu Yoma *(mts.)*, **128**, 18.40N 96.00E
Peloponnese *(f.)*, **68**, 38.00N 22.00E
Pemba *(i.)*, **102**, 5.10S 39.45E
Pennines *(mts.)*, **52**, 54.40N 2.20W
Perpignan, **58**, 42.42N 2.54E
Perth, **52**, 56.24N 3.28W
Perth, **140**, 31.58S 115.49E
Peru *(c.)*, **38**, 12.00S 75.00W
Pescara, **68**, 42.27N 14.13E
Petropavlovsk-Kamchatskiy, **84**,
53.03N 158.43E
Philadelphia, **22**, 40.00N 75.10W
Philippines *(c.)*, **128**, 13.00N 123.00E
Phnom Penh, **128**, 11.35N 104.55E
Phoenix, **22**, 33.27N 112.05W
Phuket *(i.)*, **128**, 8.10N 98.20E
Pidurutalagala *(mt.)*, **114**, 6.56N 80.45E
Pielinen *(l.)*, **46**, 63.20N 29.50E
Pinang *(i.)*, **128**, 5.30N 110.10E
Pindus Mts., **68**, 39.40N 21.00E
Pinios *(r.)*, **68**, 39.51N 22.37E
Piraeus, **68**, 37.56N 23.38E
Pirin *(mts.)*, **78**, 41.35N 23.24E
Piru, **128**, 3.01S 128.10E
Pisa, **68**, 43.43N 10.24E
Piton des Neiges *(mt.)*, **108**, 21.05S 55.28E
Pitt *(i.)*, **146**, 44.10S 176.30W
Pjórsá *(r.)*, **46**, 63.53N 20.38W
Plate *(r.)*, **38**, 35.15S 56.45W
Plenty, Bay of, **146**, 37.40S 176.50E
Pleven, **78**, 43.25N 24.39E
Plovdid, **78**, 42.09N 24.45E
Plymouth, **52**, 50.23N 4.09W
Plzen, **78**, 49.45N 13.22E
Po *(r.)*, **68**, 44.51N 12.30E
Pobeda *(mt.)*, **84**, 65.20N 145.50E
Pobedy, Peak, **84**, 42.25N 80.15E
Poland *(c.)*, **78**, 52.30N 19.00E
Pontianak, **128**, 0.05S 109.16E
Popocatepetl *(mt.)*, **30**, 19.02N 98.38W
Port-au-Prince, **31**, 18.33N 72.20W
Port Blair, **114**, 11.40N 92.30E
Port Elizabeth, **108**, 33.57S 25.34E
Port Louis, **108**, 20.08S 57.30E
Port Moresby, **140**, 9.30S 147.07E
Port of Spain, **31**, 10.38N 61.31W
Port Said, **96**, 31.17N 32.18E
Port Sudan, **96**, 19.39N 37.01E
Portland, **22**, 45.33N 122.36W
Porto Novo, **102**, 6.30N 2.47E
Pôrto Alegre, **38**, 30.03S 51.10W
Portugal *(c.)*, **64**, 39.30N 8.05W
Poso, **128**, 1.23S 120.45E
Poyang, Lake, **120**, 29.05N 116.20E
Poznan, **78**, 52.25N 16.53E
Prague, **78**, 50.05N 14.25E
Prespa, Lake, **78**, 40.53N 21.02E
Pretoria, **108**, 25.43S 28.11E
Prince Edward Island, **16**, 46.15N 63.00W
Prince of Wales Island, **16**, 73.00N 99.00W
Puerto Montt, **38**, 41.28S 73.00W
Puerto Rico, **31**, 18.20N 66.30W
Punta Arenas, **38**, 53.10S 70.56W
Pusan, **134**, 35.06N 129.03E
Putumayo *(r.)*, **38**, 3.05S 68.10W
Puula *(l.)*, **46**, 61.50N 26.42E
Pyongyang, **134**, 39.00N 125.47E
Pyrenees *(mts.)*, **64**, 42.40N 0.30W

Qaidam Basin, **120**, 37.46N 96.00E
Qatar *(c.)*, **90**, 25.20N 51.10E
Qattara Depression, **96**, 29.40N 27.30E
Qilian Shan *(mts.)*, **120**, 38.30N 100.00E
Qin Ling *(mts.)*, **120**, 33.40N 109.00E
Qinghai, Lake, **120**, 36.40N 100.00E
Quebec, **16**, 46.50N 71.20W
Queen Charlotte Islands, **16**, 53.00N 132.00W
Queen Elizabeth Islands, **16**, 78.30N 99.00W
Quetta, **114**, 30.15N 67.00E
Quito, **38**, 0.14S 78.30W

Raba, **128**, 8.27S 118.45E
Rabat, **96**, 34.02N 6.51W
Rabaul, **140**, 4.13S 152.11E
Race, Cape, **16**, 46.40N 53.10W
Rajang *(r.)*, **128**, 2.10N 112.45E
Rangoon, **128**, 16.45N 96.20E
Ras Dashan *(mt.)*, **96**, 13.20N 38.10E
Rasht, **90**, 37.18N 49.38E
Rawalpindi, **114**, 33.35N 73.08E
Ré, Ile de, **58**, 46.10N 1.26W
Recife, **38**, 8.06S 34.53W
Red *(r.)*, **22**, 31.10N 92.00W
Red *(r.)*, **128**, 20.15N 106.32E
Red Basin, **120**, 30.00N 105.00E
Red Sea, **90**, 22.00N 38.00E
Ree, Lough, **52**, 53.31N 7.58W
Reggio di Calabria, **68**, 38.07N 15.38E
Regina, **16**, 50.25N 104.39W
Reims, **58**, 49.15N 4.02E
Reindeer Lake, **16**, 57.15N 102.40W
Rennes, **58**, 48.06N 1.40W
Resolute, **16**, 74.40N 95.00W
Réunion *(i.)*, **108**, 21.00S 55.30E
Revillagigedo Islands, **30**, 19.00N 111.00W
Reykjavik, **46**, 64.09N 21.58W
Rhine *(r.)*, **72**, 51.53N 6.03E
Rhodes, **68**, 36.24N 28.15E
Rhodes *(i.)*, **68**, 36.12N 28.00E
Rhodope Mts., **78**, 41.35N 24.35E
Rhône *(r.)*, **58**, 43.20N 4.50E
Rhum *(i.)*, **52**, 57.00N 6.20W
Rift Valley, **102**, 0.00 29.00E
Riga, **84**, 56.53N 24.08E
Rijeka, **78**, 45.20N 14.25E
Rio de Janeiro, **38**, 22.50S 43.17W
Rio Grande *(r.)*, **22**, 25.55N 97.08W
Rio Grande de Santiago *(r.)*, **30**,
21.43N 105.14W
Riyadh, **90**, 24.39N 46.44E
Robson, Mt., **16**, 53.10N 119.10W
Rocky Mountains, **22**, 43.21N 109.50W
Romania *(c.)*, **78**, 46.30N 24.00E
Rome, **68**, 41.54N 12.29E
Rømø *(i.)*, **46**, 55.08N 8.31E
Roraima *(mt.)*, **38**, 5.14N 60.44W
Rosa, Monte, *(mt.)*, **68**, 45.57N 7.53E
Rosario, **38**, 33.00S 60.40W
Roseau, **31**, 15.18N 61.23W
Rostov, **84**, 57.11N 39.23E
Rotorua, Lake, **146**, 38.00S 176.00E
Rotterdam, **72**, 51.55N 4.29E
Rouen, **58**, 49.26N 1.05E
Rovaneimi, **46**, 66.30N 25.40E
Ruahine Range, **146**, 40.00S 176.00E
Ruapehu *(mt.)*, **146**, 39.20S 175.30E
Rub al-Khali *(des.)*, **90**, 19.30N 50.00E
Rufiji *(r.)*, **102**, 8.02S 39.17E
Rügen *(i.)*, **72**, 54.25N 13.24E
Ruhr *(r.)*, **72**, 51.27N 6.44E
Ruse, **78**, 43.50N 25.59E
Russia *(c.)*, **84**, 57.30N 87.00E
Ruwenzori Range, **102**, 0.30N 31.00E
Rwanda *(c.)*, **102**, 2.00S 3.00E

Saale *(r.)*, **72**, 51.57N 11.55E
Sabha, **96**, 27.02N 14.26E
Sable, Cape, **16**, 43.25N 65.35W
Sable, Cape, **22**, 25.00N 81.20W
Sado *(i.)*, **134**, 38.00N 138.20E
Sahara *(des.)*, **96**, 20.50N 5.50E
Saharan Atlas *(mts.)*, **96**, 34.20N 2.00E
Sahel *(f.)*, **96**, 14.00N 7.50E
Saimaa *(l.)*, **46**, 61.28N 28.07E
St. Denis, **108**, 20.52S 55.27E
St. Elias, Mt., **22**, 60.18N 140.55W
St. Etienne, **58**, 45.26N 4.26E
St. George's, **31**, 12.04N 61.44W
St. George's Channel, **52**, 52.00N 6.00W
St. Helens, Mt., **22**, 46.12N 122.11W
St. John's, **16**, 47.34N 52.43W
St. John's, **31**, 17.07N 61.51W
St. Kitts-Nevis *(c.)*, **31**, 17.20N 62.45W
St. Lawrence *(r.)*, **16**, 44.15N 76.10W
St. Lawrence, Gulf of, **16**, 48.00N 62.00W
St. Lawrence Island, **22**, 63.00N 170.00W
St. Louis, **22**, 38.38N 90.11W
St. Lucia *(c.)*, **31**, 14.05N 61.00W
St. Paul, **22**, 45.00N 93.10W
St. Peter and St. Paul Rocks, **38**, 1.00N 29.23W
St. Petersburg, **84**, 59.55N 30.25E
St.-Pierre and Miquelon *(isls.)*, **16**,
46.55N 56.10W
St. Vincent and the Grenadines *(c.)*, **31**,
13.10N 61.15W
Sajama *(mt.)*, **38**, 18.06S 69.00W
Sakai, **134**, 34.37N 135.28E
Sakhalin *(i.)*, **84**, 50.00N 143.00E
Salado *(r.)*, **38**, 27.50S 62.50W
Salalah, **90**, 17.00N 54.04E
Salamanca, **64**, 40.58N 5.40W
Salerno, **68**, 40.41N 14.45E
Salt Lake City, **22**, 40.46N 111.53W
Salta, **38**, 24.46S 65.28W
Salvador, **38**, 12.58S 38.20W
Salween *(r.)*, **128**, 16.30N 97.33E
Salzach *(r.)*, **72**, 48.12N 12.56E
Salzburg, **72**, 47.48N 13.02E
Samar *(i.)*, **128**, 11.45N 125.15E
Samarinda, **128**, 0.30S 117.09E
Samos *(i.)*, **68**, 37.44N 26.45E
Samsun, **90**, 41.17N 36.22E
San Antonio, **22**, 29.28N 98.31W
San Diego, **22**, 32.43N 117.09W
San Félix Island, **38**, 26.23S 80.05W
San Francisco, **22**, 37.48N 122.24W
San José, **30**, 9.59N 84.04W
San Juan, **31**, 18.29N 66.08W
San Juan Mts., **22**, 37.35N 107.10W
San Lucas, Cape, **30**, 22.50N 110.00W
San Marino, **68**, 43.55N 12.27E
San Marino *(c.)*, **68**, 43.55N 12.27E
San Pedro Sula, **30**, 15.26N 88.01W
San Salvador, **30**, 13.40N 89.10W
San Sebastian, **64**, 43.19N 1.59W
Sancy, Puy de *(mt.)*, **58**, 45.32N 2.49E
Sanday *(i.)*, **52**, 59.15N 2.33W
Sandy Desert, **114**, 28.00N 64.00E
Santa Cruz, **38**, 17.45S 63.14W
Santander, **64**, 43.28N 3.48W
Santiago, **38**, 33.30S 70.40W
Santiago de Cuba, **31**, 20.00N 75.49W
Santo Domingo, **31**, 18.30N 69.57W
San'a, **90**, 15.23N 44.14E
São Francisco *(r.)*, **38**, 10.20S 36.20W
São Paulo, **38**, 23.33S 46.39W
São Roque, Cape of, **38**, 4.00S 35.00W
São Tomé, **102**, 0.19N 6.43E
São Tomé and Príncipe *(c.)*, **102**, 1.00N 7.00E
Saône *(r.)*, **58**, 45.44N 4.50E
Sapporo, **134**, 43.05N 141.21E
Sarajevo, **78**, 43.52N 18.26E
Sardinia *(i.)*, **68**, 40.00N 9.00E
Sasebo, **134**, 33.10N 129.42E
Saskatchewan *(r.)*, **16**, 53.12N 99.16W
Saskatchewan, South *(r.)*, **16**, 53.12N 105.07W
Saskatoon, **16**, 52.07N 106.38W
Sassari, **68**, 40.43N 8.33E
Satpura Range, **114**, 21.50N 76.00E
Saudia Arabia *(c.)*, **90**, 26.00N 44.00E
Sault Sainte Marie, **16**, 46.31N 84.20W
Saumlakki, **128**, 7.59S 131.22E
Sava *(r.)*, **78**, 44.50N 20.26E
Save *(r.)*, **108**, 20.59S 35.02E
Sayan, Eastern *(mts.)*, **84**, 53.30N 98.00E
Sayan, Western *(mts.)*, **84**, 53.00N 92.00E
Scafell Pike *(mt.)*, **52**, 54.27N 3.12W
Schelde *(r.)*, **72**, 51.13N 4.25E
Schouwen *(i.)*, **72**, 51.42N 3.45E
Schwaner Range, **128**, 0.45S 113.20E
Scilly, Isles of, **52**, 49.55N 6.20W
Seattle, **22**, 47.36N 122.20W
Ségou, **96**, 13.28N 6.18W
Seine *(r.)*, **58**, 49.28N 0.25E
Seistan *(f.)*, **90**, 31.00N 61.00E
Selkirk Mts., **16**, 50.02N 116.20W
Selvas *(f.)*, **38**, 9.00S 68.00W
Selwyn Mts., **16**, 63.00N 130.00W
Selwyn Range, **140**, 21.35S 140.35E
Sendai, **134**, 38.20N 140.50E
Senegal *(c.)*, **102**, 14.15N 14.15W
Senegal *(r.)*, **102**, 16.00N 16.28W
Senja *(i.)*, **46**, 69.15N 17.20E
Seoul, **134**, 37.30N 127.00E
Sepik *(r.)*, **140**, 3.54S 144.30E
Sept-Iles, **16**, 50.12N 66.23W
Serbia *(d.)*, **78**, 44.30N 20.30E
Serowe, **108**, 22.25S 26.44E
Serra da Estrela *(mts.)*, **64**, 40.20N 7.40W
Serra do Mantiqueira *(mts.)*, **38**, 22.25S 45.00W

GLOSSARY

acid rain rain that has become more acid by absorbing waste gases discharged into the atmosphere.

arctic that part of the Earth lying north of latitude 66°32'N where for a time in summer the sun never sets and in winter never rises. It is cold and ice covered.

arid dry and usually hot. Arid areas generally have less than 250 mm (10 in) rain a year.

atoll a coral reef enclosing a lagoon.

bauxite the ore that is smelted to make the metal aluminium.

biome a major global unit in ecology, with its own plants and animals, eg savanna grassland.

bituminous coal black coal that contains less carbon than anthracite but more than lignite.

cash crop a crop grown for sale rather than subsistence.

cereal a food crop and member of the grass family.

colony a territory under the control of another country.

Commonwealth a loose association of countries that are former members of the British empire.

communism a social and economic system based on the communal ownership of property.

coniferous forest one of cone-bearing, usually evergreen trees.

conservation the management of natural resources in order to maintain their sustainable use.

constitutional monarchy a form of government with a hereditary monarch and a constitution.

consumer goods those bought for immediate use, such as food, clothes, or electrical goods.

continental climate one with a wide daily and seasonal variation of temperature, and low rainfall, usually occurring in the interior of continents.

continental drift the complex process by which the continents move their positions relative to each other on the plates of the Earth's crust. Also known as plate tectonics.

coral reef a colony of living and dead corals in the sea.

deciduous forest one of broadleaved trees, which drop their leaves in winter.

deforestation cutting down and clearing forested land.

delta the fan-shaped muddy sediment which forms where a river meets the sea.

democracy a form of government in which decisions are made by the people or those elected by them.

dependency a territory subject to the laws of another country but not formally part of it.

desert a very arid area with less than 250 mm (10 in) of rain a year.

desertification the creation of desert by overgrazing, soil erosion, or climate change.

dictator a leader taking the power of the country into his or her own hands.

empire the political organization of countries and territories in which one dominates the rest.

endemic species one that is native to a specific area.

erosion the process by which exposed land is broken down into small pieces or worn away by water, wind, or ice.

evergreen a plant that bears leaves throughout the year.

exports goods and services sold to other countries.

fault a fracture in the Earth's crust.

federalism a form of constitutional government in which power is shared between two levels: a central or federal government and a tier of provincial or state governments.

ferroalloy metals metals blended with iron in the manufacture of steel.

fjord a steep-sided inlet formed when a U-shaped valley is drowned by the sea.

fossil fuel a fuel such as oil, coal, peat or natural gas, formed from ancient organic remains.

global warming an increase in the average temperature of the Earth probably caused by the 'greenhouse effect'.

greenhouse effect the process in which radiation from the Sun passes through the atmosphere, is reflected off the surface of the Earth, and is then trapped by gases in the atmosphere. The build-up of carbon dioxide and other gases is increasing the effect.

Gross Domestic Product (GDP) the total value of a country's annual output of goods and services.

Gross National Product (GNP) a country's GDP plus income from abroad.

habitat an environment to which a plant or animal is adapted.

hardwood the wood from trees other than conifers (which produce softwoods). Hardwoods are generally stronger and less likely to rot.

ice age a geological period during which snow and ice were present throughout the year.

imports goods and services bought from other countries.

indigenous people the original inhabitants of a region.

lava molten rock from a volcano, or its later, solid form.

llanos treeless grasslands of South America.

maritime climate a moist climate generally found in areas near the sea.

Mediterranean climate one with warm, wet winters and hot, dry summers.

military regime a government controlled by the armed forces.

monarchy a form of rule where there is a hereditary head of state.

monsoon tropical wind systems that reverse direction with the seasons; also, the rain brought by these winds.

multiparty system a system of rule in which parties compete for votes in elections.

nomad a member of a group of people who migrate seasonally in search of food, water, or grazing for their animals.

official language the language used by governments, schools, courts and other official institutions in countries where there is no single common mother tongue.

one-party system a system of rule where there is no competition at elections, and all but the government party is banned.

pampas level, treeless and grassy regions in South America.

peat a thick layer of partly decomposed plant remains found in wetlands. High acidity, and low temperature, nutrient and oxygen levels prevent total decomposition.

per capita per head.

permafrost soil and rock that is always frozen.

plateau a large area of level, high land.

polar region those lying within the lines of latitude known as the Arctic and Antarctic circles. At this line of latitude the Sun does not set in midsummer.

polder agricultural land at or below sea level, reclaimed from the sea, particularly in the Netherlands.

prairie the flat grassland in the interior of North America, used for cereal crops.

precipitation moisture reaching the Earth from the atmosphere in the form of mist, dew, rain, sleet, snow, and hail.

province an administrative subdivision of a country.

radioactivity the radiation emitted from atomic nuclei. This is greatest when the atom is split, as in a nuclear reactor.

rainforest forest where there is abundant rainfall all the year. Tropical rainforests are rich in plant and animal species and growth is lush and very rapid.

republic a form of government with a non-hereditary head of state.

rift valley a long valley formed when a block of land between two faults subsides.

Romance language a family of languages all derived from Latin.

savanna a habitat of open grassland with scattered trees in tropical and subtropical areas.

sclerophyllous vegetation hard-leaved scrub, of low trees and shrubs with tough evergreen leaves, found where there is drought in summer.

sediment a layer of rock, gravel, sand or silt that has been laid down by water, ice, wind or mass movement by water or ice, and cover the bedrock.

semiarid areas between arid deserts and better watered areas, where there is enough moisture to support a little more vegetation than can survive in the desert.

softwood the wood from coniferous trees.

soil erosion the removal of the topsoil from land, mainly by the action of wind and rain.

steppe an open grassy plain with few trees or shrubs. It has low, sporadic rainfall, and wide ranges of annual temperature.

subsistence a system in which producers supply their own needs for food, shelter and so on but have little or no surplus for trade.

subtropical the climatic zone between the tropics and temperate zones. They have marked seasonal changes of temperature but it is never very cold.

sustainable development using the Earth's resources to improve people's lives without diminishing the ability of the Earth to support life today and in the future.

taiga the belt of coniferous forest and peatland in the northern hemisphere, south of the tundra.

temperate zone any one of the climatic zones in the mid latitudes, with a mild climate. Such zones cover areas between the warm tropics and cold polar regions.

tropics the area between the Tropic of Cancer and the Tropic of Capricorn. They mark the lines of latitude farthest from the Equator where the Sun is still found directly overhead at midday in midsummer.

tundra the level, treeless land lying in the very cold northern parts of Europe, Asia and North America.

wetland a habitat that is waterlogged all or enough of the time to support vegetation adapted to those conditions.

INDEX